Accounting for the Environment

Accounting for the Environment

SECOND EDITION

T400

Rob Gray and Jan Bebbington

Editorial adviser: Martin Houldin, EMAG

SAGE Publications
London • Thousand Oaks • New Delhi

SAGE Publications Ltd
6 Bonhill Street
London EC2A 4PU

SAGE Publications Inc
2455 Teller Road
Thousand Oaks, California 91320

SAGE Publications India Pvt Ltd
32, M-Block Market
Greater Kailash – I
New Delhi 110 048

British Library Cataloguing in Publication data

A catalogue record for this book is available from the
British Library

ISBN 0–7619–7136–X
   0–7619–7137–8 (pb)

Library of Congress Control Number available

Typeset by Photoprint, Torquay, Devon
Printed in Great Britain by Athenaeum Press

CONTENTS

PREFACE AND PERSONAL ACKNOWLEDGEMENTS TO THE FIRST EDITION

Within less than five years, accounting for the environment has moved from being considered the most marginal and irrelevant of topics to its present position of occupying an increasingly central role in the deliberations of the worldwide accounting profession. Further, environmental accounting is now seen as an essential element in any organization's environmental response. EC proposals in 1992 in *Towards Sustainability* recognized that accounting must change its most basic concepts and practices if full environmental information is to be a central element in management organizational decision-making. Also in 1992, the State of Washington (USA) Department of Ecology issued guidelines on how to develop accounting systems 'for pollution prevention'. Such radical proposals from authoritative non-accountancy bodies would have been unthinkable only a few years ago.

This book follows on from *The Greening of Accountancy* published by the ACCA in 1990. It seeks to answer the question 'What can/ should accountants do in response to the developing environmental agenda?' The book lays out the best accounting practice with regard to the environment around the world and provides ideas for experimentation and future development. Whilst environmental accounting has come a considerable way in a very short time, it has now reached the stage where much wider – and more open – experimentation is essential. And this requires the very closest collaboration between practising and academic accountants. This book is the result of such collaboration and should provide a basis for the practitioner in industry and in partnership to start the environmental accounting ball rolling. Beyond that, the book should provide a basis for experimentation. In addition, the formation of the CSEAR (see below) is designed to facilitate the sort of more extensive academic/practitioner collaboration that is essential if our profession is to play its full part in the mitigation of the worst excesses of environmental degradation.

We have received considerable help and support throughout the research work for this book and in the preparation of the manuscript. In particular, we would like to express our especial gratitude to Roger Adams and the ACCA, who not only funded the project but also supported it in many ways, and to Martin Houldin of KPMG who acted as editorial advisor for the book and wrote the overviews for Parts A, B and C. We are also pleased to acknowledge the help we received from Rick Clarke of KPMG, Mark Campanale of Jupiter Tarbutt Merlin, Tony Clayton of IPAD, John Elkington of Sustain-Ability, Frank Jenkins of DTI, Nola Buhr, Sue Gray, Helle Bank Jorgensen, Linda Lewis, Meg Liston, Dave Owen, Ian Thomson, Jonathon Walesby and colleagues at the University of Dundee who have all given of their time, experience and ideas in different ways.

Rob Gray
Jan Bebbington
Diane Walters
August 1992

PREFACE TO THE SECOND EDITION

The first edition of *Accounting for the Environment* caught us all rather by surprise. In the writing and publication of a text in an area about which so little was known and so few appeared to be active, we (as authors and researchers), the ACCA (as sponsors) and Paul Chapman (as publisher) were genuinely unsure how the book would be received – if at all. As it transpired, we needn't have worried. The book was popular and editions have appeared in languages other than English. The text was gratifyingly well received by practitioners, academics and students and has been a major factor in bringing new contacts to us and CSEAR from all around the globe. A second edition therefore seemed inevitable – and is, in fact, rather overdue.

Two observations dominated our approach to this second edition of *Accounting for the Environment*. The first was the realization that environmental accounting and reporting were now well established and continuing to develop rapidly. In 1992, when we put the first edition together, there was little actual practice and providing a comprehensive overview of the subject in a single text was not difficult. Now it would be impossible – the area has grown so much in less than ten years it is just too vast to fit into the covers of a single book. The second observation was that the broad themes of the first edition had held up remarkably well. As environmental accounting was only just emerging as a practice in 1992, much of the content comprised estimates of where the field was going coupled with extrapolations from the few examples of best practice that existed. This edition has been constructed on what are now firmly established practices in environmental management and environmental reporting and strongly influenced by leading-edge developments in financial and management accounting.

The basic structure of the text is not, therefore, much changed. The contents have, however, been fairly thoroughly revised. In general terms, environmental accounting now sits on three foundations: environmental management, environmental reporting and (the essential agenda setting principles of) sustainability. These are also the areas where the fullest re-writing of the text has taken place.

Two more fundamental changes in the text have also flowed from all these developments. The first edition was explicitly directed to a practitioner audience. There was little to guide the practitioner in 1992 and our first intention was to provide an introduction that would support practitioners who needed to begin the process of addressing environmental issues in their work. The world has moved on and there is now a considerable body of good material that is directly practitioner-orientated and which is a great deal more specifically focused on the detailed needs of the practitioner. These are referenced throughout the text but we have not attempted to cover ground that is now so well served by the professional accountancy bodies, environmental management specialists and so on. We have, instead, sought to provide a text that will give a broad – but still practical – introduction to the whole area for students of (especially) accounting, finance, business, management and environmental management but in a style that will still serve the practitioner who is new to the issues. The text is, explicitly, an introduction to environmental accounting, management and reporting.

The other major change in this edition is in the tone in which the text is written. The first edition exhibited a somewhat hectoring tone – with much emphasis on cajolery and the self-evident desirability of the developments we were seeking to encourage. In 1992 we were explicitly trying to encourage people to see the importance and urgency of the issues and to do so in a manner which suggested the inevitability of this new environmental agenda. This edition has been written in a more realistic frame of mind and with a simpler, more straightforward tone. It is more explicitly conscious of the difficulties of developing the environmental agenda in business and has made much more use of the significant emerging research literature in the field.

The result of these changes does, we hope, produce a text that is more easily accessible, simpler to read and more engaging to study. As with the first edition, we will again be very pleased to receive any feedback and suggestions for further editions.

It is impossible to thank, by name, all the people who have supported and influenced us, CSEAR and the world-wide network of environmental (and, increasingly, social) accounting researchers, students, teachers and practitioners. It has been our privilege to work with – and become friends with – many wonderful individuals the world over. So, beyond thanking the ACCA (and, most especially, Roger Adams without whom this book would not exist), Martin Houldin (who has again acted as editorial adviser on this edition) and David Collison (who has read and commented on the draft of this edition) and reiterating our gratitude to those we mentioned in the first edition plus our colleagues at Aberdeen and Glasgow, we would simply wish to extend a warm and heartfelt thanks to all those wonderful people throughout the CSEAR network who have made the past ten years so pleasurable and worthwhile. Thanks.

Rob Gray
Jan Bebbington
January 2001

ABOUT CSEAR AND ACCA

The Centre for Social and Environmental Accounting Research (CSEAR) was established in 1991 as an international networking centre to encourage the research, teaching and practice of social and environmental accounting on a world-wide basis. The Centre provides a mechanism for the flow of ideas, information and best practice between all with a genuine interest in any aspect of social and environmental accounting. CSEAR has both an exceptionally diverse international membership as well as an active network of international contacts and associates. The Centre's activities include research projects, publication of working papers and introductory materials for those new to the area, maintenance of a specialist library, active interaction between international members – many of whom visit the Centre – the organization of an annual Summer School and the production of a twice-yearly journal of news, reviews and articles across the social and environmental accounting spectrum. For more detail please contact the Centre at the address in the appendix.

The Association of Chartered Certified Accountants (ACCA) is one of the world's major professional accountancy bodies and funds a wide range of original and practical research. The ACCA funded the research which underpinned *The Greening of Accountancy*, published in 1990, and provided the funding and support on which the first edition of the present text was based. The ACCA has an active policy of encouraging the development of environmental and social accounting and in addition to funding research in the field has been a major participant in many of the more significant developments in environmental and social accounting in the past decade. More detail about the ACCA, its environmental and social initiatives and its work in such areas as the Environmental Reporting Awards Scheme and the Social Reporting Awards can be obtained by contacting the Association at the address in the appendix.

ACRONYMS AND ABBREVIATIONS USED IN THE TEXT

ABC   Activity Based Costing
ACBE   Advisory Committee on Business and the Environment
ACCA   Association of Chartered Certified Accountants
AEC   Association of Environmental Consultancies
AICPA   American Institute of Certified Public Accountants
APB   Auditing Practices Board
ASB   Accounting Standards Board
ASC   Accounting Standards Committee
BATNEEC   Best Available Techniques Not Entailing Excessive Cost
BCSD   (i) Business Charter for Sustainable Development (see ICC)
            (ii) Business Council for Sustainable Development (now WBCSD)
BiE   Business-in-the-Environment
BIM   British Institute of Management
BPEO   Best Practicable Environmental Option
BS   British Standard (e.g. 7750)
BSI   British Standards Institution
C&LD   Coopers and Lybrand Deloitte
CBI   Confederation of British Industry
CEAS   Corporate Environmental Accounting System
CEBIS   Centre for Environment and Business in Scotland
CEFIC   Conseil Européen des Federations de l'Industrie Chimique (European Chemical Industry Federation)
CEP   Council for Economic Priorities
CERCLA   Comprehensive Environmental Response Compensation and Liability Act
CERES   Coalition for Environmentally Responsible Economies
CFCs   Chlorofluorocarbons
CHP   Combined Heat and Power
CIA   Chemical Industries Association
CIA RCP   Chemical Industries Association Responsible Care Programme
CICA   Canadian Institute of Chartered Accountants
CIMA   Chartered Institute of Management Accountants
CIMAH   Control of Industrial Major Accident Hazard
CIPFA   Chartered Institute of Public Finance and Accountancy

CIS	Counter Information Services
CMA	Society of Management Accountants of Canada
COD	Chemical Oxygen Demand
COSHH	Control of Substances Hazardous to Health
CSEAR	Centre for Social and Environmental Accounting Research
CWS	Compliance-with-Standards
DCF	Discounted Cash Flow
DFE	Design for the Environment
DoE	Department of the Environment
DTI	Department of Trade and Industry
EA	Environment Agency (England & Wales)
EC	European Community
EC DG XI	Directorate General XI (Environment, Nuclear Safety and Civil Protection)
EEO	Energy Efficiency Office
EFFAS	European Federation of Financial Analysts Societies
EIA	Environmental Impact Assessment
EIL	Environmental Impairment Liability
EIRIS	Ethical Investment Research Service
EIS	Environmental Impact Statement
EMAS	Eco-Management and Audit Scheme
EMS	Environmental Management System
ENDS	Environmental Data Services
EPA	(i) Environmental Protection Act
	(ii) Environmental Protection Agency (USA)
EPI	Environmental Performance Indicator
EPS	Environment Priority Strategies/Earnings Per Share
EQM	Environmental Quality Management
ERA	Environmental Reporting Awards
EU	European Union
FASB	Financial Accounting Standards Board
FEE	Fédération des Experts Comptables Européen
FRC	Financial Reporting Council
FRS	Financial Reporting Standard
G7/8	The Group of Seven/Eight (major industrialized countries)
G77	The Group of 77 (lesser developed countries)
GAAP	Generally Accepted Accounting Principles
GATT	General Agreement on Tariffs and Trade
GEM	Gas Energy Management
GEMI	Global Environmental Management Initiative
GRI	Global Reporting Initiative
HMIP	Her Majesty's Inspectorate of Pollution
HMSO	Her Majesty's Stationery Office
HSE	Health and Safety Executive

IAPC	International Auditing Practices Committee
IAS	International Accounting Standard
IASC	International Accounting Standards Committee
ICAEW	Institute of Chartered Accountants in England and Wales
ICAS	Institute of Chartered Accountants of Scotland
ICC	International Chamber of Commerce
ICCBCSD	International Chamber of Commerce Business Charter for Sustainable Development
IEA	Institute of Environmental Assessment (see IEMA)
IEM	Institute of Environmental Management (see IEMA)
IEMA	Institute of Environmental Management and Assessment
IFAC	International Federation of Accountants
IISD	International Institute for Sustainable Development
INCPEN	Industry Council for Packaging and the Environment
IoD	Institute of Directors
IPAD	Institute of Policy and Development
ISEA	Institute for Social and Ethical Accountability
ISO	International Organization for Standardization – also ISO Standards (e.g. ISO 140001)
JIT	Just in Time
LCA	Life Cycle Analysis/Assessment
LDC	lesser developed country
LETS	Local Economic/Exchange Trading Systems
MNC	Multinational Corporation
MNE	Multinational Enterprise
NACCB	National Accreditation Council of Certification Bodies
NADS	National Association of Diaper Services
NGO	Non-Governmental Organization
NPV	Net Present Value
OECD	Organization for Economic Co-operation and Development
Ofwat	Office of the Director General of Water Services
PCBs	Polychlorinated biphenyls
PIRC	(i) Public Interest Research Centre
	(ii) Pensions Investment Resource Centre
PPP	Pollution Prevention Pays
R&D	Research and Development
SARA	Superfund Amendments and Reauthorization Act
SEC	(i) Securities and Exchange Commission
	(ii) State Electricity Commission (of Victoria, Australia)
SEPA	Scottish Environmental Protection Agency
SEPTIC	Single Event Pollution Triggered Incident Clause
SETAC	Society of Environmental Toxicology and Chemistry
SFAS	Statement of Financial Accounting Standards (see FASB)
SNA	United Nations' System of National Accounts

SORP	Statement of Recommended Practice
SSAP	Statement of Standard Accounting Practice
SWOT	Strengths, Weaknesses, Opportunities, Threats
TNC	Transnational Corporation
TQM	Total Quality Management
TRI	Toxic Release Inventory
TUC	Trades Union Congress
UNCED	United Nations Commission on Environment and Development
UNCTAD	United Nations Conference on Trade and Development
UN CTC	United Nations Centre for Transnational Corporations
ISAR	Intergovernmental Working Group of Experts on International Standards of Accounting and Reporting
UNEP	United Nations Environment Programme
VAS	Value Added Statement
WARM	Waste as a Raw Material
WBCSD	World Business Council for Sustainable Development
WCA	Waste Collection Authority
WDA	Waste Disposal Authority
WEN	Women's Environmental Network
WICEM	World Industry Conference on Environment Management (see WBCSD)
WRA	Waste Regulation Authority
WRAP	Waste Reduction Always Pays
WRI	World Resources Institute
WTO	World Trade Organization
WWF	World Wildlife Fund for Nature

PART A: INTRODUCTION TO THE ISSUES

Overview

by Martin Houldin, EMAG Ltd

Any accountant would be well advised to consider how his or her responsibilities are – and should be – influenced by today's environmental agenda. Quite simply any factor that can bring about change in an organization will affect accountants. This will apply just as much to accountants who work as financial advisers or auditors, as to those with different accounting and financial roles within a business.

Broadly speaking, there are three principal reasons for accountants to become involved in environment management issues.

(1) *Environmental issues are business issues:* Above all, this book seeks to show clearly that environmental issues, principally in terms of legislation and market forces, have implications for business in those areas that directly concern accountants. From straightforward profit and loss issues, to competitive advantage issues related to market opportunity and cost efficiency, to the more complex issues of asset values, contingent liabilities and environmental risk, and to investment appraisal decisions that are growing in complexity – most accountants will have some role to play.

(2) *Environmental management is inextricably linked with business management:* The 1990s saw the increasing recognition in many quarters that environmental issues need to be managed holistically within business, and be subject to normal management routines and disciplines. This notion has had a major influence on the development of standards for environmental management systems (EMS) – such as ISO 14001 – the international standard for EMS – and EMAS (the European Union Eco-Management and Audit Scheme). And these standards have, in turn, stimulated

and reinforced this systematic approach to the management of environmental issues.

There is now less talk about environmental issues as if they were new and emerging, and rather more about environmental performance. This important area of development has been re-inforced further by the ever-growing external stakeholder interests in environmental performance. This goes far beyond compliance with the law (on such matters as levels of emissions, discharges, wastes and complaints).

As a consequence there has been sustained growth in environmental reporting. However, the demand these days is for less dialogue/general description on broad issues, and much more for specific, quantified performance information.

In fact, as an issue for general management, environmental management has probably developed and grown faster, and more internationally, than any other during recent times.

(3) *Environmental issues have considerable implications for financial advisers in all their guises:* The implications for the statutory audit, particularly in the more polluting/regulated industries, are so important that financial auditors may be found negligent should they fail to recognize profit and loss account and balance sheet implications. Other auditors, with whom accountants in business must also interface, are also providing services under the general heading/label of environmental audit. Some of these 'audits' may be of more direct concern to accountants. Any major financial transactions (such as of an investment, corporate re-structuring or financing nature) will need to take into account how current and projected environmental performance and role may affect the business's prospect (and therefore its value). The continuing interest in using fiscal instruments to influence business activity also affects accountants. There will be many other examples.

The book firmly puts environmental audits into their place within the context of environmental management. Accountants, whether inside or outside the business, may become involved through the implications for their own duties. Or they may get involved by providing their skills and experience in new areas – the auditing or verification of environmental performance information as contained in corporate environmental reports is a case in point.

The first two chapters do more than introduce environmental issues as they affect accountants. A strong case is made in support of the view that accountants have a major role to play, both through their traditional roles of recording and reporting financial information and through their roles as business managers. The authors go even further to suggest that there are five ways in which accountants can contribute to environmental management (see Box).

The Roles of Accountants in Environmental Management

- Modify existing accounting systems to include environmental performance within internal management reporting.
- Eliminate conflicting elements of the accounting systems (as in investment appraisal).
- Plan for financial implications of the environmental agenda (as in capital expenditure projections).
- Introduce environmental performance to external reporting (as in annual reports).
- Develop new accounting and information systems (as in eco-balance sheets).

Research findings indicate that accountants are still not yet as involved as they should be, especially when some aspects of the environmental agenda and the attitudes of different groups are taken into account. This is surprising, when one considers the financial implications of:

- liabilities for cleaning up contaminated land;
- liabilities for being in breach of environmental legislation and regulations;
- opportunities for gaining market share over competitors who have been slower in grasping the need to change (in response, for example, to the implications of the packaging standards in the German market);
- the shift in public opinion and the growth of stakeholder interests leading to possible public relations risks or opportunities;
- developments in both national and supra-national government policy towards sustainable development. Environmental regulations are beginning to incorporate environmental management requirements. This opens up a wider group of management to the ever-developing regulatory agenda.

In spite of widespread efforts of a number of business organizations, survey results seem to show a distinct lack of interest in meeting higher environmental performance standards unless there is pressure of legislation, although, given the rapid change in the environmental agenda, it remains to be seen how reliable these results still are.

In some areas, however, there has been a significant increase in involvement by accountants since the mid-1990s. All of the major accounting firms have recognized the need to have environmental expertise available and that expertise has been employed both in supporting the various financial advisory functions, as well as in environmental management consultancy. Similarly, a significant proportion of the world's major accountancy institutes have established research programmes designed to advance both environmental accounting and reporting. In addition, supra-national accounting bodies, such as FEE (Fédération des Experts Comptables Européens), the United Nations and the International Accounting Standards Committee have been in the vanguard of both environmental accounting research and environmental accounting regulation since the early 1990s.

The real issue seems to rest with accountants in business and other organizations. What may not be fully known, of course, is whether accountants are becoming more involved inadvertently. It may be that environmental issues are being internalized, through conventional management channels, rather than specifically labelled as 'environmental issues'. This would then lead to greater involvement as a part of 'business as usual'.

A Practitioner's View

From wide experience in working with different companies on the full spectrum of the components of environmental management, it could be said that we could expect much greater interest from accountants in the near future. Indeed there are indications that this is already happening in perhaps the one area which you might expect to be in the vanguard, namely the arrangement of corporate deals/transactions.

Before delving into the body of the book, it is useful to consider the following issues.

Business and Environmental Issues

What are the business implications of environmental issues and how is business responding? The spectrum of environmental pressures (see Figure A.1) really has two broad categories: legislative (local, national, regional) and market-based. Each has implications for business and accountants.

Figure A.1 Sources of environmental pressures: opportunities and threats

Martin Houldin, EMAG Limited

Legislation

Regulation of environmental issues is growing rapidly in all countries of the world and keeping up to date with even national legislation is a specialized field in itself. For illustration, *UK legislation* involves such things as the EPA 1990, the Water Act 1990 and the Environment Act 1995. A new regime for Integrated Pollution Prevention and Control (Pollution Prevention and Control Act 1999) was implemented in 2000. As a consequence companies need to:

- invest in pollution protection;
- invest in cleaner technologies;
- change processes and products;
- establish waste minimization programmes;
- review asset values;
- spend on waste treatment/disposal.

Similarly, *EC environmental legislation* is expected to be developed to support the policy of sustainable development (such as measures to reduce emissions of greenhouse gases). Even by the turn of the century there were already some business implications:

- the nature of packaging was changing;
- packaging recovery/recycling schemes were needed;

- cost of waste treatment/disposal was rising;
- companies need to make more information available to the public;
- heavier industrial processes need to adopt environmental management practices.

Fiscal measures

Market or economic instruments to encourage environmental response – carbon taxes of one sort or another which might raise the cost of energy by 50 per cent – look increasingly likely.

Business community

Peer pressure and leadership through, for example, ICC, WBCSD, GRI, CIA, acting ahead of legislation.

Corporate customers

There are an increasing number of environmental requirements in product/service specification. Supplier evaluations are likely to include some environmental criteria. Environmental audits may be carried out. Major companies expect certification to environmental management systems standards. Product stewardship techniques have been more widely applied to cover life-cycle issues, and to promote responsible care of the use and disposal of products.

Greener competitors

Competition is developing through cost-effective response to legislation and to customer needs, high environmental profile in markets and the development of products with better environmental performance. Companies compete for recognized leadership roles in environmental management and technology fields.

Investors/financial institutions

Environmental issues mean new risks for financial institutions requiring more information from companies on: capital expenditure plans;

the environmental effect on profits; potential liabilities; and ability to cope with existing and future environmental problems.

Public concern/environmental groups

Companies need to build closer working relationships with groups who are increasingly vocal and well informed by the greater amount of information available in the public domain. Despite the (temporary?) decline in the impact of the green consumer, the impact of these groups is rising.

Environmental Accounting

What do we mean by environmental accounting? This is open to interpretation. However, for the purposes of this book it can be taken as covering all areas of accounting that may be affected by the business response to environmental issues, including new areas of 'eco-accounting'.

Environmental accounting will cover:

- Accounting for contingent liabilities/risks
- Accounting for asset re-valuations and capital projections
- Cost analysis in key areas such as energy, waste and environmental protection
- Investment appraisal to include environmental factors
- Development of new accounting and information systems to cover all areas of environmental performance
- Assessing the costs and benefits of environmental improvement programmes
- Developing accounting techniques which express assets and liabilities and costs in ecological (non-financial) terms.

But the development of the accountant's role will be set within an environmental management context. As with any new field of management, there will be differing ways of defining environmental management. One broad definition is 'the range of responses by companies to environmental issues in reviewing their environmental position, developing and implementing policies and strategies to improve that position and in changing management systems to ensure ongoing improvement and effective management'.

If we consider that the fundamental purpose of environmental management is to manage (control and improve) environmental performance, then it adds weight to the need for involvement by accountants. As ISO 14001 *Specification for Environmental Management Systems* states '*it is intended that the implementation of an environmental management system . . . will result in improved environmental performance'* (Annex A, A.1) and '*Environmental performance: Measurable results of the environmental management system, related to an organisation's control of its environmental aspects, based on its environmental policy, objectives and targets'* (Definitions 3.8).

Also, environmental management will consist of a range of functions, which in turn will influence the role of the accountant.

Environmental management functions

- Environmental review and policy development
- Objectives and targets development
- Life-cycle assessment
- Establishment and maintenance of environmental management systems to international and European standards (ISO 14001 and EMAS)
- Regulatory compliance
- Environmental impact assessment (including contaminated land)
- Eco-label applications
- Waste minimization
- Pollution prevention programmes
- Research, development and investment in cleaner technologies
- Environmental performance and issues reporting

Environmental Management and Accountants

How does all this affect different accounting roles and responsibilities? It is evident from the above introduction to the business implications of environmental issues and the definitions given for environmental management and environmental accounting, that a variety of accounting jobs will be affected. Those working as external financial advisers and auditors will be similarly affected.

By mapping environmental issues to different accounting jobs we can begin to see more clearly how accountants will be involved (see Box).

How the Accountant's Job Will Change

- *Financial accountant*
  - Balance sheet issues: valuation; liabilities; contingencies; provisions.
  - Profit and loss issues: major cost items such as waste treatment/disposal and site clean-up.
  - Annual reports: environmental performance figures.
  - Relationships with banks, fund managers, insurance companies.

- *Management accountant*
  - Business plans including new costs, capital items and revenue projections.
  - Investment appraisal to evaluate environmental costs/benefits.
  - Cost/benefit analysis of environmental improvement.
  - Cost analysis/efficiency improvement programmes.
  - Environmental performance reporting.

- *Systems accountant*
  - Changes to management information systems.
  - Changes to financial reporting systems.

- *Project accountant*
  - Investment appraisal.
  - Environmental auditing of proposed corporate deals (mergers and acquisitions).
  - Environmental assessment for planning purposes.

- *Accountants as internal auditors*
  - Incorporate environmental auditing into internal audit programmes.

As these affect accountants in commerce and industry, then we also see corresponding roles for accountants within the professions, acting as auditors or specialist advisers.

From an accountant's point of view all this could be seen as unwelcome change; however, it can equally be regarded as a great opportunity for building on the proactive, business management roles that many accountants already enjoy. Environmental issues are of real interest to accountants because of the breadth and scale of potential business issues that arise, whether profitable and/or cost-incurring.

Many of us believe that, as accountants, we have no option but to become involved in the organization's management of environmental performance at all points in the company. We do have the option, however, to get involved early and plan ahead, or to be forced to react to the negative effects of pressures, and to suffer the potential costs and disadvantages that may be the result.

CHAPTER 1

BUSINESS AND THE ENVIRONMENT

The Challenge for Accounting and Finance

In responding to the challenges posed by the environment, which is our natural wealth, all aspects of accountancy including financial reporting, auditing, management accounting and taxation will have to change. In doing so, there will be an impact on all members of the Institute whether in public practice or in commerce and industry and whether working at home or abroad.

(Mike Lickiss, ex-President of the Institute of Chartered Accountants in England and Wales, *Accountancy*, January 1991)

1.1 Introduction

The twentieth century was a period of unprecedented change. In only a hundred years the world has changed out of all recognition. Amongst the major areas of change are the factors that concern us most in this book. We have seen a vast increase in economic activity, unprecedented growth in the size and power of business organizations, breathtaking technological change whilst, simultaneously, the health of the natural environment upon which we all depend and of which we are all a part has declined to a dangerously precarious level. Whilst a substantial proportion of the populations in the (so-called) developed countries continue to enjoy an ever-rising material standard of living, an increasing proportion of the people on the planet face ever-increasing poverty, starvation and social disintegration. There is a problem here. To what extent can the privileged minority of the world's population continue to enjoy a life of rising luxury whilst the planet's eco-systems collapse and the majority of the world's people descend into poverty? This is a question as complex as it is urgent. It is an economic question: to what extent is the well-being of the wealthy gained at the expense of the poor? To what extent is the very economic and technological success the cause of the environmental degradation? It is a moral question: how can we justify such disparity and such steady erosion of the planet's health? And it is a practical question: can the declining health of the planet continue to support the high levels of material production and consumption that are the hallmarks of the success of late twentieth century financial capitalism?

This book does not set out to try to analyse and answer these questions (see Further Reading at the end of the chapter for exploration of these matters) but, rather, recognizing that these questions are substantial and important, tries to examine what we, as accountants, can do about the issues.

It is no longer contentious to recognize that there *is* an environmental crisis.[1] What remains contentious are: the extent of the crisis; explanations for the causes of the crisis; the nature of the required solutions to environmental (and social) degradation and, most relevantly here, what, if anything, this has to do with accounting and accountants.

We will return to such questions in Chapters 14 and 15 of the text. For the time being, however, it is sufficient to recognize that *all* sections of the population are implicated in environmental degradation to some degree or other – whether as consumers, producers, policy-makers, educators or whatever. Consequently, all sections of the population need to look to their activities, to assess what impact those activities have and to try to explore how, if at all, the activities can be made more environmentally benign. Although it might seem counter-intuitive, accountants have a crucial role to play in any substantial attempts to ameliorate the environmental crisis.

There are two, central, reasons why accountants must pay particular attention to environmental issues. In the first place, business and accounting are inextricably linked. If business is going to respond to the demands of the growing environmental agenda – and it is certainly doing that[2] – it needs accounting to move with it. As we shall see, two of the most significant environmental developments under-

---

[1] It is perhaps worth recording that before about 1990 it *was* contentious to suggest (a) that there was an environmental crisis, (b) that such a crisis was in any way connected with business organization, and (c) that this had any implications for accounting. It is appropriate to recognize how far business and accounting have come in a short period of time whilst also recognizing that business and accounting systems are not set in stone, do change frequently but are generally reluctant to acknowledge new demands that do not directly have an impact upon their 'normal' day to day activities.

[2] The most obvious examples of this are the international initiatives of the World Business Council for Sustainable Development (WBCSD) and the International Chamber of Commerce (ICC), see, for example, ICC (1989), Schmidheiny (1992) and Schmidheiny and Zorraquin (1996). A word of caution, however, is appropriate. In part such initiatives could be seen as attempts actually to control, rather than respond to, the environmental agenda. It is noticeable that business-based publications on the subject generally avoid engaging with the environmentalists' arguments in the debate. The most obvious example of this relates to 'growth' and whether it is the cause of or the cure for ecological desecration. No business-based publication of which we are aware has made any attempt to address carefully the 'anti-growth' arguments and evidence. For more detail on this see, for example, Elkington (1995), Mayhew (1997) and Weizsäcker et al. (1997).

taken by business (environmental management systems and environmental reporting)[3] need the full support of the accountants to be fully effective. Secondly, and much more subtly, the very practice of accounting and its current fundamental assumptions about profit, cost, success and failure are absolutely central to the environmental crisis. So much so, that it is possible to argue that, given current accounting practice, environmental crisis is inevitable.[4] (This argument is outlined in Appendix 1.1 to this chapter.)

This, then, is the central theme of the book. Accountants and accounting are centrally implicated in the declining health of the natural environment and thus should – and can – do something about it. The following chapters lay out what accountants and accounting can do. But there *is* a sub-theme to the book and that relates to the complex nature of the environmental crisis and the extent to which we can only begin to *really* do something about the state of the natural environment (and the related increases in social disintegration and poverty) if we examine the very basis of what accounting is, what it assumes about the world and what that, in turn, tells us about the nature and workings of late twentieth century financial capitalism. This sub-theme will be there in the background throughout our discussions and will re-emerge in Chapters 14 and 15.

1.2 Accountants, Accounting and the Environment

Whilst there is no doubt that accounting is not the most obvious place to start if one is seeking to address either environmental issues in general or the business/environment relationship in particular, it is equally true that without a 'greener accounting' many environmental initiatives will simply not get off the ground. Throughout this book we have treated the accountant as a member of the organization's management team and therefore seen his or her role as greater than just that of maintaining the financial information systems.

This approach will be apparent throughout the text. However, as it is difficult – if not impractical – to consider the role of accounting without giving some attention to the context within which that accounting takes place, it will be necessary to provide an introduction to the wider business/environment agenda and its implications for

---

[3] These matters are examined in Chapters 5 and 12.

[4] There are also more pragmatic reasons why accountants need to respond to environmental issues. These include changes in legislation, increasing attention given to the issues by the professional accounting bodies, the increasing impact of environmental issues on financial statements and statutory financial auditing (see Chapters 10 and 11) and the growing involvement of accountants with the development of environmental consultancy.

Figure 1.1

**Some areas where traditional accounting and finance frameworks are
potentially in conflict with environmental initiatives**

- Investment appraisal criteria
- Performance appraisal criteria
- Budgeting constraints
- Share price performance
- Reported earnings per share
- Priorities in the annual report
- Design costs
- Creation of new information systems
- Forecasting
- Assessing environmental costs
- Costs of sustainability

business and accounting. We know that accounting does not operate
in a vacuum. Accounting systems in any organization are effective
only when related to the context in which they seek to operate. For
much accounting this context is the organization itself. Therefore, to
understand the issues arising from any attempt to 'account for the
environment' we need to understand the wider management issues
within which accounting innovations need to take place as well as
some of the wider social issues which determine both the operations
of the organization and the accountability for those operations which
accounting seeks to discharge. We have therefore used Chapters 2, 3,
4 and 5 to introduce a number of the basic (but essential) environmental management initiatives in a way that should be relevant to the
accounting and finance professional. With this background, we can
then move on to those activities that are more specifically within the
functional ambit of the accountant.

The accountant's role in helping organizations to become more
environmentally sensitive will fall, approximately, into five phases.[5]
The chapters and structure of the book reflect this.[6]

---

[5] We have generally chosen to ignore any tendency for accountants to treat environmental matters as 'nothing to do with me'. Such an attitude is usually predicated upon
the grounds that their job is to record and account for financial transactions. As such, it
is argued, when the environmental issues are reflected in changed monetary values the
accountants will account for them. Such a narrow perspective would conclude that the
changing environmental agenda has no direct effect on accounting. This would still
appear to be a widely held view among accountants.

[6] This and other comments throughout the book are taken from the continuing
research undertaken by the authors, other members of the Centre for Social and
Environmental Accounting Research (CSEAR) and the wider academic and professional
community. Some of this work is specifically reflected in Bebbington et al. (1994), Gray,

(1) The existing accounting system can be modified slightly to identify the environmentally related areas of expenditure (and, perhaps, revenue) separately. The most obvious areas for this to occur are in energy, waste, packaging, legal costs and suchlike (see, for example, Chapters 6 and 7) and in land remediation and liability – especially in North America (see Chapter 11).

(2) The environmentally negative elements of the existing accounting system need to be identified and, where possible, ameliorated. The most obvious examples of this relate to investment appraisal and performance appraisal (see, for example, Chapter 8).

(3) The accounting system needs to become more forward-looking and, in the present context, to be more aware of potential issues arising from the rapidly changing environmental agenda. This will affect such matters as changing payback periods as energy costs change, looking forward to potential contingent liabilities, the potential costs of 'greener' financing, assessing the potential costs of *not* undertaking environmental initiatives, and so on (see, for example, Chapters 2 and 5–10).

(4) The external reporting function is changing. One extreme (but not unrealistic) description of current corporate reporting practice is that the accountants look after the statutory accounts and the public relations department looks after the rest. Environmental issues will not permit this hard delineation when the financial statements begin to reflect various aspects of the environmental costs, and the non-financial elements of the report need to be a great deal more substantive than self-congratulatory publicity material (see, for example, Chapters 11 and 12).

(5) New accounting and information systems will need to be developed. Whether these are physical quantity information systems or some sort of financial information system, they will need to be of a status equal to the present financial accounting systems. Experimentation and innovation will be crucial here whether one is talking about more subtle performance appraisal, the development of something akin to eco-balances and life-cycle assessment or really attempting to build a sustainability accounting system (see, for example, Chapters 4, 5, 8, 9, 13 and 14).

Throughout any process of 'greening' accountancy and finance it *is* possible to allow accountants simply to be reactive within their conventionally conceived roles. However, whilst there is a lot of evidence to suggest that accountants *are* reactive, we have predicated much of

Bebbington, Walters and Thomson (1995). Gray et al. (1998) and publications from CSEAR including the newsletter *Social and Environmental Accounting*. For further detail, please contact CSEAR (address in the appendix).

Figure 1.2

What is environmental accounting?

- Recognizing and seeking to mitigate the negative environmental effects of conventional accounting practice;
- Separately identifying environmentally related costs and revenues within the conventional accounting systems;
- Taking active steps to set up initiatives in order to ameliorate existing environmental effects of conventional accounting practice;
- Devising new forms of financial and non-financial accounting systems, information systems and control systems to encourage more environmentally benign management decisions;
- Developing new forms of performance measurement, reporting and appraisal for both internal and external purposes;
- Identifying, examining and seeking to rectify areas in which conventional (financial) criteria and environmental criteria are in conflict;
- Experimenting with ways in which sustainability may be assessed and incorporated into organizational orthodoxy.

---

the book on the belief that accountants are also professionals and can (and should) exercise professional attributes. For this, accountants need to recognize the responsibility which accounting bears for the environmental crisis[7] and, recognizing the skills and attributes which accountants bring to bear in their job, look for creative ways to mitigate the responsibility and to help organizations develop greater environmental sensitivity. Many accountants are not hostile to this view (see below) but they do not have the intention or wherewithal to put it into practice. This book is intended to help them do so. From a human, ethical and professional point of view, the accountant is committed to the 'public interest' and amelioration of the ecological crisis, and survival of the human species must fall within that interest.

Although they were, at first, rather slow to get started, the professional accountancy bodies around the world *have* undertaken a number of initiatives as a response to the developing environmental agenda. Many accountancy bodies do recognize that there is a need for a reaction – perhaps even a lead – from the accountancy profession. The impact of these initiatives on practice has also been generally slow although, as we might expect, it is in the more visible and traditional areas of accounting activity – notably the financial statements and auditing – where progress has been most marked. How far the accounting profession is able to take its environmental initiatives will depend on many factors – not least the development of

---

[7] See Appendix 1.1, Appendix 1.2 and Gray (1990d).

legislation, the demands of business and, more subtly, the extent to which accountants can begin to see the nature of their abilities and their responsibilities for what they are – rather than restricting themselves to a reactive interpretation of GAAP.

1.3 Accountants and Environmental Attitudes

It still seems to be the case that accountants are not as widely involved in the changing environmental agenda as they could be. More worryingly, there is a widespread view that the accountant's conventional approach is acting like a dead hand on environmental innovation. Conventional short-term profit measurement, performance reporting, budgetary constraints and investment appraisal are highly likely to be in conflict with more environmentally benign initiatives – in the immediate term at least.[8] For one of our correspondents, this conflict is profound and the priorities clear:

> *I was disheartened to receive your letter of 5 Jan and to learn that a pragmatic and esteemed organization such as yours had lowered its standards to worry about c--p at a time when most of the nation is facing economic hardship and your subject matter will add zero to the well-being of this country.*
> *We have therefore filed the Questionnaire in a place we believe appropriate.*
> (Finance Director, Large International Trading plc [censorship by authors])

However, experience suggests, more encouragingly, that this is a minority view and, in fact, accountants are often keen to innovate. But, of course, accountants do have a strong attachment to the conventional accounting activities – in particular, financial measurement. Consequently, the accountants too often do not involve themselves in initiatives where they have much to contribute. One of the more favourable explanations for this is that accountants are (still) largely unsure about whether they should become involved and, if so, how to contribute to the development of environmental sensitivity in the organization. There seems to be little doubt that accountants – at least in the more forward-looking organizations – are fully aware of the changing environmental agenda and of their own organization's responses to it. However, accountants more generally do appear to

---

[8] See Gray et al. (1998) for more detail on British experience here.

need guidance in the form of a lead from their company or from their professional body . At the same time, the training of accountants does encourage many to retain a deep-rooted suspicion of any attempt to dilute the 'reliability', 'objectivity' and 'unbiasedness' of their conventional activity.[9] As we have argued elsewhere,[10] this is an untenable position for the accounting profession to maintain.

These observations have a considerable importance in this book. 'Environmental accounting' is still a relatively new concept and whilst standards of best practice are steadily emerging, they have yet to be widely adopted by organizations. In part, this arises from accountants' apparent reluctance to undertake new activities for which there may not seem to be an *immediate* need. (Especially when, despite the accounting profession's encouragement, such matters do not feature widely or centrally in, for example, accounting standards or professional examinations.) But, in part, the slow adoption of environmental accounting techniques is due to the reluctance of businesses to fully recognize and embrace the environmental agenda. Accountants, consequently, are under little pressure to adopt new methods. One result of this relates to the contents and structure of the book. As environmental accounting is steadily emerging as a coherent body of knowledge and techniques, as adoption is by no means universal and as organizational experiences with approaches to environmental accounting vary widely, there is no definitive set of guidelines as to what 'environmental accounting' actually looks like. This book, therefore, draws from a very wide range of experiences; examples of best practice; experiments (both successful and unsuccessful); and practicable speculations on ways in which accounting for the environment could (and should) develop. The book has therefore been written in a way that is intended to provide the maximum available assistance to accountants wishing to begin the process of developing greener accounting and finance systems and for students and others wishing to gain an introduction to environmental issues which are – and which will need to be – central in all future accounting systems. This is *not*, however, a complete manual on 'Learn Environmental Accounting in a Weekend'. The issues are too complex and rapidly evolving for a recipe of easy answers.

---

[9] It should be clear to any student of accounting that accounting is *not* as reliable, objective and unbiased as many would wish to believe. It does not (or should not) require us to rehearse why these characteristics are rarely, if ever, present in accounting data. The continuing attachment to the motherhood myths about the nature of accounting is a perplexing and worrying one.

[10] See Bebbington and Gray (1992), Gray (1990a, 1990b), Gray, Laughlin and Bebbington (1996).

1.4 Conclusions and Developing the Accountant's Role

Research suggests that accountants are not seen as a major source of innovation – in the organization generally and in organizational response to the environment in particular. Indeed, whilst accountants *do* see themselves as potentially innovative, it is an innovation constrained within the existing financial information system. As a consequence, innovative environmental accounting has emerged only slowly. This is changing as the growing pressures on the organization (see Chapter 2) take root.[11] As a result, in the short to medium term, it seems most likely that the environmental initiative will tend to come from elsewhere in the organization. However, the rapidly changing demands upon the organization will bring an urgent demand for changes in accountants' activities. Only the far-sighted are yet ready to respond to this.

We have tried to provide support and encouragement for the accountant seeking to explore environmental initiatives and, as a result, have provided chapters on both potential and actual areas of direct relevance to the accountant as well as the broader environmental management areas. We have not attempted to be comprehensive on these latter topics, and refer readers to the works listed in the further reading sections. Our hope is, however, that we will encourage accountants to adopt the role that they *can* play in developing the environmental sensitivity of the organization and to see that it is relatively practicable to put aside some elements of their traditional – and perhaps limited – role. The book cannot answer all problems, and for this we have provided, in Appendix A, contacts at the Centre for Social and Environmental Accounting Research and contact points for many of the other appropriate and frequently excellent organizations.

Further Reading

There is a very considerable array of good books around dealing with the issues we raise throughout this text. The following are just a few examples of sources that address the issues from a variety of perspectives. (As environmental law is both country-specific and liable to change rapidly, no references are given here.)

[11] A central element in this realization of the caricature of accountants is the education and training which accounting students receive. There is a plethora of evidence now to suggest that accountants are actually inculcated into a particular way of looking at the world which not only does not encourage innovation but actively discourages it. There is some sign that this is becoming more recognized in accounting education – but we have a very long way to go yet.

General Introduction to Environmental Issues

Cairncross, F. (1991) *Costing the Earth* (London: Business Books/The Economist)

Ekins, P. (1992) *Wealth Beyond Measure: An Atlas of New Economics* (London: Gaia)

Jacobs, M. (1991) *The Green Economy* (London: Pluto Press)

Porritt, J. (1991) *Save the Earth* (London: Dorling Kindersley)

Weizsäcker, E. von (1994) *Earth Politics* (London: Zed Books)

General Introductions to Business and the Environment

Beder, S. (1997) *Global Spin: The Corporate Assault on Environmentalism* (Dartington: Green Books)

Davis, J. (1991) *Greening Business: Managing for Sustainable Development* (Blackwell: Oxford)

Eden, S. (1996) *Environmental Issues and Business* (Chichester: John Wiley)

Elkington, J. (1987) (with T. Burke) *The Green Capitalists* (London: Gollancz)

Elkington, J. (1997) *Cannibals with Forks: The Triple Bottom Line for Business* (Oxford: Capstone Publishing)

Elkington, J., P. Knight and J. Hailes (1991) *The Green Business Guide* (London: Gollancz)

Stead, W.E. and J.G. Stead (1992) *Management for a Small Planet* (Newbury Park, CA: Sage Publications)

Weizsäcker, E. von, A.B. Lovins and L.H. Lovins (1997) *Factor Four: Doubling Wealth, Halving Resource Use* (London: Earthscan)

Welford, R. (1997) *Hijacking Environmentalism: Corporate Responses to Sustainable Development* (London: Earthscan)

Welford, R. and R. Starkey (1996) *The Earthscan Reader in Business and the Environment* (London: Earthscan)

General Introductions to Accounting and the Environment

Bennett, M. and P. James (1998a) *Environment under the Spotlight: Current Practice and Future Trends in Environmental-related Performance Measurement for Business* (London: ACCA)

Bennett, M. and P. James (eds) (1998b) *The Green Bottom Line: Environmental Accounting for Management* (Sheffield: Greenleaf)

Ditz, D., J. Ranganathan and R.D. Banks (1995) *Green Ledgers: Case Studies in Environmental Accounting* (Baltimore, MD: World Resources Institute)

Epstein, M.J. (1996) *Measuring Corporate Environmental Performance* (Chicago: Irwin)

Field, D., P. Fisher and J. Oldham (1994) *The Environment: An Accountant's Perspective* (Scarborough, Ontario: Carswell)

Gray, R.H. (1990) *The Greening of Accountancy* (London: ACCA)

Macve, R. and A. Carey (1992) *Business, Accountancy and the Environment: A Policy and Research Agenda,* (London: ICAEW)

Niskala, M. and R. Matasaho (1996) *Environmental Accounting* (Helsinki: WSOY, Ekonomia) (In Finnish)

Owen, D. (ed.) (1992) *Green Reporting: Accountancy and the Challenge of the Nineties* (London: Chapman Hall)

Schaltegger, S. (with K. Mueller and H. Hindrichsen) (1996) *Corporate Environmental Accounting* (New York: John Wiley)

In addition, many of the leading professional accountancy bodies in, for example, Australia, Canada, the United States and throughout Europe, have issued various guidance and discussion of aspects of environmental accounting. There are also a number of good newsletters which keep their readers abreast of developments – amongst which are *Business and the Environment, ENDS, Environmental Accounting and Auditing Reporter,* and *Social and Environmental Accounting.* Addresses for these and other sources of further information are provided in the appendix at the end of the book.

APPENDIX 1.1
The Accountant and the Environment: a Systems View[1]

Whilst accountants use systems terminology (in, particularly, management information systems and auditing), there have been only a few attempts to take a wider systems perspective of the conventional accounting activity itself. One such view is given in Figure Appendix 1.1a.[2]

The figure is no more than a reinterpretation of what the accountant traditionally does. His or her world centres around the organization (the accounting entity – which is itself a system made up of various sub-systems; see Gray, Laughlin and Bebbington (1996) for more detail), which can be seen to be located in a 'substantive environment'. (The word 'environment' does not necessarily have ecological connotations in this context.) This 'substantive environment' is bounded with reference to only those events which the accountant traditionally recognizes – those economic events which can be described in financial terms. For simplicity, the flows that the accountant records can be categorized into three sets of inflows (debits) and three sets of outflows (credits) represented by information (e.g. debtors, creditors, ownership claims), funds (all receipts and payments) and physical resources/goods and services (e.g. labour, plant, vehicles, buildings, materials, sales).

This perspective can be used to capture all the accountant's bookkeeping and financial reporting activities, but one of the major benefits of this view is that it makes explicit the very limited view we take of the world. In Figure Appendix 1.1b, a simple representation of the social world is introduced. Now we can see the accountant's perspective rather more clearly. The organization is a complex web of interactions drawing from and contributing to the social world in many ways (both positive and negative). Because many of these interactions are either implicit, and/or embedded into the very fabric of the society (e.g. the question of personal and group rights) and/or are matters of interpretation and perception, they are not made explicit in a way that the price system – and therefore traditional accounting practice – can recognize. Traditional accounting therefore largely ignores them, as does the traditional neo-classical model of economics (see, for example, Gray, 1990c; 1992; Owen, 1990; Zaikov, 1986). It is almost certainly the case that accounting ignores these interactions *because* of these omissions by the underlying economic model. Our present concern is with environmental issues, and these are introduced into the model in Figure Appendix 1.1c. The activities of the organization in creating material well-being draw off from the biosphere some things for which prices exist (raw materials) and some things for which no prices exist (landscape, sea water). The biosphere in most cases is diminished by this. The processes of producing the man-made capital and the (presumed) subsequent material well-being as well as the subsequent consumption benefits lead to waste (immediately or eventually). This waste is injected back into the biosphere – there is nowhere else for it to go! The accountant's model cannot recognize these interactions and so they are ignored.

[1] The material that follows is a straight adaptation of the material in Gray (1990d).

[2] Figure Appendix 1.1a and subsequent figures are based upon the excellent work of Lowe (1972) and Lowe and McInnes (1971). These ideas are summarized and employed in a financial accounting context by Gray, Laughlin and Bebbington (1996). A very good critique of systems theory is provided by Hopper and Powell (1985).

Figure Appendix 1.1a   A systems view of accounting, organizations and the environment

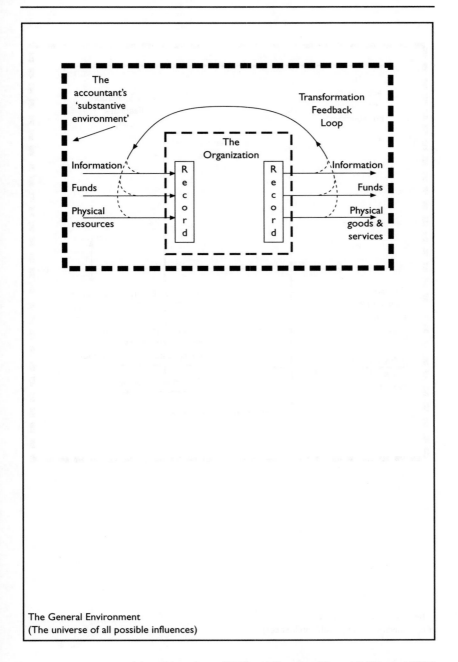

The General Environment
(The universe of all possible influences)

Adapted from Lowe (1972) and Gray, Laughlin and Bebbington (1996)

Figure Appendix 1.1b   A systems view of accounting, organizations and the environment

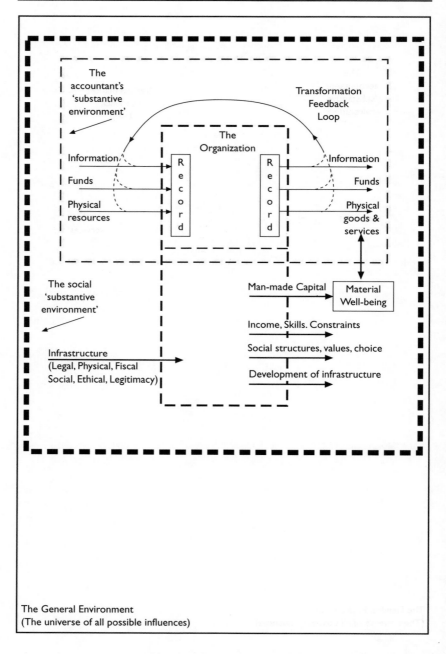

Adapted from Lowe (1972) and Gray, Laughlin and Bebbington (1996)

Figure Appendix 1.1c A systems view of accounting, organizations and the environment

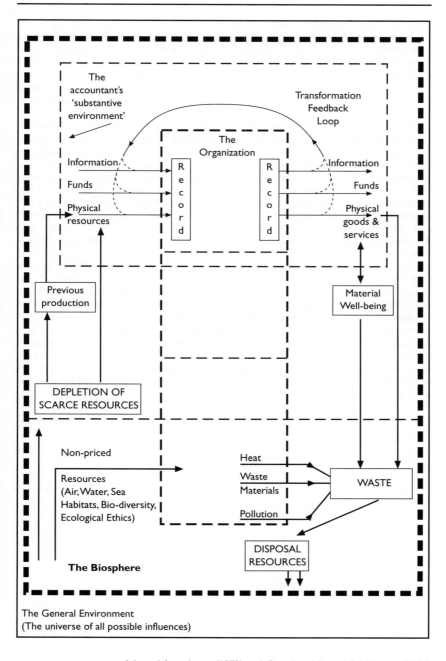

Adapted from Lowe (1972) and Gray, Laughlin and Bebbington (1996)

The problems this raises are graphically put by Yankelovich (1972), in his 'Macnamara fallacy':

> *The first step is to measure whatever can be easily measured. This is OK as far as it goes. The second step is to disregard that which can't be easily measured or give it an arbitrary quantitative value. This is artificial and misleading. The third step is to presume that what can't be measured easily really isn't important. This is blindness. The fourth step is to say that what can't be easily measured really doesn't exist. This is suicide.*
>
> (Daniel Yankelovich, *Corporate Priorities: A Continuing Study of the New Demands on Business*, 1972)

The pictures painted by conventional accounting must be incomplete – accounting can recognize only those things that can be measured, that can be measured in prices, and that are exchanged for prices. In so far as accounting is an important source of information about organizations, this incompleteness may be very dangerous. The information from the accounting system is used in a whole range of management decisions and is a major source of information to the external participants of the organization. It not only forms part of the basis of important decisions but, far more importantly and subtly, accounting helps define and measure the 'success' of actions and, ultimately, helps construct our concepts of organization and of the world itself. Accounting is thus implicated in the construction of a 'social reality' (this point is especially well developed by Hines, 1988; 1989). With regard to (for example) the environment, it is obvious that the accounting picture is one from which essential elements are missing and, if used as a basis for action and decision, it must mislead. The present environmental crisis is certainly a function of decisions taken for reasons of economic success or efficiency. To a large degree, accounting forms a major basis for the assessment of that success or efficiency – accounting is the score keeper. The 'score' takes no account of environmental matters and so, as a result, neither does 'economic' decision-making. Given the importance of accounting information and the way in which we account it seems inevitable therefore that 'economic' decisions must be environmentally malign. The environmental crisis is an inevitable result of the way we accountants do what we do. Accounting bears a serious responsibility for the growing level of environmental devastation.

APPENDIX 1.2
The Impact of the Environment on the Conventional Financial Statements

---

PROFIT & LOSS ACCOUNT

REVENUE	COSTS
Market growth	Clean-up
Market decline	Effluent/emission control or reduction
Product taxes	Waste Treatment/disposal
	Insurance
	Fines
	H & S Claims
	Plant Depreciation
	Compliance
	Waste Minimization
	Licences/Authorizations
	Research & Development

KPMG The National Environment Unit

BALANCE SHEET

ASSETS	LIABILITIES
Land Revaluations	Breach of Consents
Plant Write-offs	– fines/ actions, damages
New Plant	Remediation
Stock – net realizable value	(pollution damage)

Capital Commitments	Contingent Liabilities

KPMG Sustainability Advisory Services

CHAPTER 2

BUSINESS AND THE ENVIRONMENT

Agenda, Attitudes and Actions

2.1 Introduction

The first question for any organization considering its response to the environmental agenda is to decide the importance of environmental issues. Until an organization comes to a view on this question, it is not possible to respond in an appropriate way. This chapter will briefly introduce the elements of the environmental debate and then attempt to outline the positions that individuals and organizations are taking on the environmental agenda. This should illustrate the range of views and help accountants and management to reach responsible conclusions.[1] However, the environmental issues *are* different in nature from other 'normal' business strategic issues in that the wrong decision may have the profoundest effects for a great deal more than one's business, one's employees, management and shareholders. Attitude to the environmental issues is therefore a crucial first step in the greening of enterprise (see Figure 2.1).

2.2 The Evolving Agenda

Environmental issues are evolving so fast and developments in thinking, law, practice and attitudes are so very rapid that no one individual could keep up with them. Figure 2.2 illustrates just some of the areas that are changing and from which further change will come.

What must be grasped, is that each of these changes will produce a pressure for change – indirectly (for example, through changes in service or material availability) or directly (for example, through

---

[1] We should perhaps state that the authors share a 'deep green' view of the environmental issues in that we consider the planet to be in crisis and that the crisis must transcend other, shorter-term concerns. We know that this is a minority view. We also know it is not a view held widely in business and accounting circles. We fully respect the views of our 'lighter green' colleagues but would claim that all the evidence supports our case. We will try to be even-handed in giving 'both sides' throughout the text. For a review of 'light' versus 'dark' green perspectives on the environment see, for example, Plant and Albert (1991).

Figure 2.1

Crisis? What crisis?

- Ozone depletion
- Global warming
- Species extinction
- Habitat destruction
- Acid rain
- Desertification
- Soil erosion
- Air pollution
- Water pollution
- Land pollution
- Noise pollution
- Resource scarcity

- Third World debt
- Deforestation
- Waste disposal
- Energy usage
- Starvation
- Inequality
- Population
- Water depletion
- Toxic chemicals
- Nuclear waste
- Ethnic peoples
- Poverty

Figure 2.2

**Some issues in the changing institutional framework
(pressures for environmental change in business)**

- Supplier responsibility
- Voluntary agreements on CFCs
- Voluntary agreements on CO_2
- Eco-labelling/Eco-logo
- Waste disposal
- Contaminated land
- Superfund/CERCLA liabilities
- Packaging
- Debt-for-nature swaps
- Returnable containers
- Recycling
- Environmental disclosure
- Energy efficiency
- Environmental audit
- Environmental management systems
- Eco-efficiency

- Resource taxes
- Control of SO_x and NO_x
- Clean Air Acts
- Sustainable development
- Ethical investment
- Green consumerism
- Control of road transport
- Energy taxes
- Tradable pollution permits
- Greener employees
- Public pressure
- Organizational environmental policy
- Supplier audits
- Agreements on hardwoods
- Social audits

legislation). These pressures must be incorporated into the organization. That, in turn, will raise demands for innovation in the accounting and related information systems. All functional areas of accounting and management will be affected. Adjustment earlier in the process will avoid ill-advised change later and spread the financing of change. Thus, monitoring the agenda and all its developments (see Chapter 3) is a crucial element in coming to – and educating – one's view on the

Figure 2.3

Monitoring the agenda

At a minimum, every organization will have to monitor:

- forthcoming national law;
- existing national law and its implementation timetable;
- existing and forthcoming international agreements (e.g. the Montreal Protocol on CFCs);
- existing and forthcoming law in the countries in which one operates and in which one's trading partners operate including existing and forthcoming (e.g.) European Community directives;
- the activities of water, land, air and noise pollution agencies, changing methods and levels of enforcement, changing levels of fines and increasing tightness of consents;
- the views and concerns of one's stakeholders;
- industry agreements – one's own industry as well as those with which one deals;
- the changes in thinking about environmental issues (e.g. on sustainability); public opinion and the attitudes and actions of the pressure groups;
- the ethical position of oneself, one's employees and colleagues and one's organization *vis-à-vis* the environmental issues;
- changing knowledge – about the impact of actions on the biosphere, about the scale of impacts, about new expectations and new technologies;
- changing opportunities for funding or for organizational development;
- issues of social accountability.

ecological crisis as it influences (and will influence) business and accounting. This leads to a form of defensive monitoring of, at least, the types of data that are listed in Figure 2.3.

Figure 2.3 could be greatly expanded but captures many of the things which organizations will have to monitor in the short to medium term. One thing is certain: having let the environmental issues out of their box they show no signs that they can be returned to obscurity. The world has changed and continues to change. All organizations and eventually all professions will be greatly affected.

Every organization will need help in keeping abreast of environmental developments. For the very largest, this may often be found in-house. For all others, the plethora of publications, forums, networks, information centres and consultancies will continue to prove invaluable.[2]

---

[2] Organizations, information sources, bodies, companies etc. are listed in the appendix at the end of the book, and each chapter recommends further reading and suggests (where appropriate) specifically helpful organizations. Each chapter also contains footnotes which refer to readings and information contained in the bibliography. The lists of helpful sources are not complete, nor are we prepared to state that they are necessarily the best.

The developing business and environmental agenda has so far relied heavily upon voluntary initiatives.[3] In addition to the international agencies (such as WBCSD and ICC) each country has its own voluntary bodies. Britain especially has an abundance of them. These organizations are effectively rolling the environmental agenda along while taking a proportion of the business communities with them.

Only time will tell, however, whether this has been effective enough. There is no evidence to suggest that voluntary action alone will be sufficient to deal with the environmental crisis. Indeed, there is a substantial and growing body of evidence which suggests – quite unsurprisingly – that voluntary initiatives are having only partial success.[4] Equally though, legislative solutions are not without their own major problems.[5] But the probability is that voluntary initiatives cannot make the necessary impact when there are clear clashes between short-term business interests and protection of the environment.

A critical major factor in one's response to the environmental agenda appears to be attitude and the extent of one's education in environmentalism and ecology. More especially, our experience suggests that *what* an individual knows about the environment and *how* that individual thinks about what he or she knows profoundly affects attitudes. In particular, the extent to which one does or does not believe in the possibility of 'environmental crisis' depends largely on

---

[3] Much in keeping with the move to the political right and the more open and enthusiastic embracing of liberal economic thinking. It would be difficult to see such a move as an unqualified success. Voluntary initiatives, although useful for experimentation and clearly more desirable than regulation *if they are effective*, can be shown to be, time and time again, ineffective in that they are adopted by only a minority of organizations. Apart from any other issues, there is the problem of equity in which the 'bad' companies are saving costs which more responsible organizations are incurring in adopting the initiative.

[4] Even in the early stages of the current business–environment debate, conflict was apparent. For example, a Friends of the Earth Report in 1991 (reported in the *Guardian*, 12 July 1991) states that the voluntary action on CFC reductions is much slower than required by the target dates; the (then) Conservative UK government, previously wedded entirely to the purity of 'market forces', was finding that they do not work as required (reported in the *Observer*, 5 January 1992); whilst there is a steady flow of examples in which corporate and environmental interests are in conflict – and where the corporate interests appear usually to be the winners (reports in, for example, the *Financial Times*, 25 November 1991, on the conflict between Ofwat and the water companies, and in the *Observer*, 11 November 1990, on the conflict between a major environmental initiative in the USA opposed by many companies including three of the UK's leading 'green' organizations). More significant examples, not least the Rio+5 Conference and the Kyoto agreement on global warming, point to businesses' attempts to keep legislation to a minimum even when there is a clear environmental need for major control. For further exploration of these issues see, for example, Mayhew (1997) and Beder (1997).

[5] One widely reported example was that 'twenty years of US emission control have done little to improve air quality', especially with respect to automobiles (Bell, 1992).

Figure 2.4

The four principles of ecology

- Every separate entity is connected to all the rest;
- Everything has to go somewhere;
- You cannot get something for nothing from it;
- Nature knows best.

Source: B. Commoner (1972) 'The social use and misuse of technology', in J. Benthall (ed.), *Ecology: The Shaping Enquiry* (London: Longman), pp. 335–362

---

whether or not one can consider the elements in Figure 2.1 as isolated, individually soluble problems or whether one sees them as connected, interrelated and systemic. It is only when the elements are seen in this systemic way that a crisis – rather than a 'problem' – is perceived.[6]

2.3   The Public, Media and Politicians

Whilst each individual will come to some personal, educated view on the facts of the environmental crisis (and their ethical response to those facts), it is likely that every organization will be more immediately concerned with how the environmental issues are constructed, perceived and construed by the public, the media and by politicians. As the CBI[7] (1992b, emphasis added) put it:

> *The public debate of environmental issues is growing. The heightened awareness it brings is welcome but **can lead to issues getting greater attention environmentally than they deserve**. The CBI believes it is right for **businesses collectively to help set the agenda** by stating their priorities, by enhancing their own awareness of the environment and by working more closely with Government and all those agencies, national and international, active in the field.*

---

[6] This is known as 'systems thinking', related to general systems theory, and is apparent in most environmental books. For an introduction see Gray (1990d), from which Appendix 1.1 is taken.

[7] This quotation, and a great deal from the CBI, highlights an essential series of questions. In particular is there a conflict between business needs and environmental needs? The CBI and other business organizations (most especially the WBCSD) would generally hope that there was not. The answer depends, in part, on how 'deep green' one is. A second major problem is whether or not business has the right, the moral position or the ability to set the environmental agenda *correctly* (see below). Too much of the environmental debate is conducted in a business-knows-best climate when business cannot always know best. For discussion of these crucial issues see, especially, Welford (1997a) and Beder (1997).

Public, media and political opinion influences business practice, consumer attitudes and employee concerns and ultimately leads to regulation and the institutional framework within which organizations operate. Such opinion will have an immediate impact on organizations and, consequently, organizations employ considerable resources to advertise, influence public opinion and lobby government to limit – if not remove – such influence. On the other hand, the facts of the environment itself, no matter how pessimistically one might interpret the evidence, are unlikely to have much noticeable direct effect on organizations – in the developed world at least – for some time.[8]

Public opinion on the environment is volatile and varies from country to country, but that volatility disguises the extent to which environment concern is an enduring issue – that continues to develop but with a lower, less excitable, profile.[9]

From a business strategy point of view, the volatility of public opinion does not offer any real lead for business – except perhaps to encourage organizations to persuade the public that there is not much to worry about. In this, business – and especially multinational business – appears to be achieving 'success'.[10] However, it is clear that although the public media have perhaps reduced their excitability over the issues, the quantity and – more importantly – the quality of environmentally related journalism, investigations and general programmes continues to increase. Environmental activism is increasingly diverse, widespread, effective and well-informed.[11] Organizations are

---

[8] Although even here evidence is beginning to build up. Algal bloom, water shortages, skin cancers, asthma, acid rain, etc., etc. are increasingly visible facts of life even amongst the better off and more insulated societies.

[9] There has been a steady trickle of surveys of consumer and public attitudes to environmental issues. They, generally, show a peak of concern in the developed West in about 1990 with a slow fall-off since. However, those who remain concerned (typically a majority of respondents) tend to become more sophisticated in their reactions. One significant change is that people are beginning to recognize that part of the problem is the conflicting messages about the state of the environment, the causes of environmental problems and what individuals can do about it. Taken from (i) a MORI poll in the *Independent* in July 1990 and reported by Greg Neale to the Canada–UK Colloquium, 1991; (ii) an *Observer/Harris* poll reported in the *Observer*, 15 April 1990; (iii) a report from Barry Watson of Environics in a paper to the Canada–UK Colloquium, 1991; (iv) a report in the *Independent on Sunday*, 12 January 1992; (v) a report from MORI in *Green Futures*, June/July 1997, p. 12; (vi) a March 1995 *Harris Research Centre* report; (vii) the *MORI Business and the Environment Survey*, August 1995; (viii) *UK National Consumer Council* report, March 1996 (as reported in Sheldon, 1997, pp. 205–207).

[10] See Greer and Bruno (1996), Beder (1997), Welford (1997a).

[11] Even not so well-informed activism can have most serious impacts on organizations. Perhaps the most widely reported and analysed case in recent years must be the Shell Brent Spar crisis instigated by Greenpeace. Even vast international corporate conglomerates are vulnerable to focused activism. See, for example, Greer and Bruno (1996).

almost certain to find themselves with increasingly environmentally better-educated public, customers and employees.

The media-vaunted rise of the 'green consumer' may have cooled off but consumption habits have changed and continue to do so. As we shall see in later chapters, organizations cannot ignore the green purchaser for much longer and there is every sign – not least with the arrival of eco-labelling – that environmentally motivated consumption will have an increasing effect on organizational life.[12]

The impact of the environmentally minded employee is more complex. A 1990 report in the UK suggested that environmental issues played a part in most graduates' thinking when seeking employment.[13] However, it does seem that more widespread concerns about recession, unemployment, downsizing and greater employment insecurity more than outweigh this effect. What seems more likely is that environmental concern is of increasing significance in the highly competitive employment markets where there is a substantial skills shortage for the rare and best-potential employees.[14] Certainly, the retention and motivation of employees are closely linked to how they feel about the environmental impact of what they do. An increasing number of companies have spoken to us of the importance that they place on their employees' attitudes to the environmental posture of the company.[15]

Public perceptions of the environmental agenda are, by and large, constructed by the popular media: an increase in reportage leads to a corresponding rise in concern among an organization's public, local community, customers and employees – and perhaps even among its shareholders, bankers and insurers (see Chapter 10). And active environmental groups are increasingly successful in using the media to make known their points of view. Shell, British Petroleum, McDonald's, Nike, BHP are just some of the major corporations which have experienced such pressure. For these reasons, if for no others, every organization must monitor media attention to environmental matters and must, as far as possible, stay in tune with the developing concerns of the environmentalists (see Chapter 3).

But public concern has its greatest impact when reflected in political concern. Of course, political concern – and, indeed, political will – to

[12] For more detail see, for example, Elkington and Hailes (1988, 1989, 1998). See also Bruce (1989), Ferguson (1989), Foster (1989), Krietzman (1988), Papworth (1990a, 1990b), Redmond (1988) and especially Adams, Carruthers and Hamil (1991).

[13] See, for example, a KPH Marketing Report, 'Student attitudes to corporate responsibility and environmental issues', 1990.

[14] For more detail see, for example, Baxter and Rarick (1989), Bennett (1988), Benson (1989), Cartwright (1990) and Houldin (1989).

[15] A view shared – and much expanded upon – in Elkington, Knight and Hailes (1991, ch. 12). See also, Gray, Bebbington, Walters and Thomson (1995).

undertake significant environmental initiatives varies considerably from country to country and is notoriously fickle.[16] But, despite the best efforts of 'pure' market economists and the more benighted business interests, most countries of the world are witnessing a steady rise in environmental concern as reflected in a growing political will and, ultimately, in legislation. And just monitoring the political agenda at the national level is not sufficient. Each market into which an organization sells, or from which it buys, has its own requirements that organizations ignore at their peril. International agreements – such as the Montreal Protocol on CFCs or the Kyoto agreement on carbon emissions – inevitably have an impact at the national level. International federations are as, if not more, important still. The European Union is a particularly important example of supra-national environmental initiatives leading national governments – frequently against local inclinations.[17]

Much of this must appear self-evident and yet organizations were initially slow to respond to the changing environmental agenda. In 1990 (at the height of the first wave of public green concern) 30 per cent of companies considered that environmental issues had no relevance for their business and 50 per cent had taken no steps to adjust to the developing environmental agenda.[18] By the end of the decade, however, this percentage was down into single figures for large companies in the industrialized nations.[19]

Central to this discussion are two crucial issues:

(1) How reliable are the environmental data and the extrapolations based upon them? Are the anxieties about crisis justified?
(2) To what extent is there a conflict between the respect and protection of the environment and the more immediate material well-being of individuals, societies and companies?

[16] Witness, for example, the all-embracing nature of the New Zealand Resource Management Act and the heavy and successful lobbying by business to restrict its impact; the waxing and waning of Aboriginal land rights in Australia; the reluctance to address firmly international whaling or grasp the global warming issues so hotly contested at the Kyoto Conference; the USA 'backlash' against environmental concerns; the failure of environmental issues to carry weight in the GATT rounds or within the World Trade Organization, etc., etc.

[17] See, for example, Eden (1996, chs 5 and 6).

[18] Elkington, Knight and Hailes (1991, p. 21). A survey by the Institute of Directors (1992) – a year and a half later – suggested that 30 per cent of board members *still* foresaw that environmental issues would take 0 per cent of board time. One is reminded of horses and water.

[19] See, for example, UK figures reported in Moffatt Associates Partnership's *The 1998 Business and the Environmental Trends Survey* summarized by *The Environment Council* (July/August 1998).

These issues are both complex. The first is not one we can dwell upon significantly here. Suffice it to say that (a) to see 'environmental crisis' as only a consequence of specific data sets is to miss the essential point that 'the environment' and our dealings with it involve the most basic of ethical considerations and are as much about how society (and societies) are organized, treat each other and respect natural life as about an economic concern for continued resource use; and (b) experience suggests that each individual has to make up his or her own mind after a careful and fair examination of the available data. Our experience is that anybody spending time considering the issues concludes that the possibility of crisis (however defined) is far too real to be ignored.

However, the nature of that crisis, its causes and how it might be solved is a far more contentious matter. It is this that leads to concerns over conflict as suggested in the second of the issues above. This is a central matter covered in the remainder of the chapter.

2.4   Business Attitude and Business Response

Generally speaking, business response to the environmental agenda before the 1990s was *ad hoc*, largely determined by extant legislation and, although it varied widely between companies and between countries, the issues were rarely seen by organizations as central to their core activities. The growth in importance given to the environmental issues in more recent times has been very significant indeed. It is now possible to argue that environmental management (see Part B) is an essential element of a well-managed enterprise,[20] that attention to environmental issues is crucial in the raising of finance and the negotiation of insurance (see Chapter 10); and that environmental reporting should now be seen as a normal part of organizational accountability and communication with stakeholders (see Chapters 11, 12 and 13).

But, despite this apparent widespread acceptance of the need to integrate environment into the heart of the business, it would be foolhardy to believe either that *all* organizations have embraced what might be thought of as 'the new environmental culture' or that even adoption of the essential elements of an environmental strategy was sufficient to solve the world's environmental ills. Far from it. Except in those rare, 'leading edge' organizations where there is a genuine culture of pro-active concern for environmental degradation, 'environment' is still, far too often, a matter dealt with superficially, reactively

---

[20] See, for example, Epstein (1996) for one illustration of this.

Figure 2.5 Business posture and the environment

Business Response	Belief about the state of the physical environment		
	A **Greening as a 'passing fad'**	**B** **Environmental issues are significant but not critical**	**C** **Natural environment *is* in crisis**
1. Do nothing	OK	Perhaps lose business? Catch up costs? Legal problems?	CRISIS (No natural environment)
2. Follow law and public opinion	Costs and advantages	OK	CRISIS (Perhaps delayed? No natural environment)
3. Aim for sustainable business	CRISIS (Probably out of business)	Costs and advantages	OK?

Source: Adapted from Gray and Collison (1991b), p. 22.

and within the legal minima.[21] Some of these issues are put into context by Figure 2.5.

Ten or more years ago, most businesses would have contentedly placed themselves in square A1 of Figure 2.5. Sadly it is probably the case that many organizations are still trying to hang onto this 'do nothing and it will go away' strategy. But as more and more organizations see some of the potential benefits of 'going green' or else receive (or see others receiving) the 'nasty shocks'[22] in the form of fines, court cases, stakeholder activism, loss of business and so on (square B1 in Figure 2.5), fewer and fewer businesses remain here. Matters have now moved on and environmental issues *are* now accepted as significant – although not yet seen as life-threatening. The more sensible organizations are moving into B2 in order to follow, stay ahead of and/or exploit a changing organizational climate. Here there are a

[21] See, for example, Deegan and Rankin (1996), Gray, Bebbington, Walters and Thomson (1995) and Gray et al. (1998) for more detail and examples. Witness also the steady growth in environmental prosecutions and fines. Equally, there is no evidence that the state of the natural environment is improving and there would seem to be little evidence that major environmental 'mistakes' are decreasing in number or severity.

[22] Avoiding and/or being on the receiving end of 'nasty shocks' is a frequently stated reason for an organization undertaking a significant process of 'greening'. (See, for example, Gray, Bebbington, Walters and Thomson, 1995; Gray et al., 1998.)

range of very real 'win–win' possibilities where real economic savings can be found whilst improving the environmental impact of the organization. (This is considered in the next section.)

Looking to the future, the targets of sustainability and 'sustainable business' raise many challenges that organizations – on a world-wide basis – are as yet ill-equipped to handle. Only time will finally tell whether or not organizations should be seeking to move into C3: the costs of moving to cell C3 when one does not have to are significant indeed for the business; the costs of *not* moving to C3, if the environmentalists are right, are appalling (see Chapter 14).

2.5 Business Response: Cost or Benefit?

For most organizations, however, the environmental issues still remain a matter of judging the costs and benefits – to the business[23] – of action and inaction. Figure 2.6 illustrates a few of the areas where businesses might begin to seek a reduction in their environmental impact together with an estimate of the likely cost or benefit to the organization. There are problems with the diagram,[24] but, given that the theme from business has been that 'greening equals profit', it seems necessary at least to look at that suggestion. It *is* possible to equate certain environmentally benign activities with cost savings and profitable opportunities (we look at some of these in later chapters).[25] Indeed, many organizations have reaped such benefits from the so-called 'win–win situations'.[26]

However, there is the potential for rather more tension between environment and profit than there is congruence and, after several years of bullish 'talking up' the environment, many business leaders

---

[23] The costs and benefits to society and future generations are far more complex, and are touched upon briefly in Chapter 14.

[24] The problems include (a) the worrying idea that we assess the preferable environmental actions only on the basis of conventional profit; (b) the options for organizations in the list are over-simple; (c) the impact of costs varies across industries and over time. All industries will feel the costs eventually but it is on the innovative organizations (who tend to lead the field in these initiatives) or those upon which legal and/or stakeholder pressure first falls – typically chemicals and extractive industries – that the incidence has usually fallen.

[25] See also Ditz et al. (1995), Elkington (1987, 1997), Elkington, Knight and Hailes (1991), Epstein (1996) for many good examples of this.

[26] This term was coined in this context by Walley and Whitehead (1994). Their article and the subsequent responses in the *Harvard Business Review*, July/August 1994, remains an excellent introduction to the controversy surrounding business/environment trade-offs.

Figure 2.6 Going green: a cost or benefit?

	No change in business environment	Probable that law and PR *do* change	Environment *is* in serious crisis
Light greening			
Unleaded petrol	+£	++£	Will make very little
Catalytic converters	−£	+£	difference
Initial use of recycled products	−£	++£	
Initial recycling	£	+£	
Waste management	+£	+++£	+++£
Energy management	+£	+++£	+++£
Significant greening			
Use of public transport	+£	+£	+++£
Substantial use of alternative resources	−−£	£	+++£
Substantial recycling	−£	+£	+++£
Change investment procedures	−−£	++£	+++£
Towards sustainability			
Reduce throughput	−−−£	−£	+++£
Change products	−−−£	£	+++£
Longer-life & repairability	−−−£	£	+++£

Key: £ = Break even; +£ = Profit likely; −£ = Loss likely.

around the world have come to recognize this.[27] At its simplest, the reaping of benefits from energy and waste management, for example (see Chapters 6 and 7), will on occasions involve some considerable investment. For an organization with a cash-flow problem the option may be difficult to undertake (see Chapter 8). The costs of meeting legislation, clean-up costs (see Chapter 11), insurance costs (see Chapter 10), etc., are rising and will continue to do so. Companies that are 'environmentally impeccable' – by current standards anyway – do not always prove to be as profitable as 'dirtier' companies – a case of the 'bad' driving out the 'good' in the absence of legislation (see Chapter 10). The probability is therefore that the more substantial financial benefits from going green will – in general – be the benefit of severe loss forgone. Unless, that is, there is some very significant change in the financial, institutional and regulatory framework within which organizations operate.

Equally unclear are the strategic questions as to how 'deep' the greening will have to go, and over what time scale this will happen. It

[27] See, for example, the publications from IISD and WBCSD which illustrate this point clearly.

is quite clear that an organization that severely misjudges these questions may well put itself in dire trouble. It is equally clear that many organizations, small and large, are concerned about exactly where the goalposts are likely to settle. For all but the largest and most secure organizations this uncertainty tends to encourage a reactive stance on environmental issues. Whilst this is perfectly understandable it does not bode well for the future and clearly counsels for a stronger lead from governments.

Surveys of organizational response to the environmental agenda have produced oddly conflicting pictures about just what organizations are doing and why. The conflicting messages from business and government ('voluntary is best', 'industry is taking the environment seriously', 'more must be done') disguise a considerable gap between aspiration and actuality. On the whole the evidence is that organizations – in general – are not yet taking the environment seriously enough. The experiences from around the world are extremely mixed and, certainly, speak of different but partial responses. For example, Germany is well-advanced on environmental auditing (see Chapter 5); the United States has a sophisticated land-remediation regime (see Chapters 10 and 11); Denmark and Sweden have environmental reporting legislation whilst the UK and Canada have well-developed voluntary practices (see Chapter 12); Australia has set a lead in public sector responses on the environment; and Japan is renowned for its energy management (see Chapter 6). But these apparent advances hide a great diversity of performance in other areas. The conclusion is that only a minority of companies anywhere in the world could be thought of as operating state-of-the-art environmental strategies and management and very few indeed have come close to addressing the substantive matters of sustainable development (see Chapter 14).

2.6 Conclusions

Whilst there is little doubt that environmental matters are on the organizational agenda to stay, the progress towards a more fulsome and enthusiastic embracing of the environmental agenda has been somewhat slower than was predicted at the beginning of the 1990s. The reasons for this are various and complex. Combinations of confusion, cost constraint, ignorance, lack of political will from governments, lack of conviction about businesses role in the environment plus successful lobbying and propaganda from (a few) pro-business but anti-environmental groupings may all have played a part.

If, however, we are to arrest environmental degradation then a much more substantial – and widespread – response is crucial: for both the environment and the life of organizations. That groups such as Friends of the Earth, Greenpeace and Earth First! *and* business groupings such as the IOD, ICC, CBI, DoE, DTI, IISD, WBCSD, UNCTAD, BiE, etc. agree that business *must* respond means that even reactionary organizations *cannot* ignore the messages for much longer. That the environmentalists and the business groups differ on the extent and nature of that response is less of a surprise but, especially when married with a lack of clear political direction from many governments, certainly leads to an atmosphere of confusion within which it is easier to understand the reactive stance of many organizations.

And the accounting profession? Most of the major accountancy bodies in Europe, North America, Australasia and, increasingly, throughout all corners of the world have nailed their colours to the mast of the development of environmental accounting systems and disclosure. For most of the professional accountancy bodies, however, the issues still remain tied within the frameworks of conventional accounting reasoning and only rarely have the bodies really provided an active leadership that directly influences the practice of environmental management and accounting. But this *is* changing steadily and, consequently, accounting practices and accountants themselves are slowly – very slowly[28] – beginning to respond to the needs of the environmental agenda and, especially, its implications for their employers and clients.

This book will, hopefully, help the accountant in the field to respond to this challenge. But a word of warning. Environmental accounting, as we currently understand it, is a rapidly emerging field but one in which there is still relatively little experimentation. Whatever picture we paint here (and that can be enhanced by the additional readings) it will be an incomplete one. There is, for example, rapid change in the detailed issues surrounding the financial reporting issues (Chapter 11) but still relatively little experimentation. By way of contrast, there is considerable experimentation in environmental (and social) reporting (Chapters 12 and 13) but few countries have established any legislative backing for the activity. Consequently, there is massive diversity in the practice here. Other advances in (say) costing techniques, life-cycle assessments and eco-balances (Chapters 6–9) do not always see the light of day until some time after their inception. This book will provide a basic introduction to the principal elements in environmental accounting and management and should continue to help those in practice – as well as those researching and studying the

---

[28] See, for example, Bebbington et al. (1994), Bebbington and Gray (1995), Gray, Bebbington, Walters and Thomson (1995), Gray et al. (1998), Guilding and Kirman (1998).

issues – to undertake important steps towards understanding and application of this 'new' practice. It is *not* the whole story – that has not yet been written!

Further Reading

The readings suggested for Chapter I are equally applicable to this chapter – especially those suggested as general introductions to business and the environment.

PART B: MANAGEMENT INFORMATION AND ACCOUNTING

Overview

by Martin Houldin, EMAG Ltd

Given the range of environmental issues covered in Part A and the potential implications for business, especially where we can see the full range of business functions becoming involved, getting started can be a daunting task.

A multitude of different sources of guidance is available to companies, from books to consultancies offering varying degrees of technical and business/management skills. Much of the published material, and even some of the consultancies, tend to give advice on *what* needs to be looked at rather than *how*. The solutions offered may at first seem somewhat confusing: 'Develop an environmental policy, set objectives, carry out an environmental audit, publish a report, appoint somebody senior', and so on. Key questions such as 'Do we need to cover all activities/products/services?', 'Who in the company should be involved?', 'What kind of performance objectives and targets should be set?', can be answered only by considering each company's individual situation.

Environmental Management

While there cannot be a panacea, all of these approaches can be fitted into a framework or context of environmental management. This is worth introducing at this point.

Managing the causes of environmental impacts on business activities is for many businesses a relatively new idea, and one which calls for a change both in organization culture and in day-to-day management techniques and systems. Current thinking on environmental management is based on the recognition that it cannot stand alone as a discipline, and that environmental considerations must be integrated with normal business practices. So, environmental management is essentially about changing management practices and systems in response to the business implications of environmental issues, whether they be threats or opportunities. It is in the first stages of this change process that much 'new' work must be done. By gathering information and data about the causes of environmental impacts ('environmental aspects' – see ISO 14001), businesses will gain a better understanding of environmental performance issues. It is this understanding and information, together with knowledge of available technologies and relevant legislation and regulations, which will provide the direction for change, in terms of policies and objectives.

The starting point is to carry out a review of environmental issues (whatever it ends up being called – environmental review or audit). The aim is to understand enough about the current and planned activities of the business in relation to potential environmental impacts (on air, water, land and nature). This means looking not only at the possible environmental effects of materials and resources used, wastes and emissions, and of products, but also at business issues arising. These are likely to result from legislation and regulatory standards, market activity (such as by customers and/or greener competitors). At this stage, environmental impacts can be looked at on a cradle-to-grave basis by using a life-cycle approach; in other words considering environmental aspects and associated impacts of supplier and customer activities, from raw material to end-of-life disposal.

The results of the environmental review will provide a basis for identifying those areas where the company needs to improve its performance. This will mean forming some ideas of objectives. We will then have identified those key areas, which need to be reflected in policy and in a strategy for action. This process, although sounding simple enough, is more often than not an interactive process of doing enough work at the review stage to identify priority areas then focusing on these for more in-depth review to shape and refine policy and objectives.

Environmental policies and objectives will typically cover a range of key performance areas, and not just those that are prescribed by legislation and regulation. These can include process emissions, wastes, use of natural resources (energy, water, materials), supplier performance, product design effects (on product use and disposal), nature conservation and management systems.

While the policy can be used effectively to demonstrate the company's intent, the real measure of commitment lies in setting responsibilities and objectives at business unit and department/section levels.

As a consequence of all this there will be increasing demands for information on environmental performance.

Recent Developments

A wide range of organizations that represent, support or regulate businesses have recognized the importance of environmental management. As a result an equally wide range of 'guidelines' have been developed for different purposes by, for example, the ICC (International Chamber of Commerce), the World Business Council for Sustainable Development, the CBI and industry associations (such as the Chemical Industries Association's Responsible Care Programme). There have been similar developments outside the UK through organizations such as BAUM (Germany), GEMI (USA), and UNEP (United Nations). There is no doubt that these initiatives are influencing business awareness and thinking.

There are developments, however, which are having a more direct effect in shaping environmental management practice. At the international level, an ISO Standard for Environmental Management Systems (ISO 14001) was introduced in 1996. Since then other guidelines have been introduced within the ISO 14000 series. As of the beginning of the new millennium, over 10,000 companies, around the world, had been certificated to ISO 14001. At the European level the European Union passed a Regulation in 1993 for member states to introduce a voluntary scheme of Eco Management and Audit. Largely similar in requirements to ISO 14001, the main difference is the requirement for an environmental (performance) statement to be produced, audited (verified) and published. By the year 2000 some 2000 sites had been registered in European Union member states.

It is important to remember, however, that these standards, and other emerging guidelines (at sector level and in different areas of environmental management technique), provide only a generic framework within which companies can develop their own approaches, policies and objectives. The standards for environmental performance will always be set at the legislative or regulatory level, unless voluntarily done so at business or industrial sector levels.

While there has been strong interest in the adoption of environmental management systems, the challenge of better controlling and improving environmental performance remains. Certainly, it will take anything from three to five years for businesses to well establish environmental management so that environmental performance is being systematically and consistently managed across the organization. In addition, positive steps need to be taken for environmental performance management to become fully integrated with other areas of managing business performance.

The next major challenge is now to find ways in which businesses can contribute towards sustainable development. Sustainable development has long been an aspiration of governments; references can be found in both recent and older policy documents. A key feature of the new millennium era will be the development and implementation of policies aimed at achieving sustainability.

In summary, it is now fairly commonly recognized that we will need to achieve enormous advances in technological innovation (anything from a factor of four upwards). Only then might we be able to achieve the kind of economic growth in the world that will be needed to meet the demands of population growth and quality of life expectations, without irreversibly damaging the environment that supports life.

This will put even more demands on environmental management and performance management, as well as require businesses to devote resources (human, financial, technological) to working towards sustainability.

Management Information and Accounting

Success in implementing effective environmental management will depend on the quality of information available to managers. While companies rely on the more traditional types of management information produced on a regular basis, there is a need for new information (such as emissions, regulatory compliance data, waste statistics – including levels of recovery and recycling – and product disposal impacts) and some refocusing of existing systems in areas such as energy and wastes.

There may be practical difficulties, resulting mainly from the lack of raw data, as many companies are thus far developing *ad hoc* information streams from environmental reviews. As a starting point this is not a bad approach, but one that needs to lead fairly quickly into an analysis of environmental information requirements within the business context. This would address data sources and gaps, and identify options for developing information on different application areas. There is no doubt, however, that accounting and financial systems need to be brought more into play, both in producing better information and aiding decision-making. The question is how.

In the short term, accountants can focus on those key performance areas identified in the policy and consider their contribution while working within existing accounting and financial systems. This is likely to be in two areas. First, by *costing* those areas relevant to environmental objectives, such as waste treatment and disposal, energy, site maintenance, in such a way that makes them separately identifiable and more controllable. Secondly, by working to resolve inevitable conflicts between environmental management and traditional financial management systems. This occurs particularly in *investment appraisal*, where new guidelines need to be developed.

Accountants need to find ways of taking into account quantifiable and tangible environmental factors. Otherwise some proposals that are economically and environmentally sound, in the longer term, may be rejected. This is where life-cycle analysis may have a role to play, and accountants need to assess whether it could be a useful tool in cost/benefit analysis.

In the medium term, accountants need to reorient planning and forecasting systems to incorporate environmental improvement targets, and their financial implications. Part of this will involve assessing the need for new and/or modified information and financial systems.

In the longer term, there will be developments in eco-accounting or natural resource accounting, aimed at producing environmental accounts to reflect the full costs of production, even where monetary values cannot be assigned. The benefits of contributing towards sustainability will also need to be recognized.

Accountants in Environmental Management

Remember the old maxim: if you can't measure it, then you can't manage it!

In many companies, environmental policies and objectives are defined well enough for accountants to be able to begin to determine a role in measurement, analysis and control, and thereby contribute to environmental improvement. The chapters in Part B aim to put the accountant's role in the context of environmental management, and to give some guidance in those areas likely to be of immediate interest.

CHAPTER 3

GREENING THE ORGANIZATION

Getting Started

3.1 Introduction

There is no unique way to start an organization on the path towards increased environmental sensitivity. Environmental response is the sort of issue that *must not* be quickly delegated to some remote, peripheral part of the organization and forgotten about. It must be central to the organization's whole management function. The environmental crisis itself arises out of the basic failure of organizational structures, business ethics, economic frameworks and accounting systems to recognize 'nature'. All life, obviously, derives from and is part of the 'natural environment', but until 'environment' is inescapably enmeshed with the organization, Western industrial systems will continue to treat it as though it were something that is irrelevant at best and distinct from life at worst – and thereby destroy it. Just as health, safety and respect for one's employees have become accepted – even essential – prerequisites for responsible organizations, so too must environmental concern be considered an essential element of responsible management.

Figure 3.1

The ten steps to environmental excellence

(1) Develop and publish an environmental policy.
(2) Prepare an action programme.
(3) Arrange organization and staffing including board representation.
(4) Allocate adequate resources.
(5) Invest in environmental science and technology.
(6) Educate and train.
(7) Monitor, audit and report.
(8) Monitor the evolution of the green agenda.
(9) Contribute to environmental programmes.
(10) Help build bridges between the various interests.

Source: J. Elkington with Tom Burke (1987) *The Green Capitalists* (London: Victor Gollancz)

Where to start? Everywhere at once is the most accurate, if the most bewildering, answer. Elkington's (1987) ten steps to environmental excellence (Figure 3.1) continually prove to be a robust statement of the necessary – if not sufficient – conditions for incorporating environmental matters. The span of issues that must be considered offers just a guide to the ubiquity of green thinking.

Throughout this chapter, we will attempt to provide an overview of the areas in which an organization can make some impact on its environmental sensitivity. However, our treatment must be superficial and the reader is recommended to consult the growing number of excellent texts which develop these matters more fully. (See the further reading at the end of the chapter.)

3.2   The Forces of Change

How the many potential forces for change actually succeed in creating change and the form that such change eventually takes is not well understood.[1] The 'environment' itself is not, generally speaking, yet a *direct* force for change on organizations (in the developed world at least). The pressure for environmental change comes, principally, *indirectly* as a result of changes in consumer taste, employee and management attitudes, law, etc. This is one of the reasons management seeking to manage the 'environmental agenda' have such a

Figure 3.2

One company's approach to 'Going Green'
(1)   Develop corporate culture components on environmental matters.
(2)   Accept that the company's activities do disturb the environment and aim to minimize these and perhaps look for enhancement also.
(3)   Undertake environmental impact assessment on all major company proposals.
(4)   Provide environmental training for all levels of staff.
(5)   Build up networks with environmental groups.
Source: Reported in *Environment Update* (1990) New Zealand Ministry for the Environment, No. 17, p. 2

---

[1] See, for example, Laughlin (1991) for a general introduction to issues of organizational change and Gray, Bebbington, Walters and Thomson (1995) for an examination of environmental change in organizations. Of particular importance, however, are the forces that will resist change and, in particular, resist environmental change because of the challenge it makes to traditional ways of operating. This chapter is guilty of paying insufficient attention to these questions and the reader is recommended to look at the excellent Newton and Harte (1997).

Figure 3.3

The new 3 Rs of an environmental culture

- Reduce
- Reuse
- Recycle

Popular also are:

- Refuse
- Refill
- Repeat
- Repair
- Remediate
- Reclaim
- Return

. . . and so on.

---

problem. It is necessary to monitor the development both of environmental facts *and* of the environmental issues and knowledge in the public domain, while attempting to assess the different ways in which these might eventually have a direct influence upon the organization.

However, there are some prerequisites for change, the most crucial being the attitudes and actions of the board. The 'tone from the top' is as important in environmental matters as it is in ethical ones.[2] This becomes even more apparent when it is realized that what is needed is a *cultural* change. An organization that was previously maximizing throughput, growth, profitability, etc. will have to start minimizing a few things – a new dimension will have to enter it.

In the broadest of terms, the forces of change can come from outside the organization, the employees and the senior management. We briefly examine these in turn before looking at the accountant's role.

3.3   External Influences for Environmental Change

It is that range of pressures external to the organization which provide the greatest influence on its environmental response. As such, however, they are forces over which the individual organization has little immediate or direct control. Good management control requires, therefore, that such influences be successfully anticipated.

[2] See, for example, Baumhart (1961), Bennett (1988), Benson (1989), Ermann (1986), Hoffman (1993).

The most obvious of these pressures arises from changes in legislation and the related institutional framework.[3] Surveys of business
executives and their views on environmental change regularly cite
these factors as the principal impetus for undertaking environmental
change within the organization. Our own research has gone beyond
this, however, and suggests that the most powerful forces for change
come in the form of 'shocks', and/or from otherwise largely unexpected sources. Such shocks may be in the form of unanticipated
legislation but, more typically, tend to emerge from other actors in
the business environment. The characteristic is that they catch the
organization unprepared. It is noticeable that where environmental
issues have remained significant within an organization (i.e. had not
been given a superficial treatment) *and* have not been fully integrated
(e.g. into a TQM culture; see below) it was usually because there has
been some external shock to the system. Examples of such shocks
included the attentions of organizations like Friends of the Earth,
Greenpeace or Earth First!; an environmental disaster with attendant
fines and publicity; an environmental regulator changing its policy;[4]
even the unexpected activities of a competitor company 'breaking
ranks'; or some other substantive change forced upon the organization
from outside.[5]

It should follow, therefore, that careful monitoring of the agenda
(see Figures 3.4 and 2.3) will have the effect of encouraging change. At
least change will be encouraged once an organization recognizes that
what has happened to Exxon, Shell, ICI, Rhône-Poulenc, Fisons,
Union Carbide, BP, Nestlé, McDonald's, etc. can happen to it. Such a
shock – or potential shock – can then be treated as a matter for
aggression, of fear, of disdain or a matter for recognition that opinions
other than those of the organization have intrinsic merit and it should
seek to learn from them. Which response is chosen will depend on the
organizational culture and, in particular, the attitude of the chief
executive.

After the law and other external shocks, the pressures for change
are equally powerful and intrusive – but much less dramatic. Such
pressures include changing customer behaviour and the eco-labelling
developments, changing public opinion, initiatives from the business
community (such as the Global Reporting Initiative, see Chapter 12),

---

[3] For example, in supervision, financing, taxation, penalties, incentives, etc., although
to ignore the effectiveness of organizational lobbying against such changes would be
naive (see, for example, Beder, 1997).

[4] This can be as significant as to force a board seriously to consider whether or not
the enterprise is still a going concern (see, for example, Gray et al., 1998).

[5] Other examples from practice include instances of changes of board membership,
takeovers and privatizations which had acted as the spurs for change.

Figure 3.4

Monitoring the developing environmental agenda

The organization must be monitoring:

(1)   the emergence of environmental facts, findings and research;
(2)   the emergence of environmental issues;
(3)   the media's portrayal of issues;
(4)   public opinion;
(5)   employee views and attitudes;
(6)   the activities of environmental groups;
(7)   the activities, profile and attitudes of suppliers and customers;
(8)   draft law and directives;
(9)   business and government committees and 'think tanks';
(10)   complaints procedure and complaints received;
(11)   what is considered 'best practice' in one's industry.

---

environmental audit and ISO 14000, the developing 'supplier chain audits', producer responsibility and ethical investment. We will consider these and other pressures as appropriate in subsequent chapters. For the present, it suffices to say that monitoring, anticipating and responding to the external, environmentally related influences are therefore essential steps for the organization starting on the road to environmental sensitivity.

3.4   Internal Influences for Environmental Change: the Employees

Setting the organization on a greener path from the 'bottom up' has worked well for some companies (up to a point at least). Employees' actions have succeeded in educating senior management and can continue to do so. Equally, senior management can begin a 'light greening' process through encouraging employees in a variety of ways. This may be the most successful means of initiating the preliminary changes to the organization and its culture which will be necessary if environmental matters are to be taken seriously.

The first environmental experience for many organizations has arisen from some employee initiative that deals with the softer aspects of environmentalism. Examples have included the collection of paper for recycling in offices, canteen collections of cans and glass for recycling, transport-sharing schemes or, rather more innovatively, requests to undertake tree-planting schemes on land owned by the

Figure 3.5

Greening from the bottom up
• What do the employees of the organization think about environmental issues?
• How do you know? Why don't you know?
• Encourage and support employees to establish schemes for recycling – start with paper, cans and glass – but don't stop at that!
• Are any employees active environmentalists? Will they help the organization? If not why not? That deserves thinking about.
• Tree-planting scheme or nature reserve scheme on organizational land? Involvement with local authority?
• Give employees free time for environmental involvement.
• Suggestions from employees? Are they encouraged and acted upon?

organization.[6] The impact of such initiatives on the larger environmental programme is initially slight but in each case these small beginnings have had the effect of raising awareness among employees and of effectively introducing environmental questions into the workplace. Such an initiative may come from individuals, groups or trade unions,[7] either independently or as a result of contact through environmental groups, schools, local authorities, etc. Figure 3.5 summarizes the 'bottom-up' approach.[8]

For such initiatives to be successful, they must be seen to be encouraged – not just patronized or tolerated. Depending upon the management/employee climate in the organization, care must be taken not to appropriate a genuine employee initiative and thereby impede the motivation that originated it. For one, medium-sized manufacturing company, it was the initiative of two (very junior) employees that eventually led to a series of recycling schemes throughout the organization, a presentation to the senior management organized by the employees and, subsequently, a complete rethink

---

[6] There is increasing recognition of the importance of the land owned by organizations and that systematic stewardship of that land has great potential – both positive and negative – for issues of biodiversity. One initiative in the UK recognizes this – see, for example, *Business and Biodiversity* from the UK Round Table on Sustainable Development published by Earthwatch, Oxford in 1998.

[7] See, for example, Trades Union Congress, *Greening the workplace* (London: TUC, 1991).

[8] This 'bottom-up' approach is just one element of the wider stakeholder consultation that organizations are increasingly recognizing as a sensible part of any well-managed unit. For more detail see, for example, Gray et al. (1997), Wheeler and Silanpaa (1997) and Zadek et al. (1997).

of the company's stance on environmental issues.[9] For another (engineering) company the planting and landscaping of the site became a major factor in the organization's culture and self-image and has brought enormous benefits in terms of public relations, employee morale, contacts with schools, local authorities and local voluntary groups. IBM's 'community investment programme' is a totally embedded part of its culture, which helps define the organization and appears to be an essential element in employee self-esteem and motivation. For many schools and universities, the pressure for change has come from small initiatives from students to which, eventually, the organization has sought to respond.

The initial steps may be small, but in raising the profile of the issues, many substantive advantages accrue and environmental awareness, as a precursor to real environmental development within an organization, can successfully infiltrate all aspects of the organization. Equally, such small steps seem to be a useful – and less threatening – way of increasing the transparency of the organization and beginning the process of opening up to – and listening to – the wider stakeholder community.[10]

The response of the management is, of course, crucial. Some of the simplest but most effective (in terms of environmental sensitivity) changes have come from employee suggestions. As is the case with all aspects of organizational management, there must be a culture in which suggestions are encouraged, seen to be encouraged and seriously considered. The worldwide fame of the 3M culture and, in particular, its PPP (Pollution Prevention Pays) programme and of Dow Chemicals' encouragement to employees to form environmental groups within the company demonstrates just how far such a process can go.[11]

Taking matters further will involve providing facilities for training employees – both general and job-specific. This, in the right climate, should have a roller-coaster effect. Of course, in the wrong climate any training can be a waste of time, money and effort and counterproductive in terms of the frustration and demotivation it creates. Therefore, some degree of freedom within individuals' working lives becomes essential. There must be a degree of autonomy for issues – and even experiments – to be pursued. One company (reluctantly) gave an employee some freedom to explore the cost, use and disposal

---

[9] It is worth pointing out at this stage that many of the recycling initiatives are of dubious environmental value if not thought through. These matters are touched upon in Chapters 6, 7 and 9.

[10] These latter issues are considered again in Chapters 12 and 13.

[11] See Elkington (1987) for further information. See also Dauncey (1988), Davis (1991), Elkington (1997), Plant and Plant (1991) and Robertson (1985, 1990) for further ideas on this participative innovation approach.

of the containers and wooden pallets it used. The analysis, although somewhat naive, raised a considerable number of issues which the organization had to address. The resultant savings more than paid for the employee's time and the employee had enjoyed himself – thus lifting morale. Another company (again reluctantly) had permitted an employee doing an Open University degree to use the laboratory facilities – including technician time – to explore land contamination on the site. The results came as a shock to management and stood up to further testing. This put the organization in a position to start to address the issue well before the matter became a legal one. A third organization has encouraged a school to undertake an inventory over time of the flora and fauna on the company site. Employees are responsible for the project starting in the first place (through contact with the school) and are also involved in supervising and supporting the activity. The investigation has generated enormous interest throughout the company and has led – inevitably really – to suggestions for increasing the habitat possibilities of the site.

The openness of the organizational culture has usually been the determining factor of successful developments along these lines. With the increasing complexity of and rapidity of change in the green agenda, the organization that encourages and responds to its employees is bound to be in better shape. Indeed, an increasing number of international organizations – AT&T and Monsanto amongst them – are harnessing the specific expertise and enthusiasms of employees into 'green teams' with specialist remits to develop areas of environmental strategy for the organization.[12]

Ultimately, however, the depth and adequacy of the organization's response to environmental matters will be a function of its management and, in particular, its directorate and performance appraisal schemes.

3.5 Senior Management: the 'Tone from the Top'

If environmental issues are to be addressed seriously by any organization, they must be 'championed' within the organization by a member of senior management – ideally a member of the board. Without board representation – and/or direct and real access to it by the environmental manager – the organization is only playing at going green. The representation and 'championing' must also be backed up in a number of specific ways (see again Elkington's ten steps, set out earlier). Whilst each organization will approach the matter with a somewhat different emphasis, it must ensure that, at a minimum, the

---

[12] For more detail on such matters see, for example, Ditz et al. (1995) and Magretta (1997).

'environment' is sufficiently resourced in an active and effectual department. This may be a separate environmental department but much more usual is to tie environmental concerns to health and safety (SHE – safety, health, environment) departments, to such current procedures for the control of substances hazardous to health (or equivalent) or to the mechanisms in place or being developed for total quality management.[13] Indeed, the appointment of a senior and well-qualified environmental manager appears to be a *sine qua non* of serious environmental response.

Environmental matters *must not*, however, be located and left in PR departments. Although PR is clearly a function that will wish to cover environmental matters, the environment is not a PR issue – it is substantive and must be treated as such. Figure 3.6 provides just some

Figure 3.6

Watching the environmental issues

- Environmental policy
- Performance targets
- Management structure
- Staff awareness and training
- Public relations
- Community involvement
- Investment
- Financial implications
- Legal compliance
- Purchasing policy
- Market pressures
- Emergency/contingency plans
- Insurance
- Site and building management
- Paper use
- Equipment and furniture
- Energy sources and use
- Waste management and disposal
- Water use and discharge
- Product design
- Raw materials
- Packaging
- Process design/operation
- Emissions
- Transport and distribution.

Source: Adapted from Business-in-the-Environment (1991a) *Your Business and the Environment: A DIY Review for Companies* (London: BiE/Coopers & Lybrand Deloitte now PwC)

---

[13] Leading to 'environmental quality management' as Elkington, Knight and Hailes (1991) call it. See also environmental management systems and ISO 14000 in Chapter 5.

Figure 3.7

Identifying Environmental Priorities for your Company

L – Low
M – Medium
H – High

	Atmospheric Emissions	Water Use/ Discharge	Solid Waste	Energy	The Natural Environment	Corporate/ Market Pressures	Human Health	Accidents/ Emergencies	Legislation
Agriculture, forestry and fishing	L	H	M	L	H	M	H	M	M
Energy and water supply	H	H	H	H	H	M	M	H	H
Minerals, metals, chemicals, plastics	H	H	H	H	M	H	H	H	H
Metal goods, engineering, vehicles	H	H	M	M	L	M	M	M	H
Food, drink and tobacco	L	H	L	M	L	H	H	L	M
Pulp and paper	M	H	H	M	H	H	M	M	M
Other manufacturing	M	M	M	M	L	L	L	L	M
Construction	L	L	M	M	H	M	L	H	M
Distribution and transport	H	L	L	H	M	L	L	M	M
Communications, printing, publishing	M	M	M	L	L	M	L	L	L
Banking, finance and insurance	L	L	L	M	L	M	L	L	L
Retail	L	L	M	M	L	H	M	L	M
Marketing, advertising	L	L	L	L	L	H	L	L	L

Source: BiE (1991a) *Your Business and the Environment: A DIY Review for Companies* (Legal Studies and Services on behalf of BiE/C&LD now PwC)

indication of how substantive, and Figure 3.7 (from Business-in-the-Environment, 1991a) provides one illustration of an approach to making an initial prioritization of the issues.

Once the breadth and depth of the response the organization will have to make to environmental matters has been recognized, it becomes clear the 'environment' will be a strategic management issue for the board. Environmental response must permeate every aspect of the organization's activities and must, therefore, be bedded into its long- and medium-term plans for the positioning of the organization, its processes, structure and products. This must start from the development and implementation of an environmental policy (see Chapter 4). This must then be used to ensure that – from both an ethical and a (not entirely incompatible) business survival and strategy viewpoint – 'environment' receives as much priority as a business policy issue as do marketing, technology, product development, and so on.[14] A potential 'map' for the organization is provided in Figure 3.8 and environmental management systems are examined in more detail in a number of subsequent chapters, but particularly Chapter 5.

[14] For more guidance on this, see, for example, Davis (1991), Elkington, Knight and Hailes (1991), Sadgrove (1995), Welford and Gouldson (1993) and Winter (1988) as well as the other further reading at the end of this chapter.

Figure 3.8

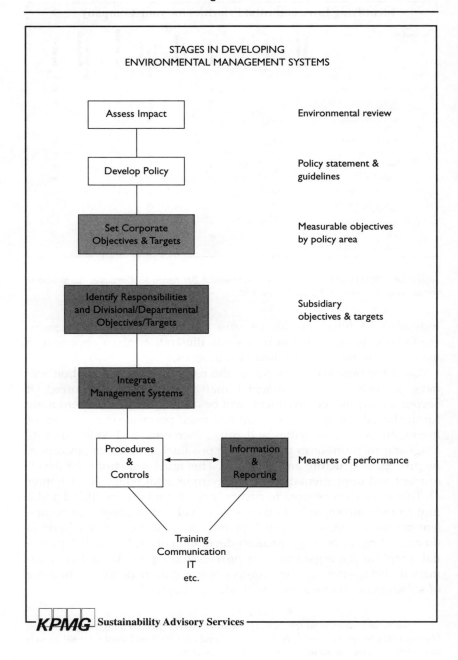

STAGES IN DEVELOPING
ENVIRONMENTAL MANAGEMENT SYSTEMS

Assess Impact — Environmental review

Develop Policy — Policy statement & guidelines

Set Corporate Objectives & Targets — Measurable objectives by policy area

Identify Responsibilities and Divisional/Departmental Objectives/Targets — Subsidiary objectives & targets

Integrate Management Systems

Procedures & Controls ⟷ Information & Reporting — Measures of performance

Training Communication IT etc.

KPMG Sustainability Advisory Services

3.6 Performance Measurement and Appraisal Systems

This is the point at which 'environment' must – if the organization is serious about its environmental impact – flow into all procedures and policies of the firm. *Most crucially* environmental issues must become a core factor in the design and operation of the financial system and the system of performance appraisal, incentives and rewards.

It is all very well having bold environmental policies (see Chapter 4), a well-developed environmental management system (see Chapter 5) and high environmental tone at board level, but if this has little or no impact on activities it amounts to no more than PR 'puff'. All people in the organization need to know that the apparent environmental obligations that organization places upon them are, *in fact*, part of the required performance. As a consequence if general performance is monitored and controlled, that monitoring and controlling must be seen to include the environmental matters as they relate to the individual or unit's activities. Equally, if a performance appraisal system is operated in the organization then that appraisal and any rewards – or penalties – attaching to it must also be seen to reflect the environmental issues. If, for example, a manager undertakes a project that is marginally less profitable than the apparently 'best' option but does it on environmental grounds, will the organization ignore, punish or reward him or her? Until that question – and the whole matter of performance appraisal – is resolved, the organization is not serious about environmental matters. And such lack of seriousness will be glaringly apparent to employees and managers who will, consequently, feel aggrieved, demotivated or simply content to ignore the environmental dimensions of their work.

There is a great deal of empty rhetoric in this area, but in amongst the (often empty) language of benchmarking[15] and performance indicators are two important specific elements: how are the environmental issues to be measured and assessed? And how are 'conventional' business measurements to be integrated and/or reconciled with environmental impacts? These are large and complex areas

---

[15] 'Benchmarking' typically refers to the establishment of targets, ideal levels of performance or acceptable minima by reference to, for example, past performance, company policy or, more typically, to the industry average or close competitors. Thus, for example, our company might have had three significant spillages last year, the industry average might be five per annum and our closest competitors might have had four such spills. In these circumstances, we might typically 'benchmark' against our previous (relatively good) record. Of course, benchmarking is only as good as the benchmarks and if our company and the rest of the industry have a woeful record we should not get too excited about unambitious targets.

Figure 3.9

Three layers of environmental performance indicators

- **Operational Indicators:** measure potential stresses on the environment, such as burning fossil fuels or converting forest resources at a paper mill.
- **Management Indicators:** measure efforts to reduce or mitigate environmental effects, such as company spending on energy efficiency or environmental training programmes.
- **Environment Condition Indicators:** measure environmental quality, such as ambient air pollution concentrations or global climate change.

. . . in a good management system, the different layers of indicators will be linked as closely as possible.

Source: Adapted from D. Ditz and J. Ranganathan (1997) *Measuring Up: Toward a Common Framework for Tracking Corporate Environmental Performance* (Washington, DC: World Resources Institute)

---

which we cannot go deeply into here.[16] Central to the first element is the care with which the key *environmental performance indicators* (EPIs) – see Figure 3.9 – that an organization uses are chosen and the way in which they are integrated with the environmental management policy (see Chapter 4), the environmental management system (see Chapters 4 and 5) and with the environmental reporting system (see Chapter 12). How the EPIs are integrated with more conventional business measurement systems is a matter much dependent upon the accountant. This seems an appropriate moment to bring accountants back into the frame.

3.7   The Accountants' Role in the Initiation of Change

Whether one is considering a large multinational company, a small manufacturing enterprise or a not-for-profit organization such as a local authority, it is clear that the crunch comes when environmental matters are in conflict with financial criteria. Organizations have dealt with issues of this type before – most obviously in the area of employee protection, health and safety. A company may consider that employee protection is a good long-term financial investment or (more typically in a TQM culture) that accidents and injuries to employees are simply unacceptable to any reasonable, responsible and ethical organization. Either way, some basis upon which 'social',

---

[16] But see the excellent Bennett and James (1998a) and Ditz and Ranganathan (1997).

'human' and/or 'ethical' matters can transcend immediate financial criteria has been established. So it is with environmental issues.

It is clear from a wide range of experience and research that until organizations embed environmental matters into the performance appraisal system, appropriately prioritized, and the incentive, reward and budgeting systems similarly redirected, environmental matters will nearly always lose out to financial criteria. (There are, of course, as we have seen, exceptions where financial and environmental criteria are in harmony, and these are likely to increase – see particularly Chapters 6 and 7. This is not true for all activities, however (see Chapter 8), and this must be explicitly recognized and addressed.)

Perhaps the best illustrations of this can be given by a specific example. One of the most 'environmentally advanced' organizations we dealt with in the early stages of the upsurge in environmental awareness by business had established environmental criteria as part of its managerial job specifications. Every six months, managerial appraisals were held on the basis of the targets set at the previous appraisal. Each appraisal concentrated on three areas, one of which was environmental.[17] The company saw itself as operating in a TQM culture and expected all target areas to be met within a framework of zero complaints (internal or external), zero notifications from the regulatory authorities, zero transgressions of consents or internal standards (whether notified or not) and a rapid recognition of suggestions from external or internal sources. Financial rewards and promotion were dependent upon these appraisals and failure to meet environmental standards was appropriately penalized. It was apparent that this had permeated the organization; employees were aware that their management were appraised upon environmental matters and that eventually environmental criteria would be built into their own job specifications. (This was warmly welcomed by the employees with whom we spoke – not least because the organization's close relationship with a number of local communities meant that employees, including management, were under pressure from friends and neighbours about the environmental impact of their employer's activities.[18]) This had forced the 'Best practicable environmental option' criteria[19]

---

[17] For example, one manager's targets ranged from the relatively trivial requirement to eradicate litter from his sites to the much more demanding requirement that he present to the board practicable proposals for eradicating – or at a minimum reducing – the pollution of water discharges from sites. This latter was regardless of consent levels.

[18] This is related to the crucial matter of transparency – the process of enabling (particularly) communities to 'see into' the organization in order to develop an informal environmental accountability. This matter is returned to in Parts C and D.

[19] See, for example, Royal Commission Environmental Approval (1988) and Chapter 8.

into investment decisions (see Chapter 8), had raised the emphasis on and detail contained in environmental impact assessments (see Chapter 5) and discussions were taking place about establishing particular allocations within the budgetary system. It also required, obviously, establishment of the appropriate information and reporting systems. These were developing as the organization experimented.

Most of this sounded like accounting, so where were the accountants?

> *The accountants? We had never thought of getting them involved. They just concern themselves with the numbers. We just tell them what to do and if they start interfering and telling us it costs too much, we simply override them. I'm not sure we'd want them involved really. They are good at their job but they'd be more likely to prevent environmental initiatives than to encourage them. I suppose I should talk to them about it.*
>
> (The Divisional General Manager, medium-sized extractive and processing company[20])

Accountants have, in general, been slow to initiate change themselves. In part this must be due to organizational expectations illustrated by the quote above. But in large part it is also due to not having previously thought about their role in environmental issues and, in many cases, appearing to be at a loss to make the connection between accounting and the environment. This response from the organization and the accountants is widespread but must be changed if organizations are to respond fully to the green agenda.[21]

The accountant as neutral at best, obstructive at worst, is illustrated by two other organizations – a local authority and an international company – both of which experienced the same problem. Both had a financial budget-driven culture, in which environmental investment initiatives naturally fell against financial return rates (see Chapter 8). Statements from the board that apparently encouraged environmental initiatives to be undertaken were not backed up by a change to the performance appraisal system and thus all environmental projects had also to meet current financial criteria; and no extra facilities, time or money were made available, so that any environmental activities that were not directly financially beneficial and/or avoided legislative complications became – in effect – voluntary acts of the employees. Naturally enough, very little (apart from falling morale) was happening.

Research suggests that accountants do see themselves as responsible for innovation as well as keen and willing to undertake initiatives

---

[20] See Gray, Bebbington, Walters and Thomson (1995) and Gray et al. (1998) for further examples of this and related attitudes.

[21] See, for example, Bebbington et al. (1994), Gray, Bebbington, Walters and Thomson (1995) and Gray et al. (1998).

in the development of financial information systems.[22] In the environmental domain, however, accountants still only rarely translate this into practice.

Interestingly, it is only when things like environmental matters are considered that the ubiquity of financial information systems within organizations becomes apparent. Figure 3.6 listed some of the areas to which the environmentally aware organization will give attention. Many will have financial implications in one form or another, in which case the accountants (and the auditors, internal and external, see Chapter 11) must be brought alongside. A number of organizations have, for example, adopted a more environmentally aware purchasing policy. Whilst imaginative approaches (and care over wastage – see Chapter 7) can ensure that less environmentally malign purchasing does not necessarily cost more, it may often do so. The accountant, the accounting system and/or the internal auditor may quickly put a stop to that if not properly integrated into the system. An increasing number of organizations have also recognized the importance of transport policy and, in particular, personal transport.[23] Private car usage is clearly heavily subsidized (financially and environmentally) in general and company cars especially so. A particularly imaginative approach is to allow all personal travel on the organization's business to receive the standard car mileage rate – users of public transport, foot or bicycle are thus highly rewarded for their effort, the organization is no worse off and its environmental impact is reduced. In two organizations we know, this system floundered very quickly because the accounting system and the internal audit personnel had not received instructions and this practice was strictly counter to existing regulations and therefore (in the case of a local authority) actually illegal. The matter was quickly resolved but where the accountants had been involved from the beginning – with an environmentally educated and aware point of view – the system ran very sweetly from the start.

Organizations cannot reduce their environmental impact and become more environmentally benign if they have a strong financial culture *and* their accountants are not in at the design stage of environmental initiative and environmental information systems. Their exclusion will prevent initiatives, their inclusion brings their undoubted abilities into the frame.

---

[22] See Bebbington et al. (1994) and Guilding and Kirman (1998).

[23] Despite the at-times reverential awe in which the sacrosanct private car is held, some companies do manage to get away from it. Body Shop is perhaps an unsurprising initiator but Ciba–Geigy is reported by Hutchinson (1991) as discouraging cars, issuing bicycles and encouraging public transport.

Figure 3.10

Getting started
(1) Adopt Elkington's 'ten steps'.
(2) Adopt the 3 (or more) Rs.
(3) Monitor the developing environmental agenda.
(4) Encourage employee initiatives and environmental schemes within the organization.
(5) Set the 'tone from the top'.
(6) Ensure that environmental concerns permeate the organization.
(7) Ensure that the company takes a multidisciplinary approach, bringing different functional managers together.
(8) Raise company-wide awareness and ensure that the environment is 'owned' across the board.
(9) Adapt the performance appraisal system.
(10) Ensure that the accounting and financial systems are in harmony with the environmental initiatives.
(11) Undertake environmental reviews.
(12) Identify and measure key environmental indicators.
(13) Begin to implement an environmental management system.
(14) Integrate the EMS with the rest of the management information systems.

3.8 Conclusions

There can be no single, ideal way in which any organization can begin the process of developing its organizational sensitivity. Each may choose a different route – some starting with an environmental policy (see Chapter 4), some with an environmental audit and the development of an EMS (see Chapter 5), others with environmental reporting (see Chapters 11 and 12). Others may wish to experiment with some of the suggestions in this chapter. However one approaches it, there is no need to do it alone. Contact with the support organizations listed in the appendix and guidance from the further reading below (and throughout the book) are essential – and economic – ways of getting started on the very difficult path of making the organization more environmentally sensitive.

Further Reading

Bennett, M. and P. James (1998) *Environment under the Spotlight: Current Practices and Future Trends in Environment-related Performance Measurement for Business* (London: ACCA)

Business-in-the-Environment (1991a) *Your Business and the Environment: A DIY Review for Companies* (London: BiE/Coopers & Lybrand Deloitte)

Business-in-the-Environment (1991b) *Your Business and the Environment: An Executive Guide* (London: BiE)

Business-in-the-Environment (1992) *A Measure of Commitment: Guidelines for Environmental Performance Measurement* (London: BiE/KPMG)

Davis, J. (1991) *Greening Business: Managing for Sustainable Development* (Oxford: Blackwell)

Ditz, D. and J. Ranganathan (1997) *Measuring Up: Toward a Common Framework for Tracking Corporate Environmental Performance* (Washington, DC: World Resources Institute)

Earth Works Group (1989) *50 Simple Things You Can Do to Save the Earth* (London: Hodder & Stoughton)

Elkington, J., P. Knight and J. Hailes (1991) *The Green Business Guide,* (London: Gollancz)

Trades Union Congress (1991) *Greening the Workplace* (London: TUC)

Welford, R. (ed.) (1996) *Corporate Environmental Management: Systems and Strategies* (London: Earthscan)

Welford, R. (ed.) (1997) *Corporate Environmental Management: Culture and Organisations* (London: Earthscan)

Winter, G. (1988) *Business and the Environment* (Hamburg: McGraw-Hill)

CHAPTER 4

ENVIRONMENTAL POLICY

Adoption, Establishment and Implementation

4.1 Introduction

All aspects of a company's operations, from accounting and purchasing, to product design, manufacturing, sales and marketing and distribution, will have an impact on the environment. Your company environmental policy should reflect your recognition of this.

(Business-in-the-Environment (1991a), Annex 1)

The primary prerequisite for an organization intending to take environmental matters seriously is the development of an environmental policy. This should typically form the basis from which all the organization's environmental interactions and policies can be developed and it will be one of the principal signals to the internal and external stakeholders of the seriousness (or otherwise) of the organization's intentions with respect to the environment. It is therefore not a matter to be taken lightly.[1]

It may be the case that an organization adopts one environmental policy for internal use but discloses to a wider public only extracts from or even a watered down version of it. Whilst it is difficult not to have sympathy for an organization nervous about offering hostages to fortune, the publication of bland policy statements (see below) or, more specifically, the refusal to open up to the environmental debate is not a constructive approach to one's commitment and contribution to the amelioration of the environmental crisis.[2]

The establishment of an environmental policy can take two main routes: development of an organization-specific policy; or the adoption of one of the publicly established 'charters'. We will deal briefly with the tailor-made experience first before spending most of the chapter on the 'off-the-peg' possibilities. But a policy on its own means little, so the later sections of the chapter will cover some of the

[1] One approach – plus discussion of some of the complexities involved – is given in a review of Compaq's environmental policy development by one of the company's vice-presidents. See R. Gilfillan, 'A policy for many functions and markets', *Environment Strategy Europe 1997* (pp. 103–104) (London: Campden).

[2] Disclosure of environmental information – including disclosure of environmental policies – is examined in rather more detail in Chapter 12.

steps towards implementing the policy – embedding it into organizational practice.

4.2 The Company's Own Environmental Policy

The primary purpose in adopting an environmental policy is as a guide to future action. It therefore needs to be informed by reliable data on the organization's environmental interactions, consist of commitments that are as specific as possible and be supported by as many mechanisms for turning the policy into specific targets as can be established. The specific targets, which should be transitory and developing, should be referred to in the policy but *not specified*; that should be done in supporting documents.[3] Figure 4.1 lists some pros and cons of developing an in-house environmental policy.

It makes considerable sense for any initial environmental policy statement to be a draft only. Once the organization has carried out environmental reviews, assessed its own environmental position and

Figure 4.1

Some pros and cons for developing an in-house environmental policy

Advantages to the organization
- It can be tailored to one's own needs.
- It can recognize what can be 'realistically' achieved in the foreseeable future.
- It can be protected and tended in the dark, away from the glare of publicity.
- Its feasibility can be assessed in privacy.
- It can be much more general and less demanding.
- It can be refined and developed in the light of experience.
- It can be easier to defend against environmental groups.
- Implementation may be cheaper.
- It can be more adventuresome if it can be kept private.

Disadvantages
- It may be bland.
- Implementation and monitoring may not be prioritized.
- Derivation of the policy is more expensive.
- It is not comparable – nationally and internationally.
- It looks like a softer option – bad PR?
- It does not necessarily encourage transparency.
- It may avoid the really difficult and important issues relating to the business.

---

[3] It should also be recognized that the formulation of the environmental policy may come after the initial environmental review (see Chapter 5). Policy, to a degree at least, does need to be informed by a sound knowledge of the actual and potential environmental impacts of the business.

Figure 4.2 Compaq environmental policy

COMPAQ

Environmental Policy

Compaq is committed to conducting its business in a manner that is compatible with the environment and protects the quality of the communities where we operate. We believe that business must work in partnership with suppliers, government, community and industry groups in an effort to protect the environment.

Compaq fosters openness and dialogue with employees and the public anticipating and responding to environmental concerns in a timely manner. Compaq is dedicated to integrating sound environmental practices into our products and services.

Compaq will continue to develop and implement programs that meet or exceed compliance with country, province or local regulatory requirements. We will continue to develop long-term plans that identify and manage environmental issues, even though the issues may not be regulated.

Key groups within the company have clearly defined roles and responsibilities for the environmental program. In addition, each employee has a responsibility to follow environmental procedures and to participate proactively in our environmental programs and committees.

Our goal is to operate our facilities in a safe and environmentally sound manner. We integrate environmental considerations into our products via the business planning process and by using innovative engineering controls, proactive programs and the creativity and ingenuity of our personnel. Through the efforts and teamwork of all employees, Compaq will continually review product designs, processes, materials, recycling and treatment technologies to reduce our chemical usage, waste production and impact on the environment.

Eckhard Pfeiffer
President and Chief Executive Officer

assessed the feasibility of its environmental goals, *then* it can turn the draft into the 'real thing' in the knowledge that the policy is feasible and can be a long-lived document. Then, but only then, the organization can consider publishing the statement.[4] (A more detailed guide to this process is contained in Appendix 4.1.[5]) Figure 4.2 provides an example of a published statement that has emerged from this process; other examples are referred to in Chapters 11 and 12.

The process of developing the environmental policy is not without its problems. One company, for example, was concerned that:

> *this emphasis on environmental policy is in danger of overshadowing other areas of policy. Isn't environmental policy just one more part of the organization's general policy? Shouldn't we be making the same fuss about health and safety for example?*

Indeed, it seems most appropriate that the organization should have a general mission and policy statement, but backed up by detailed policies in the appropriate areas – including environment and health and safety.[6] In fact, such an approach seems essential in that environmental matters will permeate the whole organization and must therefore influence, and be integrated with, other areas of policy.

If the environmental policy-making process is working successfully within the organization it will raise difficult questions. For example, should the policy state that the organization will comply with all laws or, even, go beyond them? Our experience suggests that the wider (and less cynical) elements of the public will assume that organizations comply with law. The publication of such a statement may not be seen as especially impressive. The irony is, of course, that a great many organizations either do not comply with all law or, far more commonly, have little or no idea whether or not they comply with environmental law. For this reason, if no other, reference to the law seems particularly appropriate.

Another major issue for multinational corporations is whether or not to adopt worldwide standards. Companies such as IBM, ICI and

---

[4] A statement of intent or even a very general policy can usefully be disclosed earlier in the process, of course.

[5] See also BiE (1991a), which contains a draft outline policy statement for organizations to mould to their own needs. Much more detailed guidance on this process is provided in Elkington, Knight and Hailes (1991) and see also the guide issued by 3M/ The Environment Council (1991).

[6] Whilst we might consider environmental matters should dominate all others, this is not an especially widely held view nor is it likely to achieve the sort of balanced organization that most environmental initiatives are intended to achieve. This problem of balance is captured by what John Elkington calls '*The triple bottom line*' – reflecting financial, environmental and social/community issues (see Elkington, 1997 and Chapter 14).

Norsk Hydro *have* committed themselves to such a policy even though this means that the operations in the country with the lowest environmental standards will be conducted by reference to the standards operating in the most environmentally stringent country. This is an expensive and brave policy. A number of other multinationals have consciously decided not to adopt this policy because it has a severe impact on their international competitiveness, it costs far too much, they see no need for such high standards or, as one company said, they really have no idea what sorts of environmental standards are being applied in many of their subsidiaries. Such problems – and attitudes – suggest to us that a 'worldwide standards' clause must ultimately be the target of all environmental policies.[7]

The importance attaching to environmental policies, the need for all organizations to adopt them, the need for guidance on them and, especially, the perceived need for comparability against the highest (currently feasible) standards have led to the development of the 'charters' – independently derived and publicly adopted environmental policies.

4.3 The Environmental Charters

An environmental charter is a public document with a number of primary purposes. It consists of a number of guiding principles covering areas of corporate planning, activity and control where environmental aspects should be incorporated. We shall briefly review the most widely known charters: the CERES Principles[8] and the ICC's Business Charter for Sustainable Development; look briefly at the Chemical Industries Association Responsible Care Programme; and finally touch upon a few other examples.[9]

An environmental charter has a number of advantages (or disadvantages, depending upon one's point of view) which can be summarized in Figure 4.4.

Whatever potential they may have, they must be essentially imperfect. The difficulties of interpreting and implementing the charters

---

[7] It is notable, however, that the charters we will be discussing below do not insist on this requirement. Some of the implications of this are touched upon in Chapter 15.

[8] CERES is the Coalition for Environmentally Responsible Economies. These principles were previously known as the 'Valdez principles'.

[9] Each of these charters we review can serve the purposes in Figure 4.3. However, it is quite obvious why the vast majority of companies are less then enthusiastic about adopting such policies and thus providing outside parties with a stick with which to beat them.

Figure 4.3

The primary purposes of the public environmental charters
(1) To provide information to external parties by signalling environmental intentions and commitments of the entity.
(2) To act as an internal guide for the organization of the broad areas of environmental concern – a blueprint for the development of more detailed environmental policies and practices.
(3) To act as a means by which external parties may place pressure on organizations to become more environmentally sensitive via (e.g.) providing investors with an investment evaluation tool and providing a standard that organizations can be asked to match.

Figure 4.4

Major advantages/disadvantages of signing up to the public environmental charters
(1) If sponsored by a body independent of the organization it is likely to be free of the more obvious forms of bias. As a result it is likely to contain clearer and more specific environmental objectives than the environment mission statements found in annual reports or other public relations statements.
(2) By providing a common mission statement, charters simplify the process of comparing organizations' policies.
(3) An organization can be assessed on its performance by comparison with the charter – either by the charter's initiators or some other body (e.g. Friends of the Earth, Greenpeace, EIRIS, etc.). This potential for a monitoring function permits a potential enforcement mechanism.
(4) It provides an external standard for reference by which organizations – whether or not subscribers to the charter – may be judged.
(5) It allows the existence and identity of non-subscribers to be more readily available. This leads to the inevitable questions as to why an organization *did* not sign up to a particular charter.

plus the absence (to date at least) of adequate monitoring and follow-up procedures[10] do place the charters at risk of becoming merely public relations statements rather than substantive commitments of policy. The charters are, however, widely promulgated and discussed

---

[10] Although the CBI's Business and Environment Forum in the UK did have a degree of monitoring procedures built into it, these, it would appear, proved to be expensive and difficult to administer as well as, more contentiously, exposing the less than whole-hearted approach to environmental issues by UK businesses. There was a potential source of embarrassment here as the CBI's line has consistently been that the environment is safe in businesses' hands.

and, generally, represent standards to which every organization must aspire – even if they currently represent standards that make most organizations perspire.

4.4 The CERES Principles

The CERES Principles (see Figure 4.5) were developed in the wake of the *Exxon Valdez* tragedy[11] by the Coalition for Environmentally Responsible Economies (CERES) project of the Social Investment Forum in the United States. In the UK, the Principles were launched in November 1989 by the Green Alliance and Jupiter Tarbutt Merlin[12] and have been periodically updated since.[13]

Corporations are invited to sign publicly the CERES Principles and, in doing so, provide a highly visible signal of corporate commitment to environmental excellence and to compliance with (what one analyst referred to as) 'a legal document which has direct financial consequences'. The Principles are the strictest of the public charters and the lack of general support for them by industry[14] reflects an understandable (if not admirable) preference for less stringent codes. The extent of the commitment required by the Principles prompted one public expression of why a company might refuse to sign them:

---

[11] Exxon's oil tanker the *Valdez* spilt 11 million gallons of oil into Prince William Sound, Alaska after running aground in March 1989. The devastation to the fragile ecology of the region was such that there remain profound doubts as to whether it may ever fully 'recover'. The resulting devastation to Exxon, although considerable and measured in US$ billions, was *not* fatal.

[12] Jupiter Tarbutt Merlin were one of the most active of UK ethical investment funds at the time. Other ethical investment funds (see also Chapter 10) together with a UK unit – the Social Investment Forum (the UK equivalent of CERES, formed in July 1991) – keep a watching brief on these and other principles. For more detail and background see, for example, Dobie (1990), Lander (1989), Miller (1992), the further reading at the end of this chapter and Chapter 10.

[13] CERES (1995) *Guide to the CERES Principles* (Boston: CERES). There is the suspicion that updating of the Principles has weakened them. It is a moot point whether it is better to have more companies signed up to weaker commitments or to have a charter of the very highest standard which companies may aspire to but currently fail to meet.

[14] By August 1991, only 28 organizations (principally unlisted companies and ethical/green investment funds) in the USA had signed the Principles. This had risen to over 80 by the late 1990s. This relatively low level of commitment does not prevent the use of the Principles as a potent tool in the application of external pressure on organizations via such things as shareholder resolutions to companies. For one example see KPMG, *Environment Briefing Note*, no. 8 (Autumn 1991), pp. 2–5.

Figure 4.5

The CERES Principles

We adopt, support and will implement the principles of:

1. Protection of the Biosphere We will reduce and make continual progress towards eliminating the release of any substances that may cause environmental damage to the air, water, or earth or its inhabitants. We will safeguard all habitats affected by our operations and will protect open spaces and wilderness, while preserving biodiversity.

2. Sustainable Use of Natural Resources We will make sustainable use of renewable natural resources, such as water, soils and forests. We will conserve non-renewable natural resources through efficient use and careful planning.

3. Reduction and Disposal of Waste We will reduce and where possible eliminate waste through source reduction and recycling. All waste will be handled and disposed of through safe and responsible methods.

4. Energy Conservation We will conserve energy and improve the energy efficiency of our internal operations and of the goods and services we sell. We will make every effort to use environmentally safe and sustainable energy sources.

5. Risk Reduction We will strive to minimize the environmental, health and safety risks to our employees and the communities in which we operate through safe technologies, facilities and operating procedures, and by being prepared for emergencies.

6. Safe Products and Services We will reduce and where possible eliminate the use, manufacture or sale of products and services that cause environmental damage or health and safety hazards. We will inform consumers of the environmental impacts of our products or services and try to correct safe usage.

7. Environmental Restoration We will promptly and responsibly correct conditions that we have caused that endanger health, safety or the environment. To the extent feasible, we will redress injuries we have caused to persons or damage we have caused to the environment and we will restore the environment.

8. Informing the Public We will inform in a timely manner anyone who may be affected by conditions caused by our company that might endanger health, safety or the environment. We will regularly seek advice and counsel through dialogue with persons in communities near our facilities. We will not take any action against employees for reporting dangerous incidents or conditions to management or to the appropriate authorities.

9. Management Commitment We will implement these basic Principles and sustain a process that ensures that the Board of Directors and Chief Executive Office are fully informed about pertinent environmental issues and are fully responsible for environmental policy. In selecting our Board of Directors, we will consider demonstrated environmental commitment as a factor.

10. Audits and Reports We will conduct an annual self-evaluation of our progress in implementing these Principles. We will support the timely creation of generally accepted environmental audit procedures. We will annually complete the CERES Report, which we will make available to the public.

Several of these Principles, while worthy in their aims, contain unqualified commitments to 'minimize' or to 'strive to eliminate' emissions or other environmental damage. We considered that such commitments with no regard to practicability, to cost, or to acceptable or sustainable levels of emissions are simply unrealistic if taken literally.

(Charles Donovan, Senior Managing Director of British Gas, *British Gas Views: Business and the Environment* (London: British Gas), 1991, p. 6)

Non-subscription to the Principles revolves around either a fear of the 'blank cheque' or concern about the commitment to disclosure. There is a degree of irony in this. In principle, at least, the Articles of the charter are only a combination of the basic principles of environmental quality management and environmental management systems (see Chapter 5), responsible care and public information plus (the admittedly much stricter) basic prerequisites of sustainable development (see Chapter 14), which nobody (publicly at least) will admit to being 'against'. Thus, at a simple interpretation, the Principles are tailor-made for any organization committed to less unsustainable development, environmental management systems and being ahead of legislative development.

In this sense, there should be no organization which cannot sign them.[15] And, if there is, the public could be expected to ask why. In this sense the Principles have been successful. However, the demand from industry for a milder, more forgiving environmental code with which to work led to publication of the ICC's Charter.

4.5 ICC Business Charter for Sustainable Development

The International Chamber of Commerce formally launched its Business Charter for Sustainable Development (ICC BCSD[16] – see Figure 4.6) in April 1991 at the Second World Industry Conference on Environmental Management (WICEM II).[17] It has become, as far we can assess, the most widely supported charter, with well over 1000 (principally) large organizations having endorsed it.

[15] There is some concern that not all elements of all the charters are equally applicable to every business. Certainly one would expect – from a business, as opposed to an environmentalist point of view – that an organization should assess whether the charter is relevant to the business and then set about the difficult process of prioritizing the elements of the charter. An environmentalist would argue that each charter *is* applicable to every organization. Business and environmentalists would agree on the need to prioritize but perhaps disagree on what that priority should be.

[16] Not to be confused with the (now World) Business Council for Sustainable Development – although the two organizations would appear to work closely together.

[17] For further information see, for example, Burke et al. (1991).

ICC is a non-governmental organization 'serving world business with membership in over 100 countries', whose stated purposes include:

> to represent business at international levels such as the United Nations; promote world trade and investment based on free and fair competition; harmonize trade practices and formulate terminology and guidelines for exporters and importers; and provide practical services to business.

ICC has a history of supporting business in the environmental arena. Its environmental guidelines for world industry were first published in 1974. The ICC BCSD, in contrast with the 'absolutes' contained in the CERES Principles, involves softer standards and vaguer undertakings.

Indeed, although the Charter is labelled as concerned with sustainable development, it contains nothing on this subject (see Chapter 14) and is, rather, a guide to good environmental management. The ICC BCSD is thus less stringent than the CERES Principles – especially as it requires its signatories merely to endorse its aims rather than to have reached the standards set out. For instance, ICC BCSD refers to 'no undue environmental impact' (Clause 6) and speaks of 'foster[ing] openness and dialogue' (Clause 15). The ICC exhorts business to an environmental response rather than demands one.

Further, the ICC is publicly opposed to disclosure in general (see Chapter 5) and so the 'tentative' nature of the requirements for systematic auditing and reporting comes as no surprise. While Clause 16 requires regular audits and periodic provision of 'appropriate' information, it neither insists on disclosure nor makes absolute the audit requirement. This allows organizations considerable flexibility in reporting and provides the public and shareholders with no guarantees on the quality of environmental performance or the regularity of environmental information (see Chapters 10 to 12).

Finally, ICC does not monitor compliance with the Charter. Rather, it believes that the public interest will be an adequate monitoring mechanism.[18] That is, knowing that the organization subscribes to BCSD will enable the public to evaluate its compliance with the Charter. However, given the absence of widespread public announcement of which organizations have signed the Charter and the lack of systematic audit and publication of results, how individuals will in fact be able to assess for themselves the level of compliance is unknown. In fact, as the ICC itself recognized, independent organizations such as UNEP, ethical investment funds, consultancies and non-governmental organizations (NGOs) have, to an extent, stepped into

---

[18] See, for example, the words of Torvild Aakvaag, Chairman of ICC Environment Commission, in Burke et al. (1991, p. 88).

Figure 4.6

ICC Business Charter for Sustainable Development

1. Corporate priority   To recognize environmental management as among the highest corporate priorities and as a key determinant to sustainable development; to establish policies, programmes and practices for conducting operations in an environmentally sound manner.

2. Integrated management   To integrate these policies, programmes and practices fully into each business as an essential element of management in all its functions.

3. Process of improvement   To continue to improve corporate policies, programmes and environmental performance, taking into account technical developments, scientific understanding, consumer needs and community expectations, with legal regulations as a starting point; and to apply the same environmental criteria internationally.

4. Employee education   To educate, train and motivate employees to conduct their activities in an environmentally responsible manner.

5. Prior assessment   To assess environmental impacts before starting a new activity or project and before decommissioning a facility or leaving a site.

6. Products and services   To develop and provide products or services that have no undue environmental impact and are safe in their intended use, that are efficient in their consumption of energy and natural resources, and that can be recycled, reused, or disposed of safely.

7. Customer advice   To advise, and where relevant educate, customers, distributors and the public in the safe use, transportation, storage and disposal of products provided; and to apply similar considerations to the provision of services.

8. Facilities and operations   To develop, design and operate facilities and conduct activities taking into consideration the efficient use of energy and materials, the sustainable use of renewable resources, the minimization of adverse environmental impact and waste generation, and the safe and responsible disposal of residual wastes.

9. Research   To conduct or support research on the environmental impacts of raw materials, products, processes, emissions and wastes associated with the enterprise and on the means of minimizing such adverse impacts.

10. Precautionary approach   To modify the manufacture, marketing or use of products or services or the conduct of activities, consistent with scientific and technical understanding, to prevent serious or irreversible environmental degradation.

11. Contractors and suppliers   To promote the adoption of these principles by contractors acting on behalf of the enterprise, encourage and, where appropriate, requiring improvements in their practices to make them consistent with those of the enterprise; and to encourage the wider adoption of these principles by suppliers.

12. Emergency preparedness   To develop and maintain, where significant hazards exist, emergency preparedness plans in conjunction with emergency services, relevant authorities and local community, recognizing potential transboundary impacts.

13. Transfer of technology   To contribute to the transfer of environmentally sound technology and management methods throughout the industrial and public sectors.

Figure 4.6 *(continued)*

---

14. Contributing to the common effort To contribute to the development of public policy and to business, governmental and intergovernmental programmes and educational initiative that will enhance environmental awareness and protection.

15. Openness to concerns To foster openness and dialogue with employees and the public, anticipating and responding to their concerns about the potential hazards and impacts of operations, products, wastes or services, including those of transboundary or global significance.

16. Compliance and reporting To measure environmental performance; to conduct *regular* environmental audits and assessments of compliance with company requirements, legal requirements and these principles; and periodically to provide appropriate information to the Board of Directors, shareholders, employees, the authorities and the public.

---

the vacuum to monitor, if not signatories' statements, broad environmental performance by companies. (See also Chapter 12.)

In broad terms then, signing up to the ICC BCSD is thus a relatively relaxed affair. In the words of the Environment Director of a large plc:

> *The ICC policy is a very good set of the principles that must form the basis for discussion for any company deriving its own policy. It is the discussion which is useful – not the policy itself. It is this company's nature to be in the fore front and thinking about these issues will put you in the forefront – and this will give commercial advantage.*

Ironically, one of the most interesting reasons expressed for *not* subscribing to the Charter came from one of the world's largest and most environmentally advanced companies. It believed that it was improper to sign anything which committed it to sustainable development as currently understood. Not because the company was opposed to the concept (after all, who is?), but because 'buying into sustainable development' implies also 'buying into' the major social policies that would appear to go along with it – most notably population control.[19] The directors of the company did not believe that their authority extended to such a commitment. The irony is that the ICC BCSD, despite using the term 'sustainable development', makes no attempt to demonstrate that satisfaction of the Charter is in fact compatible with sustainability (see Chapter 14).

---

[19] See Chapters 14 and 15.

4.6 Other Charters and Related Initiatives

Whilst it might be a little too optimistic to infer that the number of different initiatives directed towards the development of public (or semi-public) environmental charters is a recognition of the importance attached to this first of Elkington's 'Ten Steps', there seems little doubt that, at a minimum, such charters have kept environmental issues to the forefront of companies' and the public's attention.

As the business-environment agenda has developed there has been a steady growth in environmental charters as different organizations seek to (depending on your point of view) set the targets for ideal environmental performance or offer companies realistic but less stringent goals in environmental management. In addition to the international charters we have seen above, charters have appeared that are intended to cover either national organizations or specific sectors of organization.

Examples of national charters include the Canadian National Round Table on the Environment and the Economy's *Objectives for Sustainable Development*, Japan's Federation of Economic Organizations' *Keidanren Global Environment Charter* and, in the UK, the CBI's Environment Business Forum published the *Agenda for Voluntary Action*. The CBI's initiative (see Figure 4.7) was launched in 1992 as an explicit attempt to persuade businesses to adopt a 'responsible attitude' to environmental issues in order to demonstrate that regulation of such matters as environmental management and environmental reporting (see Chapters 5 and 12) was unnecessary. As a political initiative and as a means of keeping businesses moving forward on environmental issues it was clearly a success. As a demonstration of the superiority of 'voluntary initiatives' one might be less than entirely convinced.

Figure 4.7

The CBI Agenda for Voluntary Action

- Designate a board-level director with responsibility for the environment and the management systems needed to address the key issues.
- Publish a corporate environmental policy statement.
- Set clear targets and objectives for achieving the policy.
- Publicly report progress towards meeting those objectives.
- Ensure communication with employees, and training where appropriate, on company environmental programmes.
- Establish appropriate 'partnerships' to extend and promote the objectives of the Forum, particularly with smaller companies.

More sector-specific codes have also emerged. These include The European Petroleum Industry Association's *Environmental Guiding Principles*, the UK *Environmental Investor Code* developed by Pensions Investment Research Consultants (PIRC), the UK *Environmental Charter for Local Government* developed by Friends of the Earth, and, perhaps the best known, the Chemical Industry Association's (CIA) *Responsible Care Programme*. The CIA programme (see Figure 4.8), whilst less demanding than either the ICC or CERES Charters, is a good example of an industry-based initiative which has the value of being 'realistic' enough to be acceptable to most of that industry. It was launched in May 1989 in order to 'improve the chemical industry's performance and to enable companies to demonstrate improvement to the public' (CIA Preface to the Guiding Principles).

Figure 4.8

CIA Responsible Care Programme

GUIDING PRINCIPLES:

Members of the Chemical Industries Association are committed to managing their activities so that they present an acceptably high level of protection for the health and safety of employees, customers, the public and the environment.

The following Guiding Principles form the basis of this commitment:

- Companies should ensure that their health, safety and environment policy reflects the commitment and is clearly seen to be an integral part of their overall business policy.
- Companies should ensure that management, employees at all levels and those in contractual relationships with the Company are aware of their commitment and are involved in the achievement of their policy objectives.
- All Company activities and operations must be conducted in accordance with relevant statutory obligations. In addition, Companies should operate to the best practices of the industry and in accordance with Government and Association guidance.

In particular, Companies should:

- Assess the actual and potential impact of their activities and products on the health and safety of employees, customers, the public and environment.
- Where appropriate, work closely with public and statutory bodies in the development and implementation of measures designed to achieve an acceptably high level of health, safety and environmental protection.
- Make available to employees, customers, the public and statutory bodies, relevant information about activities that affect health, safety and the environment.

Members of the Association recognize that these Principles and activities should continue to be kept under regular review.

In addition to its industry-based origin – a response to the chemical industry's increasingly environmentally malign public image – the CIA charter has a number of noteworthy characteristics: it explicitly states the need to comply with legislation (far from being as trivial as it might appear); whilst falling short of actually committing itself to regular and widespread public disclosure, it does require that companies make information available upon demand to employees, customers, etc. – by implication – to the extent that these groups are affected by the organization's activities. In an atmosphere characterized by a reluctance to disclose, this is a welcome development (see Chapters 11 and 12); and it explicitly recognizes the developing nature of the environmental agenda and the need, therefore, to closely monitor and review any environmental policy.

It is worth also noting that the CIA's Responsible Care Programme was issued relatively early on in the modern development of the environmental agenda. It seems likely that this was motivated, in part at least, by 'good business sense' in order to provide a defensible position either against charters of the CERES requirements or against the possibility of more demanding legislative requirements in the wake of a series of chemical and chemical-related environmental disasters. Whether such small advances as the weaker and less-demanding charters, if they defuse wider and more critical debate, can be thought of as unqualified environmental successes remains a matter of judgement.

4.7 Implementing and Monitoring the Policy

The publicly launched charters are learning something that organizations which have developed their own in-house environmental policy learned some time ago: a policy on its own means virtually nothing; it must be translated into action.

The textbook approach to implementation is laid out in Figure 4.9, in which one simply follows a cookbook menu. It *is* possible to follow this approach: Alcan said in 1991 that the environmental (and related) policy drives all investment and R&D (see Chapter 8); British Telecom has regularly published its policy, targets *and* target completion dates (see also Chapters 11 and 12). Each of these steps is important. That is:

(1) Unless the policy can be turned into specifics it cannot be controlled – for example, all organizations may choose to think of themselves as sustainable without ever having defined sustainability or investigated the claim.

Figure 4.9

Implementing the policy
• Prioritize the goals of the policy.
• Prioritize the goals of the organization in terms of the policy.
• Identify interactions throughout the organization and decide how to harmonize them.
• Turn the goals into specific targets.
• Give the targets completion dates.
• Assign responsibility.
• Monitor performance.
• Feedback and reward.

(2) Unless the conflicts in the policy(ies) are examined the policy may be ineffectual – an organization may reduce emissions 'as far as is practicable', or use technology which is the most environmentally advanced 'within budget constraints'. Both statements mean nothing at all until the financial implications of 'practicable' and 'budget constraints' are adapted.

(3) Monitoring is more important than often realized. Not only does it assess performance and provide a feedback and control mechanism, it should also fulfil two further functions. First, the existence of *no* monitoring is a strong signal to employees that the organization is not serious about environmental issues. It signals that despite warm words and exhortation, performance will still be measured by the old ways, promotion will still be on the same old criteria and no resources will be made available for environmental matters. No monitoring virtually equals 'don't care'. Secondly, the monitoring should be part of a wider monitoring system that can also provide early warnings to the organization. This is worth emphasizing. We have already discussed (see Chapter 3) the need to monitor the developing environmental agenda. This cannot be a precise, technical (or algorithmic) activity. Much will depend on instinct. This instinct needs to be informed by regular reviews. For example, an organization may be apparently meeting its consents but certain areas of the organization may be having more accidents than others. This is an area that a responsible management will wish to investigate not least because it may prove to be an area of embarrassment at some time in the future. Similarly, if an organization is not making regular reviews of its activities, it needs to recognize that outside bodies may be doing so. The organization will wish to avoid the unpleasant surprise of discovering that part of its operations are

Figure 4.10

Monitoring systems (including audit and review)

- Performance against legal standards
- Performance against consent levels
- Performance against forthcoming law
- Performance against organizational ethical policy
- Performance against environmental policy
- Performance in all areas of environmental policy
- Analysis of complaints
- Highest standards audits/reviews
- Analysis of employee suggestion boxes
- Review of regular organizational data on wastes, emissions, leaks, accidents, etc.
- Review of who gets the information and when. What is done with it.

. . . all of which are elements that should be explicitly dealt with within the environmental management system (see Chapter 5).

---

breaching its mission and ethical statement or are in an area of increasing sensitivity.[20]

A monitoring system is outlined in Figure 4.10.

But all this involves time and energy. The intelligent design of information systems and the regular scrutiny of the data from the information systems are far from trivial matters. An organization can feel realistic confidence in its performance across environmental and related areas only if it has applied real manpower resources to it. Ignorance and assuming the best will no longer be enough.

4.8 Conclusions

Setting and/or adopting an environmental policy is a major step. It is the first step that an organization must take in reassessing its environmental sensitivity but it is a step requiring serious commitment, careful thought and, most importantly, systematic follow-up. The policy will set the tone for the organization and, if it is to be believed by internal and external participants, it must be backed by real commitment. Organizations are increasingly under public scrutiny and, at

[20] The experience of BP in 1989 is a good example when its activities in the South American rain forests, much to the amazement of its UK management, were suddenly front-page headlines. The company was caught unawares. Similar – and perhaps even more graphic – illustrations were provided by Shell and its extensive difficulties with, first, the disposal of the Brent Spar platform and, second, the company's alleged involvement in the oppression of indigenous people in Nigeria.

a minimum, senior management must place their organization in a position that is publicly defensible. This has two major elements: are you complying with your own professed standards? And are these standards as high as (say) the CERES Principles? If not, why not? The environment is a public matter and reluctant though organizations may be to accept that, accept it they must. The environmental policy is both the first step and potentially the most contentious. Any organization serious about its environmental impact will recognize that anything less than the best is simply not good enough.

Further Reading

Brophy, Michael (1998) 'Environmental policies', and 'Environmental guidelines and charters', in R. Welford (ed.), *Corporate Environmental Management: Systems and Strategies* (London: Earthscan), pp. 92–103 and pp. 104–117

Business-in-the-Environment (1991a) *Your Business and the Environment: A DIY Review for Companies* (London: BiE/Coopers & Lybrand Deloitte)

Business-in-the-Environment (1992) *A Measure of Commitment: Guidelines for Environmental Performance Measurement* (London: BiE/KPMG)

Elkington, J., P. Knight and J. Hailes (1991) *The Green Business Guide* (London: Gollancz)

Focus Report (1992) 'Business and Sustainable Development – the Role of Environmental Charters', *Business and the Environment*, 3 (7), pp. 2–4

3M/The Environment Council (1991) *A Guide to Policy Making and Implementation* (London: 3M/The Environment Council)

APPENDIX 4.1
Shandwick Environment:
'Creating a Corporate Environmental Policy Statement'

SHANDWICK ENVIRONMENT
CREATING A CORPORATE ENVIRONMENTAL POLICY STATEMENT

If your company wishes properly and fully to meet its environmental obligations, it must first articulate the commitment of management with a formal policy statement. This is not a large, long and complex document, but does need to be carefully thought out.

The policy, if not to be seen as empty posturing, must:

- address the agenda set by external audiences
- be seen accurately to reflect past action and future aspirations
- lead naturally to an action plan
- indicate yardsticks for measuring progress

A key audience for the policy statement is your own employees. If it is not credible and acceptable to them, it will be impossible for management to take it forward.

THE POLICY-MAKING PROCESS

Writing a policy is a multi-stage process. Not until these are complete is the organisation able to start taking position benefits from its environmental actions.

The stages are enumerated below. Although carefully ordered for clarity, many are actually carried out simultaneously.

1) Scoping
The general content of a formal policy has been reasonably well defined by environmental and industry organisations.

However, an effective environment policy is highly specific to the individual company. It must be practical and appropriate in technical scope, and cover the full range of corporate activities.

Action: Review policy guidelines by e.g. CBI, ICC, and environmentalists' proposals.

2) Establish Company-Specific Issues

Review all environmental issues relevant to your company, both now and predictions for the future. You should take account of both 'real' technical environmental impacts and public perceptions.

Action: Interview internal experts and external commentators for their views. Consultants may help, as they often have broader experience.

3) Positioning Content
For maximum usefulness, your policy must not be a pale imitation of competitor positions, nor fall

---

SHANDWICK ENVIRONMENT

CREATING A CORPORATE ENVIRONMENTAL POLICY STATEMENT

short of the expectations of activists, customers or staff. It must fit within any framework established by the parent company.

The policy needs to be phrased consistently with corporate values, habits and language.

Action: Obtain and review parent, competitor and customer policies. Interview sample of staff (all levels, but especially middle management) on their expectations. Review existing documentation, interview communications specialists.

4) Address Content

Whatever external and internal views may suggest, the policy *must* be consistent with the real level of management commitment. It must address as many areas as possible, but must not promise beyond what is intended.

Action: Interview senior management to determine extent of commitment.

5) Draft Policy

The policy is best written to last, and will therefore be quite generally phrased. It should make the firmest commitment possible.

The policy should make reference to company targets and actions, but these are better set out in full elsewhere.

Action: Prepare drafts and discuss in detail with senior management. Try to be as bold as possible with the first draft, it is more likely to get softened than strengthened as the consequences of the commitment become clear.

6) Amass Examples

To make it easier to understand the policy, it helps to describe actual examples of good environmental decisions already made. It is very rare for a good range not to be available. Often the reason for the action was not directly environmental (e.g. cost-based) but the effects are just as helpful. These examples can usefully be published in a policy booklet.

Action: Interview middle management against checklist of draft policy points.

7) Assess Present Position

Unless the extent of the company's present impact is known, progress will be difficult to identify. Measuring environmental impact is a technical matter. It can be carried out internally or with external support.

Action: Identify technical resource and priority areas to be examined. The issue analysis will be useful for this.

8) Set Targets

The policy statement defines commitment, targets define progress. Reaching targets is a clear demonstration of progress, and it is, therefore, better that they be set achievably. Targets are more credible with dates attached. They should be numerical, and can be either actual (e.g. average fleet mpg down to x) or relative (emissions to air cut by 10%).

The positioning benefit of targets varies according to the values set by receiving audiences, so targets must address perceived issues.

SHANDWICK ENVIRONMENT

CREATING A CORPORATE ENVIRONMENTAL POLICY STATEMENT

Action: Review issues in relation to operations, draft targets and discuss with management.

9) Define Action Plan
In order to meet targets and demonstrate management commitment to good environmental practice, actual action is required. Priorities must be agreed, and may be influenced by feasibility, external issues or competitive positioning advantage.

Action: Prioritise areas for action by reviewing possible options against external perceptions, ask operational managers to write action plans for approval.

10) Allocate Responsibilities
The action plans will languish unless someone is made responsible for carrying them out. Environmental improvement is no exception. Responsibility for each point of the agreed action plan should be clearly defined and progress reviewed regularly.

Action: Review existing managerial procedures and recommend structure for effecting environmental action plan.

For further information, please contact: Shandwick Environment,
Shandwick Public Affairs,
Dauntsey House, Frederick's Place, Old Jewry, LONDON EC2R 8AB
Tel: 071 726 4291   Fax: 071 726 2999

CHAPTER 5

ENVIRONMENTAL AUDIT AND MANAGEMENT SYSTEMS

Assessment, Review and Attestation

5.1 Introduction

From an organizational point of view, the only sensible response to the growing complexity of the environmental agenda is to work towards the development of a fully integrated *environmental management system (EMS)*.[1] One definition of an EMS is: *'the organizational structure, responsibilities, practices, procedures, processes and resources for determining and implementing environmental policy'*.[2]

As such, the EMS covers all aspects of the organization[3] and is the means by which the separate elements of environmental response are systematically harmonized and integrated with the other management systems (including accounting systems) of the organization. This is a great deal easier said than done. Indeed environmental management has become a whole area of study in its own right and there are now many excellent texts that provide detailed and in-depth study of the issues. (See Further Reading at the end of the chapter.)

---

[1] Whilst, in the present climate, it makes perfect rational sense for an organization to seek to 'manage' the environment, there are many political, moral and long-term matters which suggest that such an approach should not be taken for granted. That is, especially from a 'deep green' point of view, humanity is just one element of the 'environment'. 'Managing the environment' suggests that humankind is separate from it and seeks to exploit it for its own ends. It is argued that it is this very separation of humans and the environment that leads, inexorably, to the creation of environmental crises. These matters are touched upon in Chapter 14 and see also (for example) Gladwin et al. (1995, 1997). In an attempt to introduce the issues and keep matters relatively simple, this book takes a predominantly 'light green', organizational perspective. This view should not, however, be seen as unproblematic.

[2] This definition is taken from the British Standards Institution (1994) as quoted in Netherwood (1996).

[3] An EMS will not, of itself, guarantee a reduction of environmental *impact*. Environmental impact is exceptionally difficult to assess. It is important to retain the difference between environmental interactions and the impact of those interactions. Generally speaking, the lower the interactions the lower the impact – but this is not necessarily so. We touch upon this again later when we consider ecological footprints in Chapter 14.

Our ambitions in this chapter are rather more modest. We are more concerned with trying to introduce the elements of the environmental agenda as they affect organizations with the particular purpose of identifying the ways in which accounting can and should contribute to the organization's environmental response. To achieve this, we need at least some understanding of the key issues in environmental management systems and environmental audit. Consequently, we shall be seeking, in this chapter, to simply provide an overview of some of the key elements that comprise EMS and environmental audit.

The most straightforward way of doing this is, in our experience, to start with the (apparently) simpler – and certainly more discrete – activities associated with environmental audit(s) before moving on to talk about EMS in a little more detail. The chapter is structured to reflect this.

5.2   Overview of Environmental Audit

The environmental audit is both one of the first substantial steps that an organization might take in moving towards embedding environmental issues in organizational practices *and* a continuing essential element in managing and reporting on environmental issues. It is, thus, both an important mechanism that managers and accountants need to understand as well as being as convenient a place as any for beginning the process of understanding how an organization may develop its own EMS.

Thus, whilst environmental audit and environmental management are terms that have become synonymous with organizational response to the green agenda, they are rapidly developing issues of growing complexity and importance. Indeed, so important are the issues that, for example, the British Standards Institution, the European Union and the global International Organization for Standardization have all produced detailed guidance and standards for the development of organizational environmental audit and management systems. We will return to these standards (and some further discussion of EMS) later in the chapter. For now, let us start with the basic issues – like what an environmental audit is and why one might undertake such an activity.

The CBI (1990, based on ICC, 1989), for example, defines 'environmental audit' as:

> *the systematic examination of the interactions between any business operation and its surroundings. This includes all emissions to air, land and water; legal constraints; the effects on the neighbouring community, landscape and ecology; and the public's perception of the operating company in the local area . . . Environmental*

audit does not stop at compliance with legislation. Nor is it a 'green-washing' public relations exercise . . . Rather it is a total strategic approach to the organization's activities.[4]

The term covers a multitude of different (although related) activities. The first step in environmental auditing which any organization must take is the precise determination of the sort of 'audit' it wants and the range of activities the audit must cover ('scoping'). This, itself, will be determined by a wide range of factors related to, *inter alia*, the nature of the organization, its industry and markets, how far it has advanced towards embracing the green agenda and, more prosaically, whether the organization has decided it needs to seek *accreditation* under one or other of environmental auditing standards. Ultimately, 'environmental audit' should become a major and established element of an organization's environmental management systems but in the early stages it may be no more than the first tottering step towards the goal of environmental sensitivity.[5]

It therefore makes sense to recognize explicitly the range of things that are, at times, included within the term 'environmental audit' (see Figure 5.1).

Figure 5.1

Types of environmental audit

(1) Environmental impact assessment
(2) Environmental survey
(3) Environmental review, monitoring and surveillance
(4) Environmental investigation
(5) The environmental management and audit schemes – EMAS, BS7750 and ISO 14001
(6) Independent attestation of environmental information – for internal or external participants

[4] The Confederation of British Industry, *Narrowing the Gap: Environmental Auditing Guidelines for Business* (London: CBI, 1990) which is based upon the International Chamber of Commerce, *Environmental Auditing* (Paris: ICC, 1989).

[5] There is a very considerable literature and experience on environmental auditing in its widest sense. This chapter and its further reading can only scrape the surface. Other useful sources include Bins-Hoefnagels et al. (1986), Bins-Hoefnagels and Molenkamp (1989), Cardwell (1991), Dewhurst (1989), Roger Gray (1989), Greenpeace (1985) and Welford (1996). Moretz (1981) provides a useful insight on Allied Signal's approach. See also Humble (1973) and Hunt (1974) for a historical perspective to remind us that little in this area is actually new.

Each of these types of 'environmental audit' are importantly differ-ent, require different skills and have a different orientation. In addi-tion, each one may also have legal implications – something every organization needs to pay attention to.

We will, albeit briefly, examine each in turn.

5.3   The Environmental Impact Assessment (EIA)

EIAs were probably first developed in the USA under the National Environment Policy Act of 1969. This lead was initially followed by Canada, Australia, the Netherlands, New Zealand and Japan but has since become a requirement – often a legal requirement – across the globe.[6]

EIA can be defined as:

> *essentially a process that seeks to identify and predict the impacts of a new development on the environment, to mitigate them where possible and to monitor the actual impacts.*[7]

As a general statement, all major projects that are subject to some form of planning permission and which are likely to have 'a sig-nificant impact on the environment' should be subject to EIA.[8] Their primary purpose is to guide planners in coming to decisions on whether or not to permit new initiatives – such as new plants, roads or industrial activities.[9]

[6] Since July 1988 EIAs have been required throughout Europe as a result of the EC Directive on Environmental Assessment (85/337).

[7] Taken from Fuller (1991, p. 12), from which more detail can be obtained.

[8] For Europe including the UK the EC Directive lays down in Annexes I and II some indication of what this might mean. See Department of the Environment (1989d). For information on the legal issues consult an appropriate environmental law textbook. (Legal texts date especially quickly but for the UK see, for example, Ball and Bell, 1991.)

[9] Although Fuller argues that the motivation for their introduction in the EU owed as much to attempts to 'level the playing field' as to protection of the environment. However, the situation in the UK has remained far from clear in that it is not obvious that EIAs are always conducted when required and neither is the quality of the resulting environmental impact statements (EISs) as high as it should be. This situation appears to have arisen from a number of factors, including the apparent reluctance of the UK government to take an appropriate lead, the lack of accreditation of bodies equipped to produce EISs, the diversity of planning authorities to which the EIS goes and, as a result, the lack of expertise in evaluating the EIA. By way of comparison, in the Netherlands a single Impact Commission is involved in all EIAs, in Canada there has been a significant emphasis on the development of public awareness and involvement in EIAs and in New Zealand detailed guidelines are supplemented by Environmental Impact Report Audits carried out by the Commissioner for the Environment. For more detail on the UK see, for example, Ball (1991a).

Figure 5.2

Information in an environmental impact assessment

(1) A description of the proposed project and, where applicable, of the reasonable alternatives for its siting and design.
(2) A description of the environment that is likely to be affected.
(3) An assessment of the likely effects of the proposed project on the environment.
(4) A description of the measures proposed to eliminate, reduce or compensate for adverse environmental effects.
(5) A description of the relationship between the proposal and the existing environmental and land-use plans for, and standards of, the affected area.
(6) An explanation of the reasons for the choice of the preferred site and project design rather than of the 'reasonable' alternatives.

All this information would, in addition, need to be published in a form which the public can understand, to ensure effective public participation.

Source: Elkington (1982, p. 26)

Whilst EIAs are typically thought of as a legal requirement, the number of statutory environmental impact statements (EISs) is frequently being matched by the number of voluntary EISs. This arises as organizations recognize the value of the EIA – both as a means to assist the planning process and as a useful management technique as part of their wider environmental management and audit (see below).[10]

Indeed, EIAs are not seen as especially onerous by most companies with a developed experience of them and, in fact, they can speed up, simplify and remove some of the risk from the planning process. This, in turn, can increase the environmental reputation of the company and thereby assist in future planning procedures. (Figure 5.2 provides an outline of the process.)

The experience of companies such as ICI and IBM can also be useful here. Both have developed their experience over time and have

---

[10] This has brought a recognition of the need to establish guidelines and standards of good practice for EIA. This, in turn, has led to the formation of bodies that can specialize in EIAs and develop an appropriate 'professional' status in the area. There is, however, an important tension here as consultants also become the 'policemen' of standards under which their consultancies operate. This is a problem long experienced in the accounting profession whenever conflicts of independence arise (see, e.g., Sikka, Willmott and Lowe, 1989, 1991). The problem is the potential conflict of interest between consultants and the professional body on the one hand and the development of a need for independent attestation on the other. (See also Chapters 11 and 12.) For more detail on the UK experience, see *ENDS Report* 195/April 1991 (pp. 15–17), Gray and Symon (1992a).

Figure 5.3

Environmental audit checklist based on the approaches of IBM and ICI

Stage 1: Screening   assessing whether the project qualifies for an EIA and, if not, whether the organization should still undertake one.

Stage 2: The IBM approach   in three stages:

(a)   Site environmental assessment: a quick first appraisal to identify early on in the process any major issues – which may, in fact, screen out the project at an early stage.
(b)   Environmental baseline study: the basis against which to assess any changes to the environment over the course of the study and the project – for planning, EIA and 'defensive' purposes. Will include (*inter alia*) air, water, land, flora, fauna, habitat, noise, aesthetics and the community.
(c)   Prepare for the EIA.

Stage 3: The ICI checklist

(a)   Describe the project: including benefits, costs, potential issues, possible objections, legal issues, etc.
(b)   Describe possible alternatives to the proposed plan.
(c)   Propose methods to reduce environmental impact.
(d)   List possible effects on the environment
(e)   Measure the impact of the project on people, animals and their environment.
(f)   Summarize and evaluate: involving economic versus environmental 'costs and benefits'.

Stage 4: After project begins, monitor environmental impact

---

produced useful guidelines. These can be integrated to produce the checklist shown in Figure 5.3.[11]

The EIA is clearly an area in which experience and technical, legal and scientific knowledge are required. However, it must not be seen as a wholly unique activity. It differs from most other environmental information-collation activities in that it is specifically prepared for public consumption in a particular context. Whilst other environmental information is increasingly finding its way into the public domain (see Part C) much of it is prepared, in the first place at least, for management's consumption. Any organization with a well-developed environmental response and a fully functioning environmental management system will integrate the EIA process with the

[11] The information for Figure 5.3 was obtained through interviews with the companies and from other public sources (see the further reading at the end of the chapter and the appendix). Principally the same information can be found in Elkington, Knight and Hailes (1991).

other elements of 'environmental audit' to avoid duplication, to provide independent sources of data and to develop the overall organizational strategy with respect to environmental sensitivity.

5.4 The Environmental Survey

We have used the term 'environmental survey' to refer to the simplest type of environmental audit – the first step that any organization can take towards improving its environmental sensitivity.[12] Simple though it might be, it serves a number of important functions, including orientating the organization to environmental issues, beginning the process of recognizing and identifying actual and potential areas of environmental impact, and laying out an initial agenda for undertaking further environmental audits and starting the move towards a more complete environmental management. Whatever the outcome, the experience at this and later stages should feed back into the issues we have discussed in earlier chapters – for example, organizational policy statements, initial green activities and changing the corporate culture.

It is a sad fact that a great many organizations have still not recognized and taken this crucial step. Experience and research continues to show that a great many organizations – private and public – have undertaken no environmental audit and some companies still refer to themselves as either 'having no environmental impact' or as being 'environmentally neutral'. As we discussed in Part A, no organization can justifiably make such claims.[13]

In this section we suggest how any organization can undertake this first step. Subsequent sections will explore how an organization can move beyond this basic first step, while the appendices to this chapter and the further reading provide examples of flowcharts and checklists for the putative environmental auditor.

The first stage in the process may seem elementary but is often the most difficult – that is, actually sitting down and starting the

---

[12] Sometimes also called the 'scoping' audit. Costs of audit vary considerably. For example, Scottish Enterprise reckoned in the early 1990s that £1000 should be sufficient for a scoping audit. Burkitt (1990) reports that environmental audits in the widest sense would have, at that time, cost between £5000 and £400,000.

[13] It should not be thought that environmental audit and environmental impact only apply to the more obviously 'dirty' industries such as extraction and manufacturing. Environmental audits have been undertaken on banks, accountants, newspapers, universities, hospitals as well as on NGOs and community enterprises. Every organization has major environmental (and indeed social) impacts.

Figure 5.4   A 'first step' environmental audit for a small hotel

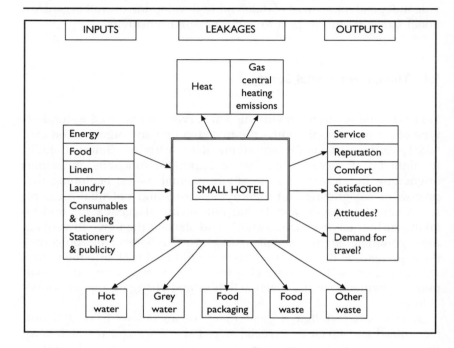

process.[14] The second stage involves no more than paper, pencil and a knowledge of the organization. Applying the 'systems perspective' we discussed in Appendix 1.1, the flows into and out of the organization are broadly identified in the first place by the proprietor or manager. An extract from the first step in one initial such 'survey' (of a small hotel) is shown in Figure 5.4.

This was not, obviously, seeking any especially profound insights into the environmental impact but encouraging the manager (or whoever) to think the process through. Each of the categories was then itemized separately (which leads to recognition of other items originally missed, e.g. use of the car, use of a coal fire).[15] Then each item and

---

[14] For small organizations this can be especially difficult and so we recommend that some third party is invited in – even if this is just an intelligent colleague or friend with a basic appreciation of environmental matters.

[15] One of the less obvious difficulties is actually identifying the materials, products and activities of the organization – see Step 3 in Figure 5.5. One useful way of making a start at this is through using the cash book which, obviously, lists what we have paid for (energy, materials, labour, etc.) and what we have sold (levels of service or goods despatched, for example). The cash book will not give a complete specification – nor provide all the detail which is needed – but it is an often overlooked first port of call.

area of activity was discussed in terms of possible impact and how that could be minimized through 'refuse, reduce, reuse, recycle and substitute'. Current practices with respect to minimizing environmental impact were itemized and a plan of action, with maintenance of additional information systems as appropriate, was detailed. The most important part of the plan was the decision to appraise performance against the plan at subsequent meetings of the directors.

Such a simple approach can have a profound effect on the thinking and subsequent actions of the proprietor/manager of the organization. It also explicitly raises two additional crucial matters:

(1) What are the costs and benefits – in hard financial numbers – of the plan agreed? In a tightly run organization, operating on small margins with no spare capital, most of the significant actions were impossible in that the organization could not afford them and stay in business.

(2) What are the crucial business success factors, beyond which the business is unable to go, i.e. the actual points of real conflict between the environmental standards and the business standards?[16]

This basic beginners' environmental survey must be refined before either relying upon it or moving on to the more sophisticated forms of environmental audit. Two of the basic ways of doing this are, first, to refine the conception of the organization into more useful sectors, for example upstream effects, people, housekeeping/office, processes, products/services, emissions, wastes and other downstream effects; and then, secondly, to separate analysis to individual sites and/or lines of business/activity in order either to repeat the exercise or to refine by reference to more local criteria.

However, the most important factor missing from the layperson's audit is any reference to law, local conditions, industry standards, consents, etc.[17] Experience suggests that larger organizations often find the law and its threat a major motivation in greening activities, but that a disturbing proportion of smaller organizations have little idea of the legal matters which govern them in this area or, more appositely, which are likely to concern them in the near future. On the other hand, smaller organizations do tend to have a much stronger

---

[16] In the case of the small hotel, one such issue was the whiteness (not cleanliness) of sheets, which was considered essential to the success of the business.

[17] A number of consultants are developing computer software for use by small organizations as a guide to self-environmental audit. The market for this sort of support is growing rapidly and new products can be expected on a regular basis. (For an illustration see *Social and Environmental Accounting*, 18 (2), 1998.)

Figure 5.5

The beginner's environmental survey

Step 1: Get started – asking for assistance if necessary.

Step 2: Draw a systems flow of the organization – identifying the major categories of inputs, outputs and leakages.

Step 3: Provide a detailed itemization of the elements in Step 2 – identifying the products and materials and the activities to which they relate. Pick up additional items involved along the way.

Step 4: Review each item with a view to minimization – refuse, reduce, reuse, recycle, substitute.

Step 5: Assess financial costs and benefits (if any) – what can the organization realistically afford?

Step 6: Identify crucial business factors – what are the issues on which you feel you cannot compromise – where the environment loses out to the business?

Step 7: Draw up a detailed plan of action

Step 8: Review progress at board meeting or equivalent

Step 9: Refine the organization – identify (as appropriate) people, housekeeping/office; processes, products/services; emissions and wastes; and repeat on site and/or business basis.

And do not forget . . .

Step 10: Identify existing and potential law, industry standards, consents as appropriate – the smaller organization relies here upon its trade association and related journals and trade magazines (but see Further Reading). This will become the first step as the organization begins to adjust.

Figure 5.6

The Eco-balance

The 'beginner's environmental audit' is a most important step towards thinking in environmental terms about the organization. So much so, that the diagram shown in Figure 5.4 is the simplest form of what is known as an *eco-balance* or the *ökobilanz*. The eco-balance is, at its simplest, a diagrammatic form of all the inputs and outputs of the organization. The inputs and outputs are then quantified and the total inputs should equal total outputs. In this way all wastes, leakages and emissions can be traced. The approach to environmental management based on the eco-balance is called eco-controlling and has been significantly developed in Germany and Austria (see, for example, Schaltegger, 1996). An example of a simplified eco-balance is shown in the appendix to Chapter 9.

sense of community and duty to the locality in which they are situated. They seem less likely to outrage local residents or attract the wrath of Greenpeace. (The steps for the beginner's environmental audit are summarized in Figure 5.5.)

As a starting point, the beginner's survey is helpful. It most certainly is not sufficient. It can provide no more than a starting point to frame and identify areas for later development. Without specialist knowledge it cannot identify legal problems, it cannot identify potential chemical hazards and so on. For this, more advanced forms of audit – leading to environmental management – are necessary.

5.5 Developing the Environmental Audit

There are, broadly, two approaches to developing environmental audit and management systems. The first is the iterative, almost trial-by-error, approach that many organizations took in the early history of environmental management. The second is to directly follow the procedures for adopting the current standards as enshrined in, for example, EMAS and the ISO 14000 series. We will look, albeit briefly, at both of these. This section will provide a broad, generic discussion of the more formal environmental audit. Section 5.6 outlines some of the broad key issues in EMS. Then Section 5.7 will consider some of the factors involved in the current environmental audit and management standards.

Whilst there are increasing forces towards standardizing the approach to developing the environmental audit, each organization is different, has different concerns and, perhaps most importantly, differs in the talents, time and cash available to it. Perhaps the first decisions any organization must make at this stage are: do we go it alone or call in outside help? And do we undertake more investigation, or are we in a position to move directly to setting up our environmental management systems?

Many organizations of every size have found that further investigation is necessary as a precursor to the development of environmental management systems. The most widely reported approach is that of calling in an environmental auditing consultancy to provide an organization-wide review. Other companies have chosen to do the matter entirely in-house – to keep the matter private whilst they start the process of getting their house into some sort of order. More common is a balance between these two – developing in-house environmental auditing team(s) and calling upon external bodies at different stages for advice and evaluation of what has been done.

Figure 5.7

Major elements in an environmental audit or review

- Identify the most important of the organization's environmental interactions.
- Assess the degree of environmental impact.
- Learn about how to deal with and reduce or improve the organization's impact.
- Identify a priority list of interactions to be dealt with (this will develop, in part, from the first two and in part in response to actual and potential changes in law and in society's attitudes).
- Establish standards and policies.
- Identify responsibilities.
- Train staff.
- Change practices and put policies into action.
- Develop environmental information systems.
- Monitor performance and performance appraisal.
- Assess performance against standards.
- Reappraise this list, starting from the top, on a systematic and continuing basis.

An outline of the basic steps as an illustration of what will be necessary in the move towards environmental management systems is shown in Figure 5.7.

By the time an organization reaches the stage of devising an 'environmental audit strategy' it is beginning to beg larger questions about its overall environmental strategy, aims, objectives and how environmental issues are to be fitted into the overall organizational context. (This we touched upon in Chapters 3 and 4 and will return to from time to time.) One approach to attempting this integration is the use of SWOT analysis.

Companies of the stature and experience of Pilkington Glass have found undertaking a SWOT (Strengths, Weaknesses, Opportunities, Threats) analysis, if done brutally and honestly, can provide useful guidance on where to place attention in the development of the organization's environmental response. Figure 5.8 illustrates generally the sorts of matters that may usefully come through such a process – to be really useful it would need to be a great deal more specific than this.

Such analysis has the distinct advantage of encouraging an organization to take a hard look at itself and begin the process of identifying where its environmental efforts should lie. However, a successful SWOT analysis presupposes a significant knowledge of the organization's activities and this cannot be assumed. Experience has shown that many companies – major as well as minor – often have little real idea of what is happening throughout their operations. This was especially noticeable in the multinationals where, for example, several

Figure 5.8 An illustration of environmental SWOT analysis

XYZ plc: 1/1/92

Environmental SWOT analysis

Strengths	Weaknesses
1. Public image	1. Public impression of greenness, visible pollution
2. Staff morale	2. Trade-offs: cost versus emissions; different types of emissions
3. Product type	3. Worldwide standards
4. Technological advantages	4. Level of recycling
5. Recycling opportunities	5. Current technological limits on greening products and processes
6. Current position in meeting consent levels	6. Transport
7. Environmental awareness in the industry	7. Toxicity of wastes
Opportunities	**Threats**
1. Products' environmental strengths	1. Legislation in all countries of operation
2. Involvement with business and environmental groups	2. Energy costs
3. Involvement with community	3. Duty of care and landfill costs
4. Recycling opportunities	4. Worldwide standards and inter-company trade
5. Use and develop employees' goodwill and ideas	5. Cost of current and future monitoring
6. Position in the industry	6. Existing good public image makes us vulnerable to accidents and other discoveries
7. Exploit R&D advantages	

household name companies might have a sound knowledge of their US and Canadian activities and a growing knowledge of their European ones but little or no knowledge of operations elsewhere. Here, there was a need to do more investigation before any more sophisticated development could take place. (As we discussed in Chapter 4, companies are recognizing that there is both a moral and a defensive case for attempting to operate worldwide standards.) Figure 5.9 provides an indication of the possible range of environmental audits.

5.6 Developing an Environmental Management System

Understanding of the role of environmental audit – and thereby making full use of the process(es) – can be achieved only within the broader context of learning to manage environmental performance. This is not simply because this may make good business sense or because limiting oneself to *ad hoc* reaction is inefficient but because 'environment' is embedded in every strand of organizational life and its impact will continue to grow. The environment is not a one-off

Figure 5.9

Forms of environmental audit

Within any particular management strategy, the following audits may be seen as the same in essence, differing only in terms of their objectives, scope, the risks they seek to assess and the management decisions which they support and inform.

- **Compliance Audits I:** Assessing compliance with current and future legal standards.
- **Compliance Audits II:** Assessing compliance with consents, industry and guideline standards.
- **Compliance Audits III:** Assessing compliance with corporate policy and standards ('Corporate', 'Policy' and 'Ethical' audits).
- **Energy Audits** (see Chapter 6).
- **Waste Audits** (see Chapter 7).
- **Site Audits:** Reviewing every aspect of a site or spot checks on sites having actual or potential problems.
- **Activity Audits:** Reviewing a particular activity or process, especially one which spans sites, business units and countries.
- **Issues Audits:** Review of corporate performance in a particular area – e.g. in the case of BP, BAT and B&Q, tropical hardwood forests and impact on habitats.
- **Takeover/Merger Review:** Assessment of potential subsidiary, associate or partner against corporate standards and any actual and potential legal issues.
- **Process Audits:** Related to the above and designed to ensure that policies, processes, documentation, responsibilities, monitoring and appraisal are in place.
- **Emerging Issues Audit:** Future scenario assessment, anticipatory and intended to assess the extent of the organization's ability to respond to new challenges.

And, as the environmental management system develops, these audits will be closely related to:

- **Process Safety Audits:** Hazards and risks arising from processes, safety and accident provisions.
- **Occupational Health Audits:** Exposure and conditions for the workforce.
- **Quality Audits:** Not only the product in use but the environment in relation to TQM.
- **Social Audits** (see Chapter 13) and even **Sustainability Audits** (see Chapter 14).

---

issue admitting of one-off solutions. Thus 'environmental audit' must become a regular, critical and analytical part of organizational management. (As we shall see in the next section, the EU and ISO are ensuring that this must be the case.)

A constant message through the book has been the difficulty – if not impossibility – of breaking down environmental response into discrete parts. Developing an organization's environmental policy and signing up to the charters (Chapter 4) required an understanding of the organization's environmental impacts. This is acquired through an initial environmental audit. To guide the environmental audit(s)

Figure 5.10   Going green

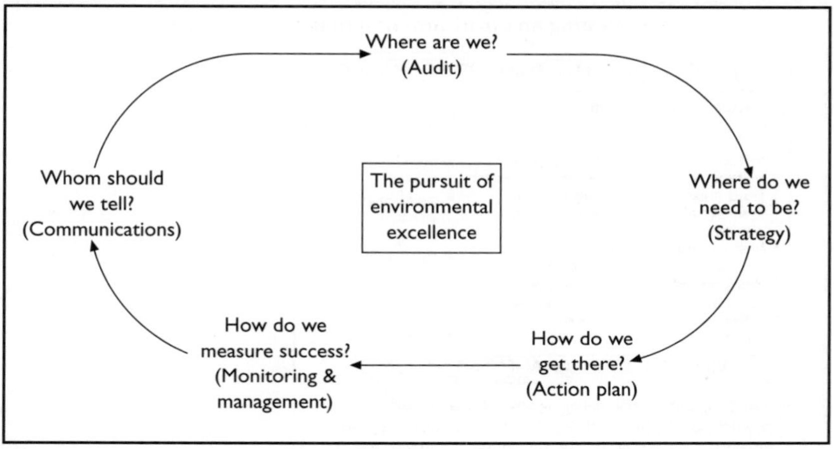

```
                        Where are we?
                           (Audit)


 Whom should          The pursuit of          Where do we
   we tell?           environmental           need to be?
(Communications)        excellence             (Strategy)


        How do we
     measure success?        How do we
       (Monitoring &         get there?
       management)          (Action plan)
```

Source: Elkington and Jennings (1991)

efficiently and effectively they must be driven by policy. The whole process is circular rather than linear. This is nicely illustrated by Figure 5.10.

In this way we can see the more developed function of environmental audit (more accurately called 'review', 'monitoring' and 'surveillance' now) as a means of assessing progress against targets and goals and as a means of monitoring new and emerging problems and searching for new and innovative ways of improving overall environmental quality – exactly the role designed for environmental audit at, among others, Hewlett Packard. Figure 5.11 provides a basic way of conceiving of this more developed approach.[18]

What any organization must be seeking by this stage is an integrated environmental management strategy similar in principle to a culture in pursuit of total quality management (TQM) – and, increasingly, good environmental management is being seen as an essential component of TQM: namely, EQM.[19] As with TQM, there is no simple method of buying in quality. The organization has to seek, in all dimensions, to be the best. This leads organizations to consider anything other than (for example) zero complaints, zero spills and accidents, zero pollution and zero waste as fundamentally unacceptable. As two medium-sized companies, making the same point, in different ways on different continents, put it:

[18] These diagrams are reprinted from KPMG, *Environment Briefing Note*, no. 5 (1990).

[19] See Houldin (1992) for an especially helpful discussion of these matters.

Figure 5.11

Developing an environmental management system

AN APPROACH TO MANAGING PERFORMANCE

ENVIRONMENTAL POLICY	ENVIRONMENTAL AUDIT	ENVIRONMENT STRATEGY
• Understand environmental impact (damage, legislation, market pressure) • Assess risks and opportunities • Identify required standards • Establish policies and goals	• Define basis for performance assesment (targets/standards) • Identify damage drivers and assess • Check performance vs standards/targets • Identify technical/ managerial solution options	Implement changes: • technical • management/ operations • training • marketing/PR • market analysis • internal care programme • establish EMS

ENVIRONMENTAL MANAGEMENT SYSTEM

Achieving the goal of managing environmental performance requires environmental objectives to be fully integrated into business activities. An enviromental system needs to be built into day-to-day management processes.

UNDERSTANDING ENVIRONMENTAL IMPACT

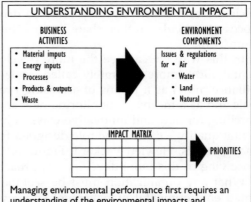

BUSINESS ACTIVITIES	ENVIRONMENT COMPONENTS
• Material imputs • Energy inputs • Processes • Products & outputs • Waste	Issues & regulations for • Air • Water • Land • Natural resources

IMPACT MATRIX → PRIORITIES

Managing environmental performance first requires an understanding of the environmental impacts and interactions between the environment and all business activities.

COMPREHENSIVE PERFORMANCE REVIEW

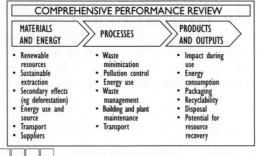

MATERIALS AND ENERGY	PROCESSES	PRODUCTS AND OUTPUTS
• Renewable resources • Sustainable extraction • Secondary effects (eg deforestation) • Energy use and source • Transport • Suppliers	• Waste minimization • Pollution control • Energy use • Waste management • Building and plant maintenance • Transport	• Impact during use • Energy consumption • Packaging • Recyclability • Disposal • Potential for resource recovery

KPMG Sustainability Advisory Services

We know we cannot achieve perfection in these things but this doesn't make mistakes and carelessness acceptable.

We are decent people. I don't soil my own home, I don't drop muck in the High Street, I don't think any of my colleagues do either. We have standards of personal behaviour. We try damned hard to make sure those standards apply to the business as well. I don't drop my crisps packet in my neighbour's garden; how can I look him in the eye if I've dropped our s..t in the river he goes fishing in? Answer me that!

This approach to environmental TQM/EQM leads IBM to apply the highest standards worldwide, and to be followed by companies such as ICI and BAT. It leads to the much vaunted initiatives such as Ciba–Geigy's six-point corporate principles, 3M's 3Ps (Pollution Prevention Pays) and Dow Chemicals' acknowledged leadership in standards of care in the chemical industry. And it leads into the whole area of *environmental performance measurement and indicators* which we have mentioned already. One interesting approach to this is shown by Rhône-Poulenc's Environmental Index.

Although not without its problems, Rhône-Poulenc's Environmental Index is calculated for aqueous effluent discharges by 'weighting the suspended solids, COD, dissolved salts, results of daphnia toxicity tests and the nitrogen and phosphorus produced by each plant by coefficients reflecting the environmental hazards posed by different components of the effluent stream and by production volumes for the period'.[20] Figure 5.12 illustrates how this material appeared in one of Rhône-Poulenc's environmental reports.[21]

As other individual organizations see the value of identifying environmental performance measures the indexing notion has grown in popularity.[22] There are, inevitably however, doubts over the accuracy of such indices in that they allow trade-off between increases in some effluent against decreases in others. In other words, they potentially lose too much information in the aggregation. They can be, thus, potentially misleading. Indeed, such are just some of the problems with any use of composite performance measurement.[23]

[20] *ENDS Report*, November 1989, p. 16. Experimentation in the UK led to its introduction in 1990 and, in recent years, Rhône-Poulenc has developed additional indices for air and for wastes.

[21] Chapters 11 and 12 cover the issues arising from disclosure. For more detail on the Rhône-Poulenc approach see *ENDS Report*, November 1989, Salamitou (1991) and various Rhône-Poulenc publications – most notably *Presence* (R-P house magazine), special issue on the environment, 1990. The company pronounces itself very pleased with the indices as a management tool for integrating the environment into all aspects of management and appraisal.

[22] The Chemical Industries Association was a major force encouraging these developments via its collation of industry data to produce environmental, distribution and energy indices.

[23] See, especially, Bennett and James (1998a) for a detailed introduction to environmental performance measurement.

Figure 5.12

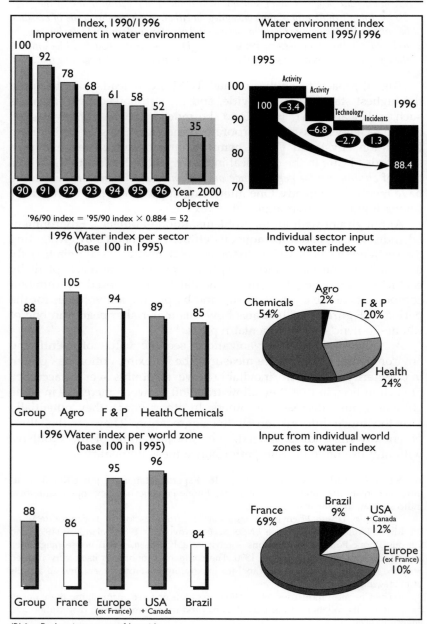

(Rhône-Poulenc is now part of Aventis)

The irresistible advance in the penetration and sophistication of environmental auditing in all its forms and its inevitable link through to environmental management systems is now being enshrined in guidance and cajolery at both national and international levels. It is to this that we now turn.

5.7 Eco-Management and Audit Scheme, BS7750 and ISO 14000

Environmental auditing and environmental management systems find their most visible manifestation in a series of (currently voluntary) guidelines that have rapidly established themselves as the indicators of 'best practice' in the field. So much so, that explicit and systematic adoption of one or more of these guidelines – together with certification by the guideline issuing body – can now be considered to be an essential element of good business management.

Whilst national guidelines on environmental auditing and EMS have existed in some countries for quite some time,[24] it was the issuance of international and generic standards which thrust environmental auditing and EMS onto the international stage as a central plank in any organization's environmental policy and strategy. There are three of these standards which we will discuss briefly here. They are the British Standards Institution BS7750, the European Union's Eco-Management and Audit Scheme (EMAS) and the International Organization for Standardization's ISO 14000 series. Whilst all three standards have much in common, there are some important differences which have been the subject of much heated debate and dispute. We will, first, outline each of the standards and then very briefly consider the contentious issues.

BS7750 is typically considered to be the first international standard for EMS and environmental auditing. Issued in 1991 (and subsequently withdrawn in 1997 in favour of ISO 14001, see below), it drew heavily on the approach and rationale used in the British Standard approach to 'total quality management' (as enshrined in BS5750). The rationale behind this was that organizations that were already certified under the 'quality' standard would find it relatively straightforward to seek certification under the 'environmental management' standard. The essential element of both the 'quality' and the 'environmental' standards was that an organization must have a systematic

---

[24] The obvious examples here are Sweden and the Netherlands. Other examples of national standards which emerged during the 1990s include the French standard X30-200, the Spanish UNE77–801 and the Irish IS310.

Figure 5.13

BS7750: environmental management systems
The standard was voluntary and adopted a similar structure and regime as employed in BS5750 on quality management systems. It required: (1)   a preparatory environmental review including an inventory of emissions and wastes from each facility; (2)   assessment of environmental impacts and the setting of improvement targets; (3)   the establishment of the targets in managerial and centre performance appraisal, responsibility and accountability; (4)   the implication is that organizations will also need to have systems in place to review the supplies of materials (see below), their products in use as well as their financial investment procedures (see Chapters 13 and 14); (5)   detailed management plans and regular audits of performance (the audits undertaken by personnel independent of the facility audited who may be members of the organization or external auditors); (6)   the whole process must be auditable; and (7)   the award of BS7750 was renewed by assessment of the organization's continuing commitment to the development of the EMS and the review and audit of those systems.

policy in place, a means of identifying key issues, a systematic monitoring of these and a commitment to continuous improvement. The details are shown in Figure 5.13.

With its emphasis on the means of *managing* environmental effects rather than on *actual environmental performance*, the standard was relatively popular with business, widely adopted and, in the broadest terms, set the template for the later standards. The European EMAS Regulation was adopted by the European Council in 1993. Unusually for a European Regulation, EMAS was established as 'voluntary' – but only after considerable successful lobbying by business interests to prevent its adoption as a requirement on all organizations.[25] Whilst the requirements for registration under EMAS look broadly comparable with BS7750 and are based on broadly the same rationale, there are a number of very significant differences. (The key elements of EMAS are shown in Figure 5.14.)[26]

Perhaps the three key elements of EMAS are its robust insistence on targets and improvement, its site-basis and its requirement for disclosure and verification. The insistence on targets and improvement means that the standard will not tolerate simply *monitoring*

[25] This is a fairly recent and relatively well-publicized example of business lobbying to overturn the decisions of a democratically elected body. There are many other such examples (see, for example, Beder, 1997 and Mayhew, 1997).

[26] This summary is derived from information provided by EuroInfoCentre Glasgow, whose help is gratefully acknowledged.

Figure 5.14

Criteria for EMAS registration
• Adoption of an environmental policy containing commitments both to comply with all relevant legislation and also to achieve continuous improvements in environmental performance.
• An environmental review to take place on site.
• An EMS to be established for the site in the light of the review and the company's environmental policy.
• Environmental audits covering all activities at the site must be conducted within an audit cycle of no longer than three years.
• The audit results will form the basis of setting environmental objectives and the revision of the environmental programme to achieve these objectives.
• On the completion of reviews and audits, the company will produce a public environmental statement and this will be validated by accredited environmental verifiers.
• The environmental statement must include description of the site and all significant environmental issues; summary of figures for pollution, waste, raw material usage, energy, water and noise; the organization's environmental policy and a description of the site EMS; the deadline for the next environmental statement; the name of the accredited verifier.

---

environmental effects – it actually requires improved *environmental performance*. The site-basis of the standard, whilst it allows organizations to develop their compliance with EMAS on a piecemeal, iterative basis, also means that 'dirty' sites (and, indeed, sites in lesser-developed countries) cannot be hidden by offsetting results against 'cleaner' sites. The issue which has created the most voluble visible opposition to EMAS, however, is that of disclosure and verification.

If improvement in the environmental performance of organizations is our principal aim, then disclosure seems an essential component. Companies need to know that their performance will be under public scrutiny based on data which has been systematically attested to. This, like the wider developments in environmental reporting (see Chapter 12), can then lead organizations to become, what John Elkington calls, 'good little goldfish'. As we shall see, many organizations have welcomed the opportunity to provide environmental disclosure – it encourages the 'good' companies to gain appropriate recognition for their activities and encourages organizations and their *stakeholders* to discuss and recognize the very real difficulties and conflicts of interest inherent in environmental-business issues. However, a great many organizations are opposed to regulated disclosure and their voice carried a great deal of sway over the introduction of EMAS. Once EMAS was voluntary, then the 'market' determines who adopts EMAS and who does not. It is difficult to find sound environmental

Figure 5.15

Outline of ISO 14000
An environmental management system (ISO 14001) must comprise:
• an environmental policy;
• an assessment of environmental aspects and legal and voluntary obligations;
• a management system;
• a series of periodic internal audits and reports to top management;
• a public declaration that ISO 14001 is being implemented.
An environmental audit (ISO 14010):
• is required to establish that ISO 14001 is being complied with.

and social reasons why a company might oppose EMAS on disclosure and verification grounds. We might well assume that such organizations either did not care about environmental issues and/or had something to hide.

EMAS remains the toughest of the environmental management and audit standards. It was adopted widely in Germany and Austria but its adoption elsewhere was more patchy. Most organizations have chosen to vote with their feet and avoid EMAS. But such companies could not, when under scrutiny for their environmental performance, simply walk away from an environmental standard – and this is where ISO 14000 comes into play.

The ISO 14000 series of standards is based (like the BS7750) on earlier 'quality management' standards (ISO 9000). The series was first published in 1996 and has grown in both number and ubiquity since then. Indeed, it is probably appropriate to say that ISO 14000 is now *the* standard for environmental management and audit. The reasons for this are not hard to find. Based in the USA and dominated by large US companies, the ISO's guidance on environmental management and audit is explicitly voluntary, far more concerned with the management systems than with environmental performance *per se* and, most especially, contains no requirement for either disclosure or rigorous verification. Figure 5.15[27] provides a brief outline of the key elements – from which the less demanding nature of the standard will be apparent.

It is a moot point whether, as its supporters claim, the less-demanding requirements of ISO 14000 will have the effect of encouraging a wider range of organizations to meet a set of minimum standards. The detractors of the ISO approach say that 'best practice'

---

[27] This summary is adapted from Krut and Gleckman (1998).

has been diluted and that the avoidance of disclosure encourages companies to 'hide'.[28]

Whilst, inevitably, there is some cause for celebration if all organizations come up to some minimum level of environmental management we should not fool ourselves that this, necessarily, leads to improvements in environmental performance or that it has much, if anything, to do with sustainability (see Chapter 14). At the most obvious level, there is no evidence to suggest that adoption of even minimum levels of environmental management has spread much beyond the leading companies (but see below). Furthermore, even if all organizations adopted EMAS, the quality of verification,[29] the partiality of reporting and failure to link environmental management and sustainability would ensure that indicators of global degradation would continue to worsen.[30] Environmental audit may well be a prerequisite for more benign environmental effects – it is certainly not the Holy Grail of sustainability.

5.8 The Supplier Audits and Eco-labelling

Eco-labelling and the supplier audit are two related issues which rely, to some degree, upon both EMS and environmental auditing. Both are predominantly 'market mechanisms' through which the purchasers of goods and services can, it is claimed, make more informed judgements about the environmental history of what is being purchased. They do, however, relate to different stages in the economic (so-called) 'value-chain'. On the one hand, eco-labelling relates primarily to purchases by end-users (and thus depends upon the quality of EMS and environmental audit in the supplying organization). On the other hand, the supplier audits are more generally concerned with the

[28] A particularly valuable critique of ISO 14001 is given in Krut and Gleckman (1998).

[29] Research conducted and published by FEE and more critical work undertaken by researchers at the University of Sheffield has raised considerable questions over both the comparability and usefulness of attestation in this context and that of environmental reporting more generally (see Chapter 12).

[30] A more subtle, though more penetrating argument has been developed by Michael Power in which he argues that 'auditing' has become the substitute for 'doing'. That is, we no longer educate, or produce or seek quality, we simply audit the fact that something along these lines is happening. For more detail see Power (1991, 1992, 1994a, 1994b, 1997). An equal and related part of Power's arguments governs the development of apparent 'professionals' to take over these monitoring (auditing) roles. There has been much jockeying (global and national) for position and prestige as being recognized as an 'auditor' or 'verifier' confers high economic value and, more significantly, the body that successfully claims to be competent to award 'verifier/auditor' status will clearly be a powerful one.

environmental effects from the source of goods and services purchased by organizations for use in the production of their own goods and services (and is, thus, an essential input to the organization's own environmental management and environmental audit).

Eco-labelling aims to permit organizations to 'badge' products and services that meet the highest environmental standards in their manufacture and operation. Such labelling is perhaps at its most active in Europe. The European Eco-Labelling Regulation was first established in 1991 and takes a cradle-to-grave approach to products (see life-cycle assessment in Chapter 9). Based upon the German 'Blue Angel' programme,[31] an eco-label will attach to a product in such a way as to ensure 'free' passage of the product throughout the countries of the EU.[32] The award of an eco-label will be taken to suggest that the total product meets the very highest standards of environmental care throughout its life – to be, in fact, the result of a total environmental quality management system. Hence the tie-in with the EMS and the environmental audit. It has been mooted that an eco-label cannot be achieved without an organization first having qualified under EMAS or ISO 14000.

Eco-labelling has proved to be a process fraught with difficulty and conflict. In essence, the potential market impact of an eco-label leads companies to be anxious about the criteria adopted in determining the label. This, inevitably, leads to lobbying and conflict. The basis of the conflict is real enough – complex products (e.g. washing machines or cars) go through so many processes and are of dubious environmental value in their use such that establishing a single indicator of 'environmental effect' is impossible. (That is, should perhaps energy, raw material or emissions be used as the basis of assessment? If all three – plus others – should be used, how are they to be placed on a common basis?) The nature of these problems becomes clearer when a life-cycle assessment is constructed and we will, consequently, revisit the issues in Chapter 9. Suffice it to say, for now, that eco-labelling is an important plank of the 'market mechanisms' approach to environmental performance improvement and whilst it remains a crucial and live

---

[31] There are many other national schemes for eco-labelling such as the Scandinavian 'White Swan' system. In the continual dilution of eco-labelling (see below) there has been an increasing anticipation (anxiety?) that eco-labelling criteria might be standardized through ISO standards.

[32] The Netherlands has also developed its own system of eco-labelling – concerned that the EU standards will be too low and too late. There have also been a number of specific industry initiatives intended (it would seem) to forestall regulation. For example, a number of travel agents joined together in 1991 to establish a Green Flag System for 'sustainable tourism and conservation'. The CIA's Responsible Care Programme might also be seen as a variation on this theme.

issue eco-labels do not look to become widely, consistently and reliably adopted in the near future.

The essence of the *supplier audit* is that products and services bought in by an organization should meet, at a minimum, the standards applied within that organization. The reasons are various and fairly obvious: defensive (a green claim for a product, service or process can be undermined by the use of non-green inputs); ethical (making claims which are untrue, misleading or mischievous and/or for which the organization has no evidential basis does not enhance its ethical stance); environmentally active (whether seen as a proselytizing activity or as part of the initiatives by large companies to help the smaller, these audits advance the level of environmental awareness in organizations); strategic (establishing supply chains, employee and competitive advantage in advance of changing law and public perception).[33]

The supplier audits, being (still) an emerging phenomenon, have no established method.[34] At their most effective they constitute an advanced form of green consumerism and rely on policy statements whereby an organization will not buy from (for example) a company that does not have the eco-audit certification. Currently, we are finding that the supplier audit is driving green awareness back into organizations which had previously ignored it. This is generally achieved by the customer educating the supplier. By the early 1990s, companies like British Telecom, the DIY chain B&Q and the supermarket chains of Gateway and the Co-op were reported as having developed major analyses of their suppliers as a step towards much tighter environmental standards.[35]

Of especial interest, however, the approach is also of increasing importance as part of *ethical audits* in which organizations seek to establish whether their suppliers conform with the organization's standards on, for example, health and safety or the employment of children. As sustainability (see Chapter 14) becomes the integrating force of public and organizational policy, integration of both environmental and social/ethical supplier chain audits becomes increasingly important. (See also Chapter 13.)

IBM (UK) has perhaps one of the longest established policies in this field and presents an especially good example. The extract from its *Environmental Programmes* shown in Figure 5.16 indicates the process.

---

[33] Such audits do not relate only to physical goods and services. Chapter 10 talks about the impact of ethical investment on the supplies of funds to companies and even established major investment institutions such as Norwich Union are establishing supplier audits for the supply of funds. This is somewhat different in emphasis – although similar in effect – to the banks instituting audits as a prerequisite of loans.

[34] But see, especially, Business-in-the-Environment (1993).

[35] See, for example, *ENDS Report*, February 1990, pp. 18–24, for more details.

Figure 5.16

Extract from IBM's policy on supplier audits

Recognizing the crucial role played by IBM UK's thousands of suppliers and subcontractors in maintaining environmental standards, a task force was established within the purchasing organization in May 1990 to review and promote supplier awareness of key issues.

- Establish supplier self-assessment environmental guidelines.
- Issue guidelines to all suppliers.
- Establish detailed environmental questionnaire for major company suppliers.
- Pilot and issue questionnaire to major suppliers.

. . . and this continues through Transport, Distribution and Car Fleet!

There is an obvious tie-in with LCA (Chapter 9) and with concepts such as the duty of care and (what ICI calls) 'Product Stewardship'. That is, what are now considered to be the standards that a responsible organization must apply require that the organization be aware of both the 'upstream' and 'downstream' effects of its activities.

Supplier audits are an increasingly significant influence on corporate environmental activity. Whilst their influence is likely to grow slowly, in the nature of so many environmental developments, they work with a ratchet effect, constantly raising standards until no organization will be able to ignore them if they wish to deal with those greener than themselves.[36] A major group in this connection will be the local authorities.

5.9   National and Local Government and Environmental Audits

Despite the difficult situation in which many civil authorities find themselves – having to regulate and monitor corporate environmental activity whilst being subject to extensive pressure and lobbying from the corporate sector – national, state and local governments are clearly an essential element in any attempts to place environmental (and social) issues at the heart of economic affairs. It was national governments which signed the 'Rio Declaration' committing them to the adoption of the principles of sustainable development (see Chapter 14) through the mechanism of *Agenda 21*.[37] This has manifested itself in the creation of national environmental and sustainable development units, more active and (potentially) powerful environmental

---

[36] See the further reading at the end of this chapter for more information.
[37] The sustainable development agenda for the twenty-first century.

agencies and, at a local level, in the empowerment of local government to develop strategies for *Local Agenda 21*.

In the very broadest terms, national and local government must now be committed to:

- environmental auditing of their own activities (energy use, purchasing, etc.);
- environmental assessment of their policies, taxation, subsidies and regulation;
- placing environmental issues at the heart of all of their spheres of influence (education, training, development, housing, health, etc.);
- working with business to move forward the social and environmental agendas to which they are committed (and which business successfully avoided through removing themselves from Agenda 21[38]);
- providing mechanisms to encourage all organizations to adopt best environmental practice through, for example, training, grants and consciousness-raising on matters such as EMS and environmental audits;
- placing firmer environmental criteria at the heart of planning issues, environmental impact assessment and other matters such as registers of contaminated land;[39]
- monitoring the state of the local and national environment itself.[40]

Amongst the most influential roles that local government can play – and the most apposite in the context of this chapter – is the insistence on the highest standards of environmental management in all organizations which are part of, supply or work with the government. Despite the considerable economic and political strains under which government often finds itself, an increasing number of national, state and local governments now require EMAS or ISO 14000 as a prerequisite for dealing with that government. The effect of this is, inevitably, patchy. And much of this patchiness seems inevitable as long as the lobbying pressures (in the broadest sense) brought

[38] For a good introduction and explanation of this point, see Mayhew (1997).

[39] See e.g. Pollock (1992) and Friends of the Earth (1990, pp. 107 *et seq.*).

[40] The 'State of the Environment Report' in which the local authority attempts to construct a comprehensive picture of the current state of the local environment. A major problem for all organizations, not least local authorities, is the establishment of systems to collect (and then collate) the data. One UK authority, for example, used the integration of environmental issues into the school curriculum as a source of data collection, setting schools to act as measuring and collection points for a variety of characteristics such as flora, noise and pollution. The implications this may have for the data are not discussed here.

by business and the lack of political will in central government continue.[41]

Despite this, the range of activities undertaken by governments is bewildering: from 'Sustainable Seattle' to 'The Bremen Declaration'; from the Friends of the Earth *Environmental Charter for Local Government* (1989) to the Australian national response to the United Nations Commission on Sustainable Development. Indeed, a UN report in 1997 identified 1812 Local Agenda 21 initiatives in 64 countries.[42] This area would justify a book in itself,[43] but the interested reader with Internet access is recommended to spend a little time browsing the astonishing array of national and local government websites where current activities are detailed.

As national and local governments overcome the initial disruption that inevitably arises from their increasing role within the development of national environmental policies and begin the process of taking a hard look at their own environmental activities, there seems little question that civil authority of whatever political hue will prove to be a most important factor in determining the environmental climate within which organizations operate. Sensible companies have long taken steps to develop a good working relationship with their local authority, and nowhere is this more true than in relation to environmental matters (see also Chapter 13).

5.10   Concluding Remarks

Environmental management and audit have been undoubtedly the major growth and development areas in businesses' response to the environmental agenda. They are now so central to organizational management that any organization ignores them at its peril. But they are also complex and demanding areas. Environmental audit touches many areas of current, proposed and possible future environmental regulation and acts as both the essential first substantial step towards environmental sensitivity and as a regular and essential part of environmental management systems. As we have seen, the related issue of independent attestation of the environmental audit and statement is

[41] Such matters, although central to the whole area of environmental change, are complex and beyond the scope of our discussion here. But for an introduction, see, for example, Beder (1997), Eden (1996) and Welford (1997a).

[42] *Local Agenda 21 Survey: A Study of the Response by Local Authorities and International Associates to Agenda 21*, The United Nations Department for Policy Coordination and Sustainable Development, February 1997.

[43] See, for example, *Sustainable Development in Western Europe: Coming to Terms with Agenda 21*, ed. T. O'Riordan and H. Voisey (London: Frank Cass, 1998).

an additional complication of the process. This, in turn, raises issues about attestation of environmental reports and the role of the statutory financial auditor. Given the already dense nature of the material in this chapter, we will not further consider these matters here. We do, however, briefly consider attestation and auditing again in Part C, where we will discuss them in relation to the information to which such audits will relate – typically external reporting.

The parting remarks we would like to make are twofold. First, with the term 'audit' having been appropriated from accountants – as was the case with 'social audit' in the 1970s and 1980s – there is a great need to take care with terminology so that one is entirely clear about the objective of the activity undertaken. Whilst the establishment of environmental auditing and management guidelines has offered an important degree of standardization in the area, it is still necessary to remember that the review, the check against standards or the investigation of potential chemical hazards each require different approaches, different knowledge of law and other source disciplines and different personnel and experiences. Clarity in these matters can save lives, money, time and a great deal of disruption and heartache.[44]

The second point is more a general warning: environmental audit as whitewash will be counterproductive in the medium term.[45] General evidence suggests that a significant minority of organizations that have undertaken an initial review either have not followed up on it or have set its parameters so loosely that the results are largely meaningless. The way in which the organizational climate is changing suggests that these sorts of approaches are not only a waste of time and money but can be seriously counterproductive. Relatedly, but more obscurely, there is the longer-term question which we raised in Chapter 2 concerning the extent to which the pressure of environmental change will require substantial alteration in organizational orthodoxy. This leads to questions of whether the relatively technical nature of environmental audit as currently constituted can and will genuinely address many of the fundamental dilemmas posed by the environmental crisis. Whilst a pragmatic stance is clearly in the current interests of organizations, this is not necessarily the only way forward or the most desirable route towards sustainability. These matters are briefly re-examined in Part D.[46]

[44] See, for example, Gray and Symon (1992a).

[45] See, for example, Gray and Collison (1991b).

[46] The interested reader is directed to the further reading at the end of this chapter and, especially, to the work of Michael Power included in the references and bibliography at the end of the book.

Further Reading

There is now a very considerable array of excellent material on the areas covered by this chapter, ranging from the general and theoretical to the specific and technical. The following are just a few suggestions with which one could begin the process of acquiring a deeper knowledge of the area.

Business-in-the-Environment (1991a) *Your Business and the Environment: A DIY Review for Companies* (London: BiE/Coopers & Lybrand Deloitte)

Eden, S. (1996) *Environmental Issues and Business: Implications of a Changing Agenda* (Chichester: John Wiley)

Elkington, J., P. Knight and J. Hailes (1991) *The Green Business Guide* (London: Victor Gollancz)

Fuller, K. (1991) 'Reviewing UK's experience in EIA', *Integrated Environmental Management*, no. 1, August, pp. 12–14

Gray, R. H. and I. W. Symon (1992a) 'An environmental audit by any other name . . .', *Integrated Environmental Management*, no. 6, February, pp. 9–11

Krut, R. and H. Gleckman (1998) *ISO 14001: A Missed Opportunity for Sustainable Global Industrial Development* (London: Earthscan)

Power, M. (1991) 'Auditing and environmental expertise: between protest and profession-alisation', *Accounting, Auditing and Accountability*, 4 (3), pp. 30–42

Sheldon, C. (1997) *ISO 14001 and Beyond* (Sheffield: Greenleaf Publishing)

Welford, R. (ed.) (1996) *Corporate Environmental Management: Systems and Strategies* (London: Earthscan), especially Chapters 3 and 4 by, respectively, A. Netherwood and R. Starkey

Welford, R. (ed.) (1997) *Corporate Environmental Management 2: Culture and Organisations* (London: Earthscan)

APPENDIX 5
Examples of Guidance on the Conduct of Environmental Audits

Appendix 5.1   CEBIS Guide to Environmental Audit

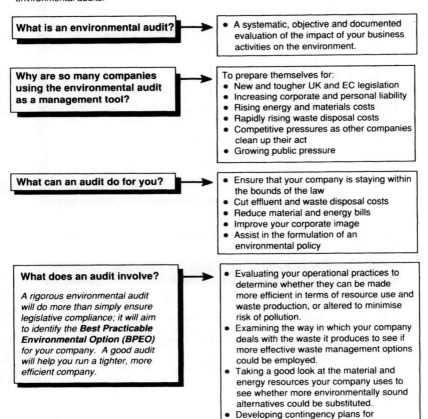

THE ENVIRONMENTAL AUDIT

Environmental auditing is playing an increasingly important role in all sectors of industry and commerce. The CBI has called for every UK company to carry out an audit, the European Commission is drafting legislation to encourage the widespread use of auditing and a growing number of large companies are demanding that their suppliers and contractors undertake environmental audits.

What is an environmental audit? →
- A systematic, objective and documented evaluation of the impact of your business activities on the environment.

Why are so many companies using the environmental audit as a management tool? →

To prepare themselves for:
- New and tougher UK and EC legislation
- Increasing corporate and personal liability
- Rising energy and materials costs
- Rapidly rising waste disposal costs
- Competitive pressures as other companies clean up their act
- Growing public pressure

What can an audit do for you? →
- Ensure that your company is staying within the bounds of the law
- Cut effluent and waste disposal costs
- Reduce material and energy bills
- Improve your corporate image
- Assist in the formulation of an environmental policy

What does an audit involve?

*A rigorous environmental audit will do more than simply ensure legislative compliance; it will aim to identify the **Best Practicable Environmental Option (BPEO)** for your company. A good audit will help you run a tighter, more efficient company.*

→
- Evaluating your operational practices to determine whether they can be made more efficient in terms of resource use and waste production, or altered to minimise risk of pollution.
- Examining the way in which your company deals with the waste it produces to see if more effective waste management options could be employed.
- Taking a good look at the material and energy resources your company uses to see whether more environmentally sound alternatives could be substituted.
- Developing contingency plans for environmental mishaps.

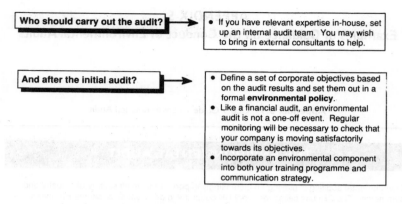

Who should carry out the audit? ➤
- If you have relevant expertise in-house, set up an internal audit team. You may wish to bring in external consultants to help.

And after the initial audit? ➤
- Define a set of corporate objectives based on the audit results and set them out in a formal **environmental policy**.
- Like a financial audit, an environmental audit is not a one-off event. Regular monitoring will be necessary to check that your company is moving satisfactorily towards its objectives.
- Incorporate an environmental component into both your training programme and communication strategy.

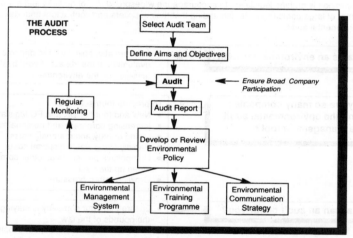

THE AUDIT PROCESS

Select Audit Team → Define Aims and Objectives → Audit ← *Ensure Broad Company Participation*

Audit → Audit Report → Develop or Review Environmental Policy

Regular Monitoring

Develop or Review Environmental Policy →
- Environmental Management System
- Environmental Training Programme
- Environmental Communication Strategy

Many companies have already reaped considerable benefits as a result of carrying out environmental audits. For example:

Sector	Action	Annual saving	Payback Period
Electronics	Recovery of copper	£27K	2 years
Metals	Recovery of foundry dust	£76K	3 months
Food	Improvement in the efficiency of water use and effluent treatment at a sugar factory	£200K	10 months
Public	Improved energy management introduced in local authority schools	£70K	2 years
Retail	Production of energy from waste	£32K	22 months

AUDIT CHECKLIST

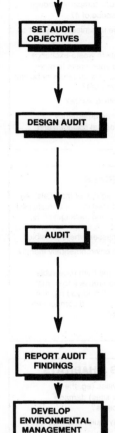

SELECT AUDIT TEAM

Team should include:
• Director or manager with access to the Board
• In-house personnel with skills in disciplines such as waste, energy, design etc
• External consultants to guide internal team, if necessary

SET AUDIT OBJECTIVES

Define what you want from the audit. Objectives may include:
• Compliance with legislation
• Financial savings
• Enhanced company image
• Increased efficiency
• Gaining a market advantage
• Protecting investment and insurance options

DESIGN AUDIT

Identify areas in which the company's activities may be impinging on the environment. These will vary according to the nature of the company's activities. A typical audit might evaluate:
• legal compliance
• waste management and emissions to air and water
• materials use
• energy use
• landscape and habitat disturbance
• transport
• noise and odour   *(see overleaf)*

AUDIT

Decide on the most effective way of gathering the necessary information to assess performance in the relevant areas. You may wish to use:
• questionnaires
• site visits
• informal interviews

Gather all relevant information as planned. Encourage staff participation and make sure that personnel are aware of, and understand, the aims and objectives of the audit.

REPORT AUDIT FINDINGS

Analyse the company's environmental strengths and weaknesses in the light of audit findings. Where improvements are necessary, cost alternatives and identify BPEOs (**B**est **P**racticable **E**nvironmental **O**ptions). Produce written Audit Report.

DEVELOP ENVIRONMENTAL MANAGEMENT STRATEGY

Decide how the company will implement necessary improvements and set a time-scale for this. Develop a mechanism for monitoring progress towards the company's environmental objectives. Environmental excellence will not be achieved overnight - prioritise. Aim to incorporate sound environmental practices into day-to-day management. Encourage staff involvement at every level.

Scottish

MAIN AUDIT CATEGORIES

The following is not intended as a comprehensive checklist to be rigorously adhered to, but rather as a guide to the type of questions the audit team should be addressing.

LEGAL COMPLIANCE

- Do you know how UK and EC regulations and standards affect your business?
- Do your current practices comply with these?
- Do you take future environmental standards into consideration when planning new projects?
- Are you aware of, and where possible do you implement, the best available technology?
- Do you keep up with the latest regulatory requirements?

WASTE

- What waste does your company produce and how do you dispose of it?
- Could your waste be minimised, recycled or eliminated?
- Could you participate in waste-exchange schemes (ie. selling your waste to other businesses to use as raw materials or buying waste in for your own use)?
- Could you recycle office waste?
- Do you have adequate emergency procedures for accidental spillages and emissions?

TRANSPORT

- Do you transport your goods efficiently (eg avoid empty vehicles)?
- What special precautions do you take in the transport of dangerous goods and wastes?
- Do you regularly maintain vehicles and plant to minimise noxious emissions?
- Could you switch to vehicles with smaller engines?
- Could you develop a strategy that minimised use of staff transport? Could you encourage car pooling or offer a 'bicycle allowance', for example?

MATERIALS

- Could you cut down on use of materials? eg: Can products be reduced in size or reshaped to minimise materials and packaging? Is packaging excessive? Are you recycling materials within processes where possible?
- Could you use more environmentally friendly materials? eg: Do your materials come from renewable resources? Could you replace toxic materials with less toxic ones? Could you replace non-recyclable materials and components with recyclable ones?

ENERGY USE

- How much energy is used in each area of your business and do you regularly review energy use?
- Could waste energy be usefully redirected?
- Could you use combined heat and power?
- Is there potential for energy saving in your business? For example, could better insulation and heat controls, more energy-efficient lighting and plant, cut your fuel bills?

LANDSCAPES & HABITATS

- Do any of your activities (eg. the development of new sites) damage landscapes and habitats?
- Are your sites as tidy, quiet and dust-free as they could be?
- Are your sites landscaped to make them look attractive?
- Do you preserve natural habitats around your sites where possible?

Appendix 5.2 Taken from ICC position paper on environmental auditing ICC Publication No. 468 Copyright © 1989 published in its official English version by the International Chamber of Commerce (ICC) ISBN 92 842 1089 5. Published by ICC Publishing SA, Paris. Available from ICC Publishing SA, 38 Cours Albert 1er, 75008 Paris or ICC UK, 14/15 Belgrave Square, London SW1X 8PS

Basic steps of an environmental audit

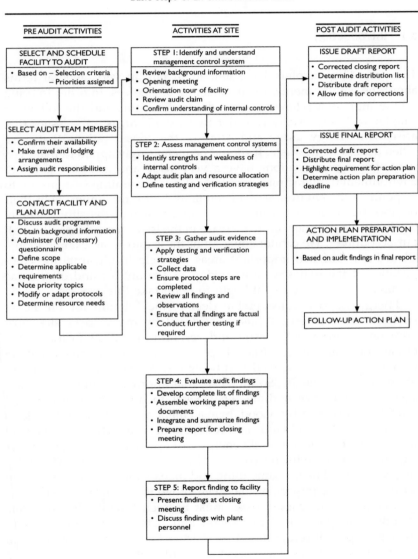

PRE AUDIT ACTIVITIES

SELECT AND SCHEDULE FACILITY TO AUDIT
- Based on – Selection criteria
  – Priorities assigned

SELECT AUDIT TEAM MEMBERS
- Confirm their availability
- Make travel and lodging arrangements
- Assign audit responsibilities

CONTACT FACILITY AND PLAN AUDIT
- Discuss audit programme
- Obtain background information
- Administer (if necessary) questionnaire
- Define scope
- Determine applicable requirements
- Note priority topics
- Modify or adapt protocols
- Determine resource needs

ACTIVITIES AT SITE

STEP 1: Identify and understand management control system
- Review background information
- Opening meeting
- Orientation tour of facility
- Review audit claim
- Confirm understanding of internal controls

STEP 2: Assess management control systems
- Identify strengths and weakness of internal controls
- Adapt audit plan and resource allocation
- Define testing and verification strategies

STEP 3: Gather audit evidence
- Apply testing and verification strategies
- Collect data
- Ensure protocol steps are completed
- Review all findings and observations
- Ensure that all findings are factual
- Conduct further testing if required

STEP 4: Evaluate audit findings
- Develop complete list of findings
- Assemble working papers and documents
- Integrate and summarize findings
- Prepare report for closing meeting

STEP 5: Report finding to facility
- Present findings at closing meeting
- Discuss findings with plant personnel

POST AUDIT ACTIVITIES

ISSUE DRAFT REPORT
- Corrected closing report
- Determine distribution list
- Distribute draft report
- Allow time for corrections

ISSUE FINAL REPORT
- Corrected draft report
- Distribute final report
- Highlight requirement for action plan
- Determine action plan preparation deadline

ACTION PLAN PREPARATION AND IMPLEMENTATION
- Based on audit findings in final report

FOLLOW-UP ACTION PLAN

CHAPTER 6

ACCOUNTING AND THE CONTROL OF ENERGY COSTS

6.1 Introduction

The preceding chapters have tended to talk in very general terms about the environmental issues affecting businesses. In order to bring a little more concreteness to our discussions, this and the following chapter will very briefly consider two specific areas – the issues that arise with energy usage and some of the considerations that arise when dealing with waste. It should be increasingly apparent that even very simple organizations have a very wide and complex range of environmental interactions. Similarly, if our accounting systems are to respond to the environmental agenda and, at a minimum, help their organizations in increasing their environmental sensitivity, there needs to be a commensurate increase in the issues we address through our accounting. We cannot cover all of these and so an examination – albeit brief – of two important areas can help to illustrate the complexities of the issues we are seeking to account for and offer some guidance on how we might begin to undertake this process.

Energy is, to a considerable degree, the fulcrum for business/environment relations. Whilst considered by many to be the most pressing environmental issue and certainly a critical factor in the pursuit of sustainability[1] (see Chapter 14), it is also the major area in which all parties are agreed that being environmentally sensitive can bring financial benefits. So much so, that approaches to energy management need have nothing whatsoever to do with environmental considerations directly. Good management practice should seek to minimize waste of all kinds and reduce unit costs, which means, *inter alia*, seeking out the minimum energy cost options. However, minimizing energy cost (reducing costs) and minimizing energy usage (efficiency) need not be the same thing and management who consider the former the more important may well prove to be short-sighted.

'Energy', as discussed here, must be seen broadly. It must thus include 'transport costs' in general and petrol and diesel costs in particular; permit recognition that every action, process, raw material and element of waste has energy embedded in it; as well as noting that heat (and thus energy) is carried away via water and other

---

[1] See, for example, Stevenson and Dowell (1990).

emissions.[2] For both environmental and financial reasons these elements must be minimized.

This chapter will introduce some of the issues connected with energy, the sorts of problems with which energy usage is connected and where the savings – environmental and corporate financial – can come from and may be likely to come from in the future.[3] We will then go on to look at ways of controlling energy usage before looking at the accounting implications and the role that accounting can play in energy minimization.

6.2 Energy: Some of the Wider Issues

The environmental issues associated with energy are complex and critical. Energy may be derived from non-renewable (coal, oil, gas, nuclear, geothermal) or renewable (wood, wind, sea, solar, hydro) sources. Western fuels are derived predominantly from the non-renewable sources.[4] Extraction not only depletes a scarce resource (which may have alternative, more sustainable uses – see Part D) and disrupts ecosystems, but itself uses energy in the process. The extracted raw material is transported and processed, using further energy, before reaching the end-users – or arriving at power stations where it is further processed before reaching the consumers in the form of electricity. Energy creation is itself very energy-intensive and therefore not energy-efficient. Its use and processing produce waste heat, by-products and emissions of gases and are thereby directly linked to the creation of acid rain, global warming, air pollution and myriad other intrusions into the biosphere. The implications of these intrusions are still very much a matter for argument but the worst-case scenarios suggest devastation of the human species – developed and lesser developed countries alike not to mention the impact on other species

[2] This is a point made and developed in Winter (1988, pp. 128–130) in relation to (a) situations in which there are charges for water and therefore the financial and environmental desire to reduce usage makes water similar in nature to energy from the business point of view, and (b) the fact that water is often raised in temperature for various reasons and thus becomes a major focus for energy recovery.

[3] With the considerable growth in the published discussion, analysis and guidance on areas of environmental management – including matters such as energy – there are now many excellent sources of further information. This chapter will not rehearse the detail of these other sources and the reader is, once again, encouraged to consult the references provided throughout the chapter – and see, in particular, footnote 16.

[4] Ekins (1992a, p. 91) suggests that in the developed countries outside Scandinavia and other countries with extensive hydro opportunities, the use of renewable energy is slight, viz: Denmark (1%), UK (2%), West Germany (5%), USA (5%), France (13%), Japan (14%), whereas Norway, for example, is 100% reliant on renewables.

and the planet as a whole.[5] The implications of nuclear power are also far from straightforward[6] and geothermal and hydro schemes raise many difficult environmental problems themselves. It would appear that no use of conventional energy in the West is entirely without its problems.[7]

Energy is also a major factor in the G7/G77 debate. In the first place, per capita consumption of energy in the developed countries is approximately seven times higher than in the lesser developed countries, and when the most profligate (USA, Canada and Australia) are compared with the poorest, the figure is many times higher.[8] It is obvious that the West has far greater capacity for savings than does the developing world. For much of the developing world's population, energy use is directly geared to basic (often, less than basic) sustenance – warmth and cooking. These activities represent a small proportion of Western usage. The increasing pressure on energy for the developing world will continue to rise with the encouragement of industrialization whilst the rising demand for timber for fuel adds the final straw to devastated woodlands – with the attendant destruction of habitat, desertification, flooding, and so on.

Clearly, all sectors of the population are implicated in this process and the efforts of government, individuals, households and business will be necessary to mitigate the worst effects before the devastation starts to have more than marginal impacts on Western life. This will involve a major shift by business. For example, CO_2 is the principal 'greenhouse' gas contributing to global warming. In the UK about 70 per cent of all CO_2 is contributed by business and transport. The principal contributors to acid rain are SO_x and NO_x. The lion's share of these emanates from electricity generation, manufacturing and heating processes and road transport.[9]

---

[5] For more detail see, for example, Friends of the Earth (1990), Porritt (1991), Weizsäcker et al. (1997) and the worldwide concern and discussion over 'global warming' and climate change. The international conference on climate change (the Kyoto conference) in 1997 was an indicator of the potential seriousness of these matters.

[6] See, again, Friends of the Earth (1990) for a summary.

[7] Unfortunately, the debate is one which tends to generate more heat than light in many forums. In the UK, for example, reading the annual reports of the major energy producers would leave one with a warm, glowing feeling that each is absolutely safe and environmentally responsible. It is not clear that the principal critical issues are being honestly addressed by the energy, producers or the politicians. There is a great deal of material on 'alternative' sources of energy but see Purkiss (1992) for a simple introduction to some of the options and Weizsäcker et al. (1997) for consideration of the wider implications.

[8] See, for example, Hutchinson (1991) and O'Riordan (1997, ch. 1).

[9] For more detail of a calm and helpful kind on this see, for example, Business-in-the-Environment (1991b).

The real irony is that the majority of the energy used in the developed world is wasted. Friends of the Earth estimates that the UK could, using present levels of technology, reduce its electricity consumption by 70 per cent. Figures such as this, while not making the very slow progress on non-renewable energy generation irrelevant, do put it into perspective. Furthermore, many developed countries – despite the scares during the 1970s 'energy crisis' – have shown little real commitment to major energy efficiency. With effective government subsidies to private road transport and very large inequalities between the different energy research initiatives, for example, the drastic change in emphasis which is needed in energy usage is still a thing of the future.[10]

6.3 Energy: Some of the Business Issues

The steadily growing concerns over energy, its usage and consequent emissions are creating a changing – but relatively unpredictable – environment for business. The most obvious source of pressure on businesses to change their approach to energy usage would be through rising energy prices but – on the whole (but see below) – this is not yet happening to any great degree. Nevertheless, many far-sighted businesses – for reasons as varied as cost-savings, good citizenship or strategic positioning – have adopted energy management plans (see Section 6.4) and or sought out alternative energy and energy-efficiency options.[11] One of the more obvious manifestations of this activity would be the (highly visible) increased use of wind power and (less obvious but more strategic) exploration of solar power.

The one development that will make the critical difference will be if energy costs are raised against the general downward trend. In addition to any energy taxation system there has been a long debate as to whether or not energy currently represents its 'true' cost. National or international law which required, for example, higher standards of electricity generation emissions or energy efficiency; which was stricter on environmental impact assessment (see Chapter 5); which required accident-free oil movement and/or a cessation of oil-tanker flushing into the seas; which required tighter standards of remediation;

---

[10] For a general introduction to energy issues and a survey of the related data see, for example, Simpson (1990, ch. 7). See also Weizsäcker et al. (1997) for sensible discussion of the issues.

[11] There is a wide range of developments – in energy-saving technologies, in building design, in computer-controlled energy monitoring systems, etc. – now available to industry.

and so on, will all reflect the environmental costs and add to the financial costs of energy.[12]

The future (and more significant) influences on business to change energy usage and efficiency seem likely to come from two major directions: global concerns over energy efficiency *per se* and increasing anxieties about emissions, pollution and climate change. That is, whilst energy efficiency and emissions control in the G7 countries have improved steadily,[13] the improvement is nowhere near enough to reverse climatic change – let alone to compensate for increases in energy use and emissions as the G77 countries increase *their* industrialization.[14]

As it becomes apparent that voluntary initiatives in business – although significant – are nowhere near sufficient to halt the reductions in energy resources, the increases in acid rain, the increased threat of climate change and so on, the regulatory regime under which business operates is beginning to change. These changes take a number of forms, the most obvious of which are 'command and control' regulations; changes in the taxation system; changes in incentives and grants and/or combinations of regulatory regimes with market instruments. Most OECD countries have an increasing experience with one of more of these[15] and that experience seems set to continue.[16]

In particular, there are two areas which are being given increasing attention with respect to the control of energy usage and emissions: the (so-called) *carbon taxes* and the new market mechanisms of *emissions trading* or *tradable pollution licensing*.

---

[12] For more detail see OECD (1989) and reports by Kehoe, *Financial Times*, 5 June 1991, p. 15, and by Durr, by Griffiths and by Hargreaves, *Financial Times*, 24 July 1991, p. 25.

[13] See Elkington, Knight and Hailes (1991) for further detail.

[14] It is important to emphasize that a significant proportion of the recorded reductions in energy usage and emissions in the West have arisen from the 'exporting' of the dirtier manufacturing processes to the developing countries for reasons ranging from the much cheaper labour to the laxer regulations over matters such as safety and environmental protection. Thus claims by the West that the developed countries are being (for example) energy-responsible, whilst not entirely unfounded, must be interpreted with considerable care. (See, for example, Brown et al., 1998; Weizsäcker et al., 1997)

[15] The UK's differential taxation (duty) on unleaded and leaded petrol (gasoline) is one such example of a successful fiscal intervention in energy usage.

[16] For a useful introduction to the issues see Ekins (1992a), and on the wider issues of economic environmental initiatives see Bryce (1990), Owens et al. (1990) and de Savornin Lohman (1991). The issues are widely discussed in the environmental economics literature – see, for example, the Pearce references in the bibliography and also Opschoor and Vos (1989). The taxation issues are dealt with in detail in O'Riordan (1997) and Flavin and Dunn (1998). There is also a journal dedicated to issues surrounding environmental taxation – *Environmental Taxation and Accounting* published by Cameron May.

Energy taxes and carbon taxes (which target the carbon content of fuels) in particular are part of a wider net of fiscal environmental incentives and penalties to harmonize good business and environmentally sensitive practices. However, the issues involved are complex. The business community has not generally supported proposals (such as those made in Europe) for an energy tax. Fear of business disadvantages – although perhaps over-played – are nevertheless real enough. Countries, similarly, fear that 'being first' with an energy tax might lead to severe economic disadvantage. Even more significant (as the UK learned to its cost), any proposals need to be framed in a way that does not penalize the poorer and less fortunate in society unjustly. That is, as the poor and less well-off spend a disproportionately higher percentage of their net income on fuel (for warmth, cooking, basic amenities and travel) any energy tax would have a disproportionately higher impact on that group. Thus, an energy tax could be a potentially *regressive* taxation initiative. This is *not* the idea at all.

Despite these problems, something needs to be done to bring the price mechanism into play to encourage – indeed force – much greater energy efficiency.

An alternative approach has been to target, not the *input* of fuels, but the *output* of emissions arising from the use of those fuels (and other materials). This approach is concerned with *emissions trading* and can be used to target specific emissions (e.g. CO_2 or SO_x) or a basket of emissions from manufacturing pollution or other activities. The idea is that an imaginary bubble is put over the company and it is issued with a permit to fill that bubble with up to x amount of specified pollutants. The 'clean' company will not use all of its licence and may trade it to a 'dirty' company – thus transferring cash from the 'bad' to the 'good'. Widely discussed in the environmental economics literature and an increasingly important factor on the agenda in, for example, the EU and UK as well as in New Zealand,[17] tradable pollution licences emerged first in the USA. The USA scheme is in two stages, intended first to bring the dirtier companies into line with basic requirements and then steadily to reduce the baseline – thus, it is argued, reducing overall pollution in a steady and manageable manner. Futures in such permits have been traded in the USA since 1992.

Industry itself has been far from homogeneous in its response with the, now familiar, pattern of some companies seeking to oppose *any* initiatives, many ignoring the issues altogether and an impressive

[17] See, for example, Gilkinson (1992a) and the New Zealand Ministry for the Environment's working paper *Technical Design Issues for a Domestic Emissions Trading Regime for Greenhouse Gases*, Wellington, 1998.

minority seeking to undertake initiatives and set the pace of change in the field.

Industry initiatives include such things as the British Gas initiative GEM (Gas Energy Management). In addition the Chemical Industries Association and Business-in-the-Environment, for example, have encouraged the experimentation with and the development and use of performance indicators. These initiatives have typically included energy performance indicators of the 'energy-use-per-tonne-of-output' type. As we shall see below, approaches of this sort have proved very successful in many companies, with major financial savings reported by companies adopting these and other methods.[18]

At the company level a lot is happening. In large part, companies that learned from the 1970s energy crisis have continued to install, develop and refine their energy-efficiency projects. For these companies, energy saving has become part of the normal way of life. For example, a medium-sized manufacturing company forecasts that the payback period on its energy-saving investments is set to reduce in the near future as energy costs rise. This has encouraged a complete rethink of its energy usage and investment strategy (see also Chapter 8). IBM has long recognized the importance of energy and, as part of its 'taking the longer view', has been adopting more energy-efficient investments. Sainsbury has been widely reported as having adopted sophisticated management of energy costs throughout its operations. Furthermore, especially for manufacturing companies, each saving in energy can lead to further savings elsewhere through, for example, a reduction in health and safety and toxic waste disposal and control concerns, reductions in wastes and waste waters, reductions in emissions to air and water and attendant reductions in further treatment and consent costs (see Chapter 7). Energy is also a major issue in recycling and life-cycle assessment (see Chapters 7 and 9), where Norsk Hydro, for example, reports 'a small energy profit' in the recycling of aluminium. For other companies, rising energy concerns provide opportunities for their technology and products – whether control technology or an increased demand for insulation or double glazing. We look at how these things come about in the next section.

Of particular note are the initiatives that companies are beginning to consider in light of the concerns over global warming. These concerns were given especial impetus by the Kyoto conference on climate change and have led to a number of responses. Many companies are now setting – and even reporting (see Chapter 12) – self-imposed targets for their reduction in emissions of greenhouse gases. Other companies – British Petroleum is a notable example – not only

---

[18] See for example ACCA (1997) and Burkitt (1990).

have set themselves targets concerning use and exploitation of renewable energy sources but have also started to use tradable emissions on an *internal* basis as a means of seeking to control energy use.[19] The third broad approach which is emerging at the time of writing has been attempts by companies to measure – and, again, to report – their individual contributions to global climate change. This ambitious, but enlightened, initiative is important for its recognition of the direct (if complex) link between large company activity and the state of the global ecology.[20] This, indeed, begins to look like the first faltering steps towards a true recognition of the exigencies of sustainability (see Chapter 14).

6.4 Controlling Energy

As we have seen, the surveys of business practice and intentions with respect to the environment have produced widely differing results. On the whole, it seems likely that whilst the majority of organizations are largely trying to ignore the issues, no well-managed company can afford to avoid having at least some form of energy conservation policy. And, as with so much else concerned with environmental matters, the impetus for change looks set to increase steadily in the coming years. What seems clear, however, is that organizations experience net benefits from energy-saving measures, often from very small initial outlays. As Winter[21] states it: 'if energy . . . [is] consistently well-managed, there are bound to be savings in costs and raw materials'.

Organizations, if they do not ignore the matter altogether, seem to follow one of three routes: piecemeal, in-house initiatives; a comprehensive, top-down approach; or a combination of the two. For example, although energy saving is not an especially big issue in New Zealand, Milburn Cement established a piecemeal set of housekeeping

---

[19] See the report on BP in *ENDS*, October 1998 (pp. 5–6).

[20] One influential example of the sort of thinking that encouraged organizations to identify their impact at the global level was a well-researched submission by NPI Global Care Investments (an ethical investment trust – see Chapter 10) to the Kyoto climate change conference. They identified ways in which companies could begin to measure their 'global warming potential' in common units that would be useful for both the management of that potential and as a useful addition for organizational environmental reporting. As more thought goes into ideas such as this we might expect to see greater understanding of the links between organizational activity and sustainability (Tennant et al., 1997). See also Ditz and Ranganathan (1997).

[21] Winter (1988) pp. 128–30. Such savings are, of course, more substantial the more substantial is the energy content of the activity. Where energy costs are a major element of overall cost, more fundamental issues like alterations in design and production scheduling may well yield significant economies.

Figure 6.1

Initial (simple and cheap) energy-saving steps
• Insulate walls and roofs
• Consider double-glazing
• Insulate boilers and lag hot-water pipes
• Check hot-water temperatures and reduce if possible
• Isolate heating systems and give local control
• Turn off lights and heat when not in use
• Use energy-efficient lighting
• Check for leaks in heating and water pipes
• Draught proofing
• Fit thermostats and time controls
• Step up maintenance of all energy-related equipment
• Maintain, upgrade, install heat recovery and heat exchange equipment
• Appoint individuals responsible for energy savings in different areas of the organization
• Ask for suggestions from all staff but specialists (e.g. heating engineers) in particular
And begin to monitor usage

initiatives to reduce office energy and encouraged its engineers to look for ways of saving energy. After 12 months of this, a full environmental audit (which included energy issues) was commissioned and this set in train more substantial, longer-term and systematic savings. Figure 6.1 illustrates some of the basic, initial steps that any organization can take to begin to save energy. Burkitt (1990) argues that lighting costs account for between 25 and 50 per cent of the average office electricity bill and energy-efficient lighting could save UK business up to £240 million ($384 million) per annum. These are not trivial amounts. However, there is a limit to how far piecemeal initiatives can take the organization's energy savings. A more systematic approach becomes necessary. If the organization has the talent in-house, it may well be able to undertake a systematic appraisal of its energy usage without outside help. Many guides to aid this approach exist. Two – from CEBIS and the UK Energy Efficiency Office – are provided in Appendix 6 and others can be found in, for example, CBI publications and the excellent Business-in-the-Environment guides.[22] Alternatively, expert advice – in either a specialist energy audit or as part of a fuller environmental audit – may be necessary. (See Chapter 5 for information about environmental audits.)

[22] A further and useful checklist plus commentary can be found in Winter (1988), whilst Elkington, Knight and Hailes (1991) and Elkington (1987) are full of examples of energy-saving initiatives by organizations. Weizsäcker et al. (1997) offer many innovative and longer-term insights into the issues.

The first step towards any systematic approach to energy efficiency is a full assessment of what energy is used, where and how it is used, and what leakages occur. Is this changing over time? This will focus attention on the areas where maximum savings can be made. (One aspect of this – the financial and non-financial accounting for energy – is dealt with below.) As ICI noted, 'We have been monitoring for some time. Now it is time to start dusting off the old stuff from the 1970s and starting to introduce some of these things.' There is no need to reinvent the wheel. Considerable expertise was assembled during the energy crisis of the 1970s and organizations should exploit that wherever possible. For example, in 1982 CIMA (the Chartered Institute of Management Accountants) published three papers representing the state of the art in energy saving and accounting with detailed illustrations from Courtaulds and Pilkington. Although not the simplest of documents they contain a mine of experience and ideas for all organizations.[23]

Fortunately, many companies are happy to share their experience.[24] For example, Business-in-the-Environment, in collaboration with KPMG, has encouraged a series of performance indicator projects. The resulting case studies are to be published and include examples of companies experimenting – and succeeding – with energy savings. British Gas and Sainsbury have been especially open about their experiences.

The Sainsbury example has been running since 1974 and claims to save well over £7 million per annum. Computer systems monitor all energy usage and associated costs in considerable detail. These are then compared with per capita and area usage data. From this, controls over heat and light can be established. All managers are shown the monthly usage costs against targets and are accountable for the difference. The benefit of a long experience in the field reflects in the company's involvement with building design, which allows efficiency to be built in so that, for example, heat is recycled and integrated systems use the heat generated by the fridges. Sainsbury claims that its stores now use only 60 per cent of the energy that would have been required ten years ago. Office space has similarly been considered. Motion-sensitive lighting and thermostatically controlled heating and air-conditioning all produce savings.[25]

There is less evidence on the types of controls that have been successfully applied in the field of transport. Inevitably, price differentials on unleaded petrol and diesel will have effects on buying decisions by companies in a way that should reduce long-term

---

[23] CIMA, *The Evaluation of Energy Use: Readings* (1982).

[24] See also Elkington, Knight and Hailes (1991).

[25] See, for further examples and explorations, Bennett and James (1998a, 1998b), Ditz et al. (1995) and Epstein (1996).

expenditure. Furthermore, constant monitoring of transport costs – including energy – would be a normal part of any good management.

This should have the effect of forcing transport miles and associated costs downwards. However, it is quite apparent that culture and financial subsidies in the West encourage private road transport over other methods and – as with energy usage – may actually lead to an increase in road miles. There seems little prospect of the majority of organizations switching to cycles and public transport[26] until there is a major switch in the financial and physical infrastructure of transport. Given the enormous effort and publicity which is pouring into energy savings in the 1990s, the absence of much sensible discussion of transport seems odd and very short-sighted.[27]

6.5   Accounting for Energy

One of the most straightforward ways in which accountants can contribute to the developing environmental sensitivity of organizations is accounting for energy. A prerequisite for control is knowing about the thing to be controlled. The first step is to separate out energy costs in the basic accounting and costing systems. This seems self-evident but one survey suggested that fewer than 50 per cent of large companies have a system to account for energy separately and fewer still actually recharge the costs to activity centres, preferring, for reasons of simplicity, to treat them as part of general overhead.[28]

Given the very wide range of accounting systems used in practice, there can be no hard and fast rules for accounting for energy but any system must have a substantial proportion of the elements shown in Figure 6.2. These elements not only start the process of collecting data upon which the control of energy costs can be based but also raise the profile of energy costs (at, for example, site, product or divisional level) in the minds of employees and management; and attempt to attribute the costs to those incurring them.[29]

---

[26] Although both Ciba–Geigy and Body Shop announced initiatives to encourage staff use of bicycles and public transport in, respectively, 1991 and 1992. Many local authorities in the UK have a policy of positively encouraging bicycle and public transport.

[27] For deeper discussion of these issues see Weizsäcker et al. (1997) and regular consultation of the Lester Brown *State of the World* series of books will provide a wider understanding of the issues at stake.

[28] See Bebbington et al. (1994), Bebbington and Gray (1996), Gray et al. (1998).

[29] As with the great majority of accounting initiatives, such suggestions work best when wedded to the management systems of the company – in this case such accounting for energy costs is best implemented within the organization's existing (and developing) environmental management system (see Chapter 5).

Figure 6.2

Initial steps in accounting for energy costs

- Codes within the chart of accounts for each source of fuel.
- Separate posting of energy invoices to accounts for oil (different sorts as appropriate), petroleum, diesel, electricity, mains gas, bottled gas, coal, etc.
- A means of assessing direct usage for recharging processes, through product costs, ABC (Activity Based Costing), site costs or whatever the organization's cost allocation basis is.
- A means of realistically allocating 'non-traceable' costs to the cause of their creation.
- The usual holding to account of activity (etc.) centre management.
- A means of presenting trends in the energy costs (see below) – this may need some re-creation from previous invoices.
- Separate identification of these energy costs within costs reports, budgets and other control and performance information.
- Some consideration of intra-organizational transfers of energy (e.g. recycled heat) and whether the effort in accounting for this and recharging it is beneficial (in environmental and/or financial terms) as a result of potential changes in behaviour.
- Cost summary and other reports should be able to identify major users of which fuels (this then becomes the target area for senior management and the investment programme).
- In so far as the accountants are involved in investment appraisal and capital budgeting some means must be established to ensure that energy investment is considered alongside other investment proposals.

This alone will not, however, lead to reduction in energy usage. Not only must there be mechanisms for ensuring that energy is actively controlled – through energy-related investments, through ensuring that energy costs form part of performance appraisal (see, for example, Chapter 8), etc. – but there must be a separate accounting for energy units as opposed to just the costs. For example, declines in energy costs may arise through changes in the nature of the business, through changes in processes and, most importantly, either through switching between fuels or reductions in per unit costs of energy. This could easily disguise a failure to increase actual energy efficiency. As with any useful costing system, the units must also be recorded so that energy targets and volume variances, for example, can be assessed. It is this combination of separate identification of fuels by both cost and units that has led to the successful control of energy by IBM, ICI, Carron Phoenix, Marks & Spencer, Tesco, Sainsbury, etc. Other companies have chosen to control only for financial or unit measurement. This is potentially dangerous. Accounting for only the financial implications does not place the organization in a position to forecast changes in fuel costs and assess their impact. Most enlightened organizations realize that energy costs will rise substantially, and that now is the time to reduce exposure by reducing usage. It is this that will, in the longer term, reduce costs consistently. Accounting only in units, whilst it may be better environmentally, rarely produces the hard cash motivators for control and does not necessarily lead to minimizing energy costs.

6.6   Accounting in Energy Units

One of the more enlightened (or crazy) ideas that emerged during the energy crisis of the 1970s was the proposal to use energy units as the basic mechanism for bookkeeping. Although the idea suffered from a number of weaknesses, it also had its advantages. The weaknesses derived from the lack of a relationship with cash in a world where financial control still predominates, and the focus upon only one element of an organization's environmental interaction. The benefit of the idea came principally from its identification of other forms of 'income', 'cost' and 'profit', ones any organization seriously intent on pursuing sustainability would recognize.

The essence of the notion was that all bookkeeping entries currently denoted in £ or $ or whatever could be redesignated in terms of the units of energy contained in their production. A complete accounting based on the idea has never been developed and some of the practical issues are certainly far from simple. But the notion of tracing energy inputs to various options is far from stupid and a shadow accounting system based on therms, BTUs, tonnes of coal equivalent or whatever could begin to inform policy-making. Banks (1977) gives a couple of examples:[30] in 1970 the automobile accounted for 21 per cent of the USA's total energy consumption; and a wooden frame house contains less than a third of the energy input necessary to produce a brick house of the same dimensions and energy efficiency.[31] Whilst market and financial logic has accepted these situations, an energy account of the two exposes the bizarre results of our taken-for-granted assumptions. Serious restructuring of energy prices, when (or if) it comes, should have the effect of reducing the disparity and encouraging the challenge of energy accounting to be taken up once again.

In addition to the potential benefits in terms of efficiency and forecasting ability that can arise from attempts to account in energy units, other real and pragmatic possibilities exist. For example, energy accounting can be a mechanism by which waste energy might be successfully tracked. One international chemical company has been

---

[30] Banks (1977). For more detail on these matters generally, see Dick-Larkham and Stonestreet (1977), Hewgill (1977, 1979) and Sellen (1980).

[31] It is not clear whether this allows for longevity and maintenance.

experimenting with this as part of its allocation of energy costs to activities. Identification of waste heat – from buildings, via smokestacks, in the waste water stream – has helped line management identify where 'their' energy costs are going and, given the high level of accountability, encouraged them to devise ways of minimizing the losses. Another possibility for accounting in energy units arose in a medium-sized extractive and building products company. Discussion on the desirability of measuring the environmental improvement arising from design and process changes led to the innovative use of 'energy units per cubic metre of buildings constructed' as an experimental performance measure. As energy was very closely correlated with the majority of the company's environmental impacts, this proved to be an especially helpful measure for which separate accounting was necessary. As with the experiments of the 1970s, we can realistically expect more imaginative developments in accounting for energy to emerge as the environmental crisis deepens.[32]

6.7 Some Issues for the Future

Energy, like most other matters relating to protection/destruction of the environment, is experiencing very rapid change. We are beginning to see more substantial experimentation with other forms of fuels including biomass, wind and solar power. This is no longer the province of specialist centres like the National Centre for Alternative Technology (see addresses in the appendix).[33] Although some countries have maintained their attachment to nuclear energy and have been slow in developing non-fossil fuels, the options available to organizations are slowly growing. The EU continues to encourage a degree of innovation in fuel usage and throughout Europe there is, at last, debate about placing restrictions upon the motor car, while in the USA companies as diverse as Xerox Corporation and CMS Energy are reported as experimenting with alternative fuels for motor vehicles.[34] No organization's energy policy is likely to remain untouched by these and the other changes in train.

Energy issues are also essential in the debates on recycling and life-cycle assessment (see Chapters 7 and 9) and the development of eco-labelling is bound to bring energy usage more to the fore of the political and business arenas. But nothing substantial will happen

[32] Readers wishing to develop these ideas are warmly encouraged to consult Odum (1996) as one of the more fully developed theses on these issues.

[33] The Body Shop has invested in wind farms in order to reduce its dependence on fossil and nuclear fuels (see, for example, Burritt and Lehman, 1995).

[34] *Business and the Environment*, May 1992, vol. 3, no. 5, p. 11.

until a more serious recognition of the issues encourages government action. Current institutional and fiscal arrangements encourage, rather than discourage, energy usage, negotiations between suppliers and users of energy have forced prices down, not up, and blanket policies on energy will hurt the poor more than the rich. To finish by putting the matter in some sort of context, Friends of the Earth remarks that the 1990 UK housing energy efficiency standards are approximately equal to those adopted in Sweden – in 1930! With a will, better information, a slightly more proactive government and, most significantly, a slightly longer-term attitude to investment payback (see Chapter 8), there are significant financial savings to be made that can only benefit our badly mauled physical environment.

Further Reading

General Introductions to the Issues

Brown, L.R. et al. (1998) *State of the World 1998* (London: Earthscan)
Elkington, J., P. Knight and J. Hailes (1991) *The Green Business Guide* (London: Gollancz)
Friends of the Earth (1990) *How Green Is Britain?* (London: Hutchinson Radius)
Weizsäcker, E. von, A.B. Lovins and L.H. Lovins (1997) *Factor Four* (London: Earthscan)

Energy, Business and Accounting

Burkitt, D. (1990) *The Costs to Industry of Adopting Environmentally Friendly Practices* (London: CIMA)
Chartered Association of Certified Accountants (in collaboration with Aspinwall and Company) (1997) *Guide to Environment and Energy Reporting and Accounting 1997* (London: ACCA)
Chartered Institute of Management Accountants (1982) *The Evaluation of Energy Use: Readings* (London: CIMA)
Odum, H.T. (1996) *Environmental Accounting: Energy and Environmental Decision Making* (New York: John Wiley)
Price Waterhouse (1991) *Energy: Containing the Costs* (London: Energy Efficiency Office)
Winter, G. (1988) *Business and the Environment* (Hamburg: McGraw-Hill)

Other Sources of Information and Assistance

The Business-in-the-Environment publications are especially valuable and (in the UK) the Association of Energy Conservation and the Energy Efficiency Office are helpful. The more obvious sources such as the CBI, the Environment Council and CEBIS all have information and guidance on the issues. (Addresses are given in the appendix.)

APPENDIX 6.1
CEBIS Environmental Checklist:
Energy Management

**ENVIRONMENTAL CHECKLIST
ENERGY MANAGEMENT**

QUESTIONS

- Has the potential for energy saving in the company been systematically evaluated?

- Have energy efficiency and conservation programmes been implemented?

- Has the potential for recovering energy from processes for re-use been evaluated?

ASSESSMENT

	A	B	C
Evaluation of potential for energy savings and implementation of action programme (ES)	No evaluation	No systematic evaluation	Systematic evaluation and energy efficiency programmes in place

If ES = A or B then action strongly recommended

ACTION MAY INCLUDE

- Undertaking an 'energy audit' to identify how much, how and where in the company energy is being used.
- Evaluating audit findings and drawing up an energy efficiency action plan.
- Implementing the action plan, starting with the zero and low cost energy saving options.
- Setting energy use targets and monitoring energy use to ensure that efficiency measures are being effectively implemented and to identify further opportunities for energy savings.

SOURCES OF INFORMATION AND ADVICE

- The Energy Efficiency Office provides expert advice. It also produces excellent guides on energy efficiency.

- CEBIS Fact Files and Helpline

APPENDIX 6.2
Energy Efficiency Office Scottish Checklist

HOW DOES YOUR FIRM MATCH UP?

Lowering energy cost is easy – if someone in the organization will face up to rising bills and the waste of resources.

Anyone can start by ticking the checklist and seeing how many 'No' answers appear.

Each 'No' can be changed to a 'Yes' with a call to the Energy Efficiency Office for some information and then a little effort to put ideas into practice.

	YES	NO
1. Is energy efficiency on the agenda of your next Board meeting?	☐	☐
2. Does the Board regularly see and review the energy figures?	☐	☐
3. Have you appointed an energy manager?	☐	☐
4. Is your energy manager in touch with the Energy Efficiency Office?	☐	☐
5. Have you carried out an energy survey?	☐	☐
6. Have you set up an energy efficiency programme?	☐	☐
7. Is it being implemented?	☐	☐
8. Have you instituted a 'good housekeeping' programme?	☐	☐
9. Have you installed a monitoring and targeting system?	☐	☐
10. Have you invested in either low or high cost efficiency measures?	☐	☐
11. Are you carrying out staff training in energy efficiency?	☐	☐
12. Do you have copies of EEO publications relevant to your energy use?	☐	☐
13. Do you read 'Energy Management'?	☐	☐

SCOTTISH ENERGY EFFICIENCY OFFICE

For free advice on the creation of your own energy efficiency
action plan, please contact us by letter, phone or fax.

We can help you to lower your fuel bills and reach higher profits
with a simple cost effective self-help programme.
Scottish Energy Efficiency Office
2nd Floor
Meridian Court
5 Cadogan St
Glasgow G2 6AT

CHAPTER 7

ACCOUNTING AND CONTROLLING FOR THE COSTS OF WASTE, PACKAGING AND RECYCLING

7.1 Introduction

The management and control of waste (together with packaging and recycling) form one of the two main areas (energy being the other) in which environmental and financial/economic considerations are often seen to be congruent. For this reason, it is one of the major areas in which corporate environmental initiatives have been undertaken. The financial benefits to be derived from an at least 'light green' management of waste can be immediate and obvious. This makes it an aspect of organization/environment interaction in which accountants can play – and are playing – a considerable role.

The concept of 'waste' has two, very distinct dimensions. We can think of these as 'wastefulness' and 'pollution'. The human/economic dimension (wastefulness) relates to using more than we need; the by-products of production; by-products in use; the disposal of the by-products; and what to do with the products when humans have stopped using them. The ecological dimension (which also includes mankind, of course) relates to the effect of this process on the capacity of the biosphere to continue functioning (pollution in its widest sense). There are intrinsic human/economic reasons for minimizing waste but these become critical when the biosphere can no longer handle the wastes we produce. This is what is now happening. The utopian dream of the greener industrialists consists of a 'closed loop' system in which *all* wastes (including all heat and emissions) are virtually eliminated and recycled back into an economic system which introduces 'new' material into the system only from truly sustainable and renewable sources. We are some considerable way from this (impossible?) dream at the moment, but it is this sort of thinking which largely underpins most approaches to waste minimization.

7.2 Some Aspects of the Wider Problem

Waste is a global problem – the OECD regularly publishes figures of the alarming rise in the annual per capita waste production of

Figure 7.1

The ubiquity of 'waste'

Waste is everywhere:

- vehicle emissions;
- heat escape and loss;
- air emissions and greenhouse gases;
- air emissions and acid rain;
- emissions and dumping in fresh water;
- dumping and emissions to the sea;
- industrial by-products;
- packaging;
- products at the end of their use;
- leakages to air, water and land;
- domestic refuse and sewage;
- abandoned and decommissioned plant and buildings.

Figure 7.2

Waste disposal in the news

Perhaps one of the prevailing images of the 1980s involved the wanderings of wastebearing vessels like the *Karin B.*, the *Deep Sea Carrier*, the *Zanoobia* and the *Khhain Sea* (the so-called 'leper of the oceans'), which travelled the globe looking for places to dispose of their waste and found that the world was no longer large enough or willing to accommodate them. Crises like these come and go but the core issues remain: how can the wastes generated by the world be dealt with in an environmentally sound manner – or, more pertinently, how can we avoid producing this mass of waste in the first place?

member countries. Not only do these many hundreds of annual per capita kilograms have to come from somewhere, they have to be disposed of – in the biosphere. And all sectors of society – agriculture, industry, households – are equally complicit in the waste problem.

Indeed the 'waste problem' is typically underestimated by us all. Weizsäcker et al. quote three, widely cited, conclusions:

> . . . 93% of materials that we buy and 'consume' never end up in saleable products at all. Moreover 80% of products are discarded after a single use . . . [and] 99% of the original materials used in the production of, or contained within, the goods made in the US become waste within 6 weeks of sale.
>
> (Weizsäcker et al., 1997, p. xx)

The 'waste problem' is thus a manufacturing, a consumption and a disposal problem.[1]

Although worldwide attempts to reach agreement on controlling the levels of wastes and associated pollution have not been especially successful, the institutional and regulatory framework of nations and trade groups is developing very rapidly. Such developments include, *inter alia*: increasing specification of what constitute 'controlled substances'; fuller guidance on their use and disposal; greater concern over the place and the medium of disposal; tightening regulation of emissions and discharges; increasing attention to the use of waste taxes to control disposal[2] and, of course, a steadily rising cost associated with all forms of waste. This has spread inexorably to controls over packaging and initiatives on recycling. These will be considered later in this chapter.

As one illustration of how the international community is addressing the issue of waste, the EU's strategy on waste management has three major strands that closely follow the principles of waste management at the corporate level.

(1) Prevention and minimization are to be encouraged throughout all processes. They are helped by eco-labelling, ISO 14001 and EMAS (see Chapter 5), and the increasing use of waste levies and taxes.

(2) Recycling and reuse: EU directives, especially regarding packaging and containers, are rapidly changing the economics of the different activities (but see below).

(3) Safety in disposal: this strand of EU policy has produced guidance on landfill, incineration and waste shipment as well as the civil liability for damage caused by waste.[3]

More clearly than for any other element of the organization's interaction with the environment, the 'terms of trade' on waste are undergoing significant change. Waste control and disposal costs are rising and show every sign of continuing to do so (see Figure 7.3). In addition to these direct cost changes, legislation will introduce a wider

---

[1] For an interesting analysis of UK waste see *Great Britain plc: The Environmental Balance Sheet* published by Biffa (the waste disposal company) in (for example) October 1997. This provides a myriad of data and details on UK consumption, waste disposal and related matters.

[2] See, for example, Chapter 15 of O'Riordan (1997) for more detail.

[3] For more detail on the legal aspects see, for example, Ball and Bell (1991), reports from ENDS and the publications from, for example, the Institute of Environmental Management/CEBIS and the Environment Council, which all carry regular updates.

Figure 7.3

Some upward pressures on waste disposal costs

1. **The sheer volume of waste generated:** This must put pressure on disposal facilities, thereby forcing up costs.

2. **Reduction in waste disposal facilities:** Includes less available local landfill sites, increased control over the sites; control over incineration and incineration plants; greater restriction over exporting wastes to other, often Third World, countries.

3. **Rising awareness of consequences:** Even domestic and other non-toxic waste is now recognized as a potential hazard.

4. **Increased transportation costs:** These reflect, *inter alia*, increased control of transport quality on land and sea.

5. **Insurance costs:** Throughout the whole waste chain, and especially transportation.

6. **Problems of safety in disposal:** Particularly of increasingly toxic wastes and especially when mixed with other wastes to produce a 'cocktail' of unknown potency or effect.

7. **Increasing 'waste aftercare':** Needs to be incorporated into waste disposal methods and therefore waste disposal costs.

8. **Increased legal costs:** Especially associated with the waste disposal organizations, these have also helped to drive up waste disposal costs.

9. **Increased taxes and levies:** By, for example, taxation on the disposal of waste, governments can encourage companies to seek economically attractive means of reducing that waste (see later).

10. **Increased raw material and energy costs:** With increased costs attached to – or increased financial incentives to reduce – the inputs to industrial and commercial processes, the 'natural' motivation of organizations to reduce costs is, it is hoped, brought into play on waste and resource minimization – often referred to as '*dematerialization*'.

---

range of penalties for infringements of waste regulations and alterations in the taxation regime are beginning to provide corporations with a steadily changing and increasing cost structure.[4]

Furthermore, as environmental issues have an impact on earlier stages in one's production chain, inputs to the organization will become progressively more expensive – as a result of which all wastage will cost more. Increased water charges – especially given water's role in much waste disposal – are a particularly good example here.[5] Finally, experience in Europe suggests that corporations that are not in

[4] See, also, for example, *Financial Times*, 26 November 1991, *ENDS Report* 202/November 1991, Porritt (1990), Smith (1991), Tinker (1985).

[5] See, for example, Litterick (1991).

the vanguard of environmentally driven developments on waste, packaging and recycling risk finding that entire national and international markets are closed to them. Such implications have the most considerable financial consequences of course.

In this chapter we must recognize that 'waste' and 'packaging' and 'recycling' are largely inseparable and little will be gained from distinguishing them. A number of issues specific to recycling and packaging do arise, however, and these will be picked up later.

7.3   Corporate Waste Management

What we refer to as waste (whether wastefulness or pollution) arises throughout the whole production and distribution process as well as in the use of product itself (see Figure 7.5 below). The essential aim, from an environmental point of view, is to *minimize* resources throughout that process. This minimization of resource use, and waste in particular, will be in keeping with the economic aims of the business – but only to a point. A considerable amount of 'waste' can be represented by the products themselves and this raises a fundamental problem for all businesses where *maximization* of throughput is the more usual goal.[6] Within the current constraints in which businesses operate, the 'light green' response is the only one that many organizations can see as 'realistic'.

Most companies that have carefully addressed the issue of waste – throughout all aspects of their operations – have found significant financial savings. There are many immediate, economic reasons (shown in Figure 7.4) for seeking these savings. The process will most typically begin as part of the general environmental review (see Chapter 5) and then progress to a specific waste audit. Figure 7.6 provides a broad guide to waste management by means of the oft-quoted 'hierarchy of waste management',[7] while Figure 7.7 is an

---

[6] This is a major stumbling block in the environmental-business debate. The evidence strongly suggests that Western individuals must make and use *less* whilst corporate success normally depends on the production and use of *more*. It is an aspect that clearly distinguishes the 'light' and 'deep' green perspectives. This is not, however, a problem that corporations can solve – even if they wish to – without some profound change in the financial, economic, social and ethical framework within which they operate. (See Chapters 14 and 15.)

[7] This is also reproduced in Chapter 10 of O'Riordan (1997) from where further information can be drawn. Examples of innovative use of wastes abound. For example, within the cement industry proposals exist to burn waste in their kilns to reduce energy bills (*ENDS Report* 200/September 1991, pp. 11–23) and Shanks and McEwan are using methane gas produced by landfill sites to generate electricity (*Financial Times*, 26 November 1991).

Figure 7.4

Why minimize waste?

Reduce
- production costs
- on-site waste monitoring and treatment costs
- handling, transport and off-site disposal costs
- raw material costs
- energy and water costs
- long-term environmental liability and insurance costs
- the risks of spills and accidents

and improve
- income through the sale of reusable waste
- overall operating efficiency
- the safety of employees
- the company's image in the eyes of the shareholders, employees and the community

Source: DTI (1990)

Figure 7.5

Some elements in the process of waste production

Quality of input
- appropriate specifications
- technical quality
- packaging of delivery
- JIT considerations
- quality decay

Quality of processing
- efficiency of conversion
- hazards in use
- heat, noise, emissions and discharges from the process
- wastage and quality failures from the process
- waste/by-products generated

Quality of output
- how important is the product?
- reliability and quality in use; length of life
- repairability
- disposability
- transport and packaging to user

Figure 7.6

> #### Hierarchy of waste management
>
> *1. Reduction:* reduction in the production of waste to the minimum consistent with economic sustainability. Prevention and minimization of wastes through use of cleaner technology, product and process redesign and better management techniques.
>
> *2. Reuse:* ensuring that materials and material objects are placed back into use.
>
> *3. Recovery:* where waste must be produced – extract from that waste all (economically) viable elements for further use through (e.g.) recycling, composting and energy production.
>
> *4. Disposal:* last resort for waste disposal but it must be carried out in an environmentally sound manner.
>
> *Source:* Adapted from Department of the Environment (1995), Elkington, Knight and Hailes (1991) and KPMG Management Consulting *Environmental Briefing Note*, no. 7/ Spring 1991

example of the sort of checklist with which any organization would begin this process.[8]

Anecdotes of corporate financial savings abound. Widely publicized experiences such as 3M's 3Ps (Pollution Prevention Pays) initiative and the Dow Chemicals WRAP (Waste Reduction Always Pays) project, whilst among the best-known and best-developed programmes, are no longer the rarity they were. The key to all or many of these programmes, though, has been that they have been tied both to a TQM culture *and* directly to the financial systems of the organization. And this has been helped by initiatives like *Duty of Care,*[9] the Chemical Industry Association's *'product stewardship'*[10] and the slowly increasing market opportunities that have arisen for the retreatment, recycling and more professional disposal of wastes. On top of which, organizations seeking either (or both of) market advantage or a more responsible attitude to their waste have undertaken original initiatives which provide some indication for the future: cooperative multi-business ventures; labelling parts in manufacture for safe disposal (and for recycling; see below); company/local authority liaisons; imaginative

---

[8] Many other examples and sources of help exist. See, for example, BiE (1991a). Appendix 7.1 also contains a checklist from CEBIS.

[9] The essence of the Duty of Care provisions is that the waste *producer* is responsible for ensuring that all waste generated is responsibly handled. This, in practice, means that the waste producer must vet and cooperate closely with the organization which will dispose, re-treat or recycle that waste. For more detail on the early stages of this in the UK, see, for example, *ENDS Report* 204/January 1992 (pp. 29–30) and Irvine (1991).

[10] See, for example, Elkington et al. (1991, ch. 7).

Figure 7.7

> **When is waste not waste?**
>
> There are a number of incidents which have reinforced the ecologists' recognition that the 'natural' state of the biosphere is unknowable and somewhat academic. Pilkington, for example, faced a fascinating and widely publicized conundrum. Keen to get rid of its waste spoil heaps for a variety of business, legal and aesthetic reasons it ran into opposition from environmentalists! The spoil heaps over time had developed a local ecology which now supported a number of species of wild orchid. What was originally 'waste' had now become part of the 'biosphere'. Conundrums of this sort are more and more frequent.

---

introduction of a nominal fee which is charged to customers to highlight the costs of disposing of unwanted or worn-out products; and so on.[11]

7.4　Accounting for Waste

There would appear to be three main ways in which organizations are accounting (in the widest sense) for waste.

The first, simplest approach recognizes the total actual and potential costs of waste management borne by the company, identifies these on a company-wide, activity or site basis, and adjusts policy accordingly. A large number of companies have followed this route – including those to whom environmental issues are a matter of complete indifference but for whom tight cost control is a central element of the organizational culture.

The second approach employs non-financial accounting as its driver and establishes a recording and communicating information system that captures physical quantities of waste. IBM's system of logging gross tonnage of waste into and out of sites and holding site management accountable for its control and reduction is of this sort. (And, of course, these two approaches are not incompatible. Waste management recommendations to companies will frequently suggest that they be used together.)

The third approach is normally the most sophisticated and the most directly related to conventional accounting. It can be best illustrated by example – here taken from the experiences of the chemical companies Rhône-Poulenc and Monsanto.

---

[11] For detail on some of these, the usual sources are recommended (see Further Reading), plus see also, for example, Coopers & Lybrand Deloitte, *Industry Briefing*, February (1992) and Hoggart (1992).

Figure 7.8

Waste management checklist

Initial review
- Inventory of wastes generated to establish baseline information (environmental review/audit).
- Sources, quantities. physical and chemical characteristics of wastes identified (see duty of care requirements).

Management responsibilities
- Establish a policy regarding waste disposal.
- Ensure a director or senior manager is responsible for wastes.
- Allocate responsibility for wastes and packaging to the appropriate level of management.

Waste minimization
- Waste considerations designed into products at the development stage.
- Separation and treatment of wastes at the source of production.
- Reuse or recycling of wastes within production process or elsewhere inside and outside the organization.
- Consideration of the environmental impact of packaging.
- Consideration of the post-consumer environmental impact of the product – that is, possibilities of taking back and recycling a product's components.

Waste management on site
- Site survey identifying inefficiencies and hazards.
- Review practice to ensure standards and practice established in policy are maintained.
- Ensure reporting procedures are adequate to monitor compliance with legal standards and policy.
- Keep appropriate records.
- Ensure safe storage of wastes on site where necessary.
- Develop emergency contingency plans where relevant, test and review these regularly.
- Ensure appropriate insurance cover obtained.

Reporting
- Internal reporting to ensure policy achieved.
- Internal reporting for performance appraisal purposes.
- External reporting of policy and performance.

Source: Adapted from *Managing Waste: Guidelines for Business* (London: CBI, 1992a)

Rhône-Poulenc is widely known for its Environmental Index (see Chapter 5), which was originally devised to monitor water quality coming off sites and later extended to all forms of waste.[12] From this, the company devised a comprehensive waste accounting system which charged all waste management costs (costs arising from disposal, insurance, gaining consents, emergency procedures, spillages,

---

[12] Closely related to the CIA's initiative in this regard.

etc.) back to line management.[13] In effect, the 'Polluter Pays Principle' was operated for each and every facility – R&D and service units included. The motivational effects were clear: line management were recognizing the 'externalities' of their activities imposed on the rest of the company, would seek to reduce it, *and*, being 'on the spot', could often devise cost-effective ways of simply reducing those costs. (Footnote 14 provides a particularly graphic example of this.)[14]

Other companies have gone a stage further. Monsanto, for example, imposed an 'internal tax' on all internally generated waste, thereby doubly penalizing – and doubly motivating – management responsible for waste production.[15]

These examples of the accounting system providing important data on environmentally related activities are mirrored in many organizations. In one medium-sized manufacturing company this had been achieved without any awareness of it as an environmental issue at all. All management were appraised on purely financial terms but the director responsible for environmental and safety issues had *carte blanche* from the board in his duties. (Again, this was principally for financial reasons based on the belief that falling foul of the regulators, the local community or the employees was simply bad, as well as unethical, business.) All identifiable costs were automatically charged back through the accounting system, whose primary goal was to allocate as high a proportion of organizational costs as possible. This was reinforced by the environmental and safety director's practice of demanding that spills, leakages, discharges and any waste materials on site were dealt with immediately by the responsible management. This might include the requirement that a process be closed down for a day or so while the problem was solved – with the obvious impact on the manager's financial performance. This led, interestingly, to very high pressure from line management to ensure that investment decisions were based on the highest health and safety standards and environmental considerations (see Chapter 8).

These illustrations are ideal examples of the way the accounting system, operating in conventional ways, can realistically contribute to the environmental sensitivity of the organization. (That the majority of

---

[13] In this the company was leaning towards the principles of ABC in its management of environmental issues. More detailed illustration, especially of the AT&T experience in this area, can be found in Ditz et al. (1995)

[14] One simple example saved a great deal of money. Waste water leaving a site was a cocktail of many chemicals. The presence of traces of certain controlled substances in the water meant that *all* the water had to be specially treated. The waste accounting system encouraged the manager to identify the point at which the traces joined the water stream and separate them out before they joined. The water then became simply 'grey water' and the volume of controlled substances needing treatment was infinitesimal compared to the total water volume. Simple, obvious and effective.

[15] See, for example, *ENDS Report* 189/October 1990, pp. 14–18.

Figure 7.9

Some steps in accounting for waste

- Separate all waste management and disposal costs to identifiable cost headings.
- Expand the obvious to take account of other waste-related matters – e.g. spillages, emergency and contingency facilities, insurance, etc.
- Develop a non-financial accounting system that tracks all wastes on to and off the sites.
- Relate the costs to the organization's waste tracking and identification system.
- Take advice from the facilities, waste or environmental director and charge back the cost to the process creating the waste.
- Develop ABC thinking if not a system, to refine and develop this process.
- Introduce these items to the lines of the budget-centre budgets.
- Recognize the strategic and investment implications (see Chapter 8).
- Consider an internal taxation of waste.
- Ensure that the performance appraisal and reward system recognizes these matters.
- Ensure that all forecasts take special notice of the rapidly changing 'terms of trade' on waste.

---

accountants – even in very large companies – are not developing the appropriate accounting systems to account for waste is disturbing).[16] But the accountant's role need not stop here. As we shall see, awareness of these matters can compel investment decisions to take account of waste in a way that may conflict with conventional investment appraisal criteria (see Chapter 8). The accountant's desire to minimize costs must not blind him or her to the fact that the waste *quantity* and the effects of that waste also need to be minimized (as we saw with energy, in Chapter 6). This needs both quantity and financial units to be accounted for. And last, but by no means least, minimizing total resource use – not just that which is identified as waste – is an almost inevitable consequence of environmental concerns which accountants, along with business management, will have to learn. It will be a painful lesson, going against the ingrained instincts that led to success in the 'pre-environmental' era. Figure 7.9 lists some steps to be taken.

7.5 Packaging

Most of what we have said above can apply equally to the specific issue of packaging. However, a number of particular developments make elements of packaging something of a special case. Packaging

---

[16] See, for example, Bebbington et al. (1994), Guilding and Kirman (1998).

has been an especially high-profile target for many consumer groups – not least because the majority of packing is single-trip and so visibly useless at the end of the trip. For the company the purposes of packaging are clear: protection in transport, stacking, enhancement of shelf-life, display, marketing and a means of communication with the purchaser. And as companies which have seriously tried to design a minimal packaging – such as Crighton's exploration of toothpaste containers – have discovered, the matter is far from simple. At the other end of the spectrum, however, Microsoft's experience in the early 1990s of being ridiculed over the ludicrous redundancy built into its packaging has spread ripples through the computer software industry and is an experience which is becoming increasingly common for companies generally.[17]

Experience suggests that significant savings – both financial and environmental – can be made from careful examination of packaging. The Business-in-the-Environment initiative helped Start-Rite to save 6.5 per cent of its packaging costs; Pilkington has saved through redesigning the way glass is transported, IBM's monitoring of incoming packaging led to productive discussions with suppliers and Bennnett and James (1998b) provide detailed reports on how Xerox and Baxter International have set about making major savings on their packaging costs.[18] As Marks & Spencer notes: 'we can no longer think of packaging as "rubbish" – our initiatives show how you can turn waste into valuable raw materials saving both money and our precious environment'.[19]

The attempts by industry to devise voluntary initiatives[20] are being rapidly overtaken by legislation, with an increasing number of countries recognizing the impact of packaging and beginning the process of developing and imposing increasingly high standards on the use and treatment of packaging materials. This trend is particularly noticeable in the EU, where initiatives on packaging have long been prominent on the political agenda.

[17] Reported in *Computer Weekly*, Thursday, 11 June 1992, p. 1.

[18] Chapters 15 and 18 of Bennett and James (1998b) are especially instructive on how two major companies have set about re-thinking their whole packaging strategy within a wider EMS framework.

[19] Manager Jack Levene, quoted in 'Waste not, want not', *M&S Magazine*, 1991, p. 47.

[20] Although there has long been scepticism about such voluntary initiatives having the necessary impact or being widely adopted. One example of this is illustrated by the Friends of the Earth report that proposals to the UK government from the packaging industry body, INCPEN, are indicative of a failure of industry to address the central issues and produce a hard commitment to reduce significantly the waste associated with packaging (*Earth Matters*, Summer 1992, p. 3).

Given the (apparent) determination of the EU and national governments in the control of packaging it might be that very little accounting for packaging is necessary. That is, organizations are having to reduce their packaging or face a major proportion of their markets being closed to them. Relatively minor details like the cost of packaging might seem to be irrelevant in those circumstances. That would, however, be a short-sighted attitide. We have already seen that adjustment to increasing environmental demands – as with other changes in a business environment – are best dealt with on a systematic and strategic basis. In this light the relatively low numbers of accountants with large firms who are involved with and/or helping devise packaging strategies and systems for accounting for packaging and returnable containers are, once again, a cause for concern.[21]

Redesigning of packaging, transport systems and the products themselves to take account of stricter legislative regimes will be very costly. Furthermore, product costing will have to recognize the extra costs involved in making, recovering and reusing the packaging. This will lead to increased use of returnable containers, which, for many, will bring back the long-forgotten skill of accounting for them. The obverse of this scenario is also of interest to accountants – can one's organization accept goods that are not packaged adequately? Will there be a market in trade discounts if you accept the packaging? It seems to be the case that any company that is responding sensibly to these developments is well down the line on redesigning and rethinking its packaging strategy. The accountant's potential contribution here is most significant, as without careful budgeting of *all* costs associated with a changing packaging regime, the organization could be unnecessarily exposed. Done properly, however, the intelligent reduction, reuse and recycling of packaging should have very real environmental benefits and, in many cases, offer significant financial gains as well. Once again, we, as accountants, have a duty to help our organizations exploit all the win–win opportunities that eco-efficiency can offer.

7.6 Recycling and Reuse

Despite the publicly expressed enthusiasm for recycling, it can be only a 'light green' response to the environmental crisis. Recycling is not a self-contained activity (it requires further energy and/or raw material

---

[21] Bebbington et al. (1994), Guilding and Kirman (1998).

Figure 7.10

Low- and non-waste technology options	
Waste/Material	*Disposition*
Chemicals and toxic metals	Reclaim, recycle, degrade, dispose
Oily wastes	Collect, recycle, dispose
Construction materials	Reclaim, reuse, reduce bulk
Domestic wastes	Biomass, fuel/CHP, reduce bulk
Paper, glass and plastics	Collect, recycle
Source: Simpson (1990, p. 83)	

input) and it is not the first resource-saving option (refusing to consume, reducing consumption and reusing resources all rank above recycling).[22]

Recycling comes in a number of forms, of varying complexity (Figure 7.11) and raises its own individual new problems for industry to face.

A number of the industry-led initiatives have been widely publicized: the collection of old computers for recovery of precious metals and components, and the car industry initiatives to take back old vehicles for recovery of materials, for example, are not only reducing demands for virgin material but forcing companies to 'design for disassembly'. In the words of one major manufacturer:

> *The recycling of . . . [product] is profitable and is encouraging designers to think about designing for recycling. For example, plastics used to have sticky labels on them but this gave problems when recycling with regard to removing the label and glue and the contamination this caused of the plastic. Now the information previously in a label is stamped on the plastic along with detailed information concerning the composition of the plastic.*

While recycling is widely recognized as 'environmentally desirable', the proportion of wastes which are recycled remains small. One major reason for this is the low prices received for recyclable materials – forced ever lower by increased demand for recycling facilities. Although aluminium recycling is profitable, for example, the margins on other materials make them a currently unattractive

---

[22] It is crucial to note that 'refuse' – although clearly the most desirable environmental option – is not one that Western society is much attuned to and one that would challenge one of the very central principles of capitalist companies – that of growth. It is always important to remember that there are many points at which current business orthodoxy (and society norms) are at variance with environmental protection.

Figure 7.11

The variety of recycling

It is useful to distinguish three levels of recycling.

(1) *'Original recycling'*: Recycling to the same quality as the virgin material, and reuse of the recycled material in the same manner as before. This is the most preferred option as only the energy taken to recycle the material is consumed. The success of this relies on energy being cheap enough to allow recycling. Aluminium is a good example of this – Norsk Hydro notes that recycling requires only 5% of the energy needed to produce the virgin aluminium from ore.

(2) *Recycling and reuse of material at a lower purity than originally*: Less preferred because extraction or production of the virgin material is still required. Further, it is less likely to be profitable, and therefore less likely to occur because the resale value at the lower level usage is likely to be minimal. This occurs where plastic bottles are recycled into carpet pile, plastic cups into coat hangers and other non-food contact applications, organic waste into compost, etc.

(3) *Recycle material into a form suitable for use as a fuel*: The least preferred option but does have the advantage of reducing the amount of waste going into landfill and may be beneficial if energy is recovered from the process.

The complexity of the recycling task also varies, from recycling offcuts of raw materials to recycling components from complete items such as electronic equipment or motor vehicles or separating recyclable items from a mix of non-recyclable items.

Figure 7.12

Typical energy savings in production from recycling

(As a percentage of energy for production from virgin raw material)

Aluminium: 95%
Steel tinplate: 74%
Paper and board: 40%
Glass: 20%

NB   These savings do not include consumer transport energy and this will diminish, if not eliminate, the savings.

Source: The WARM Report, p. 26.

---

investment.[23] Indeed, the WARM Report claims, against the predominant deregulation trend of recent years, that:

[23] See, for example, Landbank (1992). It may well be that the raw materials prices of a number of these materials do not reflect their full environmental cost: for example, the prices for paper and board are unlikely always to include the cost of replanting and managing forests; likewise, the cost of metals is unlikely always to incorporate the cost of remediation of resource extraction sites. It is therefore unlikely that current cost and price mechanisms will reflect a preference for recycling.

> *Market forces are inadequate to deal with such pressures, since a value is being placed by society on the recovered materials which cannot be justified solely (or, in some cases, at all) in commercial terms. [It is therefore necessary] to remove the element of competition from recycling . . . these recycling targets will be achieved in the most cost-effective way by cooperation rather than competition. Cooperation makes even more sense in environmental terms, by conserving resources and reducing the energy expended in collecting and sorting waste materials.*

Although voluntary (or at least, semi-voluntary) initiatives from industry are making some progress, it certainly looks as though, if the necessary targets for recycling and reuse are to be met, intervention in 'the marketplace' is necessary (see Figure 7.13). In the present situation, it will fall to accountants to seek out economic recycling and reuse options and to assess corporations' current recycling efforts financially.

Ways in which the accountant can positively contribute on the recycling front are shown in Figure 7.14.

However, it seems most likely that the range of *conventional* options that a successful organization can consider will close down somewhat as recycling begins to bite, but *imaginative* solutions and options will give the commercial advantage. The accountant's expertise will be essential here – not simply to avoid a reactionary accountant preventing imaginative options but also in thinking creatively about the financial implications of different options. Of particular importance

Figure 7.13

Incentives to increase recycling to meet existing and future targets

(1) Education.
(2) Advertising.

or the use of economic incentives:

(3) Levy on virgin materials: sufficient to fund the costs of recycling – the consumer pays for the imputed environmental cost of the product as the levy would be included in the product's price.
(4) A deposit system: on, for example, refillable containers thereby providing the consumer with an incentive to return items.
(5) Tax relief: on borrowings for investment in recycling technology is also a possibility.
(6) Grants to aid investment.
(7) Stimulate demand for recycled products: for example, subsidies may ensure that recycled materials are cheaper than virgin products, rather like the cost differentials that presently exist between leaded and lead-free petrol.
(8) Recycling credit system: such a system has been introduced in the UK. (This mechanism is dealt with below as it arises within the context of domestic waste and local authorities.)

Figure 7.14

Some possible roles for the accountant in an organization's recycling strategy

(1) Incorporating recycling costs into product cost (especially where recycling is mandatory). This requires identification of who is to bear the costs of recycling and determination of the effect of any fiscal measures on product costs. Such information would be necessary for the recycling levy proposal. Accountants would determine likely future collection and recycling costs, the volume likely to be recycled and therefore the amount of the levy needed.

(2) Separate identification of the costs and revenues arising from recycling activities is necessary to enable the assessment of the feasibility of recycling including product design for recycling.

(3) Establishing the cost of incorporating recycled materials into the manufacturing process. (For example, Procter and Gamble has reduced the environmental impact of its packaging by incorporating recycled plastic. This also expands the market for recycled plastic.)

(4) Preparation of budgets and performance appraisal that include recycling targets, quantified in both financial and non-financial terms.

(5) The viability of recycling plans and investment in recycling technologies and the related investment appraisal. Hurdle rates of return may require modification to ensure recycling targets can be met.

---

in this area is the experience of local government which, in most instances, shares the 'waste problem' with industry and has a strong incentive to develop new means of cooperation with private sector organizations.

7.7 Domestic Waste, Local Authorities and Other Operators

Households are also major producers of waste[24] which must be handled, typically by, or through, a local government organization where an increasing emphasis is being placed on recycling. This need not be the case though. Not only can local authorities take a positive role in encouraging waste minimization and reuse but a more imaginative planning and financial regime can open up more productive options. Thus, for example, our own calculations for one local authority suggested that it could, economically, buy a composting system for every household with a garden. The reduction in the waste stream could be as high as 28 per cent (although it is most unlikely to meet this), and this reduces, among other costs, vehicle and incinerator repair. A major, and well-publicized, variation on this

---

[24] And, as the ultimate consumers of most products, might be thought of as the primary producers of waste.

Figure 7.15

An outline of recycling credits
A system of recycling credits (adopted in the UK and elsewhere) is one that provides economic incentives to ensure that components of the waste stream are recycled that otherwise would not be. The idea behind this system is that anyone removing material from the waste stream should receive the sum of money that the local authority otherwise would have had to spend to collect and dispose of it. This requires the costs of waste disposal to be calculated on both a short- and long-term basis.

theme – the Ontario blue box scheme – has produced some interesting economics.[25] There is considerable opportunity for imaginative financial examination and scenario planning in this context.

Certainly local authorities face a number of difficult logistical decisions that have financial implications for which are needed accurate costings of existing and proposed collection methods; recycling options; sorting and cleaning (decontamination) of the waste stream; final disposal options; recycling levies and recycling credits (see Figure 7.15) and other incentives.[26] On top of which, some countries, like the UK, have introduced a 'landfill tax' which adds to the cost of all materials disposed to landfill. By increasing the costs of such disposal, there is a disincentive to dispose of waste and, equally, an economic incentive to both reduce waste streams and find other means of resuse. This is just one example of how the fiscal system will be used to an increasing degree to encourage the 'internalization' of external environmental costs.

Whilst colleagues in industry worry about the costs of getting waste safely (and cheaply) off-site, the local authorities share with other (private) disposal site operators the concerns of managing and maintaining disposal facilities. Indeed, how should one account for landfill restoration and aftercare costs? Problems include the build up, migration and in some cases ignition of landfill gas; leaching into ground and surface water; and other (increasingly numerous) occurrences which can be considered life- and health-threatening. These concerns (combined with national provisions in environmental legislation) result in potential, significant liabilities which may well give rise to future costs.[27]

---

[25] See, for example, Laughlin and Varangu (1991).
[26] One early market research report by Mintel found that most consumers are willing to recycle but are restricted by lack of facilities to store recyclables in their homes, or access to recycling points due to either insufficient points nearby or lack of transport to get to the designated recycling points. See *ENDS Report* 204/January 1992, p. 12.
[27] This matter of provisions and liabilities is touched upon in Chapter 11.

Future costs that may be incurred include:

- monitoring costs necessary to identify any problems;
- remedial costs for damage already done;
- costs to prevent damage from existing and potential problems;
- litigation costs that may arise within this context.

Identifying future liabilities involves looking forward and backwards over many years. For example, in one landfill, currently undergoing remedial work, domestic waste had been accepted since 1963 and studies of the likely future effects estimate that maximum concentrations of leachate were expected in 2001.[28]

Options to finance these future costs include:

(1) Taking out insurance cover (this is unlikely to be viable).
(2) Individual operators providing for costs by setting aside funds as waste is being placed in landfill. Responsibility for aftercare then rests with the individual operator.
(3) Formation of a government-sponsored aftercare fund financed by a waste disposal levy on all operators. In this case final responsibility for sites would be transferred to government. Regardless of how such a scheme would be funded, accounting issues would be raised concerning:
   (a) the existence and valuation of contingent liabilities for restoration and aftercare costs;
   (b) the valuation of waste disposal sites currently held – which would need to be revised in the light of these additional potential costs; and
   (c) the appropriate treatment of providing for costs in terms of the effect on the income statement.

There would be concerns in industry and at the government level if profitability in the waste disposal industry were to fall dramatically or if the local authorities were unable to maintain standards through exceptional pressures on costs. Waste management and recycling goals probably require the stable provision of waste treatment and disposal facilities.

7.8 Conclusions

In a literal sense, the management of waste, packaging and recycling should automatically follow from good environmental management

---

[28] See *ENDS Report* 205/February 1991, p. 11.

linked with an active and sensible approach to the management of the business. However, experience suggests that careful management of waste does not follow so naturally, and certainly the speed of change in the regulation and the economics of waste, packaging and recycling means that no organization can afford to ignore it. The need for responsive accounting and financial information systems is just as important in this area as any other – and the ways in which the accountant can become involved are rather more obvious than in most other areas (with the probable exception of energy). But the level of accounting involvement in this area is still remarkably low, which helps neither the business nor the environment.

Further Reading

Bennett, M. and P. James (eds) (1998b) *The Green Bottom Line: Environmental Accounting for Management* (Sheffield: Greenleaf)

Biffa (1997) *Great Britain plc: The Environmental Balance Sheet* (High Wycombe, Bucks: Biffa Waste Services plc)

CEFIC (European Chemical Industry Federation) (1990) *Guidelines on Waste Minimisation* (Paris: CEFIC)

Department of the Environment (1991c) *Waste Management – The Duty of Care: A Code of Practice* (London: DoE)

Department of Trade and Industry (1990) *Cutting Your Losses: A Business Guide to Waste Minimization* (London: Business and the Environment Initiative, DTI)

Ditz, D., J. Ranganathan and R.D. Banks (1995) *Green Ledgers: Case Studies in Environmental Accounting* (Baltimore, MD: World Resources Institute)

Duncan, O. and I. Thomson (1998) 'Waste accounting and cleaner technology: A complex evaluation', *APIRA 98 in Osaka: Proceedings Volume II* (Osaka: Osaka City University), pp. 648–656

The WARM System: A Proposal for a Model Waste Recovery and Recycling System for Britain. A Gateway Foodmarkets Report prepared by The Landbank Consultancy, 1992.

Weizsäcker, E. von, A.B. Lovins and L.H. Lovins (1997) *Factor Four: Doubling Wealth, Halving Resource Use* (London: Earthscan)

Winter, G. (1988) *Business and the Environment* (Hamburg: McGraw-Hill)

. . . and particularly on taxation issues:

O'Riordan, T. (ed.) (1997) *Ecotaxation* (London: Earthscan)

Environmental Taxation and Accounting (a journal published by Cameron May, London)

APPENDIX 7.1
CEBIS Environmental Checklist:
Waste Management

**ENVIRONMENTAL CHECKLIST
WASTE MANAGEMENT**

QUESTIONS

- Does your company keep a waste inventory and if not, how are the types and quantities of wastes you produce monitored?

- Have you checked whether you produce any special waste, and if so, do you know what action is required to ensure its safe disposal?

- Are you complying with the Environmental Protection Act's Duty of Care?

- Have staff been allocated clearly defined duties and are they adequately trained?

- Does the company have procedures to deal with accidental spillage of waste?

ASSESSMENT

	A	B	C
Waste Inventory (WI)	Little systematic evaluation of waste arisings	Informal evaluation of waste arisings	Detailed inventory of waste arisings
Waste Storage/Handling (WS)	No formal system in place	Informal system in place	Formal system with responsibility allocated to properly informed staff
Waste Disposal (WD)	No monitoring of waste disposal route	Monitoring not systematic	Full evaluation of compliance with Duty of Care

If WI, WS or WD = A or B then corrective action necessary and urgent

ACTION MAY INCLUDE

- Auditing all waste arisings and establishing a waste inventory.
- Checking if any special waste is produced and how it should be managed.
- Auditing waste management practices and establishing "best practice" systems for waste handling and storage.
- Defining clear responsibilities and training amongst staff.
- Checking compliance with the Duty of Care
- Setting up emergency procedures to deal with accidents or spillages.

SOURCES OF INFORMATION AND ADVICE

- CEBIS Fact Files and Helpline
- 'Control of Pollution (Special Wastes) Regulations 1980 '(available from HMSO)
- 'The Duty of Care: A Code of Practice '(available from HMSO)
- Waste Management Papers (available from HMSO)
- District Council and/or Hazardous Waste Inspectorate Scotland

CHAPTER 8

INVESTMENT, BUDGETING AND APPRAISAL

Environment at the Heart of the Accounting and Financial Systems

8.1 Introduction

Accounting and financial systems are crucial to the operations of all organizations. They provide records of what has been done and measures of the success or failure of past activities; they provide the constraints on actions and estimates of, and constraints on, resources necessary for the actions; they supply targets and measure and reward performance against those targets, and provide a substantial part of the analytical framework within which new activities are assessed and planned.[1] Whilst it is overstating the case to say that accounting and financial systems are *the* most important information and control systems of an organization, certainly few organizational activities can take place without involving accounting and finance.

We have discussed the ways in which accounting and environment can be in fundamental conflict. It follows that unless environmental considerations are embedded into the core functions of the accounting and financial systems, those functions will not only be unsupportive of organizational change towards a 'greener' orientation, but actually prevent it. This is the position the more 'environmentally advanced' organizations have now reached. Having put environmental policy in place, designed and implemented an environmental management system (including environmental review/audit), undertaken training, become involved with the green agenda and taken imaginative steps in matters such as wastes, emissions, transport, packaging and energy control, they are facing the central problem of how to ensure that environmental considerations are central to the organization's every

---

[1] It is worth just remembering that this dominance of the accounting system in organizations is not without its problems. It depends on one's point of view, but it certainly seems to be the case that an organization driven by reference to an accounting system that cannot recognize social or environmental issues is very unlikely to encourage that organization to take serious account of such matters. A critical understanding of accounting systems and their implications is, surely, something that any professional accountant or serious student of accounting should seek and embrace.

activity. An essential prerequisite for this is 'greener' management accounting and control systems.

But this is where the problems begin. Although the issue is clearly crucial, companies (or is it the accountants?) have demonstrated limited enthusiasm about incorporating environmental factors into the financial systems as they relate to, for example, investment appraisal, budgeting, design, R&D. Despite the growing number of guides and explanations for how accounting and finance might respond to and integrate environmental issues (see the further reading in this and other chapters), as Elkington et al. state: 'The language of finance, in short, has not developed fast enough to keep pace with the changes being brought about by environmental pressures' (Elkington, Knight and Hailes, 1991, p. 81).

Whilst individual organizations and industries are developing different forms of performance targets (see, for example, Figure 8.2), their integration with the traditional accounting systems is still rare.

In such circumstances without integration, the traditional performance criteria – i.e. accounting-related measures – can always be expected to dominate. Indeed, this is not a new problem. A survey

Figure 8.1

Environmental considerations must be an integral element of the management accounting and control systems

- The costing system.
- The planning system.
- The budgeting system.
- Variance analysis.
- Capital budgeting and expenditure.
- Plant maintenance.
- Investment appraisal and post-audit.
- Performance measurement and appraisal.
- Reporting and accountability systems.
- Reward systems.
- Forecasting.
- Scenario assessment.
- Options review.
- Purchasing policy.
- Research and development.
- Business cases.
- Business acquisition and development.
- Treasury management.
- Control of sub-contracting.
- Risk assessment.
- Insurance policy.
- Financing decisions.

Figure 8.2

Examples of environmental performance indicators used in industry

- Resource measures (e.g. consumption of energy, water, paper and other biological or mineral resources).
- Solid wastes measures.
- Effluents to water measures.
- Emissions to air measures.
- Efficiency measures (e.g. material utilization).
- Satisfaction measures (e.g. of customers, employees and other key stakeholders).
- Financial measures (of costs and benefits of environmental action).
- Impact measures (measures of environmental impact such as BOD, COD, etc.).
- Risk measures (including exposure to environmental catastrophe).
- Input/process measures (e.g. hours of training, percentage of sites with EMS).

Source: Adapted from Bennett and James (1998a, p. 62)

conducted some time ago found that while the accounting system might often identify – and, indeed, emphasize – the costs associated with environmental initiatives, there was no corresponding emphasis on the benefits (environmental, financial or otherwise). This has the obvious effect of discouraging rather than encouraging environmental projects, performance and initiatives. More recent work suggests that not a lot has changed.[2]

In this chapter we will briefly review the accounting and financial implications associated with embedding more fundamental environmental change into an organization. The focus will be upon a number of the functional areas in which accounting is highly involved – most especially investment and investment appraisal – but we shall also touch briefly upon performance appraisal, budgeting and R&D. (To augment the necessarily brief treatment in this one chapter, the reader is recommended to consult those sources referenced in the text and in the further reading, where a great deal more detail may be found.)

8.2 Investment Spending

Environmental pressures are forcing up corporate spending – and especially investment spending. The ICC estimated that corporate environmental spending could be expected to be between 3 and 4 per cent of turnover in the year 2000, an increase of around 50 per cent

[2] Nikolai et al. (1976) and see, for example, Bebbington et al. (1994); Epstein (1996); Gray, Bebbington, Walters and Thomson (1995); Gray et al. (1998); Guilding and Kirman (1998).

Figure 8.3

**The UK CBI's checklist of areas of environmental importance
(with financial consequences)**

- Procurement, preparation and transport of raw materials.
- All manufacturing processes.
- Maintenance, efficiency and replacement.
- Use of products and one's products in use.
- Disposal of waste.
- Recycling of used products and packaging.
- Research and development.
- Planning of product or output.
- Design of manufacturing.
- Design of residuals and reuse of products.
- Design of central waste-handling facilities.
- Design of a system to minimize waste.
- Development and planning controls.
- Local building controls.
- Aesthetic elements in design and layout.
- Local emission and effluent control.
- Quality control and product liability.
- Control of storage.
- Decommissioning and abandonment.

Source: Adapted from *Clean up – It's good business* (London: CBI, 1986)

---

through the 1990s. For the chemicals industry as well as for other 'frontline' industries such as food and metal manufacturing, the figures may well be much greater.[3] A significant proportion of such expenditures relates to capital items.

However, there is a potential conflict in the story coming from industry on this matter. On the one hand, it is clear that costs of environmental protection will rise as 'the additional cost of doing business'. These are unlikely to diminish in future years. On the other hand, the dominant message from and to industry is that environmental protection and, in particular, environmental investment bring financial benefits to the organization. Indeed, one need not look far to find a parade of illustrations of such financial benefits experienced by well-known companies.[4]

---

[3] Such estimates are based only on current anticipated environmental demands. They take no account of the potentially profound implications that any move towards sustainability will entail (see Chapter 14).

[4] Apart from the examples cited in this text, any consultation of, for example, Bennett and James (1998b), Coopers & Lybrand, Deloitte, *Industry Briefing* (February 1992), Elkington (1987, 1997), Elkington et al. (1991), Epstein (1996), as well as publications from industry representative bodies will provide plenty of illustrations.

That is, there has been – and continues to be – an upbeat rhetoric about the (what Walley and Whitehead, 1994, call) 'win–win' situations. These are the places where business can save money *and* benefit the environment. Whether these are overstated or not, such 'win–win' can only be exploited so far without major changes in market conditions and/or consumer preferences and behaviour. Certainly, it seems likely that the costs and benefits from responding (or not responding) to the environmental agenda will not fall equally upon all organizations. The management challenge seems to be, therefore, to manage (within the normal exigencies of corporate growth and profit) the unfolding agenda in such a way as to exploit benefit opportunities whilst minimizing the costs of so doing.[5]

Of more immediate concern is why companies are not exploiting these potential advantages without prompting from organizations like Business-in-the-Environment, the CBI or the ICC. In part, it must be because there *are so* many other pressures on business that the time and energy do not seem to be available to explore the available opportunities. Recognizing that, any organization – perhaps using some of the suggestions from earlier on in the book (see, for example, Chapter 3) – should be able to take steps to find the time. But that is not the whole story. First, it is quite apparent that many organizations are *still* ignorant of the growing environmental pressures and the extent of environmentally led opportunities. Secondly, the organizational structure, and in particular the size in pursuit of economies of scale, may well tend to restrict imaginative initiatives by, for example, reducing staff identification with the project or simply breeding slower, more tiring bureaucratic processes.[6] Thirdly, evaluating the BAT element of BATNEEC (Best Available Techniques Not Entailing Excessive Cost) is not a simple matter (see Figure 8.4). And fourthly, as we have discussed, the accounting and financial systems are making the NEEC dominate in BATNEEC.

It is salutary – and important – to recognize that it is a great deal easier to suggest change than it is to implement it – even when the change seems so self-evidently in the organization's interest. Organizational change is a highly complex and little understood issue. We

[5] There is still a great deal of contention over whether profitability and environmental protection (both as currently understood) are in conflict or harmony.

[6] See Davis (1991, p. 62), who is especially eloquent and persuasive on this point. The point is widely discussed in the management literature but rarely put into practice. For further examples, see Dauncey (1988) and Hutchinson (1991). Of particular importance in this context is Newton and Harte (1997), who argue that much of the green rhetoric exhorting companies to adopt the green agenda and asserting the great benefits of so doing grossly overplays its hand and shows negligible understanding of the complex processes of organizational change.

Figure 8.4

Criteria involved when selecting from existing technologies

- Low cost (recognizing that location affects cost).
- Low energy use (again influenced by location).
- Availability of raw materials.
- Availability of external markets.
- Materials balance for the site as a whole.
- Cleanliness of the process (waste quantity and type, disposal opportunities).
- Opportunity (availability of the technology, recognition of the need for the technology).
- Improved labour productivity.
- Safety of operation.
- High material yield (i.e. high eco-efficiency in materials use).

Source: Adapted from Lawrence (1991)

---

would not wish to suggest that 'greening' either organizations or accounting is a simple matter.

8.3 Investment Appraisal

Just as there is no single method of evaluating investment opportunities, so can there be no single way of incorporating environmental considerations into investment decisions.[7] The traditional investment appraisal techniques – typically, discounted cash flow (DCF), payback and, more recently, contribution to profit or EPS (earnings per share) – have a very real tendency to narrow the range of issues considered and encourage short-term, less risky options. Indeed, the widely acknowledged 'short-termism' of the Western capital markets can now be seen to be driving investment through reference to EPS (and related) criteria. The freedom for environmental initiative in such circumstances is limited. 'Payback' clearly and explicitly emphasizes the short-term. Furthermore, DCF, which should encourage a longer-term perspective, tends to discourage large projects with an expected life of more than about ten years[8] and, most importantly in an environmental context, inevitably places less emphasis on events later in the project's life. Thus, for example, a conventional DCF calculation would take little account of a plant's reduced efficiency towards the

[7] Investment, in this context, is intended widely, to include not only new capital investment and projects and processes but also R&D as well as land and new businesses (with the potential remediation and other liability issues).

[8] See Elkington et al. (1991, p. 81).

Figure 8.5

An environmental investment checklist

Do you take account of environmental requirements and implications in all areas of budgeting and investment? In particular:

- Have you taken account of environmental spend in your budget plan (both short and long term)?
- Do those lending money stipulate environmental requirements?
- Do you carry out a due diligence review of any site or business you may be acquiring, assessing possible financial or legal liabilities relating to environmental issues?
- Do you take account of environmental issues when considering new investment, e.g. in land, technology, new business areas? Is environmental performance one of your investment criteria?
- If you invest in other businesses, do you check or specify the environmental performance standards which they should meet?
- Do you invest in R&D into more environmentally sound processes and products?
- If you operate a company pension scheme have you considered how this money is invested? You may choose to invest only in companies which manage their environmental performance effectively.
- Have you considered sponsoring a particular environmental organization or programme?

Source: Adapted from BiE (1991a, pp. 28–29)

---

end of its life (with potential increases in emissions and spills) and would, literally, discount abandonment and decommissioning costs or any other environmentally related problems (such as land contamination) which might then become apparent. So, in general, a longer-term *and* more environmentally sensitive attitude to investment is required (see Figure 8.5) but traditional investment appraisal discourages this.[9]

The real irony, however, is that in a business climate changing rapidly as a result of environmental pressures (law, technology, attitudes, regulations, etc.), management must be seeking the shortest possible returns in order to stay flexible in response to those changes and to avoid the risk of being locked into obsolete, environmentally malign technology and processes. There is a real conflict here.

---

[9] There is evidence that the business community is beginning to recognize the dangers inherent in such short-term orientation. One UK initiative of relevance has been Royal Society of Arts Inquiry into Tomorrow's Company which, in addition to talking of inclusivity and consultation with stakeholders, has been trying to imagine what a longer-term perspective would look like for organizations and how such a perspective might be achieved. The Inquiry has been influential but has had only limited success. Given the ubiquity of profit and stock markets this is not entirely surprising.

Whilst there is no simple solution to the conflict, there are a number of ways in which companies have tried to overcome the problem. One approach places TQM/EQM above conventional investment appraisal. That is, quality is defined in terms of 'being the best at what we do' and incorporates, for example, a 'zero incidents' requirement in health, safety and environmental factors. The investment appraisal process, operating within this quality framework, was of the *'must we have it? can we afford it? buy it!'* type. This approach works in some organizational cultures (and, indeed, reflects a particular culture) and seems to be very successful in maintaining the highest economic *and environmental* standards.

A more traditional and strategic approach – one more suitable to larger, more bureaucratic organizations – involves driving all investment (including R&D, see below) from the policy of the organization and, in particular, from the requirements of the environmental policy. That is, capital spend is clearly strategic in nature; strategy requires actions to meet corporate policy; therefore investment must be undertaken to meet the environmental policy. This takes two forms: first, strategic, identifiably environmental, expenditure is specifically undertaken to meet legal, forthcoming and/or corporate environmental standards; and secondly, *all* capital spend proposals must include an environmental statement. Thus, all investments are screened to meet environmental standards (in exactly the same way as any sensible organization screens its investments for health, safety and so on).

This last element – screening of investments (in effect, the setting of environmental hurdles for all new spend) – is increasingly common in companies. When matched with internal EIAs (see Chapter 5) for all big initiatives and accompanied by a detailed environmental statement as an essential part of the business case for each new spend, one is beginning to move towards a more systematic internalization of environmental criteria.

However, two brief points are worth making at this point. First, an increasing number of nations are requiring that organizations operate within a BATNEEC/BPEO framework (see Figure 8.6). If organizations are struggling to find the impetus to implement environmentally sensitive investment policies, it can only mean that the regulatory regime is not biting as hard as it should and, therefore, providing an important and direct motivation to the company. Secondly, and equally important, the sort of *ex ante* processes described here do not guarantee that the environment *will* be placed at the centre of the investment process. Widespread experience shows that (a) simple financial targets can easily drive out well-meant but financially challenging environmental targets; and (b), as most organizations do not undertake *ex post* analysis of their investments, they cannot know how

Figure 8.6

The selection of a Best Practicable Environment Option (BPEO)

(1)   Define the objectives of the project.
(2)   Identify all feasible options.
(3)   Qualitative and quantitative analysis of the options' environmental impact.
(4)   Clear, objective presentation of the information relevant to the choice.
(5)   Select BPEO.
(6)   Have choice scrutinized by individuals independent of the initial choice.
(7)   Implement and monitor performance against expected/desired criteria.
(8)   Maintain an audit trail of all steps, information and individuals involved in the process for post-audit.

Source: Royal Commission on Environmental Pollution (1988) *Best Practicable Environment Option* (London: HMSO, Cmnd 310)

---

successful they are being in (in this case) *practically* integrating the environmental with economic criteria.

Accountants have a potentially important role to play here. First, if every investment must meet fixed, immutable, economic criteria under all circumstances then environmental considerations will continue to be marginalized and included by chance rather than by choice. It happens too often that accountants apply and maintain such criteria and thus prevent wider (environmentally innovative) ones from being applied. The first step, therefore, is for the accountant to bring this issue to the board's attention and have the guidelines changed in line with environmental policy. There is not much intrinsic (as opposed to PR) value in a policy that cannot be achieved because of conflict with other, more traditional criteria.

The second step is to be more imaginative in assessing the relative merits and demerits of investment proposals. In addition to the basic screening of all investments as discussed above, a number of factors can be brought into this. These are considered in the following sections.

Costs

Assessing the costs of an investment proposal is usually the least contentious element. However, a more realistic approach to cost recognition will often make the conventional 'non-environmental' projects look less attractive. When considering 'environmental' projects, or those with a strong environmentally driven content, one must be

Figure 8.7

Four-tier approach to accounting for environmental costs (typically in investment appraisal): The US EPA/Tellus Institute (TCA) Approach

Tier 0: Usual costs
- Direct and indirect costs usually associated with the project – capital, revenue, materials, etc.
- Usual (conventional accounting) costs of alternatives.

Tier 1: Hidden costs
- Conventional accounting costs usually found in overheads/general account – include regulatory costs, EMS, monitoring, safety costs – both capital and revenue.

Tier 2: Liability costs
- 'Contingent liability costs' – also hidden and which will emerge in certain circumstances – fines, clean-ups, additional regulatory costs, etc. – assessed against the likelihood of them occurring for different investment options.

Tier 3: Less tangible costs
- Qualitative costs and benefits from improved environmental management – then assessed financially.
- Loss/gain of goodwill, good deals, suppliers, customers, employees, sales price, supplier costs, advertising/image management, etc.

---

sure to compare like with like. For example, a conventional 'non-environmental' project may well have ignored or played down factors that a more environmentally centred project would incorporate. Have all the likely regulatory costs (for example, fines, clean-up, insurance) been included? Is there an adequate allowance for waste disposal and for remediation and abandonment costs? And are there issues which a 'non-environmental' project might legitimately ignore but which the organization will have to fund in some other way (for example, emission control or landscaping)? In addition, are there any aesthetic or environmental (non-financial) 'costs' which a 'non-environmental' project will incur? What are the ethical implications of this and, to be 'hard-nosed' about it, how will they affect the business, its image and reputation?

Figure 8.7 offers one, popular, framework within which an organization can begin to assess the levels ('tiers') of costs embedded in an investment decision. And Figure 8.8 provides a related, but more detailed, specification of the kinds of costs we need to consider here.[10]

---

[10] Figure 8.8 is taken from the US EPA and is explored in more detail in IFAC (1998).

Figure 8.8 Examples of environmental costs incurred by firms

Potentially Hidden Costs		
Regulatory	**Upfront**	**Voluntary**
- Notification	- Site remedies	- Community relations/outreach
- Reporting	- Site preparation	- Monitoring/testing
- Monitoring/testing	- Permitting	- Training
- Studies/modelling	- R&D	- Audits
- Remediation	- Engineering and procurement	- Qualifying suppliers
- Recordkeeping	- Installation	- Reports (e.g., annual
- Plans		environmental reports)
- Training	**Conventional Company Costs**	- Insurance
- Inspections	- Capital equipment	- Planning
- Manifesting	- Materials	- Feasibility studies
- Labelling	- Labor	- Remediation
- Preparedness	- Supplies	- Recycling
- Protective equipment	- Utilities	- Environmental studies
- Medical surveillance	- Structures	- R&D
- Environmental insurance	- Salvage value	- Habitat and wetland protection
- Financial assurance		- Landscaping
- Pollution control	**Back-End**	- Other environmental projects
- Spill response	- Closure/decommissioning	- Financial support to
- Stormwater management	- Disposal of inventory	environmental groups and/or
- Waste management	- Post-closure care	researchers
- Taxes/fees	- Site survey	
Contingent Costs		
- Future compliance costs	- Remediation	- Legal expense
- Penalties/fines	- Property damage	- Natural resource damages
- Response to future releases	- Personal injury damage	- Economic loss damages
Image and Relationship Costs		
- Corporate image	- Relationship with professional	- Relationship with lenders
- Relationship with customers	staff	- Relationship with host
- Relationship with investors	- Relationship with workers	communities
- Relationship with insurers	- Relationship with suppliers	- Relationship with regulators

Source: EPA (1995) *An Introduction to Environmental Accounting as a Business Management Tool:*
Key Concepts and Terms

Benefits

Traditionally, any investment proposal will identify the income
streams deriving from the project. Research into post-audit suggests
that these (as well as the costs) are frequently incorrectly estimated[11]
and a realistic investment proposal will test the sensitivity of the

---

[11] See, for example, Neale (1989) and Scapens and Sale (1981).

income streams. As the world becomes more environmentally aware and the regulatory framework hardens, non-environmentally sensitive income streams may well become harder to obtain, leading to either early abandonment of the project or the need to incur extra (environmental) costs to maintain those streams. Such recognition will help support the environmentally driven investment. Of more substance, however, are the non-financial benefits of environmental investment – or at least either those benefits that have no direct *financial* value (for example, protection of habitat) or where the potential financial benefits are almost impossible to assess (such as effects on morale, image, reputation, status with the regulators, etc.). It is a short-sighted (as well as a potentially unethical) policy to ignore such benefits.

Criteria Applied

Is the criterion being applied to the investment proposal the most appropriate one? We already know that conventional investment appraisal techniques encourage shorter-term projects. It is also widely accepted that criteria related to short-term accounting profit measurement are unlikely to be to the benefit of the long-term economic health of the organization. But are there other criteria, specifically related to the industry and to the particular advantages of the organization, more sympathetic to environmental matters? What organizations are perhaps striving for here is a more subtle and sophisticated use of performance indicators that are either integrated, or at least in harmony, with the traditional financial indicators. (In the present climate, of course, it is the rare organization that can ignore entirely the short-term financial and accounting measurements. In the long term, if there is one, it will be the rare organization that will be permitted to let short-term financial and accounting measures dominate environmental targets – see, for example, Chapters 14 and 15.)

Possible Options Considered

A traditional scenario in investment appraisal involves a review of possible options and then selection from a short-list. Although this will be too 'textbook' a scenario for many organizations, it does have elements of realism. What is important is whether the investment proposers *have* considered other – often more imaginative – options. This is clearly a difficult task for an organization whose staff are fully stretched and which needs a rapid decision. But everybody is learning about environmental matters and, as we saw above, creative

Figure 8.9

Suggestions for more environmentally sensitive investment appraisal

(1) Recognize that many environmentally driven investments will have financial pay-offs under conventional criteria.
(2) Recognize that conventional investment appraisal criteria act against environmental criteria.
(3) Environmental policy should drive strategic investments.
(4) All investment proposals should be accompanied by the environmental case (a mini EIA).
(5) All investments must be screened against environmental criteria.
(6) The accountant should speak with the board and have the relationship between the environmental policy of the organization and its investment criteria clarified.
(7) A more imaginative approach to investment appraisal should be adopted via the 10-point checklist.

---

approaches to investment can bring unexpected financial as well as environmental benefits. For example, the potential changes in energy prices offer a range of new investment possibilities – as well as potentially reducing the payback period on energy-efficient invest-ments. We have also seen and discussed investments which became more financially *and* environmentally interesting through the applica-tion of different energy sources, softer (alternative) technology, imagin-ative end-of-pipe waste treatment possibilities and through looking for a site-wide input from all functional areas and specialists.

Opportunity Costs

At long last it is becoming more widely recognized that there are many investments an organization cannot afford *not* to undertake. These may be strategic, they may be related to TQM, but increasingly the opportunity costs of not investing in environmentally sound cri-teria will be considerable. One of the best illustrations of this is the plant closure threat. Instances of a plant being closed in the UK due to environmental transgressions are rare indeed and the extent of the transgression must usually be enormous. This is not so in many other countries where the threat of closure is real and considerable. The costs associated with closure are obviously significant. In such a regulatory climate, an investment appraisal must take account of such opportunity costs which can make the environmental investment not only more attractive but inescapable.

Figure 8.10

10-point checklist for more environmentally sensitive investment appraisal
(1) Environmentally screen all investments.
(2) Reconsider costs.
(3) Reconsider benefits.
(4) Reconsider the criteria applied.
(5) Reconsider the possible options considered.
(6) Consider the opportunity costs.
(7) Reconsider the time horizon.
(8) Reconsider the discount rate.
(9) Consider the 'valuation of externalities'.
(10) Consider sustainable costs.

Time Horizon

Are the time horizons employed in the investment appraisal realistic? Given the climate of environmental concern, should the organization be using longer (or shorter) horizons? Does this affect the investment judgement? It should be remembered that environmental costs are certain to carry on rising. Whilst one may be able to avoid supplier audits, clean-up costs, duty of care liability and so on for one or two years, can one realistically expect such matters to be (financially) irrelevant in three or more? The forecasting element in the investment proposal becomes a critical factor (see below).

Discount Rate

Apart from the well-known problems with the discount rate in NPV calculations, discounting literally discounts the future. The whole environmental debate is about the present generation's moral failure to provide for the future. Continued use of discount rates encourages that. This is a central issue in sustainability and must be addressed by all organizations seeking to be sustainable (see Chapter 14).

'Valuation of Externalities'

By this we do not mean 'placing a value on nature' – an activity we oppose[12] – but recognizing that, first, taxation changes that reflect

---

[12] See, for example, Gray (1992).

environmental matters will force organizations to internalize some of the costs that were previously external (for example, an energy tax); and, secondly, there is a serious moral 'cost' in ignoring the effect of an investment's externalities on communities and on the planet. The investing organization will have to recognize the potentially changing price structures as *well* as the significant ethical choice that is made in ignoring the consequences of actions.

Sustainable Costs

Chapter 14 will introduce this notion in more detail but the basic idea is that we might consider that each organization, each cost centre, each investment, should be required to leave the biosphere no worse off at the end of each accounting period. An investment proposal that incorporated the costs of repairing damage to the biosphere[13] might look a very different financial proposition.

Even this brief analysis indicates that there is clearly a long way to go before investment appraisal can fully incorporate environmental criteria. The experience of companies and other organizations is that attempting to do so is a slow and painful process which runs counter to the culture and values that management have striven so hard to acquire. In many regards, it will seem very frustrating indeed for a sprinter to be tapped on the shoulder and told that he or she should really be (what must look like) leapfrogging backwards. The suggestions here may assist accountants to begin to help their organizations through this painful but brutally essential transition.

8.4 Performance Appraisal

As we saw above, all the environmental *ex ante* control in the world will be useless unless the *ex post* control also reflects environmental criteria. In a closely related context the following observation sums up a dilemma well known throughout management accounting:[14]

> *When managers see that their execution of socially responsible policies and programs is evaluated in promotion and compensation decisions, along with performance in meeting familiar profit, cost and productivity goals, they will believe and they will be motivated. For obvious and valid reasons middle managers concentrate*

---

[13] Recognizing that a great deal of the damage to the biosphere is irreparable and therefore the costs of repair are infinite.

[14] See, for example, Prakash and Rappaport (1977).

their attention and skill on the accomplishment of performance objectives for which
they know they are held responsible. They appraise responsibility in terms of
two familiar criteria. The first is what is measured and the second is what is
rewarded.

Ashen (1980), quoted in Chechile and Carlisle (1991, p. 254)

So, not only must the environmental criteria be seen to be explicitly
recognized in post-evaluation but they must also be part of the reward
system. Embedding environmental criteria into the performance
appraisal process will encounter severe teething problems until the
organizational culture swings sufficiently behind the principles. The
essence of the problem is predictable: what happens when financial
and environmental criteria conflict? There is no simple solution to
this but explicit incorporation into the reward system appears to be
the most effective. Experience shows that if no reference is made
to environmental criteria in appraisal and reward systems, when
conflict arises, the traditional financial measures always dominate the
environmental.[15]

As with the investment appraisal considerations, there are both
environmentally ethical and financial reasons for paying special attention to this area. Having raised environmental expectations, a reward
system which then encourages environmentally malign behaviour is
both unethical and extremely bad for morale. As with staff attraction
and retention so with motivation – an environmentally malign organization which does not fulfil its promises to its staff cannot expect
much loyalty or motivation. This has obvious ethical implications and
it is also quite apparent that a demotivated work force will be less
cost-effective and innovative – with the obvious financial implications.

8.5 R&D and Design

The experience of the leading companies is that, if the environmental
policy is to have any real significance, it must drive not only the
investment policy, but also the R&D effort and, ultimately, product
and process design. This clearly makes strategic sense but the short-
term pressures on business plus accountants' traditional evaluation
criteria have generally tended to discourage R&D, design and innovation initiatives.[16] And the matters are not trivial – increasing environmental demands can add significantly to the costs of a product and, as
the research into Japanese management accounting is showing,[17] the

---

[15] See, particularly, Bennett and James (1998a) and Epstein (1996) for further illustrations and exploration of these matters.
[16] See, for example, Gray (1986), Nixon (1991, 1996), Nixon and Lonie (1990).
[17] See, for example, Innes et al. (1994).

Figure 8.11

Some environmentally related design desiderata

- Minimum resource use in production and end-use.
- Minimum waste in production and in end-use.
- Minimum emissions and discharges from production and in end-use.
- Minimum use of packaging and transport.
- Recyclability of product and of production residues.
- Disassembly at end of use.
- Repairability of product in use.
- Longer life of process and product (noting the conflict here with responsiveness to the changing green agenda).

---

bulk of a product's costs are determined at the design stage. Moreover, as in many industries – pharmaceuticals, aerospace, agrochemicals, etc. – there can be a lag of many years between inception and design of a product and its reaching commercial viability, business is faced with an increasingly difficult task staring into the commercial and environmental crystal ball.

It is quite clear that R&D falls into the class of things that business cannot afford *not* to do. This is equally true for environmentally related R&D,[18] which will determine whether an organization has the products, processes and services the markets want – and which society will permit – in the near future. The 'D' of R&D closely and inevitably links with design considerations. We have already touched upon the design issues related to packaging and other waste (see Chapter 7) and it is quite apparent that design will increasingly have to incorporate a wider range of environmentally related considerations (see Figure 8.11). Indeed, US corporations are increasingly making explicit the way in which both competition and regulation are driving developments in design for the environment (DFE).[19] Techniques such as EPS (environment priority strategies) in product design (closely related to life-cycle assessment, see Chapter 9) are emerging and being developed to assist organizations with these difficulties.[20]

But there is also a positive side to this, as famously expounded by Porter and van der Linde (1995). That is, they argue, innovation is what industry is best at and where its duty lies. In their case they argue that what is needed is the right encouragement for industry to fully embrace environmental innovation and, in the aspect of the

---

[18] For more detail see Davis (1991, pp. 110–112) and Winter (1988, pp. 131–133), who provides a useful checklist for product development. Elkington, Knight and Hailes (1991, ch. 8) is especially helpful here.

[19] *Business and the Environment*, 1992, vol. 3, no. 8, pp. 2–4.

[20] See, for example, Ryding (1991).

article which made it so contentious, the authors argue that environmental legislation should be embraced by business as just such a stimulus. Whatever the outcomes,[21] it seems highly likely that design and R&D will remain a fulcrum point of tension – both positive and negative – in organizational responses to the environment.

For the accounting and financial systems the considerations are largely the same as for investment and performance appraisal (see above). In particular, accountants must guard against any tendency for the workings of their systems to prevent environmental initiatives. Strategic concerns must dominate and to the extent that the accountant is fully involved in that process in a positive and productive way, accounting will be serving its paymasters adequately.

As more is learned from management accounting in Japanese contexts, and the roles that such accounting can play in strategy and innovation, this will add to the increasing insights we are gaining about the issues facing the design of accounting systems for environmental innovation and design. Whilst there is no apparent simple best practice in the area, experience *does seem* to be leading us in a more productive direction.[22]

8.6 Budgeting and Forecasting

It is apparent that a considerable element of an organization's response to the environmental agenda depends upon its estimate of how the environmental climate is changing and will change in both the short and long term. That estimate must then be backed up by financial and other resources. This inevitably involves forecasting and budgeting. Apart from the basic bookkeeping and costing activities of accounting, the accountant's role involves constant forecasting (although often implicitly). Everything from depreciation policy, stock valuation and the calculation of debtors provisions through to the processes of budgeting and setting (and evaluating) performance targets involves a forecast of future conditions. We have already seen aspects of the way in which environmental issues will influence forecasting in, for example, investment and performance appraisal, waste and energy management and environmental auditing; similarly, the organization's management of its external relations (see Part C)

[21] See also Weizsäcker et al. (1997) in this connection.

[22] In addition to the literature on management accounting, strategy, innovation and R&D as well as that on the Japanese experience, the more detailed texts of Bennett and James (1998b), Ditz et al. (1995), Epstein (1996), Schaltegger (1996) and the increasingly helpful publications from the professional accountancy bodies (for example, CICA, 1994) will provide the interested reader with much more depth on these issues.

Figure 8.12

Some environmental factors that will be reflected in an organization's budget

- Environmental capital spending.
- Allowance for trade-off between environmental and financial criteria in investment and project appraisal.
- Provision for EIAs and environmental business cases.
- Provision for bringing all sites up to best practice standards.
- Provision for design of new information systems.
- Spending on waste management and disposal.
- Spending on energy.
- Packaging and returnable containers.
- Spending on environmental review.
- Costs associated with environmental purchasing policy and supplier audits.
- Landscaping, remediation, decommissioning, abandonment costs.
- Recognition of the associated contingent liabilities.
- Provision for emergency and spillage procedures.
- Provision for fines, insurance and other legally related costs.
- Provision for specialist review and advice.
- Provision for (temporary) plant closure.
- Transport spending.
- Environmental projects whether on-site, in-house, or in conjunction with external groups.

---

depends to a great extent on how the company expects environmental issues to affect and be perceived by its external constituents. Environmental factors must now become an explicit and central part of all organizational forecasting. We have seen that this will affect the accountant in many ways – but the most important will probably be through the budgeting process (see Figure 8.12). At its most basic, this is no more than an extension of conventional budgeting practice – slightly redesigned to make explicit a 'new' business issue. However, research still suggests that a relatively small proportion of accountants – even in large companies – have any explicitly environmental factors built into the budgeting process. Major steps need to be taken by the accounting and financial functions in this area if organizations are to be able to respond sensibly to the environmental pressures.

8.7 Conclusions

The companies that are leading the world in the development of more environmentally sensitive systems and modes of operation are themselves discovering that going further than a 'light green' gloss is difficult indeed. But they also recognize that go further they must. One major indicator of progress – and, if absent, in preventing further development – is the extent to which the accounting and financial systems incorporate environmental criteria. Those systems that lie at the heart of the organization – the budgeting and investment and performance appraisal systems, for example – have remained largely untouched by the changing environmental agenda. Until they do develop in this way, organizations will face conflicts between environmental and conventional financial factors – and in those circumstances the financial will always win over the environmental.

Further Reading

The principal sources of further reading for this chapter (and subsequent chapters) are (a) the major accounting and related texts in the field (as referenced for Chapter 1); (b) the emerging recommendation from industry and, especially, the professional accountancy bodies; and (c) the major business/environment newsletters and journals (again, as referenced for Chapter 1) but see also:

Chechile, R.A. and S. Carlisle (eds) (1991) *Environmental Decision Making: A Multidisciplinary Perspective* (New York: Van Nostrand Reinhold)
Winter, G. (1988) *Business and the Environment* (Hamburg: McGraw-Hill)

As well as the sources cited in the footnotes to this chapter – especially the Bennet and James references, Epstein (1996) and Schaltegger (1996).

CHAPTER 9

LIFE CYCLE ASSESSMENT AND THE MASS BALANCE

9.1 Introduction

This chapter examines two, related, sets of techniques which, whilst perhaps not strictly accounting techniques, have had a major impact on approaches to the way in which an organization's interactions with the natural environment are conceived of. They have a number of similarities and are both principally concerned with (a) changing how management look at – conceive of – their organization and (b) helping guide the management of the organization's environmental impact.

Both the mass balance and life cycle assessment (LCA) are manifestations of the *systems view of organizations*, which we met in Chapter 1. To recap, we know that the traditional accounting system can be seen as one systems view of the organization with its recording (bookkeeping) of the debits and credits and with its income statement and balance sheet. But this view does not capture the environmental interactions of the organization. Hence we might recognize that we need some sort of *ecological accounting*[1] which, in broad terms, echoes the traditional accounting system and provides a record and summary of the *physical interactions* of the business.

It is worth repeating here that to capture the total environmental *impacts* of any organization is virtually impossible[2] and so our

[1] The term ecological accounting is used in many different contexts to mean a wide range of different things. For our purposes, the term simply means that we are directly accounting for the physical interactions of the business with the natural environment. One of the most complete – if somewhat idiosyncratic – developments of 'ecological accounting' is provided by Schaltegger (1996), who illustrates in considerable detail the full potential – and, by implication, the major weaknesses – that may derive from taking ecological accounting to the limit.

[2] The reasons that it is virtually impossible to capture all *impacts* are many and various. The simplest are that (a) each interaction (e.g. an emission) with a complex ecology produces a potentially infinite array of consequences (e.g. water pollution changes organisms which change the nature of the environment, affect those creatures which depend on the organisms, which in turn affect water habitats, which affect the course of the water, which affects . . .); and (b) one cannot know either where the interaction will end up (e.g. will pollution of land end up in the water course or not?) or what other human or ecological mainfestations that interaction will meet (e.g. emissions of two relatively benign substances by two organizations might mingle to produce a malign substance). This is a *very* simple overview but touches upon the essential nature of systems thinking and ecology. Goldsmith et al. (1972), although a little dated, is still a good first introduction to many of these problems.

principal concern here is to try to capture as many of the *interactions* with the natural environment as we can.

9.2 The Mass Balance

The mass balance – also called the *eco-balance* or *ökobilanz* – is, in essence, a very simple idea. At its simplest, the mass balance comprises a statement of the physical quantities of inputs, outputs (products and waste) and leakages and emissions of an organization (or part of an organization). Indeed, we have already seen such an outline mass balance when we looked at the initial environmental review of a small hotel in Chapter 5 (see Figure 5.4).

To make it a 'proper' mass balance, however, that basic identification of the major elements of inputs, outputs and leakages needs to be quantified and, in an ideal world, the totals of the inputs should 'balance' with the totals of the outputs and leakages. To achieve this it is necessary to put all the physical quantities into a common unit of measurement (e.g. weight) – and this is a great deal easier said than done. The purpose of this common measurement is to enable the balancing to take place so that 'losses' can be identified. That is, it is extremely unlikely that an organization will know *exactly* everything that comes into the organization (all the inputs) and it is almost certain that it will not know where all those inputs finish up. By eco-balancing (as it sometimes called) the organization can reassure itself that it is not missing anything of major importance in its management of environmental interactions. An example of a simple mass balance is shown in the appendix to this chapter. This pictorial representation of the mass balance (what the company calls its 'green accounts') was published by the Danish Steel Works in its Annual Report in 1991 and was possibly the earliest published example of a mass balance being used as the systematic basis for an environmental report.

Once the mass balance has been completed – itself no easy task – then the organization has to *do* something with it. (That is, the mass balance can be a basis for management and reporting – not a substitute for it.) A major advantage of the mass balance – beyond its role in assisting a reconception of the organization – is that it provides a basis for the systematic derivation of *environmental performance indicators* (see Chapter 3). Not only can the elements of principal environmental interest be identified but they can be linked to appropriate inputs (for example, resource use) or outputs (for example, sales) to produce ratios which will direct the organization to focus on the *eco-efficiency* of its operations. Despite the limitations of *eco-*

efficency[3] it is generally believed to be one of the first prerequisites of environmental management and certainly it permits the organization to begin to identify targets and thus control aspects of its operations in an informed and systematic manner.

Application and development of the mass balance first emerged in Germany and Austria, where the practice is certainly the most developed.[4] It has been shown in those countries to provide a sophisticated platform from which one particular approach to environmental management (and accounting) can be developed. It certainly has wide application in particular areas such as the control of significantly toxic/controlled substances (such as ozone depleting chemicals or PCBs).

We shall restrict ourselves, here, to the more general conception of the mass balance (as shown in Figure 5.4 and in the appendix to this chapter). We will return to the ideas of the mass balance again (not least when considering environmental reporting in Chapter 12), but for now we will turn to examine – the broadly related – technique of life cycle assessment.

9.3   Life Cycle Assessment

Whereas the mass balance is an *organization-based* view, the life cycle assessment (LCA) is (usually) *product-based*. Where the mass balance attempts to identify all interactions of the organization, the LCA is concerned to try to identify all interactions associated with a product (or service).

Life cycle assessment, although it has been in existence for a couple of decades, sprang to prominence in the 1990s as the potential Holy Grail of environmental decision-making. Its aims and claims were not modest:

> *LCA is an **objective** process used to evaluate the environmental burdens associated with a product, process or activity. This is accomplished by identifying and quantifying energy and material usage and environmental releases. The data are then used to assess the impact of those energy and material releases on the environment, and to evaluate and implement opportunities to achieve environmental improvements. The LCA includes the **entire life cycle of the product, process or activity,** encompassing: extracting and processing of raw materials;*

---

[3] Not least because it does not capture *'eco-effectiveness'* – i.e. total environmental interaction. By concentrating on 'efficiency' there is aways the danger of doing efficiently that which we shouldn't be doing at all (Lowe and McInnes, 1971)!

[4] Much of the development of the mass balance is associated with IÖW and the most advanced, published examples of eco-controlling with the textiles company Kunert and the brewing company Neumarkter Lammsbrau. For more detail see Gelber (1995), Schaltegger (1996) and White and Wagner (1996).

manufacturing, transportation and distribution; use/re-use/maintenance; recycling; and final disposal.

(Fava, 1991, p. 19, emphasis added)

It is essential to recognize from the outset that life cycle analysis/ assessment – under whatever name it appears[5] – is no magic wand; is usually driven by the goals of the organization conducting it and will not automatically mean an improvement in environmental perform- ance unless conducted with that goal explicitly in mind; and it is, in effect, no more than functional application of systems theory and systems thinking. Nevertheless, the prominence of LCA means that we could not ignore it and, as a *process*, it has considerable value. Even if it only leads one to the conclusion that there can be no such thing as an 'environmentally friendly company', LCA does encourage an explicit acknowledgement and recognition of the full life cycle of any product or activity and this is a major contribution.

9.4 Considering the Life Cycle

The principle of considering the life cycle of any activity is essentially elementary. For illustration, consider a particularly simple product like a pencil. Without knowing anything of the technical issues involved in the production of pencils we can illustrate the scope of an LCA. (The addition of technical knowledge will improve the LCA – and increase the complexity – whilst more complex products will produce more complex life cycles.)

One starts from the product itself – the pencil – and then traces the life cycle forwards and backwards. An initial outline of the life cycle of the pencil is shown in Figure 9.1. A number of immediate observa- tions are possible:

(1) One must trace all raw materials (wood, graphite, paints, etc.) back, through earlier production phases, to extraction from the biosphere and recognize: (a) the ecological effects of that extrac- tion (e.g. impact on forest habitat, oxygen/carbon dioxide balance, etc.); (b) the energy used in the extraction and transportation; and (c) the energy, machines, etc. which were used to produce the means of extraction.

(2) The same process must be undertaken for all intermediate pro- duction processes.

[5] In addition to the variations of life cycle 'analysis' and 'assessment', other names meaning the same or similar things include: cradle to grave analysis/assessment; eco- balance assessment; resource analysis; environmental impact assessment (noting the potential for confusion with EIA; see Chapter 5).

Figure 9.1 A simplified LCA for a pencil (with other LCA interconnections)

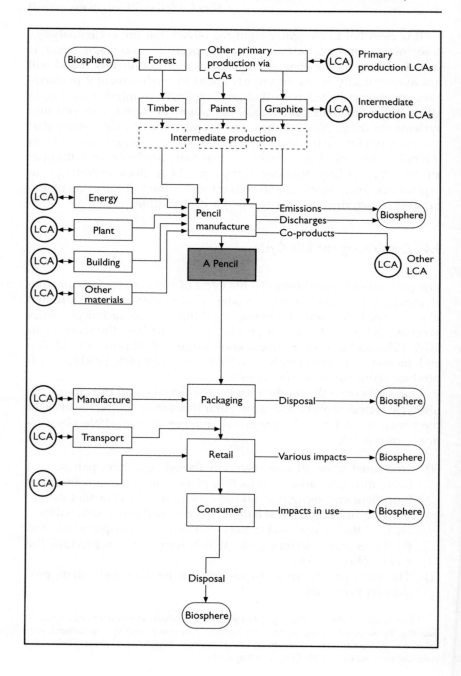

(3)   One must trace the product forward to its packaging (and *its* manufacture and disposal), transport and eventual use in the hands of the consumer.
(4)   The product must then be traced to the biospheric interactions it has in use and in disposal.
(5)   All inputs and outputs from each stage in the life cycle must be captured.

What becomes apparent is that, first, any life cycle will interrelate with many other life cycles (e.g. the paint manufacturers, the plant and machinery manufacturers, etc.) and potentially arbitrary lines will have to be drawn around systems of life cycles – the *LCA system must be bounded*; and, secondly, each LCA will involve an *infinite regress* – the wood came from a tree; the tree housed insects, was an essential element of the local soil ecology and played its part in oxygen/carbon dioxide balance; this affects bird life, the growth in the soil and global warming which in turn affects . . . and so on.

Thus, the life cycle of any product is inevitably exceptionally complicated and so no LCA *can* be complete and comprehensive. It is unlikely to catch the majority of the biosphere–product interactions and, as a result, it will rarely have much claim to objectivity. With this in mind, we can consider the stages in LCA.

9.5   The Methodology of LCA

LCA is seen as having three major stages, shown in Figure 9.2, and these are popularly summarized using Figure 9.3. The stages are relatively self-explanatory (although that is not to suggest that they are in any way simple or uncontroversial).

Figure 9.2

Summary of the three stages in LCA methodology

Life Cycle Inventory   Review of the product, identification and description of all resources, emissions, discharges and disposals throughout the cradle to grave of the product.

Life Cycle Impact Analysis   Identification, possible quantification and assessment of the human and other ecological impacts of the elements identified in the inventory stage.

Life Cycle Improvement Analysis   Attempts to reduce, ameliorate or eliminate the impacts identified through various means, including redesign or products and processes.

Figure 9.3 The popular form of summarizing the three stages in LCA methodology

2. Impact assessment
   (or environmental
   evaluation)

3. Improvement
   analysis (or
   company
   response)

1. Life cycle inventory
   (or data collection)

Life cycle inventory is usually guided by the stages shown in Figure 9.4 and it should be noted that, already, the system has been very closely bounded to exclude the infinite regress and the more troublesome ecological interactions such as habitat. The results from this phase are then collated into an assessment matrix which forms the basis for the life cycle impact analysis. (An example of a matrix is shown in Figure 9.5.)[6]

The matrix is completed,[7] first, by simply identifying those cells in the matrix which are considered relevant and then attempting some quantitative or qualitative description of the impacts.[8] This is obviously a far from simple task. There are usually widely divergent views as to the impact of various elements and these different viewpoints are often strongly held. Therefore, the results are often controversial. One approach to this task has been to assemble:

independent panels of scientific and environmental experts . . . whose task it will be to make informed and authoritative judgements about each of the main pollutants or environmentally damaging activities. These judgements will take the form of an environmental points system, reflecting the relative significance of each pollutant.[9]

---

[6] Figure 9.5 is taken from the EU eco-label process with which LCA bears a close relationship: see also Chapters 5 and 14.

[7] Each environmental medium where impact is felt should be further divided; for example, air contamination may involve a number of different pollutants – CO_2, NO_x, SO_2, NH_3, etc. Energy consumption may be further divided into source of production – non-renewable, renewable or internally generated (for example, by the incineration of wastes).

[8] The use of a quantitative method results in, what is, in effect, a mass balance.

[9] Taken from Landbank Consultancy Ltd's approach to LCA. See Carol Charlton, 'Life Cycle Assessment – making sense of environmental complexities', in *CBI Environment Newsletter*, No. 6/November 1991 (pp. 13/14).

Figure 9.4 LCA inventory analysis: a simplified framework

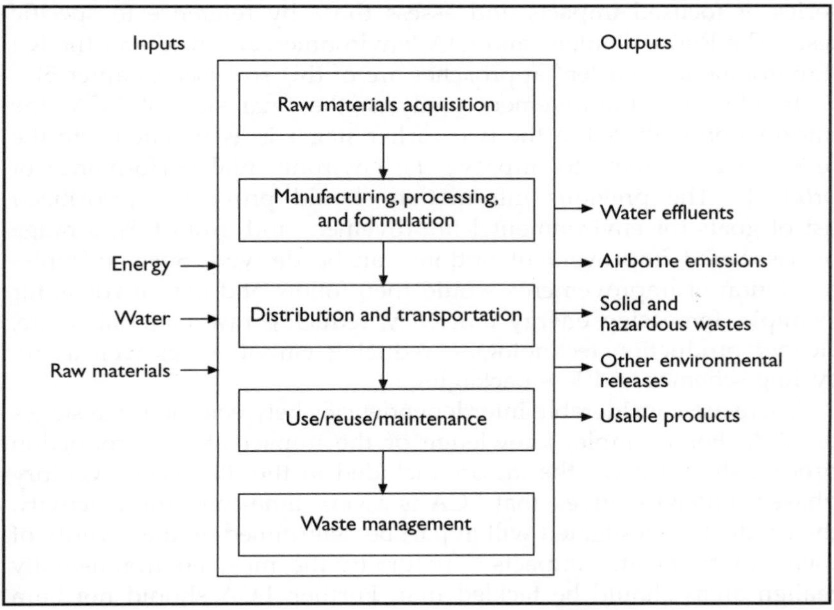

Inputs   Outputs

Raw materials acquisition

Manufacturing, processing,
and formulation   → Water effluents

Energy →   → Airborne emissions

Water →   Distribution and transportation   → Solid and
                                                       hazardous wastes

Raw materials →   → Other environmental
                                                       releases

Use/reuse/maintenance   → Usable products

Waste management

Source: Blumenfeld, Earle and Shopley, in *Prism*, 3rd Quarter (1991), p. 50

Figure 9.5 Summarizing the LCA inventory for impact assessment

Indicative assessment matrix					
Environmental fields	**Product life cycle**				
	Pre-production	Production	Distribution (including packaging)	Utilization	Disposal
Waste relevance					
Soil pollution and degradation					
Water contamination					
Air contamination					
Noise					
Consumption of energy					
Consumption of natural resources					
Effects on eco-systems					

Source: Annex 1, *Official Journal of the European Communities*, No. L 99/6 (11.4.92).

In this way a range of 'expert' opinion is obtained and 'averaged'. An alternative, but related (and far simpler) approach is to take a series of focused impacts and assess those by reference to specific tests. The Rhône-Poulenc and CIA 'environmental index' and the ICI 'Environmental burden' approaches are of this sort (see Chapter 5).

In life cycle improvement analysis, the final step of LCA, the information gathered at the two earlier stages is assimilated into the redesign of systems to improve the environmental performance of products. The previous information should provide a prioritized list of goals for environmental improvement and, from this, a range of associated improvement options can be derived. Specific implementation of improvements would then follow and may involve, for example, increasing energy efficiency, reducing raw material usage, cleaner production technologies, reducing emissions, as well as recycling schemes and less packaging.[10]

There are considerable interdependencies between the three stages of LCA. For example, knowledge of the impact of the production process should drive the factors included in the life cycle inventory phase.[11] Likewise, given that LCA is a very time-consuming activity, the products investigated will in part be determined by the severity of their environmental impacts – naturally, the most environmentally malign areas should be tackled first. Further, LCA should not be a static exercise but an iterative, dynamic one whose development mirrors the development in our understanding regarding the impacts of activities. Improvements in environmental impacts under LCA are likely to be incremental, with each LCA building on the next – LCA is not a one-off exercise to cure all environmental ills.

9.6 The Use of LCA

LCA is in continuous development but many companies are finding it increasingly useful. It has been used for purposes as diverse as assessing the impact of fertilizers, polymers and aluminium, as a basis for environmental accounting, in an attempt to find alternative sources of materials and methods of manufacture of margarine and in the construction of EIAs (see Chapter 5) in an attempt to assess the financial

---

[10] See also Chapter 6 on energy and Chapter 7 on waste, packaging and recycling.

[11] This is influenced by the limits set on the upstream and downstream effects. For example, the discharge of a very toxic substance in minute amounts warrants inclusion in LCA; however, the incorporation of this discharge in the life cycle inventory phase is dictated by the toxicity of the substance, which is in fact determined in the life cycle impact analysis.

Figure 9.6

Some inherent limitations of LCA are:

- Bounding the system: identifying the 'cradles' and the graves'. It is inevitable that the system must be bounded but too often it is done far too closely.
- Identification and measurement of impacts: the correct things must be measured and the uncertainty absorption inherent in quantification treated carefully. For example, is it more appropriate to measure a volume of discharge or the toxicity of it?
- Difficulties of information: particularly the difficulty of obtaining the information and the problems of handling so much. The drinks container LCAs involved many thousands of data points which all must be collected on comparable bases.
- Scientific ignorance and uncertainty: means that all data are complex, conditional and incomplete.
- Difficulty in prioritizing: given constraints and uncertainty – how should one identify the most immediate aspects to examine?
- Difficulties in choosing the preferred environmental/financial options.
- Problems of matching measurements made in different units, e.g. energy, weight, toxicity.

---

and environmental trade-offs in material and product use.[12] But in each case, the system of the LCA has been very closely bounded. Equally, LCA has been an essential component in the EU eco-labelling scheme's investigations into products as varied as washing machines, soft-drink containers, glass versus aluminium recycling and petrol versus diesel fuel for motor vehicles. Finally, on a global stage, LCAs have been employed in an attempt to link organizational activity to global warming/climate change (see Chapter 6). If one lesson has been learned from this experience it is that the usefulness of the approach is in its difficulty and complexity – environmental choices are rarely (if ever) simple.

There have been a number of highly publicized cases in which LCA has been at the centre of public controversy and which have served to illustrate the care with which the method should be employed. One of the most contentious cases related to Procter and Gamble's claims over the relative environmental impact of their disposable babies' nappies (diapers) compared with the more traditional material (re-washable) product. LCAs produced by Procter and Gamble were hotly contested by other parties who produced contradictory LCAs to support *their* case. Furthermore, the dispute brought out the social issues which are so fundamentally tied up with environmental matters (see Chapters 13 and 14). That is, Procter and Gamble's

---

[12] Companies which have used LCA in these ways include Norsk Hydro, Unilever, IBM, BSO/Origin (see Chapter 12), Gateway and Procter and Gamble.

Figure 9.7

Uses of life cycle analysis

Information to external parties
- Shareholders, regarding impact of their investments.
- Consumers, to assess products.
- Pressure groups regarding a product's and organization's environmental impact.
- Policy-makers, concerning environmental impacts of products.
- Other interested parties, for example ethical investors, eco-label regulatory bodies, eco-audit regulatory bodies.

Information for internal parties
- Establish comprehensive baseline information on a product's overall resource requirements and emissions.
- Help determine priorities for environmental care action.
- Provide managers with information to set targets and measure environment-related performance.
- Guide product development.
- Provide a basis for advertising claims and public relations exercises.
- EMAS/ISO 14001.
- As part of the supplier audit process.
- Aid in the selection of the 'best practical environmental option' (BPEO).

Source: Adapted from SETAC, *A Technical Framework for Lifecycle Assessments* (1991)

---

acquisition of one of the raw materials used in the disposable nappies was claimed to require the displacement of an indigenous people (the Samis) and this, in turn, raised considerable moral and ethical questions about company behaviour.[13] Until such time as these highly difficult and contentious issues implicit in LCA are resolved it is difficult to see how the method can avoid alternative LCAs arriving at contradictory results and thus undermining its credibility. But this, of course, may be the point: environmental (and social) issues are so complex that single simple answers are simply impossible. All LCA can do is help us understand this world of essential complexity.

9.7   A Role for Accountants?

Whilst LCA has been, predominantly, the domain of scientific and technical expertise, the principles of the process can be easily understood – and contributed to – by management and others with a

---

[13] See, for more information, *ENDS Report* 205/February 1992, pp. 13–15; *Green Magazine*, December 1991, pp. 11–15; Hindle (1992); *Procter and Gamble Limited Environmental Review* 1990.

Figure 9.8 Accountants and LCA

LCA checklist for accountants	Accountants' involvement
Pre-LCA	
● Establish goals of LCA	
● Identify constraints to LCA (time, cost, etc.)	✔
LCA – Inventory	
● Determine extent of products' effects (upstream and downstream)	
● Define limits of analysis and assumptions	
● Design systems to gather relevant information	✔
● Gather information	
● Audit information collected	✔
LCA – Impact analysis	
● Define impacts to be considered	
● Determine risk assessment to be adopted	
● Convert LCA inventory items into relevant impacts	
● Audit impact information	✔
● Assess impacts	
LCA – Improvement analysis	
● Establish budget available	✔
● Establish environmental priorities	
● Identify areas where significant improvements exist	
● Canvass alternatives	
● Cost and assess alternatives	✔
● Implement improvements	
● Monitor results of improvements and react where necessary	
● Audit outcomes	✔
Post-LCA	
● Assess goal achievement	✔
● Make information available to a wider consistency	✔
● Make new goals	

business systems perspective. This clearly applies to accountants whose skills and experience in evidence collection and evaluation, systems design and evaluation, and audit have a potentially important role to play in the development of LCA. Furthermore, whilst the environmental options may be seen as technical issues, the financial implications of existing activities and potential options are clearly the domain of the accountant and, as the more forward-thinking companies are beginning to learn, the involvement of accountants is an essential practical step in the life cycle improvement analysis. To date, however, accountants are rarely involved and so there is clearly a significant potential here. Figure 9.8 is provided as a guide to that potential.

9.8   Conclusions

Accountants should really know better than anyone the dangers of accepting the claims of a technique and, even more so, accepting numbers and answers that come from little-understood techniques. LCA is an essentially simple and sensible process but one that cannot fulfil its claims and aims. Like budgeting and cost–benefit analysis, the principal benefit lies in the process of undertaking the exercise rather than in believing the answers that come out of that process.

This is also an apposite point to raise some of the wider issues which are implicit in much of our discussion so far (and will be examined in more detail in Chapters 14 and 15). That is, a great deal of what environmental management is seeking is *eco-efficiency* – frequently (if misleadingly) described as 'doing more with less'. Efficiency is a ratio of input to output. High levels of efficiency can be achieved (for example, ratio of energy per unit of output, raw material usage per unit of production, etc.), but if sales are rising then the *total* environmental impact (what we might call the *eco-effectiveness*) will still rise. This notion of *eco-effectiveness* (which we only coin to high-light the limits of *eco-efficiency*) is captured by other notions such as *ecological footprint*.[14] At a simple level, our ecological footprint is the amount of physical space needed by an individual, an organization or an activity to support them. We, in the West, make enormous foot-prints. As long as companies grow faster than their eco-efficiency, their ecological footprint gets bigger[15] – and the environmental impact rises. A concern with *eco-efficiency* can disguise this basic fact of life. One of the important advantages of mass balances and LCAs is, if they are used sensibly, that they bring this essential ecological fact of life to the attention of the organization and to the forefront of manage-ment thinking. Whether the organization can do anything about it, as we will see in Chapters 14 and 15, is a moot point.

Further Reading

Blumenfeld, K., R. Earle and J.B. Shopley (1991) 'Identifying strategic environmental oppor-tunities: a life cycle approach', *Prism*, 3rd Quarter, pp. 45–57.

[14] Other concepts are also used and these vary from ecological rucksacks to esti-mates of ecological systems carrying capacities. These are beyond our scope here, but see, for example, Dauncey (1996) and Wackernagel and Rees (1996).

[15] And there is more than a little concern that Western footprints are already far too large.

Department of the Environment (1991) *Giving Guidance to the Green Consumer – Progress on an Eco-labelling Scheme for the UK*, a report by the National Advisory Group on Eco-labelling (London: DoE)

Epstein, M.J. (1996) *Measuring Corporate Environmental Performance* (Chicago: Irwin), pp. 34–43

Institute of Environmental Management (1998) 'Eco-efficiency: towards more sustainable business practice – Part II: Focus on life cycle assessment', *Institute of Environmental Management Journal*, 5 (3) June (whole issue)

Schaltegger, S. (with K. Mueller and H. Hindrichsen) (1996) *Corporate Environmental Accounting* (New York: Wiley)

Society of Environmental Toxicology and Chemistry (SETAC) (1991) *A Technical Framework for Lifecycle Assessments* (London: SETAC)

Welford, R. (ed.) (1998) *Corporate Environmental Management: Systems and Strategies*, 2nd edn (London: Earthscan), ch. 8

See also *ENDS Report* and Institute of Environmental Management publications, which carry regular pieces and updates on LCA.

APPENDIX 9.1
The 'Green Accounts' from Danish Steel Works Ltd,
Annual Report 1991

MASS BALANCE (TONNES)

GREEN

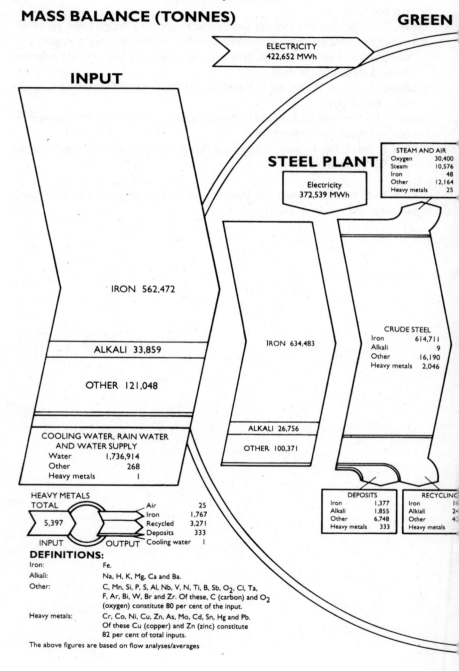

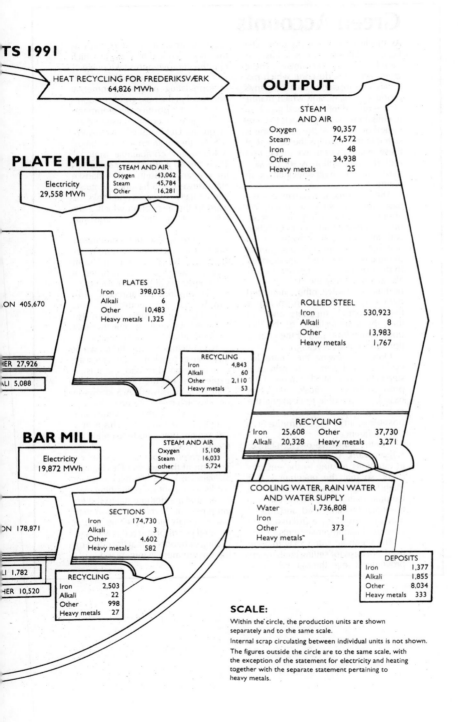

TS 1991

HEAT RECYCLING FOR FREDERIKSVÆRK
64,826 MWh

OUTPUT

STEAM
AND AIR

Oxygen	90,357
Steam	74,572
Iron	48
Other	34,938
Heavy metals	25

PLATE MILL

Electricity
29,558 MWh

STEAM AND AIR

Oxygen	43,062
Steam	45,784
Other	16,281

ON 405,670

PLATES

Iron	398,035
Alkali	6
Other	10,483
Heavy metals	1,325

ER 27,926

LI 5,088

ROLLED STEEL

Iron	530,923
Alkali	8
Other	13,983
Heavy metals	1,767

RECYCLING

Iron	4,843
Alkali	60
Other	2,110
Heavy metals	53

RECYCLING

Iron	25,608	Other	37,730
Alkali	20,328	Heavy metals	3,271

BAR MILL

Electricity
19,872 MWh

STEAM AND AIR

Oxygen	15,108
Steam	16,033
other	5,724

COOLING WATER, RAIN WATER
AND WATER SUPPLY

Water	1,736,808
Iron	1
Other	373
Heavy metals	1

ON 178,871

SECTIONS

Iron	174,730
Alkali	3
Other	4,602
Heavy metals	582

DEPOSITS

Iron	1,377
Alkali	1,855
Other	8,034
Heavy metals	333

LI 1,782

ER 10,520

RECYCLING

Iron	2,503
Alkali	22
Other	998
Heavy metals	27

SCALE:

Within the circle, the production units are shown
separately and to the same scale.

Internal scrap circulating between individual units is not shown.

The figures outside the circle are to the same scale, with
the exception of the statement for electricity and heating
together with the separate statement pertaining to
heavy metals.

Green Accounts

As the first steel manufacturer, Det Danske Stålvalseværk A/S has prepared »Green Accounts«. These green accounts describe which materials are supplied to the Company's production plant, and which materials are turned into finished goods or to emissions, waste products to be recycled or waste. At the same time is stated in main groups the content of these materials of heavy metal, iron etc. The description is set up as a mass-balance sheet specified upon elements.

The green accounts are meant as a basis for an objective discussion about further reductions of the strain on the environment in connection with the Company's activities, as all materials which may be detrimental to the environment is being supplied to the Company through raw materials, alloys, energy etc. Thus it is important to involve other interested parties in the discussion, including the Company's suppliers and not least the manufacturers of the products which form part of the circulation of steel for recycling.

Only by viewing the entire life cycle of steel and each individual step in the use of steel to many of the products on which modern society is based, is it possible to continue the recycling of steel with the lowest possible strain on the environment as a consequence.

It is the objective of Det Danske Stålvalseværk A/S to show openness in questions relating to the environment, so that the uncertainty that might exist in connection with the Company's influence on the environment may be eliminated, and instead may give room for a discussion on how to obtain improvements.

The green accounts may thus be used as a basis for setting goals for improvements, e.g. through increased recycling of waste products, just as they may be used to show at which rate the improvements take place.

The Company is actively involved in formulating new environmental goals so that the next green accounts may reflect a positive development.

The green accounts presented are unique for Det Danske Stålvalseværk A/S. Neither in Denmark nor abroad is found any comparable material. There are no guidelines or standards for »Green Accounts«. Det Danske Stålvalseværk A/S has thus ventured into a totally new area and looks forward to the inspiration which a debate about the green accounts may result in.

The green accounts statements can be documented based on quantities from the year 1991 and from analyses, which a.o. are included in the Company's application for voluntary environmental approval. The aim is that independent auditors should be able to audit and sign also the green accounts, an objective that will be pursued in the coming year.

No conclusions may be drawn at this stage as to whether the green accounts are good or bad, but it is an expression of the fact that Det Danske Stålvalseværk A/S knows in detail which materials are being supplied and which are leaving the Company's production plant. This is in itself a major prerequisite to create improvements.

The green accounts are also an expression of the fact that Det Danske Stålvalseværk A/S' production plant works as a giant recycling filter. Materials that are detrimental to the environment and which come in with raw materials etc. are either tied in finished goods or steered towards recycling or depots so that the effect on the environment is minimized.

PART C: EXTERNAL RELATIONS

Overview

by Martin Houldin, EMAG Ltd

We started by saying that accountants have a role to play in environmental management because of the potential business implications of environmental issues. For example, the contamination of land will affect assets and liabilities, as well as incurring cost through possible breach of consents and/or the requirement to clean up. Also, we have suggested that companies can benefit financially either through opportunities to increase market share and/or market new products, or through greater cost efficiency in areas such as waste treatment and disposal. Clearly, these are subjects that should be of direct interest to accountants.

The accountant's role may therefore depend on his or her responsibilities, and take a number of forms, ranging from being involved in environmental audits through the internal audit programme, to appraising investment proposals with an eye to the environmental benefits, to the analysis of waste and energy costs in order to encourage their reduction, and to the provision of information to support environmental management.

There are two other key areas that need attention from accountants, particularly those in senior positions: the interest in environmental issues from the financial services sector; and the trend towards more corporate environmental reporting. Both are continuing to generate significant activity in major companies.

Financial Services

Relationships with different parts of the financial services sector are important to all companies. Here we are talking about banks and other commercial lenders, insurance companies, fund managers and investment companies (such as merchant banks, venture capitalists).

We need to cover each of these, although all have a broadly common interest in how environmental issues will affect the company's financial position.

Banks are interested both from the point of view of their credit risk and any potential liability falling to them. Risk is primarily a question of whether the assets are worth enough to provide adequate collateral, and whether the business is a going concern. Two important environmental issues have a direct effect on these aspects. First, the need to meet higher regulatory standards will require investment in plant and equipment, and possible write-off of existing plant. This, as well as the possibility of markets being affected, is a key going-concern issue. Secondly, potentially contaminated land can lead, at best, to asset devaluation and, at worst, to major clear-up operations and liability for other damage caused. (This, in turn, could lead to annual charges.)

Banks are therefore looking at the effect of environmental issues on a business, and questioning whether land assets provide adequate security in existing loan agreements. Clearly, these issues are equally important for new business. Banks – and, indeed, any lender – must also face the prospect of the liability for damage being passed to them in the event of liquidation and foreclosure.

Insurance companies are also involved in risk but from a different perspective. There is perhaps more focus on the possibility of major contamination or pollution incidents, especially those that could affect human health. General insurance cover is now almost completely unavailable, and companies need to seek specific environmental cover. Where this can be obtained, the cost will be high and companies will need to meet stringent standards before insurers will grant it.

All investors will be interested in these questions of going concern, risk and potential liability. Fund managers and investment analysts, with their eyes more on share price and profit forecasts, are beginning to raise detailed and searching questions about the financial implications of environmental issues, whether revenue or cost. Companies are still finding it difficult to answer these questions, partly because plans are not yet in place (but perhaps should be) and partly because their financial systems are not geared up to providing this kind of analysis. They will need to be in the not-too-distant future.

Investment companies, which aim to acquire a major equity stake, are taking steps to ensure that all these issues have been thoroughly investigated and provided for where necessary. Of particular interest to them is the extent to which the company's management have adequate procedures and systems for managing environmental risk and performance. These are therefore issues for senior accountants in the company seeking finance.

Merchant banks advising companies involved in mergers and acquisitions, management buy-outs and similar transactions are now advising their clients on the appropriate due diligence steps to take prior to completing the transaction at a given price. Accountants on both sides of these corporate transactions will need to be involved in – and on top of – the issues.

Companies in all these financial services sectors are already actively involved with addressing each of these issues. Whether they call them credit reviews, risk management assessments, investigations, valuations, or due diligence reviews – they are essentially dealing with the same set of questions. Senior accountants need to be prepared to tackle these issues, and may see the benefits of planning ahead.

External Reporting

Disclosure in financial accounts

. . . will fall into a number of areas:

- contingent liabilities;
- provisions;
- extraordinary or exceptional charges against profit;
- operating and financial review comments;
- profit and capital expenditure forecasts for shareholders' circular.

We are witnessing significant growth in the extent of external reporting of environmental performance and/or attributes. This part deals, quite rightly, with the questions concerning how environmental issues will affect the financial reporting aspects of the annual reports as well as with the reporting of non-financial information.

There still seems to be little likelihood of much in the way of introduction of specific environmental disclosure requirements within financial statements or of specific environmental accounting standards outside North America. Most accounting bodies believe that existing accounting standards, together with current exposure drafts, are generally adequate for the job. The various accounting standards and auditing practices bodies have, however, undertaken to provide guidance on these matters. But other forces – such as the European Commission's interest in public access to information – may, however, change this situation in the longer term. There is no doubt that recognition of environmental issues within the financial statements is becoming a more important issue for accountants.

Environmental reporting developments and wide recognition of the possible implications of environmental issues for accounting have been the main drivers for the growth in environmental accounting activity among the different institutes of accountants and representative accounting bodies. We will continue to see considerable effort expended by the profession in monitoring, informing and educating their membership on environmental matters.

Non-financial reporting, in the shape of separate sections in the annual report, or in special environmental reports, continues to increase. There is tremendous variety, however, starting with a simple statement of intent or mission (which could barely be termed a policy), to full statements of policy and objectives, and moving towards (in stages) reports on performance with statistical back-up. The direction of developments in this field is undoubtedly to report on performance and achievement rather than intent. This essential emphasis on performance, plus the exceptionally influential Global Reporting Initiative, is moving reporting towards so-called 'sustainability reporting' by companies – which shows all the hallmarks of the central concern for the twenty-first century.

What role there is for accountants remains to be seen, and perhaps depends on different company situations. Accountants will, however, need to be alert to any financial information contained in the environmental sections, and to ensure consistency. And the stick is that if companies do not voluntarily disclose environmental information, external parties – the 'social audits' – will.

There is no doubt that there are many external issues in which accountants need not only to become involved but, in some cases, to play a leading role. It is true that at the time of going to press, the external relationships, and their implications for accounting and financial information, are *probably the more important, and certainly more visible* where there is most activity.

CHAPTER 10

THE GREENING OF FINANCE

Bank Lending, Insurance and Ethical/Environmental Investment

10.1 Introduction

As with the supply and purchase of goods and services (see Chapters 3, 6 and 7), the supply and purchase of funds are also influenced by the developing environmental agenda. For the banks, there is increasing concern over the security of loans and the potential for lender liability, for insurers increasing concern over what is and is not commercially insurable, and, for the investment community, there is increasing evidence both of a concern to exercise some environmental criteria in decisions to buy shares and of environmental criteria playing a crucial part in mergers, acquisitions and management buy-outs. The implications for companies and other organizations are considerable. Not only are there the problems of (*inter alia*) an increasingly restrictive short-termism and difficulties in attracting funds for environmental initiatives which may not offer conventionally attractive rates of return (see Chapter 8) but such funds as can be attracted are more and more likely to have demanding environmental conditions attached. Broadly speaking, in addition to having to meet increasing environmental standards and struggling to persuade financiers to take a broader view of environmental initiatives, enterprises are being faced with two further – and somewhat different – sets of pressures. First, there is the purely commercial pressure from banks and insurers concerned about their own exposures and, second, there is a growing awareness among investors of the importance of ethical and environmental matters – a development led by the major green investment funds. The whole pattern of funding to and from enterprises is in the process of changing.

On the face of it, this connection of environmental concerns with the financial community might seem surprising – after all, banks, insurance companies and investment funds (for example) are not major polluters are they? All organizations, as we know, have direct environmental impacts as soon as they use materials, property, energy, etc., but this is not the essential point for the financial industry.

Financial institutions have considerable influence on the environmental and sustainable development (see Chapter 14) agendas – whether for good or ill depends on one's point of view.[1] Ultimately, regardless of the motives, ethics and intentions of corporate management, the financial community's demand for returns – and its power if it doesn't obtain the returns it wants – is such that it holds the ultimate power in capitalism. (Given that capitalism is about capital why should that surprise us?) Similarly, the financial industry has, traditionally, operated in an amoral vacuum in which the only concern was financial returns – not how those returns were derived. Therefore, any attempt to change the way in which organizations operate must take account of how one might seek change in the financial structures of the world. There is growing evidence that the financial community is beginning to take some (albeit relatively small) interest in such matters and, counter-intuitively, is actually acting, in some cases, as a force towards greater environmental sensitivity.[2]

This chapter will attempt to provide a brief introduction to these issues. We will begin with a résumé of the issues facing lenders and borrowers. This will raise further questions about insurance issues. The chapter then reviews the experiences of the developing and increasingly important ethical/environmental investment funds.

Before we begin – a brief word of warning. This area in particular is changing very rapidly with myriad local, national and global initiatives starting up and disappearing all the time. What follows is necessarily brief and general and you are recommended to pursue the references and further reading for further detail.

10.2   Bank Lending and Environmental Liability

In an area of very rapid change and wide-ranging national differences, banks, particularly during the 1990s, found themselves forced to take a very close look at environmental factors as they affected their lending policy. From the banks' point of view the problem has three elements:

(1)   Is the business to which the bank is lending likely to find itself involved in serious environmental problems which will increase its costs and make its servicing of the loan problematic?

---

[1] See Schmidheiny and Zorraquin (1996) for a particularly optimistic discussion of the financial community's positive role. See, for example, Mayo (1993), Rich (1994) and Welford (1997a, chs 5 and 6) for alternative views.

[2] For a more developed and theoretical case about finance and environmental responsibility see Owen (1990).

(2)   If the business goes into liquidation and the bank becomes the owner of the property of the company (actual or *de facto*) what are the possibilities of environmental liabilities attaching to that property – especially land – for which the bank will be liable?

(3)   Can the 'polluter pays' principle require the bank – as a *business associate* – to take part in any business clean-up costs, even if the business is not in liquidation and the bank has not foreclosed?

The consequences of this problem have been that some companies have found obtaining loans more difficult, the requirements attaching to the granting of the loan have been more stringent and, in many cases, the costs to the enterprises in environmental audits and legal costs, for example, significantly increased the price of the finance.[3]

The issue first emerged in North America over the clean-up of contaminated land. Under the 'Superfund' legislation (see Chapter 11) organizations owning contaminated land could be held liable for its being cleaned up – a potentially massive liability. Banks whose loans were secured on such land began to find themselves the owners of significant liabilities: the US environmental authorities could come after them for the clean-up costs. This extended to Canada and has also gone beyond contaminated land to such things as hazardous products, toxic spills and failures to comply with environmental legislation. Although the legislation governing the nature of such liabilities varies considerably from country to country, some form of legislation on contaminated land, on civil liability caused by waste and the polluter pays principle is increasingly the norm.[4] The minimum requirement for industry arising from these developments is to have a sound environmental audit regime and a well-developed EMS (see Chapter 5).[5,6]

[3] A report in 1992 outlined the serious difficulties a number of established businesses were having in persuading banks to grant loan finance – due not to doubts about the core business or normal business exposure risk but to environmental considerations (David Lascelles, 'Only clean and green borrowers need apply', *Financial Times*, 27 March 1992, p. 19). See also Bömke (1997) and Maltby (1995).

[4] See Chapter 11 for more detail on this and references which develop the ideas. For an introduction to the banking view see, for example, Kopitsky and Betzenberger (1997), Rowley and Witmer (1988/9) and Singh (1989).

[5] One survey of American banks showed, *inter alia*, that 16.7 per cent had abandoned property rather than taking title because of environmental concerns; 62.5 per cent had rejected loan applications based upon the possibility of environmental liability; 88.1 per cent had changed lending procedures to avoid environmental liability; 13.5 per cent had incurred clean-up costs on property held as collateral; and 45.8 per cent had discontinued loans to certain businesses because of fear of environmental liability. (American Banks Association survey 1991 based upon 1741 community banks, reported in Bernard Simon, 'Sharks in the water', *Financial Times*, 27 November 1991, p. 16).

[6] There is an especially interesting case study which examines various elements of the liability, lending decision and financial institutions relationship. See Napier (1992). For further detail see also Thompson (1992) and Neil Bennet, 'Clean-up costs force banks to rethink lending', *The Times*, 14 January 1992.

The situation in the USA became more critical still in 1990 with the decision in the *Fleet Factors* case, in which the lender was held responsible because it participated 'in the financial management of a facility to a degree indicating a capacity to influence the corporation's treatment of hazardous wastes'. A bank did not have to exercise that capacity to be liable. Such judgments send shock waves through the banking community and, whilst the liability situation is still not entirely clear in many countries, it is clear that bank lending on a worldwide basis is having to address some fairly critical matters.[7]

Beyond the banks' very rapid reaction to the spectre of *their* potential liability and an active lobbying of governments to act to limit banks' liabilities, the public response of the banks, their development of their own environmental strategies and their development of their own environmental reporting (for example) has been (typically?) conservative, reactionary and minimalist.

Given the critical role that banks play in the economy, this is perturbing because the environmental agenda is demanding a significant change to the banks' *modus operandi*. Not only are there the direct and potential financial problems but the environment raises important ethical questions that financiers cannot dodge for much longer:

> The business of moving money is inextricably linked to the movement of raw materials, finished goods, labor, and ultimately, to the quality of our environment . . . the movement of dollars, pounds, and yen may also involve the creation of toxic wastes, ozone depleting chemicals, global warming gases, and other environmental disruptions . . . Banks that do not take an active stance on environmental issues may instead find themselves reacting defensively to a host of societal, financial and regulatory pressures.
>
> (Sarokin and Schulkin, 1991, p. 7)

The banks' traditional reluctance to respond to environmental issues has been placed under direct pressure with the launch of the UNEP *Statement by Banks on the Environment and Sustainable Development* for the 1992 Earth Summit (see Chapter 15). By the late 1990s, only 90 banks (after considerable lobbying and cajolery by UNEP) had signed up to the Statement and even these – which could be considered to be the leading banks in terms of environmental practice – had rarely more than a piecemeal and reluctant response to the environmental agenda. The conclusion seems to be that any significant contribution to the sustainability agenda (Chapter 14) by banks is some way off.[8]

---

[7] A UNEP report based on a worldwide survey of banks (UNEP, 1995) found that 70 per cent of respondents considered that environmental issues had had a material impact on their business and 80 per cent perform some degree of environmental risk assessment. US banks were the most likely to be active in the environmental risk assessment field.

[8] Hill et al. (1997).

But not all is gloom. Whilst the high-profile, international banks drag their heels on the environmental agenda a number of smaller banks have been setting the pace. In the UK, the Co-operative Bank (see Figure 10.1) has made a major virtue out of its ethical policy.

Figure 10.1

The Co-operative Bank Ethical Policy.

"Can a bank exert a positive influence on the future of the World? Can you? Together we can at least try. We can stand up and let our views be known. We can show that behaviour that is unacceptable to society should not be acceptable in business. We can act as a force for a change."

Terry Thomas, MD Co-operative Bank

1. **We will not** loan. invest or supply financial services to countries governed by oppressive regimes.

2. **We will not** help finance companies that manufacture and export arms and weapons to countries that oppress their people.

3. **We will not** invest in any business involved in testing cosmetics on animals.

4. **We will not** support any person or company that causes animal suffering through intensive factory farming.

5. **We will not** offer financial support to a business. farm or other organisation engaged in the production of animal fur.

6. **We will not** support any organisation involved in blood sports.

7. **We will not** invest in or loan to manufacturers of tobacco products.

8. **We will** try to ensure that none of our services are exploited for the purposes of money laundering. drug trafficking or tax evasion.

9. **We will** help and encourage all our business customers to adopt a pro-active stance on the environmental impact of their own activities.

10. **We will** actively seek out individuals. commercial enterprises and non-commercial organisations that have a complementary ethical attitude.

11. **We will** extend and strengthen our Customer Charter in order to maintain our high standards of customer confidentiality.

12. **We will** continuously re-appraise our customers' views on all of these and other issues and develop our ethical stance accordingly.

The **COOPERATIVE BANK**

081406

Across Europe, organizations as varied as (for example) the Triodos bank, Mercury Provident, the Ecology Building Society, SbN bank and the Union Bank of Switzerland have all undertaken significant environmental and ethical initiatives that have demonstrated – and continue to demonstrate – what a responsible financial sector might actually look like. Until the approaches taken by these smaller financial institutions become the norm, the financial sector will continue to act as a major impediment on, rather than an impetus for, the sort of fundamental change which the environment – and sustainability – requires.

10.3   Risk and Insurance

At its crudest, this growing concern of the banks can be seen as the development of a new kind of risk, one the financial community must manage if it is to continue operating. As a form of risk,[9] environmentally related liabilities are extremely far-reaching, potentially very expensive and largely unpredictable – if for no other reason than that the law is changing so fast as to make future liability an unknown quantity. But companies (and banks) turning to their insurance companies are facing problems – not the least of which arise from the insurance industry's experiences of the 1980s and 1990s that the writing of environment impairment liability policies was a major loss-maker and pollution cover virtually impossible to provide as developments seemed to try to shift liability from corporations to insurers as 'the last deep pocket' upon which environmental protection agencies could draw.[10]

The major problems seem to centre around the insurers' unwillingness and/or inability to cover all possible risks. Whilst it may be possible to insure for future events, those relating to past activity are often uninsurable. Sudden and accidental pollution can be covered but gradual pollution cannot. Injury, damage, compensation costs may well be insurable but it is unlikely that an insurance company will want to look at clean-up costs. Increasingly, insurers will insure only sites that have been inspected/environmentally audited and will provide strict exclusion clauses governing activities and standards. And so many potential environmental problems are unforeseeable, whether due to legal changes, general ignorance, unexpected results of the chemistry cocktail one is working with and so on. One can therefore expect a continually changing situation in insurance markets.

---

[9] No distinction is drawn here between risk and uncertainty.
[10] For more detail see, for example, Hester (1991).

In the meantime, organizations must look much more closely at the insurance cover they have and undertake some reassessment exercises. (A helpful checklist from CEBIS is included in Appendix 10.1.) The environmental insurance an organization does have is likely to cost more because:

(1)   although the insurance companies are learning to separate out various risks, the overall risk is rising and this will increase the cost to the customer;
(2)   this insurance cover is likely to be for a smaller proportion of the total risks of the corporation; and
(3)   the prerequisites for acquiring environmental risk insurance will be environmental audits and high standards of environmental management throughout the facility to be insured.

It would seem that enterprises must recognize too that insurance is not the best way in which to manage environmental liability – it is too costly, too partial, does not cover all current areas of potential environmental risk and is not capable of covering the wide range of possible situations that could arise. High insurance costs will actually encourage corporations to improve their environmental management, using risk cover as the final safety net.

Consequently, in recognition that the very proper caution of insurers over environmental risks can be turned to positive advantage UNEP established the *Statement of Environmental Commitment by the Insurance Sector* to which, by the late 1990s, there were 60 signatory companies.[11] The UN initiative was an attempt constructively to exploit three 'win–win' possibilities. First, it is recognized that if insurance companies demand best environmental practice of their clients – on such matters as transport, accidents, occupational health and so on – this will act as a very positive incentive to companies to adopt such practices. Secondly, insurance companies are major investors in their own right and have a major responsibility to ensure the prudent management of their investments. It is therefore in their interests (and they have the power to demand) that companies adopt procedures to minimize environmental risk. Finally, and on a much larger stage, there is an increasing belief that economic activity (and its associated pollution) is a principal cause of global climate change (see also Chapter 6). Insurers are finding themselves facing a massive increase in claims deriving from natural catastrophes from extreme weather conditions. It is therefore in the insurers' interests (as well as the interests of society and the environment) to encourage, by any means possible, practices that reduce industrial impact on the climate.

[11] See Schanzenbächer (1997).

This should, in turn, reduce (or at least not further increase) the risk exposure that the insurance industry faces in this area.[12]

10.4 The Environmental Influence of Financial Institutions

There seems little question that the banks and insurance companies are driven by conventional business motives – an improving risk/ return trade-off, with steady growth or, at least, no contraction. The motivation would seem to owe nothing to ethics or to concern for the environment in any intrinsic sense. Nevertheless, the general impact on organizations of financial institutions exercising the gravest caution over environmental matters has been enormous, and shows every sign of growing. That is, because of banks' and insurance companies' fears over profit and risk, other organizations will, of necessity, have to undertake environmental audits, set in place rigorous environmental management systems and, perhaps most significantly, move away from the more environmentally risky activities. Self-interest is driving a significant rise in environmental sensitivity. It is this sort of observation that, quite justly, is used to bolster the case for a 'market' and 'voluntary' approach to the environmental sensitivity of organizations. However, not all in the garden is completely organic and uncontaminated.

The developed economies[13] are already facing situations, as we have seen, in which the environmental and profit criteria appear to be in conflict. As we saw in Chapters 5 and 8, environmental management requires a proactive and creative approach to investment. This is possible only when the providers of the funds are willing to recognize other, non-financial criteria and/or take a longer-term view of the investment, loan or whatever. There is not yet much evidence of this. In fact, it has been argued that financial institutions in general, and banks in particular, see themselves as 'amoral' – as environmentally neutral. This is clearly not the case.[14] Ultimately, financial institutions have the greatest power over organizations, can greatly influence them in positive ways and profoundly hinder them in negative ways. This is critical because it largely determines the extent to which

---

[12] See, for example, Annighöfer (1997).

[13] And this begs questions about the relationship with G77 countries. This is addressed briefly in Chapter 15.

[14] See Sarokin and Schulkin (1991) for the case with respect to banking. In general terms this view can be supported by the wider case made against economics and accounting, which is summarized in Appendix 1.1.

organizations can become more 'ethical' and more environmentally sensitive. Thus, can the board adopt a path towards sustainable development if this is likely to reduce profits and dividends? It seems likely that the capital markets in general, and the banks and institutional and individual shareholders in particular, at the very least offer a constraint upon managerial discretion and, at a maximum, encourage the pursuit of profit, dividends and interest to dominate other ethical or environmental objectives.

The development of environmental sensitivity will frequently be costly and limit an organization's options, and the capital markets, shareholders and other providers of funds will have to recognize this. They become crucial to any discussion of how organizations may become more environmentally sensitive.

These issues also raise ethical questions of the justice of investors (perhaps alongside other providers of funds, material and labour) taking a return from an organization which has caused environmental degradation.[15] This raises questions as to the rights of capital's objectives to (perhaps) dominate all others, which – in turn – leads to a questioning of liberal economics.[16] This also leads to practical questions as to whether our present institutional arrangements will actually permit managers to undertake anything other than the most superficial greening of their organizations – even if they wished to. Perhaps most importantly, however, in recent years there has been a tendency in the West to reinforce the idea that the financial community is self-interested and greedy – in fact to suggest that investors had a duty to put profit above all else.[17] We believe we have shown that such a dominance by profit may ensure environmental crisis and risk the end of the species.

It is these matters that we wish to concentrate upon for the remainder of this chapter – to introduce the role of the shareholder to our discussions of environmental sensitivity, to review the extent to which we might expect shareholders to take stands on ethical and environmental matters and thereby to lead organizational management and,

---

[15] This issue is returned to in Part D, when the question of sustainability is examined. This concept suggests that it is possible to conceive that shareholders' dividends are currently paid out of *natural* capital.

[16] See Parts A and D; but see also, for example, Beder (1997), Gray (1992), Korten (1995), Welford (1997a).

[17] Typically, see Friedman (1962), but see also Benston (1982a, 1982b) and Walton (1983). The majority of financial accounting textbooks reinforce this idea, usually implicitly; textbooks on business finance reinforce the idea explicitly. It is little wonder therefore that accountants, in general, might see accounting profit as a God-given goal and anything which conflicts with it, such as the physical environment, as the stuff of heresy. See Gray *et al.* (1994).

finally, to outline the way in which ethical and environmental investment is developing.

10.5 Do Shareholders Care About Ethics and the Environment?

For nearly twenty years, researchers have attempted to assess whether
social responsibility (including ethical standards and environmental
issues), social disclosures, economic and accounting performance and
the performance of share prices were related. This attempt consisted
of a number of strands which, in the particular context of this chapter,
were directed towards assessing whether shareholders rewarded,
penalized or were indifferent to companies with a better than average
social (and/or environmental) performance. The elements are reflected
in Figure 10.2.[18] In broad terms, the research is inconclusive but seems
to suggest that investors *do* care about social disclosure and social
performance *only* when it will affect financial performance, and to the
extent that investors care about the intrinsic ethical positions of organizations, they care very little. Attempts to isolate the 'environmental'
element of 'social' have produced broadly similar results.

These are depressing, if unsurprising, results. Depressing in that
they suggest that the most environmentally sensitive management
will be excessively limited in the environmental options available to
them and no lead on environmental matters can be expected from

Figure 10.2 Social responsibility and shareholders

Characteristic	Social Performance	Social Disclosure	Accounting Profit	Stock Market Performance
Social Performance		No relationship	Slight relationship	Slight relationship
Social Disclosure			Slight relationship	Possible relationship
Accounting Profit				Positive relationship
Stock Market Performance				

[18] See, for example, Gray et al. (forthcoming) for an up-to-date review of these
studies.

shareholders unless it repays them financially. Whether or not chief executives would like to invest in improved technology for environmental reasons, they could not persuade their institutional shareholders and other City stakeholders that investment was justified.

The profound ethical question this raises is among the most important that accounting, finance, economics, business and the environmental agenda must face up to, but although we have touched upon the matters (see Parts A and D), we must leave this to others to discuss and move on to the more direct issues.[19] This leaves us with two broad questions: is it in the financial self-interest of shareholders to respond to environmental sensitivity? And are shareholders really so very selfish and greedy? In response to the first question, we saw in Part A that although some organizations would make financial gains from the environmental agenda, this was likely to be fairly short term and involve being only 'light green'. Substantial greening was likely to incur financial costs in the short term, at least for most organizations. However, far more likely is that those organizations that *do not* respond to the environmental agenda will face very substantial costs – up to and including liquidation.

The more interesting question at this stage is the extent of the self-interest exhibited by investors. The emergence of the ethical and green funds represents an intriguing phenomenon in this connection.

10.6 The Emergence of Ethical and Environmental Investment

Socially responsible, or ethical investment, funds were first launched in the USA in the early 1970s, and by the late 1980s controlled $50 billion in assets.[20] In the UK, such ethical funds came to prominence with the launch of the Friends Provident Stewardship Trust in 1984. By 1995 the UK ethical funds controlled about £912 million in assets.[21] The upsurge in green awareness in the late 1980s gave the ethical investment market a considerable boost. In the USA this followed the *Exxon Valdez* Alaskan oil spill and the launch of the CERES Principles (see Chapter 4) by the Coalition for Environmentally Responsible Economies (CERES) as a part of the US Social Investment Forum.[22] The impact of the funds is not related just to the amounts that they

---

[19] For more detail see, for example, Beder (1997), Jacobson (1991), Korten (1995), Lehman (1988), McGoun (1997), Owen (1990), Owen et al. (1987), Reilly and Kyj (1990).

[20] The Dreyfus Third Century Fund was established in 1972 (see, for example, Chastain, 1973).

[21] WM Research (1996).

[22] For further information on the early history of these funds see, for example, Dunham (1988, 1990), Edgerton (1989), Harte et al. (1991), Lander (1989), Mitchell et al. (1990), Owen (1990), Perks et al. (1992).

Figure 10.3

Negative criteria operated by UK ethical/environmental funds

- Poor environmental record
- Poor working environment
- Repressive regimes
- Tobacco
- Alcohol
- Armaments
- Gambling
- Animal exploitation, experimentation and furs
- Nuclear
- Sexually explicit or violent media
- Complaints upheld by the Advertising Standards Authority
- Drugs
- Political donations

Source: Adapted from Harte, Lewis and Owen (1991) and Perks, Rawlinson and Ingram (1992)

---

invest – their influence has encouraged local government funds, pension funds and others to adopt ethical or environmental criteria in their investment decisions.

The small but significant and growing proportion of the capital markets which is willing to undertake investment on other than purely financial grounds[23] is a phenomenon of increasing interest. Most significantly, though, the evidence is mixed about the extent to which 'ethical investors' actually do sacrifice financial returns. Reports have suggested that the stronger the definitions and criteria used by the fund, the more likely it is to 'underperform' against a non-ethical/environmental portfolio. The ethical/environmental funds are still, however, a relatively new phenomenon and it would be too early to jump to definite conclusions. Certainly any fund looking for 'totally socially responsible' companies or 'totally environmentally friendly' companies will have a very small portfolio indeed. At a minimum, therefore, it is possible to conclude that an investor may be 'slightly ethical/environmental' to no financial detriment. Stronger views are likely to be costly. Indeed, the Body Shop – once the darling of the UK

---

[23] It is possible to hypothesize that the inconclusive nature of the studies on the relationships between social disclosure and performance, and accounting and economic performance, which we referred to earlier, could have arisen from two 'capital markets' – one wholly geared to financial return and one geared to a mix of financial and ethical considerations which introduced 'noise' into the markets. That the financially orientated group clearly dominate is not much of a surprise – see, for example, Business-in-the-Environment (1994).

green funds – notes that there is no such thing as an environmentally friendly company – only more or less environmentally sensitive.[24]

10.7 Criteria and Information for Ethical/Environmental Investment

The ethical/environmental funds operate both 'positive' and 'negative' criteria in selecting companies in which to invest. The negative criteria are easier to operate: they involve avoiding companies active in certain sectors or involved with countries, incidents or activities selected by either the investor or the fund managers as inappropriate. Figure 10.3 lists the negative criteria of UK funds – in approximate rank order of emphasis given by the funds. As Perks, Rawlinson and Ingram (1992) point out, these negative criteria need to be refined in order to make them operable – for example, 'alcohol' may be avoided altogether but this will exclude all major grocery retail chains, companies that make and supply home brewing kits, etc. The firmness with which the criteria are applied varies considerably.

Positive criteria raise more difficult problems, not least because information is difficult to obtain. Figure 10.4 lists the positive criteria operated by the UK funds – again in approximate order of emphasis. Once again, Perks, Rawlinson and Ingram (1992) identify the lack of precision with which these characteristics are defined and the variable manner in which different funds apply them.

There are two immediate implications arising from studies of the ethical and/or environmental investment movement. First, it is very difficult to assess the extent to which the trusts actually comply with their own standards – just how green are the green trusts? The answer obviously varies from trust to trust, but when one studies lists of those companies that find more favour with the ethical/environmental investment funds it becomes apparent that finding green companies proves a very difficult issue. Often the best that one can hope for is 'greener' companies – those that tend to be in the forefront of *current* environmental (and/or ethical) standards rather than those that represent ideal types. This, is turn, often leads to an emphasis on companies engaged in, for example, some environmentally related activity (e.g. waste disposal) or 'cleaner' energy systems. This does tend to

---

[24] For more detail see Burman (1990), Dobie (1990), Dunham (1988, 1990), Harte et al. (1991), Luther and Matatko (1994), Luther et al. (1992), Perks et al. (1992) and, in particular, the report in *The Independent on Sunday*, 23 February 1992 ('The best and the worst of ethical funds'), in which the strictness of ethical criteria is identified as a financially detrimental factor – to be solved by being less ethical! For a more theoretical analysis of the issues see Mackenzie (1997).

Figure 10.4

Positive criteria operated by UK ethical/environmental funds

- High standards of environmental awareness.
- Promotion of employee welfare.
- Equal employment opportunities.
- Useful contribution to community welfare.
- Provides environmentally beneficial goods or services.
- Provides socially beneficial goods or services.
- Has good customer relations record.
- Makes substantial charitable donations.
- Involvement in specific sectors (e.g. medical and health care; education).

Source: Adapted from Harte et al. (1991) and Perks et al. (1992)

---

indicate the difficulty that ethical/environmental funds have in finding 'mainstream' industrial and commercial activity which meets even relatively mild environmental criteria. Put more forcibly, few conventional organizations can meet even embryonic environmental standards – an observation that has potentially critical implications for the future of the environment and business (see Part D).

However, to see the green funds only in terms of their actual investments is to underestimate their impact. For example, a number of the better-known funds are a major force in campaigning for a raising of the environmental agenda and they have been instrumental in raising issues on a far wider platform than simply those companies in which they invest. Many environmental funds have been driven by a more developmental and campaigning role beyond simply advising investors.[25] In effect, the campaigning funds are acting on the financial supply chain in the same way as we saw the more active commercial companies acting on the supply chain for goods and services (see Chapter 5). Unfortunately, few of the trusts yet try to exercise direct influence upon the companies although there is evidence to suggest that this is beginning to change.

The second of the questions that arose from studies of environmental investment relates to the information available to the investment managers and the implications that this has for the external reporting regime. Both Harte, Lewis and Owen (1991) and Perks, Rawlinson and Ingram (1992), for example, found that the annual report was the most frequently used source of information for the investment decision but that this document gave negligible guidance

---

[25] This is especially true of the Ethical Investment Research Service (EIRIS). Also, for example, the Ethical Investors Group pledge to give 50 per cent of their profits to designated charities or groups.

on the ethical/environmental matters by which final selection was to be made. Whilst the funds use other sources of information – including direct contact with the companies – this does not remove the crucial question as to whether or not annual reports *should* provide usable data about an organization's ethical/environmental performance; after all, a major justification for annual reports is that they guide investment decisions. When ethical/environmental issues are introduced to a decision previously made without regard to ethical considerations, the annual report fails to fulfil its purpose.[26] This issue is addressed further in the following chapters.

10.8 The Future for Ethical/Environmental Investment?

There have been a number of major factors which have restricted the development of ethical/environmental investment – the willingness of the investor and the lack of information are only two of them. Of equal, or even greater, importance has been the law's restriction on how investment bodies invest their funds. Although the law governing investments varies from country to country, there are still too many situations like the UK where, at its simplest, investments that fall under the Trustee Investments Act 1961 or similar place the investor under a fiduciary duty to pursue maximum financial return. More especially, it is *illegal* for the trustees to forgo a higher return on ethical grounds.[27] As a result, a significant proportion of potentially ethical/environmental investment is apparently closed off to the major funds in the capital markets. *However*, this situation does not prevent a fund from exercising ethical influence over the 'owned' company – a rare but, happily, growing practice.[28]

All the evidence seems to suggest that ethical/environmental investment will continue to grow. It is no longer a fringe activity but there still remains a massive counterweight of inertia, law, financial self-interest and thoughtless ignorance (this last predominantly perpetuated through education and textbooks) against which the ethical or environmental investor has to struggle. At times this has forced individuals or groups to side-step the whole process entirely.

[26] For more detail see Harte (1988), Harte et al. (1991), Perks et al. (1992), Rockness and Williams (1988).

[27] The situation facing charities in the UK was less draconian but still restrictive. However, a judgment handed down in 1992 does appear to have loosened the restraints for charity trustees.

[28] One of the best sources of information on this area is the Pensions Investment Resource Centre – see the appendix for contact details. See also, for example, Sattar (1997), Sparkes (1995), Ward (1991).

The UK, like other countries,[29] has seen a small but steady development in structures designed to enable investors to put money directly to work in ways that meet their personal ethical/environmental criteria. The most widely noticeable of these has perhaps been the exceptionally influential Traidcraft, but other organizations such as the Centre for Alternative Technology, Shared Interest and the Ecology Building Society have also achieved a considerable amount. The first three, for example, undertook share flotations in the late 1980s and early 1990s; all three were reasonably successful *despite the fact that none of the three could realistically promise either capital growth or income.* Although small organizations, these three do point to the fact that direct and serious ethical/environmental investment does and can exist and they demonstrate that there is nothing immutable, God-given, morally superior, legally established or inevitable about the widespread, modern and amoral belief that investors are – and *should be* – rich people growing richer, and that the job of accounting is to serve them in this pursuit. Traidcraft, Shared Interest and the Centre for Alternative Technology, plus myriad organizations outside the UK, demonstrate that any conflict between economic value and ethical and environmental value can be resolved if humanity is put before greed.[30] The ethical/environmental investment trusts are also attempting to demonstrate this painful but critical lesson.

10.9 Conclusions

The providers of funds exercise a critical amount of power over organizations. Whilst much of this can be restrictive upon any management attempting to develop an organization's environmental sensitivity beyond the lightest tinge of green, there are signs of environmentally positive actions flowing both from the self-interest of banks and insurance companies and from the rather more altruistic motivations of the ethical and environmental investor. However, as long as the providers of funds are seen, and see themselves, either as amoral or as duty-bound to seek the maximum profit over all other considerations,

---

[29] See, for example, the illustrations and proposals for 'alternative economic systems' in Dauncey (1988, 1996), Ekins (1986, 1992), Plant and Plant (1991), Robertson (1985, 1990) and Weston (1991).

[30] See, for example, Ekins (1986, 1992b), Plant and Plant (1991), Robertson (1985, 1990). There is also a growing interest – and practice – in alternative economic and financial arrangements from credit unions to LETS. The New Economics Foundation (see the appendix) is a useful source of information in this area.

the full response that any organization could make to the environmental agenda must remain a muted one.[31]

Further Reading

This is an area in which keeping abreast of the very rapid changes is essential. The following references can provide no more than an introduction to some of the issues.

Lascelles, D. (1993) *Rating Environmental Risk* (London: Centre for the Study of Financial Innovation)

Leggett, J. (ed.) (1996) *Climate Change and the Financial Sector: The Emerging Threat – the Solar Solution* (Munich: Gerling Akademie Verlag)

Maltby, J. (1995) 'Not paying for our past: Government, business and the debate on contaminated land in the UK', *Business Strategy and the Environment*, 4 (2), pp. 73–85

Miller, Allan (1992) 'Green investment', in D.L. Owen (ed.), *Green Reporting: Accountancy and the Challenge of the Nineties* (London: Chapman & Hall), ch. 11

Rich, B. (1994) *Mortgaging the Earth: The World Bank, Environmental Impoverishment and the Crisis of Development* (Boston, MA: Beacon Press)

Rowley, D.A. and T.L. Witmer (1988/9) 'Assessing environmental risks before booking a loan', *Commercial Lending Review*, 4 (1), pp. 53–64

Sarokin, D. and J. Schulkin (1991) 'Environmental concerns and the business of banking', *Journal of Commercial Bank Lending*, February, pp. 6–19

Sattar, D. (with A. Gozzi and C. Church) (1997) *Green and Ethical Pensions: A Report for Local Authorities* (London: UNED-UK)

Schmidheiny, S. and F.J. Zorraquin (1996) *Financing Change: The Financial Community, Eco-Efficiency and Sustainable Development* (Cambridge, MA: MIT Press)

Sparkes, R. (1995) *Ethical Investor* (London: Harper Collins)

Ward, Sue (1991) *Socially Responsible Investment*, 2nd edn (London: Directory of Social Change)

Further information about EIRIS, Jupiter Tarbutt Marlin, Traidcraft, Shared Interest, the Ecology Building Society and the Centre for Alternative Technology can be found by writing to the organizations whose addresses are given in the appendix. The Traidcraft story is reported in Adams, R. (1989) *Who Profits?* (Oxford: Lion)

---

[31] An apposite footnote to this chapter is that the UK academics' pension fund, the USS, adopted an ethical policy at the begining of 2000. As a result of changes in UK law plus the activities of the pressure group Ethics4USS, this large and influential investor has accepted that it must consider the principles of the companies in which it invests – a hopeful start for the millennium.

APPENDIX 10.1
CEBIS Environmental Insurance Checklist

ENVIRONMENTAL INSURANCE

As environmental legislation tightens and environmental liabilities grow, companies are increasingly turning to their insurers to cover environmental risks. The insurance industry's previous experience, however, is making it cautious, and any company hoping to buy comprehensive pollution insurance cover is likely to be disappointed. Almost all insurance policies now contain a clause specifically excluding liability for gradual pollution and cover "sudden and accidental" incidents only.

CURRENT POLLUTION INSURANCE

Insurance cover for damage caused by pollution is distinguished according to whether damage was a result of a single incident or gradual pollution. Two types of policy, both limited in their coverage, are currently available in the UK.

'Sudden and Accidental'
Nearly all standard public liability policies now restrict coverage to 'sudden and accidental' incidents and exclude all claims for damage caused by gradual pollution. A 'Single Event Pollution Triggered Incident Clause' (SEPTIC) is often written into standard liability policies, but even then, the cover this offers is limited. Cover is restricted to third party liability and is effectively on a 'claims made' basis. Claims made policies require that the incident is caused, discovered and filed as a claim within the same, one year, policy term.

'Gradual Pollution'
Liability cover for gradual contamination and leakage is available through 'Environmental Impairment Liability' (EIL) policies. However, cover is on a 'claims made' basis only and the excess payable by the claimant is often substantial (currently £25,000–£100,000). Applicants must provide a detailed description of the history of the site and processes operated on it, and may need to undertake a full environmental audit at their expense. Many EIL policies specifically exclude coverage for pollution liability resulting from non-compliance with environmental legislation.

NB Some companies and trade associations are assessing their pollution liability risks and developing their own contingency funds to cope with this. The Chemical Industries Association, for example, has developed its own EIL policy, and a limited liability scheme is available to members of the National Association of Waste Disposal Contractors.

POLLUTION INSURANCE TRENDS

In response to possible compulsory pollution insurance resulting from proposed European Community legislation on civil liability and waste management, the Association of British Insurers is considering a scheme of "pollution ratings" as a means of assessing risk before issuing environmental impairment liability insurance. Assessment for the ratings is likely to include the applicant's potential for pollution, including the size of the operation and any previous claims records; the level of pollution control in place, including the installation of pollution abatement equipment and management and workforce attitudes to environmental safety; and the value of the environment that may be polluted.

LIMITING YOUR LIABILITY

For most companies, insurance cover for 'gradual pollution' is likely to be prohibitively expensive. If this is the case, the most sensible precaution you can take is to minimise risk at source. Even those companies applying for pollution liability cover will have to satisfy the insurers that they are taking comprehensive steps to keep their environmental risks to a minimum.

MINIMISE RISKS →

- Identify and assess what environmental risks exist within your company's operations. This should involve an environmental audit of company activities.
- Evaluate how your operations could be adjusted to minimise risk.
- Evaluate the potential to move towards alternative processes, procedures or materials that reduce environmental risk.
- Establish clearly defined procedures, including staff training, for the safe handling and storage of materials, substances and products.
- Set up a comprehensive site monitoring programme to help you discover problems before they become irreparable.
- Establish procedures to ensure that emergency incidents or accidents are dealt with quickly and efficiently.
- Allocate responsibilities and train personnel to minimise the exposure of risk to themselves and the environment during both normal operating conditions and in the event of an emergency.

ENSURE LEGAL COMPLIANCE →

- Set up systems that ensure legal compliance. Should a pollution incident occur, being able to demonstrate that appropriate steps had been taken to ensure legal compliance will count in your favour.
- Keep up-to-date with relevant UK and EC legislative developments. If you operate outside the UK, be aware of environmental legislation which may affect you.

SET UP MANAGEMENT SYSTEMS →

- Establish and maintain effective environmental management systems. This might include setting up procedures to monitor, document and review all aspects of the company's operations from 'cradle to grave' including resource use, process emissions, and waste management.

CHAPTER 11

EXTERNAL REPORTING AND AUDITING I

Reporting within the Financial Statements

11.1 Introduction

The two areas in which the environmental agenda has encouraged the greatest development in organizational practice are probably those of environmental management systems and environmental reporting. We have already looked at environmental management systems (EMSs) in Chapter 5. This chapter, and the two following, will look at some of the major themes in environmental reporting.

The reporting and disclosure of information relating to an organization's interactions with the natural environment can be thought of as falling into three broad categories: reporting through the statutory financial statements; reporting through other parts of the annual report or through stand-alone environmental reports; and reporting of information about the organization by bodies independent of that organization. This chapter will review the first of these. Chapter 12 will introduce self-reporting by organizations through the annual report, environmental reports and other media (such as the press and the Internet) and Chapter 13 will look at, *inter alia*, the way in which third parties (governments, NGOs and pressure groups, for example) make public data about organizational activity.

At the outset, there are two general points we should emphasize. First, this three-way distinction between approaches to environmental disclosure is, inevitably, a bit arbitrary. Nevertheless, such distinctions are, in our view, the most useful when first approaching the area of external environmental reporting. The distinctions rest on (a) information, the reporting of which directly affects accountants and auditors in their traditional – and typically statutory – roles as preparers and auditors of financial statements under companies law; (b) reporting *by* the organization of information (in both financial and non-financial terms) that falls outside the accountants' 'traditional' ambit – such information is usually voluntary disclosure but, in an increasing number of countries, this is slowly changing to become required, mandated disclosure; and (c) information which is reported *about* the organization and over which the organization has very little control. This last category is frequently referred to as the 'social audits'.[1]

The second point relates to: the rapidity of developments in the area covered by this chapter; the diversity of views about such developments; and the variety of responses by different accountancy bodies, governments and supra-national bodies (such as the United Nations). In deference to these factors, this chapter, inevitably, concentrates on giving the broad themes and an overview of developments. For more specific and timely data the reader is recommended to consult the further reading at the end of the chapter and to monitor closely the work of the relevant accountancy bodies. Just how central accounting for environmental issues will be to the future preparation and attestation of financial statements is, currently, impossible to judge.

This chapter is organized in the following way. We look, first, at the general issues of how and to what extent environmental issues will (and could) influence financial statements. Then we take a broad look at the response of law, the accountancy bodies and other organizations to this potential. From there we take a brief look at how corporate financial statements are reflecting environmental issues before examining some of the implications for the statutory financial auditor.

11.2 Why Financial Accounting?

> *First we [accountants] can encourage companies to develop innovative environmental policies, to disclose them in the financial statements and to keep them regularly updated . . . We must measure up to the environmental challenge if we are to fulfill our duty as a profession to promote the public interest. We forget at our peril that we do not own our natural assets, we merely hold them in trust for future generations.*
>
> (Lickiss, 1991, p. 6)

Financial accounting and, in particular, the reported profit figures in financial statements lie at the very heart of the environmental crisis. The central reason why accounting is so closely implicated in the environmental crisis is that a company, an industry, an economy[2] can be showing very positive 'success' indicators in the form of profits and

---

[1] This, as we shall see in Chapter 13, is an unfortunate term and is also used to mean many different things.

[2] The 'economy' issues are typically measured through Gross National Product (GNP). The problems with – and limitations of – accounting measurement are equally critical for national income accounting. We do not deal with these issues here but see, for example, Ayres (1998), Daly and Cobb (1990), Ekins (1986, 1992a), Weizsäcker (1994).

growth whilst, simultaneously, polluting the air and the sea, laying off staff, destroying habitats, disrupting communities, etc., etc. That is, profits – and other accounting measures of success and failure – only capture – as we saw in Chapter 1 – one aspect of organizational and economic life. Consequently, shareholders, managements, governments and so on are not only being misled by these 'success' signals into thinking that 'all is well' but also increasingly seeking to use these indicators to guide their activities, decisions and policies. As long as profit signals 'success' the environment – and societies – will suffer.

There are three basic reasons why accountants should be concerned by this situation. There are the *moral/ethical reasons* – we as decent people need to recognize that our professional expertise is not only giving misleading signals but is actually encouraging environmental (and social) dislocation. There are the – related – *professional reasons* that one major product of our activities is clearly acting against the public interest and that our 'accounts' of organizations are seriously incomplete. Finally, there are the more *pragmatic, economic reasons:* management and shareholders are taking decisions based on seriously incomplete and misleading information. As many environmental issues will, in time, affect income and cost streams (and thus the economic well-being of the organization) its management and shareholders–decision-makers need information to guide them in this area.

Whilst the first two reasons are the most persuasive to our mind – and should be the most persuasive to the minds of accountants and policy-makers – it is, sadly, the third set of reasons which primarily informs the considerations of how financial statements should best reflect environmental issues. (We will go along with this point of view for most of the chapter and return to the wider issues at the end.)

Before addressing the detail of how environmental issues might influence the financial statements one further point must be stressed. In the deliberations of accountants on environmental issues and financial statements the focus is, almost exclusively, on how environmental issues can fit within GAAP (Generally Accepted Accounting Principles) and not on the, far more compelling, question 'how can GAAP be adjusted to appropriately reflect environmental issues?' That is, the accountant's approach is to take the existing categories of accounting (typically the main themes in the income statement and balance sheet) and examine how, within the bounds of current practice, each might be tweaked to accommodate the environment. That the environment is a far bigger issue than conventional accounting (and thus won't 'fit' into current accounting categories) is rarely – if ever – considered. Thus, when we are examining 'environmental issues' in this chapter we are *not* looking at the environment itself but rather at those manifestations of the environment which are affecting the financial measurement of economic events at a material level. We are *not* looking at habitat destruction but rather at what we might be fined for destroying habitat. We are not looking at contributions to climate change but rather at what we might have to spend to comply with future laws on emissions . . . and so on. This is a *major* limitation of accounting approaches to environmental (and, indeed, social) issues. (We return to these questions at the end of this chapter and in Chapters 13, 14 and 15.)

11.3 How is Financial Accounting Affected?

We outlined in Chapter 1 the financial statement categories that could – and probably would – be affected by the changing environmental agenda. However, within GAAP, environmental issues are not fundamentally different in nature from any sort of change in the business environment: that is, changes in the business environment lead to changes in costs, liabilities, income, etc., and these changes, in turn, are reflected in the financial numbers of the enterprise through the normal bookkeeping and accounting systems. As with any other change in the business environment, such changes in the financial numbers need, within conventional accounting thought at least, only be separately identified if they are in some way *material* or if regulations, for some reason or other, require their separate identification.

Thus, many organizations are facing increases in their waste disposal costs, increases in the costs of plant to accommodate environmental improvements, increased administration costs to meet the requirements of EMS and so on. (One influential analysis of such costs is provided in Figure 11.1.).

Within a conventional view of GAAP there is nothing here to attract our attention. One could argue that only when the changes lead to potentially significant (i.e. *material*) impacts on the financial numbers do they warrant attention from GAAP.

However, many environmental costs can prove to be material and yet others are of such a nature that they may prove to be material in the future. We are referring here, not just to the actuality – or threat – of such major events as Bhopal or *Exxon Valdez* but also to less obvious matters which, at the extreme, could involve the closure of an organization for its inability to meet some environmental legislation.[3] The best illustration of what this can mean is probably the experience with 'Superfund' in the United States.

---

[3] See Gray et al. (1998) for examples of this.

Figure 11.1

Examples of costs of environmental measures and environmental losses

Costs of Environmental Measures:
- Expenditure aimed at preventing, reducing or recycling effluent/emissions/wastes.
- Costs of producing more environmentally friendly products.
- Costs charged under polluter pays principles.
- Costs incurred in restoration or remediation of water, soil or land caused by normal operating activity of organization or past activities at a site.
- Clean up of pollution as a result of an accident.
- Costs incurred in research and development, assessments and impact statement preparations and site investigations and assessments.
- Costs incurred in environmental administration such as policy development, management structures, information systems and environmental audits.
- Costs incurred to assist resource recycling, reuse, substitution or increasing the efficiency of resource use.
- Costs incurred to recycle, reuse or reduce waste production.
- Costs incurred in support of wildlife conservation, replanting forests or restocking fish supplies.

Environmental losses:
- Fines, penalties and damages arising from non-compliance with environmental laws or consents.
- Costs incurred where facilities have been shut down due to environmental concerns.
- Assets of the entity which cannot be recovered due to environmental concerns.

Source: Adapted from CICA (1993, pp. 9–11)

11.4 US Superfund

Superfund is not just a crucial issue in its own right but has had a major impact on accounting thinking around financial accounting and environmental matters.

In 1980 the United States issued the Comprehensive Environmental Response Compensation and Liability Act (CERCLA)[4] and ushered in a new era of environmental management with very specific accounting implications. CERCLA was designed to force 'responsible parties' to clean up land contaminated through dumping, waste storage, leakages, etc. To enable this to happen where the 'responsible party' was unable to find the costs of clean-up (remediation), CERCLA established a 'superfund' – 88 per cent of which came from industry – to pay for the process (hence the more common reference to this Act

---

[4] As amended by the Superfund Amendments and Reauthorization Act of 1986 (SARA).

and similar proposals as 'Superfund'). By 1988, the US Environmental Protection Agency had identified 27,000 potential sites for clean-up at an estimated $25 million per site. Of the 27,000, only 10,000 had been inspected, a little over 1000 were on the National Priority List, 124 sites had remediation processes in operation and 43 had been cleaned up.[5]

The potential of Superfund is immense: as Roberts, a commissioner with the US Securities and Exchange Commission, noted:

> *While the aggregate numbers concerning potential environmental costs are staggering, what is almost as frightening is the massive amount of acknowledged environmental cost that has yet to be reflected in corporate financial statements.*
>
> (Roberts, 1993)

In addition, a 1992 Price Waterhouse survey claimed that 62 per cent of large US companies had known environmental liabilities not yet recorded in their financial statements. The situation prompted one commentator to state:

> *The situation in the United States is so serious that it threatens the solvency of the whole insurance industry as well as the solvency of many major corporations in the US. The EPA has estimated the cost of cleaning up the 27,000 waste disposal sites in the US would approach one trillion dollars.[6]*

The accounting issues that arise from Superfund are fairly direct and cover the making of provisions for remediation,[7] contingent liabilities and how to account for a fixed asset which suddenly acquires a negative value.[8] The matter focused the mind of accountants on environmentally related matters like never before.[9] The issue spread first to Canada,[10] next to Europe and, in one form or another, is having some form of impact in most accounting regimes.

[5] See EPA Superfund Advisory, US EPA OS-110 (Washington, DC: Office of Solid Waste and Emergency Response), Summer/Fall 1988. See also, for example, Arthur Andersen (1990), Price Waterhouse (1992, 1994), Wheatley (1991). It is said that the only people cleaning up under Superfund are the lawyers.

[6] Wheatley (1991, p. 208).

[7] Remediation is a term (derived from remedy) coined to refer, in this context, to restoring of land (usually) to its situation pre-pollution damage (however that is determined).

[8] See, for example, Newell et al. (1990). However, the issue also spread further than accounting and corporations. Banks with loans secured on land found themselves identified as liable 'responsible parties' and insurance companies would find themselves having insured, effectively, uninsurable losses. For more detail see Rowley and Witmer (1988/9), Sarokin and Schulkin (1991) and Singh (1989). See also Chapter 10.

[9] For detail on the US experience and the accounting implications see, for example, Epstein (1996, Appendix A), Surma and Vondra (1992), Zyber and Berry (1992).

[10] Where in 1990 the Accounting Standards Steering Committee approved 'Capital Assets', which requires that provisions be made for removal and site restoration costs. (CICA Handbook Section 3060; and for more detail see Hawkshaw, 1991).

Consequently, we find that a significant proportion of the attention given to financial accounting and environmental issues centres around those high-profile issues that have been so starkly illustrated by Superfund: liabilities, contingent liabilities and provisions. (Although, as we see below, this is by no means the whole story.)

A major spillover from these (principally land contamination) issues has been in the mergers and acquisitions market. An acquiring company that has not undertaken environmental audit to ascertain the potential environmental liabilities of its target can find itself in the most serious financial problems. This had the effect, not surprisingly, of instilling some much needed caution into the market for mergers and acquisitions.[11] All deals in this area can, thus, be potentially affected by environmental factors as the prices and costs in these markets slowly adjust to accommodate these new threats. In effect the whole of corporate finance is beginning to feel the wind of this change – with attendant effects on the financial director's role.

11.5   The Response of Accounting Regulators

What is probably the most significant and longest-standing initiative in the development of environmental reporting within a conventional financial accounting framework has come from the United Nations Centre for Transnational Corporations Intergovernmental Working Group of Experts on International Standards of Accounting and Reporting (UN CTC ISAR).[12] The Ninth Session of UN CTC ISAR (1991) made detailed recommendations as to the types of environmental disclosure that corporations should undertake.[13] The intention of the UN CTC ISAR was that these recommendations should be adopted by sovereign governments. To date there has been a patchy response. The recommendations from the Ninth Session are summarized in Figure 11.2.

Figure 11.2, although a UN recommendation, gives a broadly representative indication of the current thinking in the profession and elsewhere about the sorts of numbers that ought to appear in the annual report – and particularly in the statutory part of the annual report. Subsequent guides on environmental disclosure – especially in

---

[11] This caution has also extended into management buy-outs. See, for example, 'Buying trouble', *KPMG Dealwatch*, 91 (2), 1991, pp. 3–7.

[12] Now part of the United Nations Conference on Trade and Development (UNCTAD).

[13] See papers E/C.10/AC.3/1991/5.

Figure 11.2

**Recommendations for environmental financial reporting
from the UN CTC ISAR's 9th session**

In the directors report:
- Environmental issues pertinent to the company and industry.
- Environmental policy adopted.
- Improvements made since adopting the policy.
- Enterprise's environmental emission targets and performance against these.
- Response to government legislation.
- Material environmental legal issues in which the enterprise is involved.
- Effect of environmental protection measures on capital investment and earnings.
- Material costs charged to current operations.
- Material amounts capitalized in the period.

In the notes to the financial statements:
- The accounting policies for recording liabilities and provisions, for setting up catastrophe reserves and for disclosing contingent liabilities.
- $/£ amount of liabilities, provisions and reserves established in the period.
- $/£ amount of contingent liabilities.
- Tax effects.
- Government grants received in the period.

Europe[14] – have typically included a selection of the financial numbers suggested by the UN.

Although we would still appear to be some way from a majority of countries adopting the UN guidelines, elements have started to appear in country legislation[15] and the debate – especially in the

---

[14] For an especially useful introduction to the issues for accounting in a European context see Ball and Maltby (1992).

[15] The amended Enterprises Act of Norway 1989 actually requires the board of directors' report to include physical information about emissions and contaminants and information about plans to clean up activities. In the USA, the SEC S-K Regulation Item 101 requires enterprises to disclose the material effects that compliance with environmental laws may have on capital expenditure, earnings and competitive position. Item 102 requires disclosure of certain existing estimates of current and future environmental expenditures. Item 103 requires disclosure of any significant environmental, administrative or judicial proceedings that will have an impact on the enterprise. The Superfund Amendments and Reauthorization Act 1986 also requires disclosure of environmental risks arising from activities. For more detail see Newell et al. (1990). For more detail on the US climate in general see, for example, Dirks (1991) and Rabinowitz and Murphy (1991). The Ontario and Quebec Securities Commission require listed companies to include the financial or operational effects of environmental protection requirements on the capital expenditure, earnings and competitive position of the company for the current year and a forecast of impact for future years. Legislation is also in place in, *inter alia*, Sweden, Denmark, the Netherlands and Korea with other countries, including Australia and New Zealand, actively debating the issues at the time of writing.

accounting profession – although still some way from supporting mandatory disclosure (within the financial statements or elsewhere), has moved on to many of the technical issues which surround the tentative integration of environmental issues into the financial statements.

That is, as the environmental debate – in accounting as elsewhere – begins to mature we need (in a GAAP world) to start to be rather more specific about what can and cannot appear in financial statements and, having decided this, how we will treat and disclose such environmentally related accounting items. At its most basic, if we decide that we need to consider environmental liabilities, contingencies and provisions, how are these different (if at all) from other liabilities, contingencies and provisions? Why might our existing accounting guidelines, standards and so forth not be sufficient?

It *is* possible to argue that within a very narrow definition of the traditional accountants' world, existing accounting guidelines and standards *are* sufficient to cover environmental matters. However, the very size of the potential financial impact of the issues, their ubiquity and unpredictability appear to have combined with a growing realization about the parlous state of the natural environment and its critical importance to life[16] to force a wider consideration of how financial accounting and environmental issues might be combined.

Once again, the UN has been in the vanguard of developing thinking on how to approach the regulation of accounting and environmental issues. Figure 11.3 is an extract from one of the UN's draft guidelines and gives a flavour of the issues involved and how the UN's thinking has been developing.

Related to the UN–ISAR work has been the consistent work from a number of the professional accountancy bodies (of which a little more below), and Figure 11.4 is provided to give a further illustration of the issues exercising the profession and their approach(es) to them. The work of the UN is now increasingly reflected in the discussions and deliberations of the national professional accountancy institutes and standard-setting bodies. Initiatives focused on the interface between financial accounting and environmental issues are now relatively commonplace in the institutes' research and technical departments and committees in, for example, the USA (AICPA), Canada (CICA), UK (ACCA, ICAEW, ICAS), the Netherlands (NIVRA), Australia (ICAA), etc. Even international bodies such as IFAC and, especially, FEE in Europe have been consistently and notably active. This activity increasingly reflects itself in the standard-setting bodies. Whilst these bodies are still (generally) reluctant to address environmental matters

[16] Such an elementary statement needs to be made because it does seem that it is taking many people a very long time to appreciate such a simple and essential fact.

Figure 11.3

UN–ISAR Accounting Guideline – Environmental Financial Accounting (adapted extract)

Recognition of environmental costs
- Environmental costs relating to damage should be recognized immediately and charged to income.
- Environmental costs should only be capitalized if they meet specific criteria (provided in draft).
- Future site restoration costs should be accrued and capitalized as the damage is incurred.
- Environmental costs which are part of an asset should be included with that asset.
- Environmental costs that do not meet the asset recognition criteria should be expensed immediately.

Recognition of environmental liabilities
- An environmental liability should be recognized when the enterprise is obliged to incur an environmental cost and cannot avoid that cost.
- Environmental damage – even when there is no immediate duty to remediate – should be disclosed in the notes to the accounts.
- Costs relating to remediation or removal of long-lived assets should be recognized as a liability at the time of the damage.

Recognition of recoveries
- Recovery expected from a third party should not be netted off but separately recorded.
- Expected sale of property should not be netted off against an environmental liability.

Measurement
- Best practice should be used to estimate liabilities and where this is not possible this must be explained in the notes to the accounts.
- Net present value may be used to estimate certain liabilities and this should be disclosed.

Disclosure
- The enterprise should separately disclose
  - its categories of environmental costs
  - environmental costs charged to income
  - fines and penalties
  - environmental liabilities with accompanying detail.

Source: Adapted from UN–ISAR Accounting Guideline – Environmental Financial Accounting Draft, July 1997

---

as a separate, stand-alone issue, their pronouncements of such matters as provisions, liabilities, impairment of fixed assets and so on increasingly reflect recognition of – and concern about – the impact of environmental matters. Of especial note, perhaps, the IASC itself is showing an increasing awareness of the issues.

However, with such extensive attention to the pressing impact of environmental issues on financial statements only slowly finding its

Figure 11.4

Environmental costs relating to current accounting periods

Costs related directly to current period benefits
Costs of environmental measures that relate directly to benefits received in the current period and that should be charged to it include: treatment of waste products; costs of hazardous waste disposal; clean-up costs related to current operating activities.

Costs related indirectly to current period benefits
Environmental costs that bear only an indirect relationship to benefits of the current period include: ongoing environmental administration, compliance, assessment and audit activities; and employees' attendance at study groups and seminars *re* environmental issues.

Costs viewed as 'period' costs or losses
Many environmental costs incurred will simply be viewed as 'period' costs or losses. These include:

- Costs that do not have sufficient ties to future benefits and therefore cannot be capitalized or deferred. Example are: research cost for the redesign of products and processes to (i) prevent and abate damage to the environment, or (ii) conserve non-renewable and renewable resources; donations to programmes related to the environment; and recycling programmes.
- Costs that are related to the activities of, and benefits received in, prior periods, but that do not qualify as prior period adjustments. Examples are: clean-up of a polluted site that has been abandoned; decision to clean up was made by management; clean-up costs related to prior period activities in excess of the estimates recorded in prior periods (benefits received in those prior periods); clean-up of a non-owned site previously used, the clean-up being required as the result of new laws or regulations.
- Costs that do not yield any benefits, that is losses.
- Fines or penalties for current non-compliance related to operating activities.

Source: CICA (1993, p. 20)

---

way into specific mandatory statements about environmental disclosures within the financial statements, one inevitably is led to ask to what extent financial reporting practice is addressing such issues.

11.6   The Environment in Financial Statements

Given the central importance of financial statements (to organizations, shareholders, directors, other stakeholders and to society) and the clearly significant growth in concern over environmental issues, you would be quite within reason to expect the one (the environment) to be reflected in the other (the financial statements). Sadly, this is rarely the case. Throughout the 1990s, you could study the vast majority of financial statements and be led to conclude that the natural environment had no relevance to the vast majority of organizations. Hence our concern at the start of this chapter – and, indeed, in Chapter 1 – that the (environmental) price of (economic) success is not being recognized and society is being misled.

The reasons for this situation are relatively obvious – the majority of companies (and, indeed, the majority of accountants[17]) will not willingly undertake *voluntary* disclosure. (The pros and cons of voluntary disclosure are considered in Chapter 12.) Until there exist law and accounting guidelines requiring disclosure of environmental issues in financial statements it will be the minority of companies (and accountants) that seek to advance good financial reporting practice on their own initiative.[18] *But,* thankfully, a small but increasing minority do just that.

Well over 50 per cent of the world's very largest companies make some reference to environmental issues in their annual report – this proportion grew steadily (if slowly) throughout the 1990s.[19] However, not all such references are related to the financial statements – or even financial in nature. One survey[20] – echoing other research in the area – found that less than 20 per cent of these very large companies included environmental costs in the financial statements or the notes to the accounts. The majority of these were, not surprisingly, companies based in the USA where SEC regulations have continued to drive the measurement and disclosure of, *inter alia,* environmental liabilities, provisions and contingencies. This, therefore, suggests that outside the USA the proportion of all (even) medium and large corporations mentioning environmental issues in their financial statements is very low indeed and, of these, the majority are likely to be in the chemical, forestry or oil and gas industries.

One of the better examples of the type of disclosure one might look for in financial statements in provided in Figure 11.5.

Even when we look for financial data relating to environmental issues contained elsewhere in corporate reporting (e.g. in the other

[17] See Bebbington et al. (1994), Guilding and Kirman (1998).

[18] We have already mentioned the problems of whether or not environmental matters are covered by the *materiality* thresholds. In part, this decision relies upon an organization *knowing* the extent of its actual and potential environmental exposure. Even large, well-run companies do not always know this information. For more detail see, for example, Gray et al. (1998).

[19] KPMG (1996) reports the variation in countries from 95 per cent of the top 100 companies in Norway and 86 per cent in the USA to a lowest (of the countries surveyed) of 39 per cent of the top 100 companies in New Zealand.

[20] These figures are taken from the KPMG *International Survey of Environmental Reporting 1996.* Other surveys such as Adams et al. (1995, 1998) and other United Nations (ISAR) and KPMG surveys plus others reported in (for example) *Social and Environmental Accounting* would confirm this broad pattern of reporting.

Figure 11.5   Zeneca Group plc 31 December 1996

Extract from Accounting Policies

Environmental Liabilities

Zeneca is exposed to environmental liabilities relating to its past operations, principally in respect of soil and groundwater remediation costs. Provisions for these costs are made when expenditure on remedial work is probable and the cost can be estimated within a reasonable range of possible outcomes.

Extracts from Notes Relating to Accounts

18 Provisions for Liabilities and Charges

GROUP	Employee benefits* £m	Reorganization environmental and other provisions £m	Total £m
At beginning of year	296	241	537
Profit and loss account	61	55	116
Net amounts paid or becoming current	(37)	(82)	(119)
Other movements, including exchange	(33)	(25)	(58)
At end of year	287	189	476

*Includes provisions for unfunded post-retirement benefits (Note 30).

No provision has been released or applied for any purposes other than that for which it was established.

34 COMMITMENTS AND CONTINGENT LIABILITIES

Environmental

Zeneca has environmental liabilities at some currently or formerly owned, leased and third party sites in the US. Zeneca, or its indemnities, have been named under US legislation as a potentially responsible party ('PRP') in respect of a considerable number of sites (although Zeneca expects to be indemnified against liabilities associated with certain of these sites by the seller of the businesses associated with such sites) and actively participates in, or monitors the clean-up activities of sites at which it is a PRP. Stauffer Management Company, a subsidiary of the Company, established in 1987 to own and manage certain assets and liabilities of Stauffer Chemical Company, which was acquired that year, has identified a number of environmentally impaired sites for which it may have responsibility that will, in aggregate, require significant expenditure on clean-up and monitoring.

The requirement in the future for Zeneca ultimately to take action to correct the effects on the environment of prior disposal or release of chemical substances by Zeneca or other parties, and its cost, pursuant to environmental laws and regulations, is inherently difficult to estimate. The Group has provisions at 31 December 1996 in respect of such costs in accordance with the accounting policy on page 44. Although there can be no assurance, management believes that, taking account of these provisions, the cost of addressing currently identified environmental obligations, as Zeneca currently views these obligations, is unlikely to impair materially Zeneca's financial position. Such contingent costs, to the extent that they exceed applicable provisions, could have a material adverse effect on Zeneca's results of operations for the relevant period.

parts of the annual report or in the environmental report) the numbers are again very low indeed – and are as likely to refer to capital expenditure related to environmental exigencies as they are to more shareholder-relevant figures of provisions, liabilities and contingencies.

Although progress is slow, all the signs point towards an eventual insistence upon some form of recognition of environmental issues in the financial statements. An increasing number of countries are following the example of Norway, Denmark and Sweden in establishing legislation governing general environmental reporting (see Chapter 12) while the lead set by, for example, the USA and Korea[21] in requiring environmental recognition in financial statements is increasingly difficult to resist. Also, as we have seen, standard-setting bodies and the accounting profession are moving inexorably closer to firm guidance on the area. One major source of the pressure to move towards some firming-up of the best advice on the extent to which financial statements need to reflect environmental issues is the statutory auditor.

11.7 Statutory Audit of Financial Statements

The 'truth and fairness' of the financial statements – an elusive quality at the best of times – is not made easier to assess by the environmental liabilities, provisions and contingencies issues. Furthermore, there are other elements of the accounting system which are driven by environmental matters and which may have a direct impact on the financial statements.[22] These include:

(1) *Obsolete stock* – through, for example, changing tastes or developments in legislation or other standards. Costs of storage and/or disposal of certain chemicals, for example, may also rise, with attendant implications for assessments of net realizable values.

(2) *Production assets* – changing legislation may make existing processes illegal or require additional costs, the life of assets may be shortened under BATNEEC, or changes in demands and/or standards relating to the product may decline. All of these will reduce the life and terminal value of the asset.

---

[21] For information on the Korean situation see, for example, Choi (1998).

[22] This list is adapted from David Pimm's *The Environment and the Auditor*, a discussion paper from Coopers & Lybrand Deloitte (as was), 1990.

(3) *Depreciation policy* – to reflect changing conditions or life of productive assets.

(4) *Viability of product lines* – may be put into question through changing taste, standards or legislation. This may raise going concern issues.

(5) *Additional costs of production or processes* – ranging from increasing upstream costs (through, say, changing standards on extractive industries or an energy tax) through to costs of pollution abatement equipment and the costs of waste disposal. These must be anticipated, perhaps provided for and questions of capitalization of certain expenditures considered.

(6) *Catch-up and potential legal costs* – how should significant costs incurred or, more difficult, major potential liabilities arising from legislation be considered? This clearly relates to the remediation, abandonment and contingent liability issues discussed above.

What, however, is an auditor to do when a company will not disclose these things and thereby impairs what little truth and fairness the financial statements might claim?

Such matters as these also have potential legal implications and, in particular, affect the auditors' duty to investigate, and perhaps report upon, illegal acts of an auditor's clients. The problem, however, is that until the organization has a well-established EMS and full documentation of its environmental interactions how is the auditor to assess the risks associated with environmental issues?

Figure 11.6

Some areas in which the statutory financial statements and audit will need to reflect environmental considerations

- *Contingent liabilities:* especially on contaminated land but also spills and unauthorized emissions.
- *Provisions:* especially for remediation, abandonment and decommissioning costs (cf. the oil and gas company practice) but also waste disposal and recycling commitments as well as potential catch-up, insurance and legal costs.
- *Reserves:* especially for catastrophes.
- *Valuation of fixed assets:* especially land and buildings.
- *Depreciation policy:* to recognize, for example, shorter life of productive assets under rising BATNEEC considerations.
- *Additional capital costs associated with productive assets:* especially the need to incur additional costs to bring existing plant within current standards.
- *Obsolete inventory and inventory costs:* including stock made obsolete through environmental concerns, storage and disposal costs of environmentally malign materials and recycling commitments.

These matters are clearly far from trivial and are exercising both the accounting firms and the auditing profession. Research in the UK[23] has demonstrated that the more auditors know about environmental issues, the more they are concerned about them. Such concern, however, tends to be more prevalent in the larger firms of accountants who, typically, have consultancy and technical departments who can keep them abreast of issues. There must remain a continuing anxiety that the smaller and medium-sized firms and their clients are more exposed to environmental risks than they currently believe. This suggests the need for the auditing profession to take a lead in producing much needed guidance. This is something the profession has come to recognize.

Both national and pan-national auditing bodies[24] have given increasingly careful attention to the ways in which environmental issues might have a financial impact on the activities of clients and the implications this can have for auditing procedures. In addition to the technical matters of verifying the evidence underlying environmental provisions, liabilities and contingencies, audit procedures now need to take explicit cognisance of potential, but 'hidden' environmental problems. In standard audit procedures the auditor needs both to (a) assess that an adequate EMS is in place and functioning appropriately and (b) add environmental issues to the overall risk assessment of the client. These are, of course, easier said than done but the sense of a hidden but ticking environmental time-bomb somewhere amongst one's clients is causing increasing anxiety for the audit profession.

As if this were not enough, auditors *qua* auditors[25] are increasingly involved in the attestation of environmental reporting outside the financial statements.[26] Such reporting might include stand-alone environmental reports, other disclosures in the annual reports, reports under EMAS (see Chapter 5) and even, on occasions, embryonic 'environmental accounts'. (See Chapter 12 for more detail.)[27] This additional attestation is a minefield and traditional auditors are entering that minefield with, generally speaking, an understandable

---

[23] See Collison (1996), Collison and Gray (1997), Collison et al. (1996).

[24] See, for example, AICPA (1991), APB (1992), CICA (1994), FEE (1993), IAPC (1995).

[25] As opposed to the management consultancy arms of the bigger accountancy firms.

[26] It is more typical for environmental reports – where they are attested, to be audited by management or environmental consultants. As an increasing proportion of environmental reports are attested, simple inspection of a selection of environmental reports will demonstrate this (see also Ball et al., 1998). However, not only are auditors being requested, on occasions, to audit the financial data contained in an environmental report, they are also involved from time to time with both environmental (see Chapter 12) and social (see Chapter 13) reports.

[27] For more detail see, for example, Collison (1996) and Kamp-Roelands (1996).

caution. The problem is that whilst the tenets of evidence, information systems and control that are so central to traditional auditing need be no different *in principle* when applied to environmental reporting, auditors have traditionally relied upon such things as accounting standards to define the reported documents on which they were to express their opinion about truth and fairness. There is no such definition of an environmental report and therefore less clarity over what it is that the auditor is trying to attest to. Whilst this need not be an insurmountable problem, it *does* add to the environmental concerns with which auditors need to be familiar. (We return, briefly, to this issue in Chapter 12.)

11.8 Implications for the Future?

There are several important themes in any consideration of reflecting environmental issues in financial statements. The first of these is determining what the financial statements are actually *for*. If, as is usually assumed to be the case, the dominant purpose of financial statements is to inform shareholders (and, perhaps, other financial participants) about matters affecting the financial probity of the company and any likely effects on the financial value of its dividends and share price, then the key issue is assessment of any material financial risk that environmental issues pose for the organization. For that to happen the company, its accountants and its auditors must *know* what environmental exposure exists. That, in turn, requires two things: (i) a well-developed EMS that is orientated towards both day-to-day matters (for example, emissions) and strategic matters such as long-run potential problems; and (ii) some means of communication between the environmental manager (who runs the EMS and can therefore be expected to know about the organization's environmental interactions) and the accountant (who will determine what does and does not appear in the financial statements). Research in the UK[28] has demonstrated that this latter point – the communication between accountant and environmental manager – is one of the most crucial in determining whether the financial statements do or do not reflect significant environmental issues.

But this assumes that, not only are financial statements simply to inform shareholders, but also environmental issues are not *qualitatively different* from other issues. Whether you are environmentally concerned or not, that is a debatable point. If environmental issues *are* qualitatively different then a different attitude to disclosure needs to

[28] See Gray et al. (1998).

be taken and, in particular, different materiality thresholds need to be established.

Furthermore, if we can consider that environmental issues are so important that they need to transcend the current limitations of GAAP, we are led to see accounting as more than a simple recording process. That is, we can begin to recognize that a major effect of accounting and reporting is to make things *visible*[29] – and by so doing, to make other things *invisible*.[30] The disclosure of, for example, energy costs, waste disposal costs, legal compliance costs, costs of packaging, fines for breaking (for example) consents, etc., represents a simple and cheap way of reflecting some of the environmental aspects of the organization within the financial statements.

Taken together with increasing thought and attention being given by the professional accountancy bodies to the recognition of environmental issues in financial statements, using the financial statements to make environmental issues more visible (and thereby draw the financial community's attention to *their* involvement in environmental degradation) means that existing GAAP, if treated creatively, can offer significant scope for moves towards a process of beginning to reconcile some of the existing conflicts between financial and environmental demands. One outline suggestion of how GAAP-related accounting might better reflect the environment is shown in Figure 11.7.[31]

Ultimately, however, reporting and accounting for the environment cannot be entirely satisfactory within a conventional financial accounting framework. Not only will financial statements – for the foreseeable future at least – remain primarily an economic construct within which environmental (and social) issues will always be subservient, but environmental issues are very much bigger and very much more important than any GAAP-type framework can recognize – let alone cope with. In order to fully recognize environmental issues in organizations and perhaps even to develop some real environmental accountability, other forms of environmental (and social) accounting and reporting (both financial and non-financial) become necessary. Alternative (non-GAAP) approaches to environmental reporting are the

---

[29] See, for example, Gray (1992), Hopwood (1986), Laughlin (1991).

[30] Thus, for example, the flurry in the UK over the disclosure of R&D expenditure came down to whether or not companies were willing to emphasize this number and, thus, emphasize the activity. The presence of R&D in a set of financial statements draws attention to the issue. It is the same with labour-related expenditure. The UK has a fairly healthy level of disclosure of labour-related expenditure and this has the effect of raising the importance of that issue and, one hopes, of recognizing the importance of labour itself. So it can be with environmentally related expenditures and income.

[31] One especially valuable and very detailed guide to environmental reporting both within and without GAAP is *Environmental Performance Evaluation and Reporting by Private and Public Organizations* written by Craig Deegan and Marc Newson and published in Sydney by the New South Wales Environmental Protection Agency in 1997.

Figure 11.7

**Suggested practical approach to financial environmental accounting
and reporting**

The United Nations recommendations
- disclosure of accounting policies
- cost of current environmental expenditure
- environmental expenditure capitalized in the period
- liabilities, provisions and reserves
- contingent liabilities
- tax effects
- grants received

Develop disclosure with the auditor in mind
- reconsider *provisions* for remediation and abandonment
- provisions for inventory, accelerated depreciation, new investments, etc.
- actual and provided-for legal costs

Make the environment more visible
- disclose energy (including transport) costs
- disclose waste handling and disposal costs
- disclose legal compliance costs
- consider packaging costs
- consider the disclosure of environmental fines

---

focus of Chapter 12. (Chapter 13 then looks at social reporting whilst Chapter 14 widens our concerns to consider the exigencies of sustainability.)

Further Reading

From a practical point of view, without doubt the most important further reading one can do is to monitor the activities of one's own accountancy profession and the activities of the relevant standard-setting, auditing and pan-national bodies. The better professional accountancy journals tend to try to keep their members abreast of developments such as these. Equally, there is a lot of good work going on in the United Nations ISAR group and access to their activities would repay effort. To monitor such developments on a wider scale, the two sources we find most useful are the newsletters *Environmental Accounting and Auditing Reporter* published in the UK by Professional Information Publishing and edited by Roger Adams of ACCA, and *Business and the Environment* published by Cutter Information Corp. in the USA. The following are a few suggestions that take analysis of the issues a little further.

Abdolmohammadi, M., P. Burnarby, L. Greenlay and J. Thibodeau (1997) 'Environmental accounting in the United States: from control and prevention to remediation', *Asia-Pacific Journal of Accounting*, 4 (3) December, pp. 199–217

Collison, D., R.H. Gray and J. Innes (1996) *The Financial Auditor and the Environment* (London: ICAEW)

Epstein, M.J. (1996) *Measuring Corporate Environmental Performance* (Chicago: Irwin/IMA)

Gamble, G.O., K. Hsu, C. Jackson and C.D. Tollerson (1996) 'Environmental disclosures in annual reports: an international perspective', *International Journal of Accounting* 31 (3), pp. 293–331

Gray, R.H. et al. (1998) *The Valuation of Assets and Liabilities: Environmental Law and the Impact of the Environmental Agenda for Business* (Edinburgh: ICAS)

Society of Management Accountants of Canada (1992) *Accounting for the Environment: Management Accounting Issues Paper 1* (Hamilton: CMA)

Surma, J.P. and A.A. Vondra (1992) 'Accounting for environmental costs', *Journal of Accountancy* (USA), March, pp. 51–55

United Nations Centre for Transnational Corporations (1992) *International Accounting and Reporting* (New York: United Nations)

CHAPTER 12

EXTERNAL REPORTING AND AUDITING II

Environmental Reporting outside the Financial Statements

12.1 Introduction

Environmental reporting is now a major feature of business activity. Throughout the decade of the 1990s it grew from almost nothing to become one of the most important manifestations of business–environment interactions. Although still by no means a universal practice, corporate environmental reporting is undertaken, in some form or other, by most big companies. And what makes this such a remarkable phenomenon is that, by and large, environmental reporting remained a voluntary activity through this period of its growth. Such an upsurge in activity, supported by, *inter alia*, a wide array of interest, dedicated conferences and codes of practice, is virtually unprecedented in corporate reporting.[1]

In Chapter 11 we examined environmental reporting within the confines of GAAP. In this chapter we will attempt to provide a brief overview of the vast array of practice, guidance and developments that go to make up environmental reporting more generally. Such reporting can take, in theory at least, an almost infinite range of forms. The most common, and those upon which we will concentrate in this chapter, are:

- Reporting in the annual report (or associated documents) but outside the statutory financial statements.
- Reporting through stand-alone environmental reports – typically published as separate booklets and/or published on the Internet.[2]

[1] The nearest equivalent would be the development of employee and employment reporting (together with the value added statement) in the 1970s. There is an important lesson to be learned from this as, with few exceptions, such reporting is now scarce as it did not (except in rare exceptions) pass into corporate legislation. Whether environmental reporting can continue as a voluntary activity, decline or pass into regulation is a yet undecided question. (For an overview of these surges and decline in interest in voluntary reporting see, for example, Gray, Owen and Adams, 1996.)

[2] In some countries – notably Germany and Austria – this reporting is undertaken through EMAS (see Chapter 5). We will include such EMAS reporting here under the broad category of stand-alone environmental reporting. (For more detail see Kamp-Roelands, 1996; Schaltegger, 1996.)

In addition, environmental reporting takes place through, *inter alia*, company videos, advertising, product packaging, conferences, company websites, 'educational materials' and so on. We will spend little time on these forms of reporting as they can, to a degree at least, be treated as special cases of stand-alone environmental reporting.

Given the inevitable 'visibility' of environmental reporting, it seems likely that most readers will be familiar, to some degree at least, with what corporate environmental reporting looks like.[3] It *is* a diverse activity and might typically include such things as: outlines of the organization's attitude to the environment, glossy pictures of 'bits of the environment', reference to EMS and environmental audit, tables showing selected data on the levels of emissions and wastes produced by the organization and suggestions about levels of environmental investment. Later in the chapter we will look at suggestions for what a full environmental report should contain and provide a couple of illustrations of such reporting. The discussion in this chapter will, however, make more sense if one is familiar with – and/or has examples to hand of – the better examples of corporate environmental reports.

At the outset, it is worth emphasizing that environmental reporting is a vast field. It could probably fill a book on its own. All we can try to do here is to give an overview of the field and some flavour of its key elements. Consequently, the chapter will first look at why organizations voluntarily report and the growing pressures to disclose; then we will look at the incremental stages that organizations can (and do) take in developing their environmental reporting before moving on to look at current reporting practice. We finish with a few speculations on where environmental reporting will be going in the future.

12.2 Why Report on the Environment Voluntarily?

An organization might voluntarily report information for many reasons: to develop corporate image; to legitimize current activity; to distract attention from other areas; to discharge accountability; to forestall legislation. Some of these are summarized in Figure 12.1.

There is also some evidence to suggest that some organizations find it to their advantage to develop their reporting ahead of regulation in order to give themselves time to create the necessary information systems and to build up the expertise necessary in a new area of reporting.

---

[3] If not, the footnotes to this chapter plus the further reading at the end of the chapter give suggestions on how to overcome this omission.

Figure 12.1

Reasons for voluntary disclosure or non-disclosure

Disclosure
- If not done voluntarily it will become mandatory
- To provide impetus to internal developments
- To legitimize current activities
- To distract attention from other areas
- To develop corporate image
- To build up expertise in advance of regulation
- Positive impact on share price
- Reduction in perceived (company and information) risk
- Political benefits
- Competitive advantage
- Shareholders' and other stakeholders' right to know
- To explain expenditure patterns
- The desire to tell people what the company has done/achieved
- Forestall disclosure by other parties

Non-disclosure
- Obverse of the above
- No need/motivation to do so
- Wait and see
- Cost
- Data availability (and related costs)
- Secrecy
- Absence of demand for the information
- Absence of a legal requirement
- Never thought about it
- Prioritizing areas for disclosure

One research study[4] takes a more systematic approach to the problem and suggests that any organization considering voluntary disclosure will assess the relative costs and benefits. That study found that benefits were a function of: the information's positive impact on share price; the effect of any reduction in perceived risk arising from the information; and 'political' benefit arising from changed perceptions of government, employees, shareholders, etc. The costs were both direct and indirect. The former were those arising principally from data collection and processing,[5] and attendant auditing costs. The latter arose primarily from any loss of competitive advantage plus any negative impacts on share prices and 'political' perceptions. Interestingly, that study showed that environmental disclosure was

---

[4] Gray, Radeburgh and Roberts (1990).
[5] Wright and Kaposi (1992) suggested that an average plc will spend over £100,000 on design fees and production costs alone.

perceived by companies to have a very slight net cost but there was no loss of competitive advantage.

After all, the costs of disclosure should not be great and can be reduced to relatively trivial sums. (This does, of course, assume that the organization already knows the relevant environmental data and no organization can justifiably admit to not knowing such data these days.) The 'political' costs vary greatly from country to country[6] whilst the benefits to the organization can be not inconsiderable (in terms of stakeholder trust, staff morale, strategic emphasis on internal environmental initiatives and so on[7]).

Motives for voluntary disclosure, therefore, are unlikely to be simple. Our own experience suggested that disclosure depends, primarily, upon the culture of the company as reflected in statements such as 'the company discloses because shareholders and other stakeholders have a right to the information' or 'we wish to demonstrate stewardship and a responsible management'.[8]

However, it is unrealistic to expect all companies voluntarily to disclose information. At a most basic level one can ask why any individual or organization should do something – additional to their already busy lives – when there is no compulsion to do so. A selection of quotations from senior managers in large companies illustrates this nicely (see Figure 12.2).[9]

History shows time and time again that, whatever the motivation for disclosing or not disclosing, the fact is that voluntary initiatives follow a general, predictable – and entirely unsurprising – pattern. That is, the initiative is taken up by a few innovative, leading companies. Then the majority (but *not* all) of the larger companies (typically the transnational corporations) become involved and then, unless the issue passes into legislation, it begins to fade away. At the end of the 1990s, environmental reporting was at these crossroads – some countries were legislating while others were waiting to see if the issue would 'go away' (see below).[10]

---

[6] In the UK there are very few examples of organizations suffering as a result of publishing data. The only problems have tended to arise when the organization publishes 'greenwash' data which no one believes.

[7] See, for example, Gray, Bebbington, Walters and Thomson (1995) for an exploration of these issues.

[8] There are an increasing number of good publications about why organizations should, could and do produce environmental reports. Many of the more useful come from the UNEP/SustainAbility project (see below) and one such example is SustainAbility/UNEP (1998) *Engaging Stakeholders 1998: The Non-Reporting Report* (London: SustainAbility). Academic papers which look at this area include Bebbington et al. (1994) and Bebbington and Gray (1995).

[9] For further examples, see again SustainAbility/UNEP (1998).

[10] See Maltby (1997) for a nice analysis of these and related issues.

Figure 12.2

> **Why should organizations disclose voluntarily?**
>
> ● *'In the end, why should industry put its head above the parapet and disclose levels of organizational activity? What are the advantages? Where do you stop? Why not call for reporting of health and safety as well? It is only one part of the organization's mission'* (a major energy company)
>
> ● *'Not all the data is available and the company is getting used to collecting it. We will then disclose it a bit at a time to lessen the trauma'* (a major chemical company)
>
> ● *'Our holding company are obsessively secretive and very keen to minimize the information in the accounts'* (a medium-sized manufacturing company)
>
> ● *'We are just waiting to see what happens. There is no point in jumping the gun'* (a major extractive company)
>
> ● *'We are a low key company and it [environmental activity] was something we were doing anyway. We never thought to make much fuss about it. It is the nature of the company not to make too much fuss about things'* (a major electronics company)
>
> ● *'It is proving difficult to identify and isolate the figures'* (a major consumer products company)
>
> ● *'It gets excluded by the accountants. I don't suppose we have ever seen it as that important really'* (a medium-sized engineering company)
>
> ● *'I don't know really. I hadn't thought about it'* (a small electronics company)

Thus, the reasons for organizations undertaking environmental disclosure are complex – and the reasons for their ignoring it are understandable (if hardly laudable). There is no question that legislation is essential to codify and settle the area and to bring the laggard organizations in line with the leaders. That voluntary environmental disclosure went so far so quickly owed a great deal to the foresight of some companies to see both the need and the value of undertaking environmental reporting. This was, however, coupled with a – possibly unique – social and business environment which brought a steadily increasing pressure to bear on organizations to address environmental reporting issues. We look at that now.

12.3   The Pressures to Disclose

If the motives of organizations voluntarily undertaking environmental reporting are complex then the range of influences which played upon those motives are more complex still. Just a few of the more visible influences are listed in Figure 12.3.

Many of the influences in Figure 12.3 are self-explanatory but what

Figure 12.3

Examples of influences on organizational disclosure of environmental data

Business and market influences
- Customer and supplier pressure (1–3, 5)*
- International competitiveness
- Peer pressure – i.e. from other companies (1–4)
- Employee considerations (1–4)
- Environmental policies (4, 5)
- Public relations (1–4, 13)
- Stakeholder pressures (13)

Social pressures (1–3, 13, 14)
- Personal and family beliefs
- Media attention
- Schools and education
- Stakeholders

Industry and voluntary initiatives (2–4, 12)
- United Nations – UNCTAD ISAR and UNEP (with SustainAbility)
- The Global Reporting Initiative
- Signing up to Charters (e.g. ICC Business Charter for Sustainable Development) (4, 14)
- EMAS (5)
- Industry initiatives – e.g. the Chemical Industries Association
- Country-specific influences (e.g. in the UK: ACBE, Business in the Environment, UK Environment Business Forum)
- Eco-labelling
- Environmental Reporting Award Schemes (e.g. ACCA)

Legislation and regulation – and the threat thereof
- Freedom of access to information (2, 3, 11)
- Environmental impact assessments (5)
- Environmental protection acts and environmental protection agencies (2, 3)
- Developing legislation in Australia, Canada, Denmark, Indonesia, Korea, Norway, Sweden, Netherlands and discussion of such regulation in (e.g.) the UK and New Zealand (2, 3)

*Note: the numerals indicate chapters in this book where further detail can be found

---

is remarkable is that they, together, provide an intense atmosphere in which the demands upon organizations to involve themselves in environmental reporting became really quite significant indeed. More arresting still is that many of the more influential forces raising the demands for environmental reporting actually come from the business community itself.[11] However, such involvement of business in their

---

[11] Not that we should get *too* bullish about this. Reporting is still a minority sport and none of these developing influences has succeeded in encouraging the business community to desist from attempting to lobby against the introduction of mandatory environmental reporting.

own 'regulation' is almost certainly a double-edged sword – whilst it *has* meant that the initiatives have been well received and respected, it also probably explains why the more demanding requirements of environmental accountability have been largely absent from the various mechanisms used to cajole business into adopting a voluntary reporting regime.[12]

There are two, closely related, influences from Figure 12.3 which we should give attention to here: the 'codes' or 'guidelines' on environmental reporting which are issued from time to time; and the public evaluations made of corporate environmental performance and reporting.

Environmental Reporting Guidelines

Once environmental issues are a matter for public debate and the business community has begun (for whatever reason) to engage with that public debate, it becomes more difficult for any individual organization to state publicly that it does not intend to disclose data about its environmental performance. If we are to believe that the environment is safe in the hands of business, why would they not provide us with information? If an organization does not wish to report (and how many really do?) what better way is there to wriggle out from the situation than explaining that it is too difficult – or that they do not know how to do it. The extensive array of environmental reporting guidelines effectively closes off this excuse.

But why did so many guidelines arise in the first place? Some were issued by campaigners of varying hues in order to encourage organizations into environmental reporting and, indeed, to close off excuses for non-reporting. Others – often those constructed by business groups themselves – were issued for more complex reasons. At least one of these was to provide evidence that (a) business was taking the matter of environmental reporting seriously and (b) to intimate that there was no need for regulation because business groups, by issuing guidelines to their members and colleagues, were establishing the grounds for a voluntary framework of environmental disclosure. To a degree this strategy worked – regulation *was* forestalled. But to an extent it backfired – why continue to produce guidelines in the face of overwhelming evidence that companies are not complying with the

---

[12] Recall that the ICC Business Charter for Sustainable Development speaks almost exclusively about environmental management and, although it encourages environmental disclosure, it does not require it as a prerequisite for being an ICC signatory.

ones that are already issued?[13] And how many guidelines can industry need?

To give a flavour of these guidelines – as well as to provide one step-by-step approach that organizations can take to build up their environmental reporting – some of the key elements from what is currently considered to be 'best practice' are summarized in Figure 12.4.

The details in Figure 12.4 are synthesized from the many extant guidelines on what environmental reporting should entail.[14] The majority of the guidelines are broadly similar in orientation and only really differ in any substance on the extent to which: they address sustainability; relatedly, whether or not they recognize the social dimensions of environmental protection and sustainability;[15] and how they deal, if at all, with the matter of *completeness*. (That is, how can a reader assess whether or not all matters of import are included in the report? The principal means of determining this is through the use of a mass balance which, as we saw in Chapter 9, is relatively uncommon outside the northern European and Scandinavian countries.)

The extent of the overlap between the majority of the guidelines suggests that the issuance of yet further guidelines is a redundant activity for which it is difficult to find any obvious and sensible explanation. There certainly does not seem to be any remaining substantial argument why environmental reporting should not be incorporated into the legal reporting frameworks of countries (as we are

[13] It is difficult not to be a little cynical about this. For illustration, the *100 Group of Finance Directors* – a UK body of the FDs of the largest UK companies – issued environmental reporting guidelines which, as far as we have been able to assess, not a single signatory to the guidelines actually complied with.

[14] Examples of both menu-type lists of what should be found in an environmental report and step-by-step guides for organizations are legion. Some of the better known include the *Public Environmental Reporting Initiative (PERI) Guidelines* – an industry-based initiative whose guidelines were first published in 1994; and *The Global Reporting Initiative* – a multi-sector cooperative venture bringing together different interested parties. Other suggestions are provided in ACBE (1996), ACCA/Aspinwall (1997); CICA (1994), EFFAS (1994), GEMI (1997), KPMG (1997), Deegan and Newson (1997) and UNCTAD ISAR (see Chapter 11). Companies have employed other standards – such as the CERES Principles (see Chapter 4) as a basis for reporting. Of equal relevance is the work of FEE's Environmental Task Force which has worked towards the construction of a *Generally Accepted Framework for Environmental Reporting* which, inevitably, has useful links with the representation of environmental issues in financial statements. The debate over the first fruits of that initiative have carried over from the late 1990s into the present century.

[15] Sustainability is considered in Chapter 14. *The Global Reporting Initiative Sustainability Reporting Guidelines* are intended to move organizations towards 'sustainability reporting' and are an evolving set of guidelines. See Bebbington (1999) and www.globalreporting.org for more detail.

Figure 12.4

Guidelines for Environmental Reporting

POLICY
(1)   Statement of environmental policy (see Chapter 4).
(2)   Key environmental impacts.
(3)   Steps taken to monitor compliance with policy statement.
(4)   Statement of compliance with policy statement.

PLANS AND STRUCTURE
(1)   Structural and responsibility changes undertaken in the organization to develop
        environmental sensitivity (e.g. VP of environment, committees, performance
        appraisal of line managers).
(2)   Status of EMS and levels of accreditation.
(3)   Plans for EMS activities – introduction of EIA, environmental audit, projects,
        investment appraisal criteria, etc.
(4)   Stakeholder consultations and responses thereto.

FINANCIAL (see Chapter 11)
(1)   Spend on environmental protection – capital revenue, reaction to/anticipation of
        legislation, voluntary/mandated, damage limitation/proactive (enhancement)
        initiatives.
(2)   Pattern of future environmental spend – both to meet legislation and that which is
        voluntary, capital/revenue split.
(3)   Actual and contingent liabilities and provisions (e.g. 'Superfund' type problems),
        impact on financial audit, impact on financial results.
(4)   Details of environmental fines.

ACTIVITY
(1)   Overview of resource use, emissions and wastes in, for example, a simplified mass
        balance.
(2)   Procedures for, results of and issue of compliance with standards report.
(3)   Environmental audits and issue of summary/results.
(4)   Environmental performance indicators and trends therein.
(5)   Targets and progress towards them.
(6)   Analysis of dealings with regulatory bodies/fines/complaints.
(7)   Awards/commendations received.
(8)   Analysis of investment/operating activity influenced by environmental
        considerations.
(9)   Analysis of voluntary (e.g. community) projects undertaken.

SUSTAINABLE MANAGEMENT (see Chapter 14)
(1)   Identification of critical, natural sustainable/substitutable, and man-made capital
        under the influence of the organization. Transfers between categories.
(2)   Examination of social justice issues and social account.
(3)   Examination of all unsustainable activities.
(4)   Estimates of 'sustainable costs' (i.e. which would have to be incurred to 'return the
        organization to same position it was in before the activity').
(5)   Assessment and statement of input/output resource-flows and changes therein.

ATTESTATION AND AUDIT
(1)   Attestation of the environmental report and criteria used.
(2)   Statements made under EMAS and recognition of context and limitations.

beginning to see happen) and the energy expended in developing the guidelines could be more productively spent in ensuring that the reporting itself took place.

Consequently, the various means that have been established for monitoring the levels and quality of environmental reporting are especially important.

Monitoring and Evaluating Environmental Reporting

There are, again, a wide range of means employed to monitor and assess the extent and the quality of environmental reporting. One of the most important of these is, of course, systematic research by academics[16] but such research does tend to be both somewhat dated by the time it appears and not as well-publicized as it might be.[17] Of more direct influence on the reporting process have been the well-publicized cooperative initiatives from (*inter alia*) professional bodies, NGOs, academics and consultants.

Such initiatives tend to be, broadly, of two sorts: formal monitoring processes; and environmental reporting award schemes. Whilst there are a number of each, for illustration we will concentrate on just one of each: the UNEP/SustainAbility monitoring process and the ACCA Environmental Reporting Awards Scheme (ERAS).

The ACCA's ERAS was the first such national award scheme (as far as we are aware) and was instituted in 1991 in the UK. (It has since been emulated by other countries and the ACCA is one of the founding bodies behind the pan-European environmental reporting award scheme.) The purpose of the ACCA scheme was to identify and reward companies that had undertaken especially innovative environmental reporting and, thereby, to identify 'current best practice'. Such exemplars of best practice could then act as a guide to other organizations undertaking environmental reporting. (An indicative outline of the criteria used in the judging of the environmental reports is shown in Figure 12.5.)

The award scheme witnessed a steady increase in both the levels of

---

[16] There is considerable worldwide research into environmental (and social reporting). For an overview see, for example, Gray et al. (1996), and for reviews, updates and summaries of such research see *Social and Environmental Accounting* published by CSEAR.

[17] Why this might be and whether it is a weakness of academic research or not is a complex question beyond our scope here but, for an introduction to that debate, see, for example, Whittington (1995) and Gray (1996).

Figure 12.5

Indicative outline of ACCA ERAS judging criteria

(1) **Basic minima:** including environmental policy, management commitment and systems, impact of core business.

(2) **Quantitative disclosure:** including factual data, bad news as well as good, historical trends, commentary and explanation.

(3) **Performance and targets:** including performance against targets and explanations of variances.

(4) **The financial dimension:** including link to the annual report and financial statements; liabilities, provisions and environmental expenditure.

(5) **Verification:** including 'meaningful' external verification with explanation of limitations and scope.

(6) **Beyond compliance:** including examination of sustainability, LCA, mass balances, EPIs, additional channels of communication, stakeholder consultation, etc.

---

environmental reporting and the general quality of that reporting[18] but, despite its avowed intention to be positive about environmental reporting, nevertheless was forced to recognize the limitations of much of the reporting that occurred. In this, there were two principal themes: environmental reports rarely gave information to allow a reader to assess the *completeness* of a report; and non-reporting companies were escaping scrutiny and, in effect, gaining a 'free ride' on those innovative organizations which voluntarily undertook environmental reporting.[19]

The ACCA's initiative (and those which followed in other countries as diverse as Canada, Australia and the Netherlands) has had an undoubted positive impact on the development of environmental reporting and much of this has been due to its positive attitude to the field. However, if ACCA is one of the 'carrots' for environmental reporting, experience suggests that there also needs to be a 'stick'. This

[18] The ACCA ERAS is reported upon annually and examples of those reports are published in *Certified Accountant* (now *Accounting and Business*) in Adams, Owen and Gray (1997), Gray and Owen (1993), Gray, Owen and Adams (1995), Owen and Gray (1994) and Owen, Gray and Adams (1996). These reports provide more detail on the state of play, the criteria used and also provide a useful source of illustrations for the better UK reports in any one year. If one is wishing to look at environmental reporting in the UK, these articles are a useful starting point. Similar information can be obtained on other reporting awards schemes from the organizing bodies. For example, the pan-European awards scheme published *The First European Environmental Reporting Awards Scheme 1996/97* under the joint imprimatur of ACCA (UK), Royal NIVRA (Netherlands) and FSR (Germany).

[19] Other problems which the ERAS identified included a lack of independent verification, a lack of consistency in identifying targets and reporting performance against them, a tendency either to ignore sustainability or to trivialize it and a reluctance to acknowledge the social dimensions of environmental reporting.

Figure 12.6

UNEP/SustainAbility Stages in Company Environmental Reporting*

(1) **Green glossies:** Environmental reports largely devoid of substantial content, newsletters and videos, short statements in the annual report.

(2) **One-off:** One-off environmental reporting often linked to the first environmental policy.

(3) **Descriptive:** Annual reporting linked to EMS but more text than figures.

(4) **State-of-the-art:** Provision of full TRI performance data on an annual basis, input/output data for service companies, corporate and site reports, available on disk or on-line. Environmental report is referred to in the annual report.

(5) **Sustainability:** Sustainable development reporting which addresses carrying capacity, environmental, social and economic aspects of corporate performance, sustainability indicators and full cost accounting.

*These categories have been, and continue to be, subject to further refinement, revision and expansion. See the UNEP/SustainAbility project for more information.

---

was provided by the more formal monitoring schemes of which the UNEP/SustainAbility initiative is probably the most systematic and wide-ranging.

The UNEP/SustainAbility initiative started in 1994 and evolved from a relatively typical overview and cajolery exercise[20] into a much more directive activity referred to as the 'Engaging Stakeholders' project.

The Engaging Stakeholders project had a number of elements, including a model of the stages in environmental reporting (see Figure 12.6) and an exploration of what various stakeholders looked for in environmental reporting – and the rather meagre extent to which those desires were satisfied.[21]

By 1997 the Engaging Stakeholders project had derived a list of *The 50 Reporting Criteria* and a related scoring system which made for a systematic and public evaluation of the largest companies' environmental reporting quality.[22] Given that the project sampled those companies active in the reporting process from across the world and across sectors, the report shows the *very* best that corporate environmental

---

[20] See the first report – *Company Environmental Reporting: A Measure of Progress of Business and Industry Towards Sustainable Development*, Technical Report No. 24 (Paris: UNEP, 1994), which was researched and written by John Elkington and the staff of SustainAbility.

[21] See UNEP/SustainAbility, *Engaging Stakeholders Volume 2: The Case Studies* (London: SustainAbility, 1996).

[22] The criteria are listed in, for example, UNEP/SustainAbility, *The 1997 Benchmark Survey* (London: SustainAbility, 1997). The criteria are not greatly different from those elements in Figures 12.4 and 12.5, although they do provide more detail and a guide to how the individual items are weighted.

reporting has to offer. Even these companies fell well short on a number of criteria and that suggests that the many thousands of very large companies that were not included are producing little, no, or exceptionally poor, environmental reporting. (And this ignores the vast number of SMEs which are likely to be doing nothing at all.)

By the end of the 1990s the project had gone a further, very innovative, step and had turned the full gaze of publicity onto those companies that were 'non-reporters'.[23] By matching high profile companies that *were* reporting with similar high profile companies that *were not*, the project was able to ask publicly why the non-reporting companies were failing to keep up with developments. It was a systematic and successful attempt to embarrass companies (and their chief executives in particular) in an especially reasonable but uncompromising manner.

So the very diverse pressures on organizations to disclose environmental performance data – and the sophistication of that pressure – continue to increase. This has been (almost uniquely) successful in encouraging voluntary corporate innovation in the field and, more significantly, in keeping environmental reporting high on corporate agendas. This pressure will continue to be important until all countries follow the lead of Denmark, Sweden and others in turning the voluntary nature of environmental reporting into much-needed legislative requirements. When we look at environmental reporting practice it is easy to see why such legislation is needed.

12.4 Corporate Environmental Reporting Practice

As we remarked at the outset of this chapter, non-GAAP related environmental reporting typically comes in two forms: reporting within the annual report, and stand-alone environmental reports.

Reporting through the Annual Report

Environmental disclosure in the annual report tends to be fairly superficial. Whilst a very few companies have employed the annual report to give intense, concise summaries of the background and data

---

[23] SustainAbility/UNEP, *Engaing Stakeholders: The Non-Reporting Report* (London: SustainAbility, 1998).

relating to their environmental performance,[24] the majority of companies' discussion of the environment within the annual report tends to be fairly superficial. Typically such reporting ranges from some bland assertions about the 'importance of the environment' or 'why we are good to the environment' to more significant, but partial reviews of environmental policy, environmental audits and EMS with, typically, a few elements of selected environmental performance and financial data such as environmental spend.

Reporting of this sort grew steadily during the 1990s[25] and is now very common amongst the larger companies. (A review of the annual reports of the larger and higher profile companies in most countries will reveal examples of this sort of reporting.) Not only is such reporting a predominantly large company phenomenon (typically dominated by the largest 100 in a country) but there tend to be sector variations with, typically, chemicals, oil and gas and pharmaceutical companies more likely to provide substantial data whilst retail, service and financial companies are less likely to do so. By the beginning of the present century it was generally the case that whilst a significant minority of those companies outside the top 100 in any of the major industrialized countries would also be reporting, by the time one got below the largest 300 or so companies, environmental disclosure was relatively scarce. Experience suggests that only legislation will change this pattern.

There is still controversy over the best place for a company to report about the environment – the annual report or stand-alone reports. Our view is that it is essential that environmental (and, as we shall see in the next chapter, social) issues are given substantial attention in the annual report. Organizations are *not* only economic entities – they are social and environmental as well, and certainly have significant social and environmental impacts – or 'externalities'. One can argue that the externalities are part of the price by which the economic gains have been won and should, therefore, be shown alongside the financial statements.[26] In this way we can begin to

[24] One particularly interesting example is the small Scottish company Inveresk, who showed how the annual report could be used to provide significant environmental information without the major step of developing a complete environmental report.

[25] For more detail on the levels of reporting either one can consult the academic literature (one source of information about this is *Social and Environmental Accounting*) or one can turn to the professional, NGO and/or consultant publications that cover such material. The UNEP/SustainAbility project referred to above is one such source. KPMG (1996) is another example. There are many such examples and they change rapidly over time.

[26] This is *not* necessarily an argument that all environmental (and social) interactions should be expressed in financial terms to ensure comparability. This is a highly controversial issue.

recognize what John Elkington[27] calls the *'triple bottom line'*. That is, an organization has a social and environmental as well as an economic dimension to its performance. Accounting only measures the economic. A successful company – one that society and future generations can support – should be seen to be measured across the spectrum of its activities. In this way society can recognize and reward good all-round performance and/or react accordingly if the financial and economic success (as shown in the measure of profit) is won at the expense of society and the environment. Only if the annual report gives equal weight to these three dimensions can we begin to expect organizations – and society – to act accordingly.

But reporting through the annual report alone is frequently not sufficient – the data needs further exposition in some form of stand-alone environmental report.

Reporting through an Environmental Report

The primary focus of attention in environmental reporting tends to be upon the stand-alone environmental reports. These reports are frequently very carefully designed, glossy and voluminous documents and are often published alongside the annual report.[28] They will contain, to varying degrees, the sorts of information mentioned in the figures earlier in this chapter (although they may well not be organized in the same way as the lists are).

Publication of environmental reports, although, predominantly, still a large company phenomenon, is less widespread than 'reporting on the environment' in the annual report. For example, the KPMG (1997) survey of the 100 largest companies in each of 12 countries, found that 23 per cent produced environmental reports in 1996. Now, while the number of companies that have *actually* produced such reports will be somewhat higher because not all companies who report do so every year, we should not lose sight of the fact that this refers to the world's very largest companies. It tells us that the vast majority of companies do not produce any environmental reports at all.[29] So, whilst the number of organizations reporting is rising steadily,

---

[27] See Elkington (1997).

[28] For students reading this, if you do not already have examples of environmental reports, it is essential to obtain a few copies of such documents yourself by writing to the Company Secretary of some of your more favoured companies.

[29] There are many surveys of environmental reporting practice available so little more detail is required here. But to illustrate the point, the SustainAbility/UNEP (1998) report mentioned above states that in 1993 100 multinational companies had produced environmental reports. By 1998 that number had risen to 600 – but, this still left 34,000 MNCs which had not produced environmental reports. And that is just MNCs.

it is doing so very slowly indeed. It isn't difficult to see, therefore, why so many guidelines on reporting are redundant – we can at least be grateful that the number of reporting companies is rising a little faster than the number of environmental reporting guidelines!

Although, as we have seen, the pressures to disclose are extensive they are pressures that the majority of organizations appear to be able to resist. This is odd, in that the majority of companies that have undertaken voluntary environmental reporting have found it to be to their benefit. Whilst it would be difficult, if not impossible, to undertake a formal cost–benefit analysis of the pros and cons of environmental reporting, a broad-brush approach will show that there are very few real 'costs' and some very substantial benefits accruing from the activity. Figure 12.7 provides a list of the costs and benefits that arise most frequently in discussions with companies.

Figure 12.7 Some costs and benefits from the development of environmental reporting

	Potential costs	Potential benefits
To the company	• Design and format • Printing and distribution • Increased risks • Distraction from real issues • Increased enquiries • Negative reactions to information • Increased attention from pressure groups • Not believed • Decreased favour in financial community • Licence to operate open to scrutiny	• Public relations • Encourage transparency • Employee morale • Self-belief in culture • Diversion from real issues • Smokescreen • Forestall legislation • Increased cooperation • Better stakeholder relationships • Educate public • Educate investors • Focus on information collection • Experimentation • Keeping oneself better informed
To society	• Higher prices • Lower wages? • Lower dividends? • Constraint of business growth • Diversion from real issues • Smokescreen • Forestall legislation • Too much information	• Increased accountability, transparency and democracy • Better relationship with business • Choice about conflicts • Decisions about sustainability • Value of experimentation • Better informed • 'Market' better informed

Experience shows that most of the costs either do not or need not arise. If reporting is undertaken seriously – that is, without an attempt to deceive – then the reactions of stakeholders and pressure groups tend to be positive. (After all, these groups have the vast majority of non-reporters to give their attention to.) The data costs should be trivial (that is, a company should already know its environmental impact). The cost of collating and editing is the one unavoidable cost but this need not be that significant. And that just leaves design and printing costs.

It is essential to recognize that there is no fundamental need for environmental reports to be cleverly designed and expensively printed. The choice to do so is entirely the organization's own and it will do it for its own reasons whatever they be. They are *not* costs of environmental reporting. Cheaply produced reports are, surely, a perfectly adequate means to discharge the accountability and to pro-vide the detail behind the annual report data. If even these costs bother an organization, it can simply turn to the Internet.

Reporting on the Internet

As the World Wide Web grows and a rapidly increasing number of people have access to it, it comes as no surprise that organizations are using the Internet, not only to advertise but also to report. At the turn of the century there was an explosion of reporting on the web and environmental reporting was an important element in that.[30] The attractions of such Internet reporting of environmental (and, increas-ingly, social) data are obvious in terms of the cost savings and the ease of access for an increasing number.[31] There *is* a downside to such reporting, however. Internet-based environmental reports can be updated easily by the reporting organization.[32] This has obvious advantages to the reporting organization and does ensure that data is timely. *However*, it also means that one does not have a permanent record of the data, and comparisons year on year are somewhat more difficult.[33] Furthermore, despite the hype, there are still many millions of people who do not have easy access to the Internet and so if all reporting was web-based it would be a worrying anti-democratic development. However, Internet environmental reports are a great

[30] See SustainAbility/UNEP, *Engaging Stakeholders: The Internet Reporting Report* (London/Paris: SustainAbility/UNEP, 1999) for an excellent introduction to this area.
[31] See the further reading section at the end of this chapter for one means of accessing such reports.
[32] Such electronic environmental reports are also often not dated and so it can be difficult to assess to what precise period the data relates.
[33] This is problem which is especially acute for researchers.

source of exemplars for reporting organizations, monitoring agencies and students alike.

Because of the widely accessible nature of environmental reports – whether through the Internet or not – we have not included illustrations with this chapter. However, some illustrations might be valuable and so we offer some in the last part of this chapter but use them to provide (in the case of Norsk Hydro – in the next section) some history and insights into the reporting process itself and (in the case of BSO/Origin – in Section 12.6) one example of imaginative reporting that attempts to link the environmental data with the financial statements.

12.5 Norsk Hydro (UK) Environmental Report

Norsk Hydro was one of the first companies in the world to produce a systematic environmental report – and certainly one of the very first to respond to the growing wave of environmental concern in the late 1980s. The report has historic value as well as having interest in its own right.

Norsk Hydro is Norway's biggest industrial group. In an environmentally conscious country like Norway, the company was sensitive to its environmental record and believed itself to be an environmentally responsible organization. A spate of bad publicity in 1987 following from the actions of environmental activists caused the company to take a hard look at its environmental interactions. The results were not good. Initially the company was understandably defensive about this but, in 1989, as part of its strategy to reclaim its reputation, it published a fairly comprehensive report of its Norwegian activities. In 1990 Norsk Hydro published a further report covering all the group's activities, worldwide, and in the same year Norsk Hydro (UK) became the first of the overseas subsidiaries to follow suit – to considerable public attention.[34]

The UK report provides an introduction to the UK group (Norsk Hydro (UK) is not an especially high-profile company in Britain) and then goes on to review environmental interaction in each of the company's business sectors. For each sector, background data on the company is provided, together with information about environmentally sensitive elements – e.g. emissions and discharges, raw materials and hazardous substances. Further data is provided on

---

[34] See, for example, D. Thomas, 'Turning over a new green leaf', *Financial Times*, 24 October 1990. For more detail see ENDS Report 185/June 1990, pp. 13–15.

the regulatory frameworks within which the company operates,[35] the standards it must meet (where appropriate) and data on levels of activity. Figure 12.8 is an extract from the section on polymers and gives an indication of the style of the report.

Of course, the report can be faulted. Most notably, it is patchy and not consistent between sectors. However, as the company remarked, this is due to data not being collected, collated and reported on a consistent basis at that time plus a degree of selectivity as to what was thought important. However, any quibbles are far outweighed by the strengths of the report. It gives both 'good' and 'bad' news because 'people do not believe squeaky clean' and, *most significantly of all*, the report was subject to an independent 'audit' which was published as part of the environmental report – 'because journalists are a cynical bunch'. The complete audit report from Lloyd's Register is shown in Figure 12.9.

The publication of the environmental report was a gamble by Norsk Hydro (UK) – one undertaken principally on the grounds of improving the company's PR profile. The gamble has paid off. There has been none of the environmentalist backlash that was feared and the estimated cost of US$50,000[36] has more than repaid itself in terms of PR and publicity, awareness of the company, attitudes of the employees and a raised awareness among management of the environmental factors involved in the company – especially those requiring attention. The relatively low cost to the company arises because the data was virtually costless. The company – as part of its TQM culture – already emphasized health and safety reporting, particularly as part of an initiative to reduce accidents, and had already developed some environmental reporting within the organization.

> *We can now say, having put our head above the parapet and not had it shot off, that the importance and value of openness and transparency in the way it leads to increased understanding, better public relations and reduced antagonism greatly outweighs the costs – which owe more to industry's fears than to reality.*
>
> (John Speirs, Norsk Hydro (UK), in interview, May 1991)

Norsk Hydro was the first winner of the ACCA ERAS award and has gone on to produce further reports, in different formats – but *not* on a regular annual basis. Whilst the standards of environmental

---

[35] These are the UK regulatory agencies and legal frameworks and at that time included: the National Rivers Authority and the Scottish River Purification Boards; Her Majesty's Inspectorate of Pollution; the Health & Safety Executive (HSE) and the Health & Safety at Work Act 1974; the Control of Substances Hazardous to Health (COSHH) Regulations 1988; the Control of Industrial Major Accident Hazard (CIMAH) Regulations 1984 and the Notification of Installations Handling Hazardous Substances Regulations 1982.

[36] This was in 1990 and excludes staff time. The print run was 10,500.

Figure 12.8 Extract from Norsk Hydro (UK) 1990 Environment Report

P O L Y M E R S

Dust levels in the resin and compounds plants are checked regularly with personal monitoring systems and during 1989 the programme was considerably enlarged. This increased programme has revealed minor plant and sampling faults which led to questionably high figures in some cases. Remedial projects to improve operational and sampling procedures will bring much improved results in the future.

The personal monitoring programme also includes checks on exposure to heavy metal compounds in appropriate areas.

Compounds Plant Monitoring for Heavy Metals

Measurement	Occupational Exposure Limit	Plant Area	1988	1989
Mean Cadmium Level (mg/m³)	0.05	Compounds	0.005	0.002
Mean Lead Level (mg/m³)	0.15	Compounds	0.174	0.004

The comprehensive personal monitoring system, which uses samplers worn by the workforce, is backed by a biological examination service, supervised by the works doctor. He assesses the results obtained from regular blood and urine samples, which are processed by an independent laboratory, and advises the company and the workforce about the optimisation of working practices to maintain good health. Under the COSHH regulations, workers' medical records will be kept for at least 30 years. During 1989 these biological monitoring procedures revealed no abnormal results.

Safety

HPL encourages the development of high individual and collective safety standards and the provision at all times of a safe, healthy, accident-free working environment. Corporate goals have been set for a reduction in the number of lost-time injuries (LTI) and recent performance is as follows:

	1986	1987	1988	1989
LTI per million hours worked	24	9	8	7

To achieve and consolidate excellence in the field of personal safety involves major changes to procedures and attitudes developed over the years.

HPL has engaged independent Safety Management Consultants to:

a) evaluate the present safety management system and help management understand how they can modify and strengthen their approach so as to reduce injuries further.

b) provide training in the techniques of creating and sustaining a successful management safety audit system.

The quality of the Safety Management System at Aycliffe has been recognised by the award in 1987 of a Sword of Honour by the British Safety Council.

Hazard

HPL is a top-tier CIMAH site (see page 7), because its business is polymerisation and it keeps liquefied VCM under pressure on the premises at Aycliffe.

The regulations require that HPL prepare a 'safety case' which analyses, identifies and minimises the hazards in operations. Such a case has been prepared and lodged with the HSE. It sets out HPL's plans for dealing with emergencies as they may affect the site and the surrounding area, and must be reviewed every three years.

These plans have been developed in close co-operation with the local authority, the police and the fire brigade. Local residents within a designated area have been kept fully informed of all HPL's plans and are well briefed on what to do in the unlikely event that an emergency occurs. In accordance with HPL's policy of openness, the company has arranged open days for the families of staff and for the public.

Her Majesty's Inspectorate of Pollution (HMIP)

The responsibility for monitoring the effect of HPL's operations on the earth, air and water within and around the site is shared between HMIP and Northumbrian Water. Air pollution is the prime concern of HMIP and HPL works closely with them.

The vent stacks from the PVC resin plants have to be monitored regularly for both VCM and dust, and all three plants perform well inside the consent levels:

Figure 12.8   *(continued)*

P   O   L   Y   M   E   R   S

	Consent Levels	Performance	
		1988	*1989*
Mean VCM Emission (kg VCM/tonne PVC)	0.25	0.03	0.013
Mean Dust Emission (mg/m³)	0.115	0.01	0.004

In addition to the monitoring of dryer plant stacks there is a comprehensive programme of fence line monitoring for VCM agreed with HMIP. During 1989, 75 measurements were made with the following results:

Range of VCM Levels (ppm)	N.D.*–1.43
Mean Value (ppm Time Weighted Average)	0.084

*Not Detected

Northumbrian Water

This body is concerned with possible contaminations of ground water and of water leaving the site. HPL has every reason to avoid the contamination of ground water since use is made of water from a bore-hole on site. Regular checks are made on the quality of the water taken from the bore-hole. The liquid effluent leaving the site is governed by a 'Consent to Discharge Trade Effluent' given by the Northumbrian Water Authority. Additional legislation is presently coming into force including the Water Act 1989 and new Statutory Instruments arising from EEC directives. The 1989 performance is summarised below:

	Maximum Consent Level	Performance	
		Mean	Maximum
Suspended Solids (ppm)	400	110	394
Sulphate (ppm)	1200	114	600
Sulphide (ppm)	1	0.10	0.75
Chromium (ppm)	5	0.44	2.5

While these values are within the existing consent levels, HPL is planning continuous improvement so as to yield much lower levels. Attention has been concentrated upon reducing the level of suspended solids and the 1990 levels are already proving to be substantially better.

The Role of PVC

PVC has characteristics which make it superior to many competing materials. This section describes these attributes, relating them both to PVC production and to the impact of PVC production on the environment. The essential raw materials are oil and common salt, both basic commodities available in bulk supply. Catalytic 'cracking' of crude oil yields ethylene which is reacted with chlorine from salt to form vinyl chloride monomer. This in turn is polymerised to form PVC.

The production of PVC and its processing into end products require substantially lower energy inputs than are needed for competing materials such as glass, steel and concrete. In use PVC is non toxic, of long life and lightweight. There are many applications where these attributes provide economic advantages to users: in sewage and water pipes (where only one-sixth of the energy used to produce and lay cast iron pipe is needed for PVC pipe); as a bottling material (mineral water packed in PVC bottles takes 40% less fuel to transport than water transported in glass bottles); and in PVC packaging (in which food has a longer shelf life than in paper, a material which uses more energy in its production).

PVC bottles used for food and toiletries.

Figure 12.9   Norsk Hydro – Audit Report

L L O Y D ' S   R E G I S T E R

Scope

This assessment results from Norsk Hydro (UK) Ltd requesting Lloyd's Register to review and independently comment on its environmental practices and performances with specific reference to:–

- Legislation compliance.

- A check on figures presented in this report to ensure that they give a true and fair view.

- The environmental monitoring and operating procedures at the sites visited, namely Hydro Polymers at Newton Aycliffe, Hydro Fertilizers at Immingham, Golden Sea Produce at Oban, Scotland, and Hydro Aluminium Metals and Alupres at Bedwas, Wales.

The method used for assessing the monitoring and operating procedures is Lloyd's Register's Environmental Assurance scheme, which sets guidelines for environmentally excellent companies (see box on page 28).

Summary of findings

The following are Lloyd's Register's findings based on the material submitted, the appearance of the sites visited and opinions formed during the visits:–

- The sites visited all comply with existing legislation and consents where these exist. The compliance is better than the minimum legal requirement in most cases.

- The figures in this report were found to give a true and fair view of existing environmental monitoring data.

- Hydro's performance in the UK, based on the criteria laid down in Environmental Assurance, is good. Their actions and investments are consistent with a company whose aim is to reduce the environmental impact of its operations. Half the business units have an environmental policy and the rest are developing one. Consideration of environmental impact forms part of operations, and of assessments for plant expansions, on all the sites visited. The management of environmental improvements is a continuously evolving process, a fact of which Hydro is fully aware.

Commentary

Hydro operates in a wide range of industries in the UK from chemical and mechanical engineering through to food production. The sites visited span the total spectrum of operation.

The objective of this section is to support the finding that Hydro companies in the UK are well aware of the impact of their operations on the environment and to demonstrate their commitment through positive action and innovation to meet the challenge of solving existing and future environmental problems. This will be done by highlighting the strengths and weaknesses with examples of areas of good practice and areas where improvements are being instigated. Areas where certain of the Hydro operations do not completely meet the Environmental Assurance guidelines for excellent behaviour will then be identified.

Examples of good practice include:–

- The central environmental policy found at Hydro Polymers and Hydro Fertilizers. In addition Hydro Polymers has a mission statement which covers behaviour towards the environment.

- The regular environmental reports on all sites, both to site management (monthly) and to business unit HQ in Norway (quarterly).

- The achievement of doing substantially better than the maximum level set for Best Practical Means (BPM) on vinyl chloride monomer (VCM) and dust emissions from the PVC resin plant.

- The design of the ammonium nitrate plant to produce nearly zero emissions at Hydro Fertilizers. This involves the use of modern dust extraction technology.

- The effluent treatment plant at Golden Sea Produce. This plant biologically cleans process water. The site also has a plant producing animal food and saleable fish oil from all other waste.

- The complaint handling on all sites. The procedure and policy are clear, and any complaint is investigated. The complaint is followed up if the complainant has identified himself/herself.

- The strong involvement in the local community exemplified by the open days at Hydro Polymers, the environmental liaison committee with local councillors at Hydro Fertilizers, the involvement with local schools at Golden Sea Produce.

Figure 12.9   *(continued)*

L L O Y D ' S   R E G I S T E R

Examples of areas where improvements are being implemented include:–

- The effluent treatment plant at Alupres. The plant neutralises the anodising chemicals and filters out solids prior to discharge to sewer. The plant is in operation, but there are some teething problems.

- The development of a new settling tank design for Hydro Polymers' PVC resin plant. The aim is to reduce further the suspended solids in the effluent stream and to recover product.

- The extensive internal and external noise surveys at both Hydro Aluminium Metals and Alupres. These resulted in action to reduce the noise level where current plant layout permitted. Further improvements are being considered.

- The trials on the use of the small fish, wrasse, to combat the problem of the salmon louse. Success would result in the use of dichlorvos being substantially reduced.

- The survey of air emissions at Hydro Aluminium Metals. This has led to the stack height being increased to its structural maximum to try to reduce the risk of the stack plume impacting on the nearby footpath. The problem is not completely solved, so other means of minimising the impact are being investigated. In addition, a stack emission monitoring programme is to be conducted.

- The aim of initiating regular internal environmental audits. These would be in addition to the existing safety and house keeping audits. For certain plants there will in addition be corporate environmental audits in the near future.

The above are all examples of positive practices and actions. Lloyd's Register's Environmental Assurance standards are set as guidelines for excellent companies. There are a limited number of areas where Hydro in the UK does not fully meet these standards. In all these areas Hydro does comply with existing legal requirements and the recommended actions are not company wide but site specific. The following actions are suggested by Lloyd's Register to improve these areas:–

- An investigation into options for waste minimisation at Hydro Fertilizers, Hydro Polymers, Alupres and Hydro Aluminium Metals.

- A monitoring survey of liquid effluent at Alupres; this will allow confirmation of management's expectation of content and will improve their understanding of the operations' environmental impact.

- A monitoring survey of air emissions at Hydro Polymers' PVC compounding plant; there should also be a survey of surface drains in relation to drum handling and storage to ensure that the potential for an incident, whereby a spill is washed to the local river, is minimised.

- Investigation of other disposal options for the small quantity of fullers earth/talc with traces of ammonium nitrate from Hydro Fertilizers' plant.

- Long term investigation by Hydro Fertilizers into the continued reduction and/or alternative disposal of the contaminant in the liquid effluent, which discharges under an existing consent into the Humber.

Conclusions

Lloyd's Register found that Hydro's UK sites understand well the environmental impact of their operations. There were clear signs of the effort expended to limit the environmental impact of the operations. Overall Hydro appears to be ahead of individual industry standards.

Environmental Assurance and Lloyd's Register

Lloyd's Register is a significant technical, inspection and advisory organisation as well as the world's premier ship classification Society. We have over 200 years of experience at providing independent advice and technical services to industry. Our engineers and specialists are recognised throughout the world for their integrity. The Society operates with no financial, political or commercial constraint and can therefore offer an independent, preventative auditing and validation service. Environmental Assurance is a scheme that has as its main focus a comprehensive technical and management audit, which is derived from guidelines for environmentally excellent behaviour.

Lloyd's Register carries out environmental assessments on all kinds of plant.

reports have risen over the years, it is significant to note that the first Norsk Hydro report not only set a standard for its time but set a standard that the majority of companies and other organizations are still aspiring to.

Perhaps the only real advantages that arise from the voluntary environmental reporting experiences of the 1990s are that it does permit organizations to learn about how best to undertake the activity and, in turn, it *does* encourage experimentation. Experimentation is still needed and particularly in reporting for sustainability (touched upon briefly in Chapter 14) and in the integration – or at least harmonization – of environmental (and perhaps social) and financial reporting.

12.6 Experimentation and Integration

When the current wave of environmental reporting started to break in the early 1990s there was not much in the way of very clear ideas about what it should look like. There were the UNCTAD guidelines and there had been, from time to time, suggestions from researchers.[37] In the end, though, the experimentation and the lead in development in environmental reporting came predominantly from the companies themselves. In the UK and Canada, for example, the emphasis tended to be upon the identification of performance against targets whilst, as we have seen, in northern Europe the mass balance (or *ökobilanz*) tended to predominate.

What was missing, at least from a traditional accountant's point of view, was some way of linking the performance in the financial statements with the data presented in the environmental report. We have already mentioned the need to be able to understand to what extent an organization's economic success has been bought at the cost of the natural environment and society. *This does not mean that environmental and social issues should be valued in financial terms, however.*[38] But

---

[37] One suggestion in the literature was for all organizations to report on the extent to which they had complied with (legal and other) standards. More detail and the arguments in support of the compliance-with-standard approach are given in Gray, Owen and Maunders (1986, 1987, 1988, 1991). Other suggestions included the adaptation of the French *bilan social* (see Christophe and Bebbington, 1992) and attempts by Dierkes and Preston (1977) and Ullmann (1976) to capture the essential environmental elements of an organization in a single statement.

[38] This question of whether or not social and environmental issues should be expressed in (reduced to) financial terms is a hotly debated one. In broad terms economists tend to favour such valuation of the social and environmental aspects of activity whilst environmentalists and ecologists tend to profoundly dislike the idea. We are firmly in the 'do not value nature' camp.

it *does* mean that readers (including management) will need to be able to seek ways of trading off economic benefit against environmental degradation, for example. Given the ubiquity of financial measurement and the predominance of profit as a measure of 'success', it was inevitable that someone would try to place environmental issues in the same statement as financial measurement.[39] One influential such attempt was by BSO/Origin.

BSO/Origin[40]

BSO/Origin is a Dutch company whose experimental environmental accounts are especially notable in that they attempt to link the economic and environmental activities through financial numbers reported in an amended *value added statement*. The previous, most remarkable experiment in this direction of reporting information which attempted to link the economic and the 'non-economic' was the social accounts produced by management consultants Clark C. Abt in the USA in the early to mid-1970s. These accounts from Abt attempted to show a fully integrated set of financial and social accounts through both a profit and loss account and balance sheet. The experiment was one from which a great deal was learned but much more experimentation is necessary to determine whether or not the idea could be fully operationable. The impression gained from the Abt experiment was that whilst much could be done, the resultant numbers were so confusing as to verge on the meaningless. Nevertheless, the Cement Corporation of India did produce and publish a set of Abt-based social financial statements in 1981. This demonstrated that you could do this – even if you could not be entirely sure what it was you had done when you finished.

The BSO/Origin company, again a management consultancy like Abt, has continued the experiment but has cleverly avoided a number of the Abt pitfalls by focusing on the value added statement (VAS).

[39] Over the years there have been a number of experiments (notably in the USA) to integrate social and environmental costs into a financial statement. All have lessons for the development of forms of environmental reporting and from which companies such as BSO/Origin could learn to avoid reinventing wheels and thereby save money and resources. Most of these experiments were many years ago now. The most notable of these were the experiments by Linowes, Eastern Gas and Fuel Associates, Philips Screw, First National Bank of Minneapolis and Clark C. Abt and Associates. For more detail see, for example, Belkaoui (1984), Estes (1976), Gray, Owen and Maunders (1987).

[40] The following is adapted from Gray and Symon (1992b) but see also Huizing and Dekker (1992), who review the 1990 accounts, and *ENDS Report* 210/July 1992, pp. 19–21, which also reviews the 1991 accounts. Although the company continued its experimentation, these comments apply specifically to the 1990 and 1991 accounts.

The VAS is both a more focused statement than the constantly debated profit and loss account and balance sheet and, in addition, has the advantage of explicitly recognizing that shareholders are neither the only participants in, nor the only contributors to, organizational activity. The VAS was originally devised either as (depending upon one's point of view) a labour-centred attempt to demonstrate the contribution of labour to the financial success of the organization, or as a business-centred attempt to indicate the share of the organization's financial success that the employees received. BSO/Origin places the environment in the position of labour and, most notably, takes the business-centred, rather than an environment-centred, position. In fact it comes as no surprise to learn that, by reference to its own calculations, BSO/Origin still shows a net value added (as opposed to value lost) after allowing for environmental factors.

In addition to the statutory financial statements and the usual review of operations, BSO/Origin's rather splendidly designed 1990 annual report contains a seven-page (13-page if the pictures are included) essay entitled 'Pulling our planet out of the red' plus three pages of environmental accounts together with five pages of explanatory notes. The essay is among the most coherent, brief expositions of a mid- to deep-green position one is likely to find as well as being (as far as we are aware) the most direct and honest assessment of the corporate/environmental relationship from a company. It is well worth reading for this alone.[41] However, the essay's principal purpose is to explain the thinking behind the environmental accounts.

BSO/Origin's starting point is that environmental crisis requires that we begin to recognize that economic value added has been achieved only at the cost of environmental degradation. If we are to know the real value added (*sic*) then we must deduct the ecological value lost (*sic*). The company then goes on to argue that ecological impact can occur at three stages: direct from the company, downstream from the company (i.e. via the consumer) and upstream from the company (i.e. the supplier). But what should be included? BSO argues that it is essential for all companies to produce environmental accounts if any real progress is to be made. This is because only then can we avoid the double-counting of, for example, impacts that arise from the products the company purchases for use. Very clear rules are needed to establish which ecological impacts can be determined as falling to which organization – that is, to allocate carefully the ecological impact of activities between the organizations and individuals involved in (say) the extraction of the raw materials, the processing,

---

[41] The 1991 report is introduced by an invited essay on anthropology and the devastation of ethnocentrism.

the manufacture and the use of the end product.[42] An important point is made in this context: any company can reduce its apparent direct impact by (for example) switching from fuel oil heating to electric heating and thereby handing the responsibility for the emissions back to the supplier.

BSO is very clear that its decisions as to what to include and value and what to exclude are largely arbitrary. This clarity is very valuable to future experimenters as well as to users of these accounts, who are therefore able to add in or deduct items at their discretion. The company assumes that it causes little downstream negative impact and, given the nature of its business, suspects that the downstream effects will, on balance, be ecologically positive. The downstream effects are thus ignored. The upstream effects (suppliers) are ignored because those matters should be dealt with in the supplier's environmental accounts and there is too little information for BSO to establish impact. The company does, however, make two exceptions: in the use of energy supplied to the company and in the supply of waste-processing facilities which the company purchases. The essay then concludes with some explanation as to how the different ecological impacts were valued. The impacts are imaginatively derived but all impacts are not valued on the same bases. The calculations are shown in more detail in the explanatory notes accompanying the environmental accounts.

The accounts themselves provide a detailed breakdown of the ecological value lost. This is shown as 'Cost of environmental effects' (itemized between various emissions and wastes) less 'environmental expenditure' (being the net expenditure undertaken by the company). The net value lost is then shown against the conventional economic value added by the company to produce a net value added. (This is summarized, based on the 1990 accounts, in Figure 12.10.)

BSO/Origin, wisely, claims little for these accounts (which are not audited). On the down-side, the company recognizes that the accounts are partial, subjective and, in effect, add possible apples to approximate pears and subtract the result from hypothetical oranges. One would be ill-advised to place any weight on these accounts. However, with very good reason it *does* claim that experiments such as these are essential if business is to contribute to sustainability and that some experimentation is preferable to inaction. BSO further suggests that there is much value in the process itself of undertaking this kind of analysis. It is for these reasons that we believe that the BSO/Origin experiment deserves wide attention and the company deserves significant applause for the attempt. These environmental accounts from BSO/Origin (an extract from the BSO/Origin 1990

---

[42] The issues discussed here are also apparent in the concerns in life cycle assessment – see Chapter 9.

Figure 12.10

Valuing ecological impact with BSO/Origin in the early 1990s

Putting financial numbers to ecological impact must choose between, typically: the cost of preventing the ecological impact; the cost of repairing the ecological damage; the value lost to society from the ecological impact. BSO/Origin, in common with most experiments, mixes the three. Consider the following:

NO_x and SO_2 emissions
NO_x emissions are 'valued' at Dfl.10 per kg NO_x. This appears to be a reasonable assessment of the costs of reducing NO_x emissions. This does not measure 'ecological impact'. SO_2 on the other hand is 'valued' using a hybrid method. viz. 'the impact of both NO_x and SO_2 . . . is essentially associated with acid rain . . . Since 1kg SO_2 contains 1.44 times the acid equivalent of 1kg NO_x its environmental impact can be calculated on a proportional basis, giving a costing of ($1.44 \times$ Dfl.10 = Dfl.14 per kg SO_2). This is the value we have used for SO_2.' Thus an estimate of its ecological impact is derived by taking a figure for the cost of prevention and multiplying it by a factor of its impact. The resultant number means little if anything at all. It *does* not capture ecological impact.

Waste water
The 'value' of the ecological impact is taken to be an estimate of the cost of returning the waste water to drinking water. (The calculation is not a full ecological impact calculation because it makes no attempt to account for ecological impact – e.g. destruction of habitat, health hazard, etc.). The calculations are based upon domestic water cleansing costs, noting the special nature of the company's effluent (e.g. heavy metals) and measured in terms of Dutch 'inhabitant equivalents'. BSO/Origin estimates its water waste costs twice this figure, namely Dfl.48 per inhabitant equivalent.

These calculations employ three different bases to produce financial numbers. They are not comparable. For the accounts to have more meaning the calculations will have to be performed on a consistent basis.

Accounts is included in Appendix 12.1) were not the only attempt at financial and environmental integration – although they were perhaps the most colourful and the most widely known. Other companies – perhaps most notably the North American companies, Baxter Health Care and Ontario Hydro[43] – also entered the experimental phase with different approaches to capturing the environment in financial terms.

In our view such experiments are at least as valuable for what they fail to do as for what they achieve. It seems highly unlikely (even if it were desirable) that any unique organizationally based valuation system can properly capture environmental (or social) interactions in any sensible way. Like many 'failed' experiments, we learn a lot more about the nature of organization–environment interactions through the process of the experiments – and this is valuable. If we also learn

---

[43] See Bennett and James (1998b) for an introduction to the experiences of these two companies.

that we cannot (in addition to shouldn't) try to value the environment then the experiments have shown us a great deal.

12.7 Conclusions

The enormous strides in environmental reporting during the 1990s have continued into the present decade. These strides were especially remarkable in that most of the developments were undertaken voluntarily. However, despite these strides, environmental reporting remained, on the whole, a large company activity.

A number of major lessons were learned from the decade of experimentation: a 'single financial bottom line' including the environment is not only undesirable but probably impossible; the mass balance provides an excellent – and possibly the only – means of providing an indication of completeness; environmental performance through time and against targets developed to be a major focus of interest in corporate environmental disclosure; and so on.

But there remained a number of problems. The *completeness* issue was certainly a major one. Readers could rarely assess whether the most important data was being disclosed. Equally importantly, the focus on emissions and waste – which so often was the core of environmental reporting – failed to consider total resource use, impact on levels of consumption and all the other, more subtle issues which arise when a sustainability, rather than a narrow 'environmental' perspective, is adopted.

In general terms, the problem was that it *was* practice which led the way and so, like so much accounting, there was no coherent theoretical framework underpinning the environmental reports which developed over the period. Reports were trying to be good PR,[44] legitimating devices, usable for management control, perhaps discharge some accountability and so on. Such a range of purposes suggests that no single one will be successfully achieved.

Moving into the future, this combination of incompleteness and lack of coherent theory is likely to get worse rather than better. That is, if

[44] This and previous uses of the term 'public relations' have largely been pejorative and, strictly speaking, should have been accompanied by the term 'empty' or 'bad' as qualifiers. Public relations at its best must work with truthful, honest and complete conceptions of the organizations' activities and is a clearly essential part of the transparency, accountability and communication. Good public relations is a prerequisite for any sort of organization–community partnership and for a resolution of conflict between the different stakeholders in the environment and economy. Too often, however, PR has come to mean the painting of soothing gloss on a situation regardless of any relationship with truth, integrity, honesty or public interest. It is in this sense that the pejorative use of PR is intended.

environmental reports are successful (in management's terms) in convincing society that the environment is safe in business's hands they deflect attention from the very issues that are at stake – the nature of growth and consumption and the whole range of sustainability issues.

At the turn of the century there was a growing tendency to label environmental reports as 'sustainability' or 'sustainable development' reports.[45] But, as we shall see in Chapter 14, emissions and wastes are a relatively small part of sustainability. Given that no one fully understands sustainability, by definition any report labelled a 'sustainability report' will be seriously and misleading incomplete. And what are such reports for? Whilst organizations have every right to use their channels of communication (including reporting) to further their own ends, there is no reason for those external to the organization to trust such statements. Furthermore, as we saw in Chapter 11, the alleged 'independent attestation' of such reports only confounds the misleading tendencies.

It seems to us that, ultimately, all environmental reports (and eventually reporting for sustainability) must be about the discharge of accountability and must be judged against that criterion. Despite the major strides over the past two decades, it is not clear that environmental reporting has, actually, advanced the principle of accountability. It is, surely, quite unreasonable to expect companies to undertake such duties voluntarily. For the discharge of (environmental and social) accountability we need the supra-organizational bodies – the state, the UN, the EU and so on – to start taking their responsibilities seriously and lay down the new (environmental) rules of the corporate game. It is ill-advised to expect the world's organizations to play by a set of rules when one is (deliberately?) unclear about what those rules really are.

Further Reading

There is now considerable material available with which to develop an understanding of environmental reporting – much of which has been referenced in this chapter. Monitoring the publications of the various bodies and organizations closely linked with environmental reporting – including ACCA, EIRIS, KPMG, PIRC, SustainAbility, UNCTAD, UNEP – is essential. To keep abreast of company developments access to environmental reports is recommended and the Internet is as good a place as any to begin this process. The CSEAR website (see addresses at the end of the book) provides links to both company websites and, more particularly, to other websites that provide often extensive, further relevant links. Monitoring academic research is also important and the CSEAR website plus its newsletter, *Social and Environmental Accounting*, provide an overview of academic and practitioner developments in the field.

[45] This tendency is particularly encouraged by the *Global Reporting Initiative (GRI)*.

APPENDIX 12.1
Extract from the BSO/Origin 1990
Annual Report

Cost of environmental effects in thousands of guilders

Atmospheric emissions

	Emission	Unit cost	Total
		Dfl.	
Natural gas for heating purposes			
NO_x	456 kg	10 Dfl./kg	5
CO_2	483 t.	100 Dfl./t.	48
Total			53
Electricity consumption			
SO_2	7,934 kg	14 Dfl./kg	111
NO_x	6,202 kg	10 Dfl./kg	62
Particulate emissions	667 kg	10 Dfl./kg	7
CO_2	2,515 t.	100 Dfl./t.	252
Total			432
Road traffic			
NO_x	20,585 kg	40 Dfl./kg	823
HC	14,948 kg		
CO	55,452 kg		
CO_2	7,232 t.	100 Dfl./t.	723
Total			1546
Air traffic			
NO_x	1,160 kg	10 Dfl./kg	12
CO_2	317 ton	100 Dfl./t.	32
Total			44
Waste incineration			
SO_2	300 kg	14 Dfl./kg	4
NO_x	369 kg	10 Dfl./kg	4
Particulate emissions	254 kg	10 Dfl./kg	3
HCl	692 kg	13 Dfl./kg	9
CO_2	277 t.	0 Dfl./kg	0
Total			20
Subtotal			2,095

	Emission	Unit cost		Total
			Dfl.	
Atmospheric emissions (subtotal)				2,095
Waste water				
Water treatment	277 inh.eq.	48 Dfl./i.e.	13	
Transport	277 inh.eq.	12 Dfl./i.e.	3	
Residual water pollution			27	
Total waste water				43
Waste				
Company waste production				
Quantity	377 t.			
Recycled paper	— 146 t.			
Net waste	231 t.			
Collection	377 t.	80 Dfl./t.	30	
Incineration	231 t.	100 Dfl./t.	23	
Residual waste after incineration				
Bottom ash	23 t.	100 Dfl./t.	2	
Fly ash	7 t.	200 Dfl./t.	1	
Subtotal			56	
Power station waste production				
Fly ash	64 t.	200 Dfl./t.	13	
Water treatment waste production				
Sludge	4 t.	500 Dfl./t.	2	
	dry matter	dry matter		
Total waste				71
Grand total				2,209

Environmental expenditure in thousands of guilders

	Dfl.	
Fuel levies (Netherlands)		
Natural gas (heating)	1	
LPG (cars)	18	
Power station fuel	8	
Total		27
Water treatment and refuse collection charges, sewerage charges and other environmental taxes		138
Private-sector waste processors		51
Total		216

Value lost
in thousands of guilders

	Dfl.
Cost of environmental effects	2,209
Environmental expenditure	− 216
Value lost	1,993

Net value added
in thousands of guilders

	Dfl.
Value added	255,614
Value lost	− 1,993
Net value added	253,621

The Environmental Accounts form part of BSO/Origin 1990 Annual Report. For more information please write to BSO/Origin, P.O. Box 8348, 3503 RH Utrecht, The Netherlands.

CHAPTER 13

SOCIAL ACCOUNTING AND REPORTING AND THE EXTERNAL 'SOCIAL AUDITS'

13.1 Introduction

Our focus in this book has been on environmental issues and the natural environment. We have examined these issues primarily from the point of view of organizations (and especially companies) and how they interact with the natural environment. We have then attempted to show how accounting is – and can be – involved in the relationships between organizations and the natural environment. But to properly understand the relationships between organizations, accounting and the environment we would really need to consider in much more detail a number of other 'systems'. Such systems would include the broad political, economic and financial systems by which we tend to organize our economic life – predominantly the system known as 'capitalism'. In addition, we would have to try to introduce both a deeper understanding of how organizations actually function and a more refined explanation of how society operates. In turn, we would need to consider how society influences and is influenced by the ways in which organizations operate.

To try to attempt all of this in a single text would be over-ambitious.[1] However, to ignore such issues altogether would also be remiss of us.[2] The more one tries to understand any one system – be it accounting, organizations, the environment, or whatever – the more one comes to realize that to understand any one element we really need a good grasp of the central issues in those other systems – systems which, far too often, we just leave as taken for granted. These taken-for-granted assumptions are legion – and often hide crucial but unexamined issues. Why is economic growth considered to be unquestionably desirable? Is it right that the world's largest companies are now larger – and certainly economically more powerful – than many countries? We tend to assume that democracy is a 'good thing' but why do we not, therefore, worry that economic democracy is largely a fiction as economic power is focused in so few hands? Why do parts of the world's population live in luxury whilst the

---

[1] See Gray, Owen and Adams (1996), especially the first three chapters, for an introduction to these issues.

[2] The following, very brief overview of the issues can be supplemented by the suggestions listed in the further reading at the end of the chapter.

majority live in poverty? Why is so much environmental degradation, species extinction and social dislocation and exclusion seen as a 'necessary evil' of economic 'progress'.[3] And so on.

These are 'big' questions and are not easy to answer. But it is difficult to consider any aspect of organizational activity, accounting and, most especially, the environment without at least some sensitivity to these issues.

We will come back, albeit briefly, to such matters in Chapters 14 and 15 but, for the moment, let us return to organizational–environmental issues and examine whether any consideration of the 'environment' can sensibly be separated from consideration of the 'social'.

To echo issues we raised in Chapter 1, why are we concerned by environmental issues at all? The simple answer is that (a) we, as human beings, are part of the natural environment and depend upon it for our existence; and (b) it is our social, economic and financial systems – significantly influenced by accounting – that are one of the (if not *the*) principal causes of the environmental degradation we see around us. This simple answer then leads us, inevitably, to recognize that our concern for the natural environment can be partly an ethical one (that is, it is 'wrong' to, for example, damage the natural world and thus to either threaten other species and/or place peoples in destitution and poverty) and partly an instrumental one (that is, damaging the environment threatens our own health and well-being as well as placing the environmental foundation of economic activity in jeopardy).

Thus, whilst we may, very properly, be anxious about the environment for intrinsic ethical reasons, our predominant concerns are as likely to arise from a recognition of both the *social* reasons why the environment is being degraded and the *social* impacts of so doing. Consequently, whilst we *may* wish to consider environmental issues in isolation from other systems, it is very difficult to maintain a distinction between, for example, the environment and social concerns. These social anxieties and, in particular, the social consequences of organizational activity tend to be the concern of something called *social accounting*.

There are four basic reasons for paying at least a little attention to social accounting issues in a text dedicated to accounting and the environment. *First*, as we have seen above, the distinction between environmental and social issues is basically an artificial one. *Secondly*, as the environmental reporting phenomenon gained momentum it, inevitably, drew in social accounting concerns. Consequently, the late 1990s saw a significant re-surgence in interest in social accounting

[3] For more detail see, for example, Beder (1997), Eden (1996), Weizsäcker et al. (1997).

issues.[4] *Thirdly,* as we shall see in Chapter 14, a concern with environmental issues leads, inevitably, to a concern with sustainability – and sustainability demands that equal attention be given to both environmental and social concerns. *Finally,* one of the important drivers for the environmental movement has been (as we have seen throughout the book) the activities of pressure groups, NGOs and the like. One of the more powerful tools in the pressure group arsenal is the so-called *social audit* which forces accountability upon reluctant organizations.

We have briefly touched upon the first of these issues, and Chapter 14 will introduce sustainability in more detail. This chapter, therefore, will concentrate on the second and fourth issues above. The first part of the chapter will provide a short overview of social accounting and reporting whilst later sections will briefly introduce the social audits.

13.2 A Brief Introduction to Social Accounting

Social accounting is a diverse activity and has been an active area of research and practice since, particularly, the early 1970s. It is principally concerned with offering, if not an alternative, then a complementary form of accounting to the dominant economic and profit-orientated emphasis of organizations. Whilst social accounting can be (and is from time to time) used by organizations to support management decisions (in much the way as EMS functions), it tends to be driven predominantly by a desire to increase the accountability of organizations. Organizations are actively accountable to finance providers and that accountability is primarily concerned with economic activities of the organization. But every organization has many other stakeholders with (at least potential) rights to information and they – and the finance providers – have information needs which extend beyond only the financial activities of the organization. Thus social accounting – and in particular external social reporting – tends to be concerned with providing all stakeholders with information about the social and environmental activities and impacts of the organization.

---

[4] One particular manifestation of this began in mainland Europe where companies' reporting on the environment automatically covered reporting on health and safety issues. Health and safety issues are 'environmental' in that they deal with part of the organization's effect on (particularly local) environments but they are also 'employee' related (in that employees are the most exposed to health and safety risks), 'community' *and* 'customer' related. Health and safety issues are therefore general social issues and the reporting of them demonstrates the artificiality of maintaining distinctions between the different areas of activity and disclosure.

Historically, social accounting was seen as concerned with community,[5] employee,[6] consumer[7] *and* environmental issues. To these issues might be added involvement with other countries, fair trade and trade with repressive regimes, transfers of wealth between the developed and developing countries and so on. As environmental reporting began to take on a life of its own, some of these other issues were briefly forgotten but are now being recognized as essentially part and parcel of the same concerns.

Whilst social reporting has, over its life, taken very many different forms, the dominant form has been the reporting of social information by organizations – and especially companies – through the annual report. Such reporting has both voluntary and mandatory elements to it and it varies considerably from country to country.[8,9] The general trend over time has, however, been to increase the mandatory social disclosure required of companies. Consequently, the annual reports of most large companies and the majority of all companies (especially, but not exclusively, in the industrialized West) will contain some social information about, for example, numbers of employees, policy of racial and sexual equality, or community giving. In addition, it is increasingly commonplace to see voluntary social (alongside the environmental) disclosure of varying quality in the annual reports of the largest companies.

The general trend of increasing social disclosure by companies now means that for many of the largest organizations, in addition to the environmental disclosure, there is likely to be between four and six pages of relevant social information. Throughout the 1990s, as might be expected from the discussion in Chapter 12, this non-environmental social disclosure was generally swamped by the reporting on the environment.

However, such piecemeal disclosure, like the patchy reporting of environmental issues in company annual reports, falls significantly

---

[5] Community concerns included such diverse matters as involvement of the local community, local economic regeneration, involvement with voluntary organizations, contributions to charities, schools and local enterprises and concerns over impact in Third World countries.

[6] Employee issues have included concern over employment conditions, equal opportunities, redundancies, training and union matters.

[7] Consumer issues have concerned such matters as access for disabled and disadvantaged consumers, consumer protection, health and safety issues and product quality and value for money.

[8] For an overview of many of these issues and the range of social disclosure across different countries see Gray, Owen and Adams (1996) for an introduction and for references to more detailed work in the area.

[9] The longest established requirement for systematic corporate social reporting (as far as we aware) is the French legislation governing the *bilan social* which has been an established part of company reporting since 1977.

short of providing a full and usable 'social account'. So, in precisely the same way that the more adventurous, innovative (and, possibly, responsible?) companies developed their piecemeal reporting into full stand-alone environmental reporting, so by the end of the 1990s a few companies were beginning to publish equivalent 'social reports'.

13.3. The Resurgence in Social Reporting Practice

The current re-awakening of interest in social accounting was led, by and large, by a group of what are often called 'ethical businesses'. Whether or not we believe all businesses to be ethical in one way or another, the vast majority do not place ethical issues at the forefront of their strategy and objectives. Some businesses do so, however. In the late 1990s, a number of organizations, most notably Body Shop (the UK-based toiletries and cosmetics company), Traidcraft (the UK-based fair trade company) and Ben and Jerry's (the US-based ice-cream company) followed through on their high-profile campaigning on ethical issues with the production of corporate social reports. These reports were experimental attempts to provide the reader with a comprehensive overview of the social and ethical performance of the organization during the period in question. They covered such matters as employee and customer satisfaction, key issues in community involvement as well as attempts to assess how well they had performed against their own ethical standards. Perhaps the most striking feature was that each report gave prominence to the views of stakeholders about the organization's performance and its ethical and social successes and failures.[10]

Had the phenomenon of producing such social and ethical reports been restricted only to such 'ethical businesses' it would have been interesting enough. But what was remarkable was that the interest in such reports spread to mainstream businesses.

The motivation for mainstream businesses beginning to employ social reporting and accounting was diverse. In part it was the experience with environmental reporting, in part the rising importance of

---

[10] These reports are not the only such 'ethical business' reports of the late 1990s. For more detail on these and other related initiatives see Zadek et al. (1997) and Gonella et al. (1998). The way in which the reports were developed was greatly influenced by the New Economics Foundation and, as time went on, the newly formed Institute of Social and Ethical Accountability. This influence, in turn, derived a lot of its initial impetus from 'social auditing' work being carried out in the social, non-business sector where attempts were being made to provide organizations (such as community businesses, social organizations, charities and the like) with performance assessment tools by which they could assess and justify their non-economic performance. For more detail on this see, for example, J. Pearce (1993, 1996) and Spreckley (1997).

sustainability and, in part, the raised profile of social accounting given by the reports of the 'ethical businesses'. But an important additional motivation was, without doubt, a series of high-profile public issues that arose for the companies concerned. The most widely known and best documented example is that of Shell.[11] Shell was subjected to extensive public pillorying – on alleged environmental grounds – over its decision to sink the Brent Spar oil platform at sea. The debate was heated, acrimonious and tended frequently to miss the central point but it disturbed the company greatly. Hardly had this furore died down than Shell was, once again, hauled into the public spotlight for its alleged involvement in, amongst other things, the displacement (and execution) of indigenous peoples in Nigeria. Shell responded in a number of ways but, most significantly, the company realized it had to look to its social legitimacy. One mechanism it employed to achieve this was the publication of an attempt at an open and comprehensive social report.[12]

There was hardly a flood of social reports immediately following the Shell publication but an increasing number of companies have since adopted a much more positive attitude to their social account- ability[13] and, perhaps more importantly, social reporting has been placed firmly back on the public and business agendas where it belongs.[14] Social accounting has never been more important. Not only is the need for systematic and significant social accountability greater than it has ever been but the exigencies of sustainability place social accounting on a par with environmental reporting as an essential plank to the future.[15]

---

[11] Other companies were also subject to high-profile public pressure leading to greater involvement with social reporting. Examples include British Petroleum, the Australian company BHP and the mining and minerals company Rio Tinto.

[12] Shell (1998) *Profits and Principles: Does There Have to Be a Choice?* followed by *The Report to Society* by Shell (UK).

[13] Other companies include British Petroleum (a company which had always main- tained a higher than average presence in social reporting), Grand Metropolitan, South African Breweries, SbN Bank (another of the important pioneers of social reporting), the Cooperative Bank, Interface and Skandia.

[14] The turn of the century also saw the emergence of a *Social Reporting Awards Scheme* organized by ACCA and the Institute for Social and Ethical Accountability (ISEA) and which echoed the earlier environmental reporting awards schemes.

[15] See Gray, Owen and Adams (1996) for much more detail on social accounting and Zadek et al. (1997) and Gonella et al. (1998) for an overview of these recent develop- ments. All three give illustrations from practice and a more critical review of develop- ments plus guidelines on developing social accounting are provided in Gray et al. (1997). (See also the web addresses given in Further Reading to Chapter 12 where examples of social accounting can also be found.) Sustainability is introduced in Chapter 14.

13.4 Introduction to the External Social Audits

A major feature of any society with claims to be a democracy is the flow of information that should educate and inform the *demos*. However, access to information, rights to information and willingness to part with or share information are far from equal in any but the most mythically egalitarian society. Therefore, a related feature of those nations that we would normally consider to be democracies is the 'external social audit'. This is a broad and imprecise term which we will use here to refer to the preparation *and publication* of information about one organization by a body independent of that organization.[16] And in this context it can be seen variously as an independent demonstration of concern about the lack of information in a particular area; a healthy manifestation of a democracy seeking to balance up the information asymmetry; and/or a means of extending the current boundaries of accountability.

Whatever the purpose one might ascribe to them, they exist and succeed in presenting information about organizational activity in a very different way from that in which an organization might choose to speak of itself. Within the context of this section of the book they may best be seen as (i) an indication of the limitations of current external self-reporting practice by organizations and (ii) as a mechanism that will increase an organization's accountability whether it wants it or not.

13.5 A Brief Background and History of the Social Audit

The principal reason for considering the history of the social audits is the rich mine of experience that it represents – both for the 'social auditors' (to avoid the reinvention of wheels) and for the 'audited' organization (which can assess the extent of the challenge, threat or opportunity offered by these things).

The genesis of external social audits is typically attributed to the late 1960s and early 1970s in the USA (for example, Ralph Nader and the consumer movement; the Council on Economic Priorities) and in the UK (for example, the Consumers' Association, Social Audit Ltd and Counter Information Services). These were very different sorts of organizations but they all succeeded in increasing the information in

[16] This may be seen as too limiting a definition; see, for example, Geddes (1992). As with 'environmental audit' the term audit is widely and confusingly used. Geddes, for example, prefers to use it in the context of a wide sense of any collecting and collating of information for use in a campaigning context. He thus includes 'needs' auditing, for example. We shall remain with our slightly more restrictive use of the term here.

the public domain – in the words of Stephenson, a member of the Council on Economic Priorities:

> *it appears that government cannot effectively evaluate and regulate big business. And it seems unwise to place the burden of corporate conscience on executives who are responsible for maximizing profit, or on the stockholders who are normally motivated even more singularly by profits. The best place to start correcting this situation is in making more information available to the public.*[17]

The UK's experience derives, initially, from that of the USA in that the early example of Ralph Nader (and Nader's Raiders) provided a model for consumer and related activism which influenced the founders of the UK's Consumers' Association,[18] Social Audit Ltd (and its research arm the Public Interest Research Centre)[19] and Counter Information Services. The Consumers' Association, although primarily consumer orientated, was an important early example of the social audit as a mechanism for challenging the passivity of the individual in the face of the growing power of organizations and their capacity to exploit advertising and the nature of choice.

Social Audit Ltd was a more complex organization[20] originally established to demonstrate that a full social audit was a feasible proposition. The intention was to publish data covering an organization's interactions with employees, consumers, community and the environment in the interests of a wider accountability and the presentation of a 'balancing view'. The essential reasoning behind this was that organizations in general – and companies and government departments in particular – are successful at presenting their own point of view to the public at large. What was needed was a mechanism for presenting an alternative – and hence 'balancing' – view. The first fruits of Social Audit's endeavours were published in the early 1970s in the *Social Audit Quarterly*, which, whilst not quite fulfilling the ambitions of the authors, remains a particularly good source of information (see Figure 13.1) on both the ways of collecting and presenting

---

[17] Stephenson (1973, p. 69).

[18] The Consumers' Association was, and to some extent remains (see, for example, Geddes, 1992, p. 224), a campaigning consumer-based organization concerned with assessing quality, value for money and the ethical basis of the supply of goods and services to the end-consumer market through its magazine *Which?*. Concerned with more than just the 'best buys' in consumer products, the Association sought (fairly successfully) to empower the consumer and to widen the scope of the accountability of organizations to the users of their services and products.

[19] This 'PIRC' should not be confused with 'PIRC' established in 1986 – the Pensions Investment Resource Centre.

[20] By the late 1980s Social Audit was a much smaller and lower-profile organization and one that was much more focused in its attentions. It now concentrates primarily on the activities of drug companies and, in particular, the use, control and marketing of drugs in the lesser developed countries.

Figure 13.1

Some areas covered by Social Audit Ltd's *Social Audit Quarterly*

- Tube Investments Ltd (including an exercise in trying to encourage social action by the shareholders of the company)
- The Alkali Inspectorate (as was)
- Cable and Wireless
- Coalite and Chemical
- Avon Rubber Company Ltd

plus general reports on matters such as:

- armaments and industry
- social costs of advertising
- company law reform

---

information and the difficulties of collating reliable and comprehensive data without the cooperation of the organization concerned.[21] Commercial exigencies were largely responsible for the cessation of the full, formal, social audits and the last manifestations of Social Audit Ltd's wider social role were a series of books and pamphlets in the late 1970s and early 1980s which remain, although dated, a continuing source of direction on the collection and use of information for employees and consumers.[22]

Counter Information Services were a much more radical outfit,[23] concerned more with the 'good story' and the empowering of labour than with anything that might conventionally pass for accountability and dialogue. Nevertheless, they represented a thorn in the side of industry for many years – particularly during the 1970s (see Figure 13.2).

The particular relevance in the present context of these bodies was that each covered environmental issues in its data gathering and publication. Social Audit's and CIS's reporting often contained a very significant element of environmental data. For example, the CIS report on Rio Tinto Zinc contained a number of serious observations – usually drawn from *The Ecologist* magazine – about the environmental performance of RTZ (now Rio Tinto) in general and one of its sites in particular. Social Audit pioneered both the use of local authority pollution data and the reporting of emissions against consent levels –

[21] For more detail, see Gray, Owen and Adams (1996), Gray, Owen and Maunders (1987) and Medawar (1976).

[22] See Frankel (1978, 1981, 1982), Medawar (1978).

[23] They described themselves as a Marxist Collective of journalists. For more information see, for example, Gray, Owen and Adams (1996), Gray, Owen and Maunders (1987) and Ridgers (1979).

Figure 13.2

> **Some subjects covered by Counter Information Services
> and the 'Anti-reports'**
>
> - Rio Tinto Zinc
> - Courtaulds
> - Consolidated Gold Fields
> - British Leyland
> - Ford Motor Company
> - GEC
> - Unilever
> - Lucas
> - National Health Service
>
> and reports on, for example:
>
> - South Africa
> - nuclear technology
> - the Queen's Jubilee
> - women in society

with explanations as to the biological implications of the consent levels themselves. These are innovations in data use and reporting to which we are only now returning and it is wise to remember that the emergence of environmental emissions data into the public domain is not a new phenomenon.

Apart from Social Audit and CIS, environmental issues played little role in the social audit movement (in the UK) throughout the 1970s and into the early 1980s. The emphasis in this period tended to be on the social consequences of the worst excesses of Thatcherism and, in particular, on the shadowing of plant-closure decisions.[24] In general, the 'social audit movement' is, was and remains a diffuse and intermittent activity. The campaigning role is often best served by the combination of investigative journalism and the pressure groups – in the environmental domain this typically means organizations such as Friends of the Earth, Greenpeace, Earth First! and the other (often *ad hoc*) protest groups.

Meanwhile, in the USA, the existence of the Council for Economic Priorities (CEP) has provided a consistency and regularity to the social auditing process. The CEP has been actively campaigning for over twenty years. Its purpose is to research, collate and publicize information about organizational activity as it affects society[25] across a wide

---

[24] For more detail see Geddes (1988, 1992), Gray, Owen and Maunders (1987), Harte and Owen (1987) and Haughton (1988).

[25] See, for example, Miller (1992).

spectrum of social issues – including the environment – and it has produced more than 100 reports on such matters as waste disposal, nuclear energy, air and water pollution, military spending, occupational safety. The long life of the CEP has enabled it to build up a reputation, experience and a reliable methodology in the collection and reporting of data. One major effect of this has been to produce streams of data about such matters as pollution which other researchers have employed in the assessment of the social and environmental performance of corporate America.[26] Whilst it is not clear where the funding for such an arrangement could come from, there is little question that other countries need this consistent and reliable source of data if sensible debate – other than simply controlled by the corporations themselves – is to be possible.[27]

13.6 The External Social Audit: Present and Future

The diffuse nature of activities falling within the term 'social audit' should be apparent by now. This situation seems likely to continue and the plurality may in fact be a healthy phenomenon reflecting a vital and changing area of public concern. However, the very patchy and intermittent nature of the efforts to bring information into the public domain does tend to undermine its effectiveness. There are some signs that this state of affairs is changing. Not only are there now established campaigning information sources such as (in the UK) ENDS, EIRIS and PIRC, but the environmental organizations and the ethical/environmental investment movement themselves are becoming much better established whilst new institutions – most notably the Institute for Social and Ethical Accountability – are springing up and standards for the social and ethical performance of organizations are beginning to emerge.[28]

[26] This had the effect of encouraging researchers – especially in accounting and finance – to keep alive the debate about the social, environmental and economic consequences of corporate activity in a way that is simply not possible in the UK and elsewhere.

[27] For more information see Council for Economic Priorities (1973), Shane and Spicer (1983). The CEP has also played an important role in the ethical/environmental investment movement (see Chapter 10) and, to an extent, we can see organizations like EIRIS in the UK taking on the CEP role.

[28] The first of these was SA8000. Issued by CEP and based on the International Labour Organization, the Universal Declaration on Human Rights and the UN Convention on the Rights of the Child, SA8000 lays down guidelines for the human element of sourced goods – primarily about whether organizations should buy from organizations employing child labour. Early 2000 saw ISEA's issuance of the 'foundation' standards on social reporting – AA1000.

Such issues are important. With many organizations it is often the 'external shock' that has prompted them to take a serious and hard look at their environmental activity. There can be little doubt of the increasing efficacy (or irritant depending upon one's point of view) represented by the campaigning organizations (Friends of the Earth, Greenpeace and so on) and their 'social auditing' activities. Other organizations have set up consultation procedures with elements of the broad 'social audit' movement – whether prompted by a past conflict, fear of a future conflict or genuine desire to develop environmental sensitivity is not clear. But the very presence of campaigning bodies – including some of the more campaigning environmental consultancies such as SustainAbility – has a substantive effect on the level of environmental awareness and avoids the onset of complacency.

With the growth in the number of widely established and reliable information services and the increase in campaigning organizations anxious to collate and publicize such data, there is a sense that countries are just beginning to make the first substantial move towards a greater (if reluctant) transparency. This process is encouraged and reinforced by other developments such as the work of local authorities and the newer campaigning publications.

Local government has played important roles in the past in developing local accountability[29] and continues to play a major part in determining the extent to which initiatives on, for example, transport, planning and the monitoring of environmental performance are received and applied. In addition, local government is central to the implementation of *Local Agenda 21* – part of the primary policy documents that emerged from the Rio Conference. Furthermore, local communities, with or without the support of local government, are important sites for the development of new 'community business' initiative and even new economic arrangements like LETS.[30] However, what is far from clear, as yet, is how the potentially conflicting roles of 'development' – meaning economic growth and expansion of traditional forms of employment – and enhancement of the environment will be reconciled.[31] Already, local enterprise companies, for example,

---

[29] For example, during the 1980s in the UK, local authorities played an active role in the conduct of social audits primarily directed towards what were seen as the excesses of private development and the social impact of decisions by private companies. For further detail see, for example, Geddes (1988, 1992) and Harte and Owen (1987).

[30] Local Economic Trading Systems in which communities with little or no money exchange their own 'currency' – for example, a fictitious unit like an 'acorn' – or a measure of labour hours for goods (for example, home-grown vegetables) or services (repairs, baby-sitting, etc.) to generate their own local economy. For more detail see, for example, Harker et al. (1997) and Kretzmann and McKnight (1993).

[31] See, for example, Gray and Morrison (1992).

established to regenerate business development, are facing, with the appropriate local government authorities, the tensions about jobs and growth versus environment and longer term social considerations. At the present time, unfortunately, the tension looks a real one, and one in which, typically, we can expect the conventional economic criteria to win over environmental concerns.

The 'green consumer' has probably been a major force on the process of organizational environmental sensitivity. Consumer boycotts and related activism have a long (and, at times, successful) history.[32] Whilst the notion of 'green' and 'consumer' are probably contradictions and the effect they can achieve (and have achieved) must be relatively superficial in the short term, the movement has certainly raised awareness, brought new products to the market and set in train effects of a far wider influence than the recycling of toilet rolls and the phosphate-freeness of washing powders.

The upsurge of interest in the late 1980s brought a steadily growing interest in environmental and related issues as represented in consumer choice and products and, with it, came a rapid increase in demand for new information which the campaigning bodies and the journalists were pleased to supply.[33] The rise in the number of campaigning bodies also rose steadily, which in itself increased the information-demand and the related pressure on organizations to disclose such information. Perhaps the most interesting 'social audit' manifestation in this regard was the development of new, campaigning journals such as (in the UK) *The Ethical Consumer*, *The Green Magazine* and *New Consumer*. *The Ethical Consumer* provides an assessment of companies and products based upon a wide set of criteria (see Figure 13.3) – far wider than just 'green' issues – that are a serious attempt to link the consumer with the people, countries, processes and effects that produced the product now being purchased and consumed. If environmental (and related) issues are to be sensibly addressed, this recognition of the connection between all forms of consuming and the social and environmental impacts is essential. *The Ethical Consumer* is a particularly powerful indicator of the potential for social auditing both to educate and to develop accountability.

---

[32] The consumer boycotts related to apartheid in South Africa are perhaps the best known and claimed as the most successful. Other major successes have focused around 'natural' foods, 'natural' beers, genetically modified (GM) organisms and the cruelty to animals campaigns.

[33] In the UK a consumer movement specifically targeted at environmental issues can probably be dated from Elkington and Hailes's *The Green Consumer Guide* in 1988. See Elkington and Hailes (1988, 1989).

Figure 13.3

> **The *Ethical Consumer* criteria for evaluation of products and companies**
>
> - Animal testing
> - Armaments
> - Environment
> - Irresponsible marketing
> - Land rights
> - Nuclear power
> - Oppressive regimes
> - South Africa
> - Trade union relations
> - Wages and conditions

New Consumer (a British publication, now sadly defunct) operated in a similar way, although one of its most pronounced influences was as a result of the publication of *Changing Corporate Values* in 1991.[34]

This text represents a really significant piece of research, collating information about 128 companies (only 79 of which are British). The information was drawn together from a variety of sources including, most significantly, a questionnaire to the companies themselves. (Their willingness or otherwise to respond to the questionnaire is noted in the text.) Figure 13.4 provides an illustration of the range of material and its presentation. The text alone represents a major data source just crying out for further research to assess its impacts.

13.7 Some Concluding Remarks

There are a number of crucial differences between 'social reporting' and 'environmental reporting' – at least on the surface. At first glance, environmental issues are relatively straightforward, 'hard', factual issues not tied up with political ideology, and they offer, to the enterprising companies, some clear economic savings through eco-efficiency. Social issues, by contrast, are messy, complex, highly charged with ethical concerns and clearly very political. Whilst, as we are beginning to see, environmental issues are nowhere near as isolated or as simple as they first appear to be, much of the early impetus for environmental reporting had this relatively simple-minded view of the issues. Consequently, organizations could just 'get on with it' if they were so minded. How, though, might a complex

---

[34] Adams, Carruthers and Hamil (1991), and see also Adams, Carruthers and Fisher (1991), which acts as a product-orientated version of the same research.

Figure 13.4 Extract from Adams, Carruthers and Hamill (1991), *Changing Corpporate Values*

Disclosure

This rating indicates whether the company completed the New Consumer or CEP questionnaires, whether the company provided New Consumer with information over and above that in its annual report, to what extent the company went beyond minimum statutory disclosure requirements in its annual report and other material, and whether the company provided comments on its draft profile or entered into a dialogue with New Consumer concerning the issues covered.

	Well above average
	Above average
	Average
	Below average
	Well below average

Ethnic

This rating indicates to what extent the company encourages the placement and advancement of members of ethnic minority communities within its organisation. The existence of some form of ethnic monitoring to evaluate policy is one factor taken into account as is a detailed equal opportunities policy. Support for Fullemploy, specific initiatives, recruitment and the number of ethnic minorities in senior positions particularly at board level, are all represented in the rating. No allowance has been made for cultural or immigration factors in different nations determining the level of minorities in the general population of the country of the parent company.

	Above average
	Average
	Inadequate information/ below average

Women

This rating indicates to what extent the company encourages the advancement of women within its organisation. This assessment includes aspects of personnel policy such as maternity leave, career breaks, crèche provision, job share and specific training, as well as recruitment and promotion policy and the number of women in senior positions, particularly at board level. No allowance has been made for cultural factors in different countries determining the role of women in management.

	Well above average
	Above average
	Average
	Inadequate information/ below average

Community

This rating is not based purely on the extent of the company's cash charitable giving in relation to profit. Secondment of staff, gifts in kind, facilities provided for staff to engage in community service are all taken into account. Membership of Business in the Community and the Per Cent Club in the UK are regarded as indicators. A general assessment of the percentage of charitable giving in relation to pre-tax profit comprises an element of the rating, though there is no allowance for traditions of corporate giving in different countries. There is, for example, a quite different perception between North American and many European countries on the place of corporate charitable giving.

	Above average
	Average
	Inadequate information/ below average

Figure 13.4 (continued)

Environmental impact

This rating indicates to what extent the company's activities have a significant effect on the environment. Those companies involved in the production of biomass, together with the extractive and manufacturing industries, are more likely to feature in this category.

| xxx | Major environmental impact (chemical, oil and mining companies) |

| xx | Significant environmental impact (clothing, pesticides, electrical goods, pharmaceuticals, agricultural goods and motor car manufacturers) |

| x | Above average impact (tobacco, fast food, soft drinks and brewing) |

Environmental action

This rating indicates particular initiatives the company is undertaking to reduce environmental impact or improve its environmental performance or sensitivity. Significant indicators here are the existence of a written environmental policy or an environmental office or officer.

| ✓✓ | Concerted environmental action |

| ✓ | Some environmental action |

| * | Inadequate information |

South Africa

Here an indication is made of the degree of a company's involvement, if any, in South Africa.

| Y | The company has a significant operating subsidiary in South Africa |

| Y | The company has some type of licensing agreement or trading activity/sales office in South Africa |

| y | A retailer offering South African products for sale in the UK |

Other countries

This rating indicates whether the company has operating subsidiaries in developing countries

| Y | Significant operating units in the Third World |

| Y | Some operating units or major licensing agreements in the Third World |

| y | Purchases a significant volume of products or raw materials from Third World countries |

Figure 13.4 (continued)

Respect for life

This rating indicates to what extent a manufacturing company uses animals in testing its products.

✓	Has not used animal testing either in-house or through outside contractors for products or their ingredients in the last five years
*	Insufficient information to rate
xx	Products are currently tested on animals, but only pharmaceutical or medical products
xxx	Non-medical products are currently tested on animals

✓	Products have been tested on animals in the last five years, but the company is funding or carrying out research into alternative methods of testing
✓	Products have not been tested on animals in the last five years, but ingredients have

Politics

This rating indicates whether the company has contributed financially in the period 1986–90 (many companies only make political donations in the period running up to a general election) to support political purposes within the United Kingdom as defined by Schedule 7 of the *Companies Act*.

C	Recent donations to the Conservative party or free enterprise support organisations
L	Recent donations to the Labour party or associates
E	Currently subscribes to, or has not confirmed a lapse of recent subscription to, the Economic League.

Respect for people

This rating indicates whether the company produces or retails alcohol or tobacco or is involved in the provision or promotion of gambling.

A	Manufactures alcoholic drinks
A	A significant retailer of alcoholic drinks
a	Some alcohol sales
T	Manufactures tobacco products

T	A significant retailer of tobacco products
t	Some tobacco sales
G	Provides substantial gambling services
g	Provides limited gambling services

Military

This rating indicates whether the company produces a significant volume of military equipment or provides essential goods or services to the military in the UK or elsewhere.

M	Has significant military sales (above £25m)
m	Has some military sales (between £5m and £25m)

Please note that the ratings are applied, unless specified otherwise, to the whole company group. Because of the very large number of acquisitions by major companies and the growth of conglomerates over the last twenty years, many brands listed in the product group section will be found to have unexpected affiliations. These ratings are intended as a very approximate guide; for further detail about how they have been compiled please refer to Appendix A.

Figure 13.4 (continued)

THE BODY SHOP INTERNATIONAL PLC

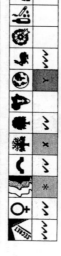

The Body Shop Group produces and sells natural-ingredient skin and hair care products and related items, both through its own shops and through franchised outlets. It has grown from its first retail shop, opened in Britain in 1976, to nearly 500 outlets in 37 countries. The company was founded by its current managing director, Anita Roddick. She opened the first shop in Brighton, selling a handful of natural toiletries adapted from materials she had seen used in less-developed countries.

Of the 151 shops in the UK, 115 are franchises, as are 320 of the 338 overseas outlets. Franchises are owned and run by the franchisee on a five-year renewable agreement. Franchisee credentials and motives are thoroughly assessed on ethical as well as financial grounds; however, the company makes no stipulation as to the pay and conditions of the staff in the franchised shops.

The Body Shop 'vigorously promotes a "green" and "ethical" image, and would seem to back this up in practice. Now truly a world-wide company, the USA is The Body Shop's youngest market and is operated by a subsidiary — The Body Shop Inc. Other subsidiaries include Eastwick Trading BV in the Netherlands, Colorings Ltd (a make-up and beauty range) in the UK, Jacaranda Productions Ltd (producing corporate, educational and training programmes for both The Body Shop and a wide range of external clients), and Soapworks Ltd.

The company sets out its mission statement as follows: 'The Body Shop cares about humanising the business community; we will con-

tinue to show that success and profit can go hand in hand with ideals and values. Profit is the lubricant to make things happen and the vehicle to help people — hence our philosophy of "profits with responsibility". We believe that a successful business has an obligation to educate and to inspire — we want to help initiate a new age of compassion and humanity. This is not hyperbole; it can, and already has been, translated into action.'

Financial data for the year ending 28 February 1990

Turnover	£84m
Profit before tax	£15m
Turnover by region:	
UK and Eire	£57m
Other EC	£7m
Rest of Europe	£4m
Australasia	£3m
Asia	£2m
USA	£6m
Rest of North America	£6m

Major shareholders: J.B. McGlinn has 30% of the ordinary shares. T.G. Roddick (chairman) and A.L. Roddick hold approximately 30.2% of the ordinary shares.

The Body Shop's annual report provides a substantial amount of information about the social initiatives, personnel and purchasing policies of the company, and the New Consumer group also completed the New Consumer questionnaire. The company has made social responsibility its unique selling proposition, and in this context it was felt appropriate to ask some supplementary questions about the effectiveness of its 'social' policies; these questions were answered in some detail. The overall level of disclosure by the Body Shop was amongst the highest of all the companies in the survey, which accounts for the detail given in this profile in comparison with the company's relatively small size.

In the twelve-month period to the end of February 1990 the average number of employees was 1,265. This figure does not include employees in franchised shops. Some 200 part-time staff are employed in the UK, and their benefits are harmonised pro-rata with their full-time counterparts. The company states that it operates a harmonised-benefits system across all grades of employees.

The Body Shop stresses its commitment to a high level of training, much of which is sales and customer-service driven, but which also seeks to inculcate 'Body Shop values'. These are set out in a ten-point *Charter*, and emphasise honesty, integrity, concern for individuals, animals and the environment. It states that 'Our policies and our products are geared to meet the real needs of real people both inside and outside the company.'

In the year ending 28 February 1990 the chairman and highest paid director were paid £110,000 and £172,000 respectively, representing 8% increases on the previous year. The company states that the entry level salaries of office/clerical and manual staff are £8,000 and £7,500 respectively. The company awarded basic pay increases of 10% and 8% in the last two years.

A private health insurance scheme, formerly for directors only, has been extended to all staff and all staff have the opportunity to join the scheme if they wish to contribute themselves. There is disability insurance, a subsidised crèche (for which, for example, staff on £10,000 per annum

pay £30 per week), and a staff discount scheme. In 1989 the company introduced a pension scheme for employees with one years' service, and it has also introduced bonus schemes for staff relating to effort'. According to the company the rate of staff turnover for its directly-owned shops is 7.5%, extremely low for the retail sector.

Staff are encouraged to maintain the principles of the company's *Charter*, and employee involvement is encouraged. The company commented that it 'does not have a policy of discouraging unions among its staff, but the necessity has so far not arisen.'

There is a limited share option scheme which is open to all staff after one year's service (this is currently being reviewed); eligible employees are granted options to purchase shares. At 5 April 1990 287 employees held shares in the company through its share option scheme. The company does not operate any form of direct profit-sharing scheme.

There are two women, the managing director and the communications director, on the board, but no members of ethnic minority communities. Of the fifteen highest-paid employees who are not directors, at least one is a woman. The company does not make a written equal opportunities statement but says that it does operate an equal opportunities policy. 'There is no discrimination on the grounds of age, race, religion, or sex. Men and women are employed in the same jobs in shops, offices warehouse and production sites.' The company does not appear to operate any equal opportunities monitoring procedures. It offers paternity leave at the rate of ten working days after one year's service, and supports the work of the Fullemploy Group.

In the year ending 28 February 1990 the company made cash charitable donations of £163,000. The Body Shop Foundation

organization embrace social issues in all their messiness without rapidly running into political ideology and a major questioning of the organization's *raison d'être*? This is the challenge for social accounting. If it is driven by a systematic concern to develop organizational accountability there is less of a problem – it is still difficult but systematic social accounting can be done.[35] It is, however, much more difficult for an organization to see the self-evident benefits of a clear and transparent approach to social accounting. Consequently, there is an even greater danger with social accounting than with environmental reporting of the resultant disclosures being rather hollow and self-congratulatory.

Whilst we wait for politicians to get around to recognizing that a democracy *needs* social *and* environmental accountability, we find that we have to rely on the increasing impact of the external 'social audits' to keep the accountability agenda moving forward. This is crucial for companies and other organizations because it means, at its simplest, that if the companies do not develop their own accountability, there is a growing and increasingly able body of expertise 'out there' that will be happy to do it for them. If there are carrots for environmental and related disclosure (see Chapters 11 and 12), here is another of the sticks.

Further Reading

Adams, R., J. Carruthers and S. Hamil (1991) *Changing Corporate Values* (London: Kogan Page)

Geddes, M. (1992) 'The social audit movement', in D.L Owen (ed.), *Green Reporting* (London: Chapman and Hall), pp. 215–241

Gonella, C., A. Pilling and S. Zadek (1998) *Making Values Count: Contemporary Experience in Social and Ethical Accounting, Auditing and Reporting* (London: ACCA)

Gray, R.H., D.L. Owen and C.A. Adams (1996) *Accounting and Accountability* (Hemel Hempstead: Prentice Hall)

Stead, W.E. and J.G. Stead (1992) *Management for a Small Planet* (Newbury Park, CA: Sage), esp. chs 7 and 9

Zadek, S., P. Pruzan and R. Evans (1997) *Building Corporate Accountability: Emerging Trends in Social and Ethical Accounting, Auditing and Reporting* (London: Earthscan)

Plus a number of examples of social reports are available on the Internet through the CSEAR website address given in the appendix at the end of the book.

---

[35] See, especially, Gray et al. (1997) for exploration of these matters and the further reading to this chapter for guidance on different approaches.

PART D: FUTURE DIRECTIONS

Overview

The law doth punish man or woman,
That steals the goose from off the common,
But lets the greater felon loose
That steals the common from the goose.

(Anon)

This book has been written with a very specific eye on not just what is practicable but also what business and politicians currently consider to be achievable. By the turn of the century there was an increasing acceptance of the need for sustainability or, more usually, 'sustainable development'. But – and it is an important 'but' – the way in which most businesses and politicians were thinking about sustainability suggested that they had only the slightest understanding of what it meant. For most business and political commentators 'sustainable development' was seen as entirely compatible with current means of economic organization. If such commentators are wrong in this – and we believe that they are – then the resultant self-delusion that humanity was heading towards sustainability – when it was doing quite the opposite – could be the most important (and possibly the last) mistake we ever make. One is struck by thoughts of Nero fiddling whilst Rome burns.

If, on the other hand, the deeper green view (to which we subscribe) proves to be the more accurate perception of the state of the planet and the causes of that state then humanity faces a stark choice between allowing current business and political views to prevail *or* seeking a sustainable future. The two are almost certainly not compatible. This section begins the process of examining the reasoning behind such a view and the implications it has for microeconomic activity.

CHAPTER 14

ACCOUNTING AND REPORTING FOR A FUTURE

Sustainability, Accountability and Transparency

14.1 Introduction

Sustainability: Treating the world as if we intended to stay

Throughout the book, we have tried to review the recent history, identify current practice, highlight best practice and estimate some of the major influences that can be expected in the near future. In this chapter we take a harder look at the direction in which future developments *must* move if the environmental crisis is to stand any chance of mitigation.[1] In particular, we focus upon **sustainability**[2] as the key concept guiding mankind's future interactions with the environment. Whilst the essence of the concept – and the related notion of sustainable development – may appear simple, it is a profoundly difficult concept either to understand or operationalize. In fact, it may be that sustainability *cannot* be either understood or put into practice within our current economic and philosophical frameworks.[3] If this is so,

---

[1] Much of the work which appears in this chapter was originally prepared for the International Institute for Sustainable Development. The work and ideas of Tony Clayton and Paul Ekins have also influenced the development of our ideas. Their support and encouragement is gratefully acknowledged.

[2] We will tend to use the term 'sustainability' here. Increasingly, however, the term 'sustainable development' is replacing sustainability as the preferred term. One of the dangers of the term 'sustainable development' arises from the negative connotations of 'development' – to mean growth, exploitation and all the things that have led to the environmental crisis itself. This, in turn, can lead to a state of mind in which sustainable development is viewed entirely from a 'business as usual' point of view. This need not be the case of course. We tend to think of sustainable development as the process by which we move away from *un*sustainability – an idea we gratefully borrow from Ian Thompson and Olwen Duncan.

[3] The key to addressing sustainability is to recognize this complexity. The further reading at the end of the chapter will provide more detailed and subtle insights than can be provided here.

then the challenge of sustainability really will (to use a sadly over-worked cliché) become one of the greatest challenges the West could possibly face.

This chapter will introduce the concept of sustainability and some of its basic implications before going on to try to operationalize the term – first within an economic framework and then within an accounting one. It will be argued that moves such as this make sense only in a framework of accountability and transparency, which are then explored.

14.2   What is Sustainability?

The concept of 'sustainability' rose to prominence following the Brundtland report in 1987.[4] It became, very rapidly, the core concept in any discussion of human interaction with the physical environment. Further, on the face of it, it is a concept that is universally accepted as a desirable, even essential, yardstick by which to assess human actions. However, there is considerable disagreement over its precise meaning, over the actual operationalization of the concept and over its implications for the way in which human life is ordered. The general definition of sustainability is *not* in dispute, namely that humanity must:

> *ensure that [development] meets the needs of the present without compromising the ability of future generations to meet their own needs.*
>
> (WCED, 1987, p. 8)

However:

> *a large selection of quotations from recent writing on sustainability shows that there is no general agreement on exactly what sustainability means. This fuzziness is useful in forging a consensus to promote sustainable development but it also obscures the political, philosophical and technical issues that still remain unresolved from the 'environment versus growth' debate of the early 1970s.*
>
> (Pezzey, 1989, p. 1)

Whilst the basic idea of sustainability is self-evidently good sense and one with which few would wish (publicly) to disagree, identifying and assessing the detail of the concept has proved immensely difficult. Part of the problem is the very newness of the concept to

---

[4] United Nations World Commission on Environment and Development (WCED) (1987).

Western humans[5] with the result that Western intellectual tradition has little reliable experience or equipment with which to address and examine the term. The profundity of its implications is only just becoming apparent and these are not, generally, widely appreciated. Where they are understood, the likely impact they would have on Western lifestyle often makes the practical implementation of sustainability ideologically unacceptable. Thus, Pezzey (1989) arrives at his conclusion that there are broadly three levels of problems in addressing 'sustainability': what does the term mean? what is ideologically and politically acceptable? how do we put it into practice? We shall attempt to cast some light on these questions.

There are two basic points we should make at the outset, however. First, although in common with much discussion of sustainability we will tend to place a greater emphasis on the environmental aspects of the concept, sustainability is both an environmental and a *social* concept. Secondly, we believe that sustainability can only be understood if (a) we are willing to accept that sustainability may require the most fundamental re-think of the way in which we socially and economically organize our lives (i.e. the current mechanisms of financial capitalism) and (b) we accept that our current ways of living, especially in the so-called developed world, are probably currently *un*sustainable.[6] We can illustrate these points quite simply.

We know that sustainability relates to both present *and* future generations and that it requires that the needs of people are met. Those needs are both social and environmental. It is common to refer to these social and environmental needs as, respectively, *eco-justice* and *eco-efficiency*[7] (which we have met already). We also saw in Chapter 5 that eco-efficiency (which captures the notion of reducing material and energy inputs per unit of output), although a useful concept, needs to be distinguished from *eco-effectiveness* (which captures the idea of reducing our overall ecological footprints). For sustainability to be achieved we need to feel confident that *all* elements – eco-justice, eco-efficiency and eco-effectiveness – are met for *both* current and future generations. These elements are summarized in Figure 14.1.

---

[5] Evidence suggests that the so-called First Nations had the concept of sustainability embedded into their very culture. Western 'enlightenment' separated humans from the implicit acceptance of the notion but put nothing explicit in its place. It is the very obviousness of the concept that has led to its acceptance but which has also caught Western thought unprepared to incorporate it in any substantive way.

[6] There is considerable literature on these issues. See particularly Beder (1997), Gladwin et al. (1995, 1997), Johnston (1996), O'Connor (1997), Redclift (1992), Weizsäcker et al. (1997), Welford (1997a).

[7] We have been unable to isolate the first coining of these terms but their provenance is usually attributed to the WBCSD.

Figure 14.1   Do we currently satisfy the conditions for sustainability?

Conditions	Satisfy the needs of the current generation?	Satisfy the needs of future generations?
Eco-justice	**NO** – income inequality is growing, many millions live in and die from poverty	**NO** – present trends will make matters worse, very little evidence to suggest otherwise
Eco-efficiency	**NO – but some possibly positive signs if one is optimistic**	**POSSIBLY – if one is optimistic**
Eco-effectiveness	**NO** – all evidence suggests that global impact of production and consumption is worsening	**NO** – no evidence to suggest a change of direction

Much of the evidence referred to in Figure 14.1 comes from the United Nations conference organized five years after the Earth Summit (sometime referred to as Rio+5) which concluded that all the major sustainability indicators had worsened since the Rio Summit. The only conditions that *might* possibly be satisfied – and only then if one was very optimistic – were those relating to eco-efficiency (and eco-efficiency is irrelevant in the face of declining eco-effectiveness). It is a depressing scenario but leads unerringly, we would argue, to the belief that not only are the world's present ways of organization unsustainable but they are becoming more so.

The purpose of this is *not* to try to depress you but to recognize that if we have a problem to solve we should be reasonably clear that we are trying to solve the right problem.[8] Eco-efficiency and EMS are part of the problem but they are *not* the problem. The problem is much deeper than that.

Before turning to look at sustainability and its operationalization in more detail, there is one further point we should clarify. It is essential that we be perfectly clear that whichever way we choose to define sustainability, we can never know whether or not we have reached it. That is, the point at which the planet achieves sustainability and whether that point has been passed or has yet to be reached is simply *un-knowable*. Given any particular definition of sustainability (see below), at any given time, the planet has some maximum carrying capacity. The planet may be able to sustain that definition for some

[8] Once again we recommend reading Weizsäcker et al. (1997) for a gloriously upbeat approach to the radical change necessary to meet the exigencies of sustainability.

element of the life on it, for some period of time; it might be able to sustain into the foreseeable future; or it may be unable to sustain the way of life desired in the definition. That is, given some pre-determined acceptable level of life on the planet Earth we cannot know to what extent that level is (a) achievable and (b) maintainable, i.e. sustainable. It is also unlikely that humanity – with its present science anyhow – can ever know that point. This does not stop us trying to define the area into which it might fall. After all, the human species may be well past the carrying capacity of the planet and if we can infer any data about this it seems sensible to try.

14.3 Trying to Identify Sustainability

One simple way of attempting to conceptualize the dilemma of sustainability is shown in Figure 14.2. The wavy horizontal lines purport to capture the range of long-term carrying capacities under differing assumptions, levels of economic activity, population, etc. In the crudest terms, the straight lines represent the economic growth patterns of the different nations of the world – with some nations (e.g. Australian Aborigines in their original natural environment) barely rising off the zero economic activity line. The diagram is clearly dangerously simple but enables us to highlight a number of important points. First, we have only circumstantial evidence as to whereabouts on the 'average global economic growth' line we currently sit. The most widely held assumption is that we are somewhere *above* point a. If this is so, humanity's way of life is currently unsustainable. Secondly, the point at which the G7 nations passed the point of sustainable activity, point b, was some time in the past. Thirdly, although contestable, most commentators suggest that it is the Western ways of life which are the least sustainable – left to their own devices, many LDCs would still be within the bounds of sustainability. Fourthly, and crucially, there is not a single point of sustainability – it is a band depending on a wide range of assumptions and beliefs.

Sustainable for what?

Who or what do we wish to sustain? All existing species or just humans? All existing species but *not* humans? We are clearly failing to sustain all existing species when the rate of species extinction is accelerating.[9] For a 'deep green', sustainability must mean that species

[9] Which, of course, it must logically do given the principles of ecology.

Figure 14.2

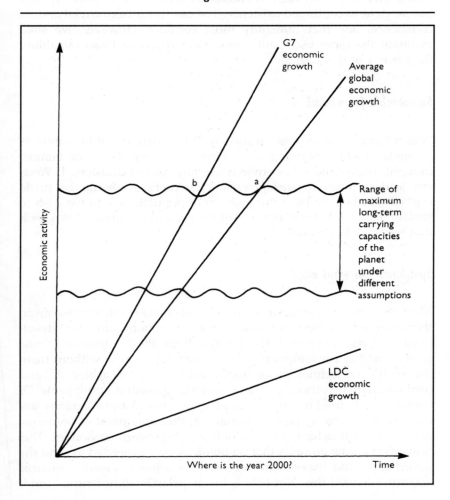

other than humans are sustained. When the problems of whether or not other species have ethical rights under concepts of justice[10] (for example) we find ourselves faced with an ethical (rather than instrumental)[11] dilemma as to the relative rights of humanity *vis-à-vis* other species and the planet itself. For many commentators, the fact that it is humanity that is desecrating the planet and causing the species extinction places the moral burden on to human beings. Many would argue

---

[10] See, for example, the issue as discussed in Rawls (1972) and developed in, for example, the *Journal of Ecological Ethics*. For an especially helpful discussion in the context of accounting see Lehman (1995, 1999).

[11] See Gray (1992) on this issue.

that, even if humanity has any choice in the matter, the human species has no right to continued existence. The case is far from trivial and, in conscience, one that humanity must consider. However, we shall maintain the more usual anthropocentric approach to sustainability for the rest of this chapter.[12]

Sustainable for whom?

Which humans do we wish to sustain? It is apparent that humanity as a whole is not sustaining itself when so many die from famine, drought, floods and other environmentally related disasters. If Western leaders mean to sustain only Westerners, it should be made explicit. Further, we have the problem of population – do we wish to sustain (e.g.) 80, 100, 150 per cent of the present population? Who is it that we wish to sustain?

Sustainable in what way?

Most Western commentators consider that 'sustainability' must mean the sustenance of Western civilization at an economically more developed stage than at present. This has two elements: that more economic growth, higher consumption, etc. are essential because without them the wealth and technology for sustainability cannot be achieved;[13] and because anything other than more economic growth is unthinkable. Of course, this is fundamentally unjust unless the rest of humanity are encouraged to reach and be sustained at the same point of economic development as achieved by the 'advanced' Western economies. This is justified on the grounds that economic wealth is needed to fund the remediation and investment necessary to achieve 'green' economic activity. We reject this. Not only is this hopelessly ethnocentric[14] but it

---

[12] We do this for a number of reasons. First, we recognize that, for many readers, the concepts of anthropocentrism and its alternatives will be new. We do not wish to alienate readership at this stage. Secondly, the issue of human versus other species is complex and although critically important (we tend to think we fall only just to the side of giving humans certain, but very restricted, rights over the planet – we are [just] anthropocentric), we are not sure that this is the place to hold the debate. Thirdly, the issues of sustainability from an anthropocentric point of view are quite complex enough to illustrate the range of problems that must be forcibly addressed if it is to be approached.

[13] For illustrations of this kind of 'thinking' see, e.g., Burke et al. (1991), Hart (1997), Magretta (1997) and Schmidheiny (1992).

[14] That is, it assumes that advanced Western capitalism is the only reasonable and desirable form of existence. There might be some serious doubts about this assertion (see, for example, Gladwin et al., 1995, 1997).

is without foundation. There is *no* evidence to suggest that by increasing the very process which caused the environmental degradation (economic growth as currently measured) humanity will reduce the degradation, whereas cases to the contrary abound.[15] At its most brutal and simple, the pursuit of economic growth as currently conceived in the hope that it *might* solve the problems seems to us too high-risk a gamble.

Sustainable for how long?

It is also fairly obvious that life (as we currently understand it) on Earth cannot last indefinitely. It is also clear that virtually *any* use of finite raw materials is ultimately unsustainable. Furthermore, it is apparent that there is no fixed, steady state in nature and in ecology – species become extinct regardless of what humanity does and natural 'disasters' occur and change (e.g.) climatic conditions independent of human interference. Decisions, in any definition about sustainability, need to be made about what 'reasonable' future we might envisage for the race.

Sustainable at what level of resolution?

Whilst, for the species and life as a whole, sustainability is a global concept this does not necessarily provide an excuse for nations, regions and even corporations to ignore the concept. It is looking increasingly likely that international governmental agreement of any substance on sustainability will not be forthcoming. This means any moves towards sustainability will be achieved by the unilateral actions of nations, regions, corporations, individuals and action groups.[16] At the level of the corporation, accounting can play a major part.

These are obviously not easy questions and are further complicated by the wide disparity of views on:

(1) the nature and the extent of the environmental crisis;
(2) the degree to which environmental problems are systemic rather than isolated phenomena;

[15] See, for example, Anderson (1991), Daly (1980), Daly and Cobb (1990), Ekins (1992b), Goldsmith (1988), Goldsmith *et al.* (1972), Robertson (1978), Welford (1997a).

[16] In Scotland, for example, WWF commissioned a study from Dr Tony Clayton of IPAD to examine the meaning and implications of sustainability at the level of the Scottish nation. Scottish Natural Heritage, a quango charged with maintaining the country's natural heritage, is also required to act in a manner that will enhance the sustainability of the nation. (See Clayton and Radcliffe, 1996.)

Figure 14.3

Some examples of current environmental pressures

Most environmental pressures are increasing exponentially. Thus mankind is faced with an accelerating:

- rate of ozone depletion
- rate of species extinction
- rate of habitat depletion
- rate of increase in technological catastrophe and scientific ignorance
- desertification
- deforestation
- income inequality
- social disintegration and exclusion
- incidence of acid rain
- depletion of fishing stocks
- decline in the planet's waste-sink-absorption capacity
- erosion of soil
- pressure on water resources
- rates of poverty and starvation
- rate of usage of non-renewable resources, etc., etc.

---

(3)   the causes of the crisis; and, as a result,
(4)   the level of effort which must be directed towards environmental issues; and
(5)   the form that effort must take.

These are scientific and psychological problems – scientific, in that our knowledge is woefully inadequate[17] and psychological in that differing world-views seem to predispose people to different interpretations of the same data.[18]

Then we have the problem of political or ideological differences: 'Whose problem is it?' This may take many forms at many different levels. For example, where we sit on the markets-versus-regulation debate; our attachments to growth and non-growth; the fears that electorates may be displeased by promises of *reductions* in material

---

[17] And is likely to remain so. It can be argued that whilst scientific knowledge is increasing, so is scientific ignorance. This latter arises from, for example, the rapidly increasing number of new compounds. Such new compounds are created faster than it is possible to examine all possible effects of the compound's introduction to other chemical, biological or physical environments. Hence the increasing ignorance.

[18] A less generous interpretation might be that we are observing two manifestations of collective psychosis in which pro-ecology views reflect other dissatisfactions with industrial life whilst the anti-ecology views are motivated by a deep reluctance to consider uncomfortable conclusions (see Gladwin et al., 1997).

well-being as currently measured; and, in particular, the conflicting perspectives of the G7 and G77 countries all add heat and steam, but little clarity or light, to the resolution of critical debates.[19]

If we could resolve these issues, we still have the question: 'Which problem are we addressing?' That is, the predispositions we bring and the intellectual frameworks we employ have considerable influence on how we define a problem and, therefore, on the problem we attempt to solve. Consciously and unconsciously, most approaches to environmental (and, increasingly, social) issues are greatly influenced by economic thought. Whilst environmental economics has provided a vast literature and contributed greatly to our understanding of the relationship between the global economy and the environment, environmental economics does not speak with a single voice. Furthermore, it is far from clear that economics, *by itself*, can offer complete insights and thus coherent solutions. Economics with (*inter alia*) its conventional attachment to particular ethical positions and particular assumptions about human nature, its focus upon prices, its preference for markets over regulation, its relatively narrow conception of what constitutes 'efficiency' and its assumptions about wealth distribution and (usually) the necessity for economic growth must, by definition, give us only partial insights into complex social and political problems raised by the environmental crisis.[20] So whilst economic reasoning can take us a long way in understanding the issues at stake[21] it cannot necessarily offer either complete truths or especially direct and practicable solutions.

At the corporate level, although there are many layers to this complex issue, two points are apparent. First, corporate uncertainty as to how far to take the environmental (and social) issues and really how to respond to the above confusion seems perfectly understandable. On the other hand, however, corporations control a dominant proportion of world economic activity as well as being the major mechanism through which technological change comes about, exercising a major influence over society's range of choice, holding much of the international power, controlling much of the world's resources and representing a significant element in employment – with all the influences that entails. Therefore any discussion about solutions to environmental crisis and of progress towards sustainability must include the

---

[19] But, yet again, see Weizsäcker et al. (1997) for an unusual clarity on these matters.

[20] For more detail see, for example, Ayres (1998), Daly (1980), Daly and Cobb (1990), Douthwaite (1992), Gorz (1989), Gray (1992), McKee (1986), Pearce (1991b), Raines and Jung (1986), Reilly and Kyj (1990), Tinker (1984), Turner and Pearce (1990).

[21] See especially Pearce et al. (1989) and Pearce (1991b), and for a more 'radical' view see, for example, Anderson (1991) and Ekins (1992a, 1992b).

corporations.[22] It is here that accounting, reporting, auditing and related matters have to make their contribution.

14.4 Caveats, Cautions and Environmental Management

One further way of articulating the 'what is sustainability?' question is shown in Figure 14.4. Its principal value at this point is that it focuses upon *unsustainability* as that is the most effective and practical way of moving towards sustainability. We might identify all actions as falling into one of the following categories:

(1) clearly sustainable;
(2) unclear but *potentially* unsustainable;
(3) clearly unsustainable.

The majority of the actions that are generally deemed 'economic' will normally fall into the last two of those categories – i.e. potentially or clearly unsustainable.[23] If this is so, and the absolute point of 'sustainability' cannot be known, attempting to identify and develop activities that are both 'economic' and entirely environmentally benign is virtually impossible. The best one can hope for without a major paradigm shift and a revolution in how humanity orders its activities is to seek out activities that *are less unsustainable*. Most forms of personal transport are unsustainable, but transport by rail will normally be less so than by private car. Most economic production and consumption is ultimately unsustainable but energy- and materials-efficient manufacturing based upon the 'reduce, reuse, recycle' principles will be likely to be less unsustainable. And so on.

If this analysis is correct – or even broadly realistic – then there is one, quite crucial conclusion to be drawn from this. The general concern in the West to develop 'greener' organizations is quite unlikely to come close to achieving sustainability except under the most restrictive and optimistic of assumptions. More especially, the

---

[22] A point made, for differing reasons by, amongst others, Schmidheiny (1992) and Hawken (1993). For an alternative interpretation – with especial emphasis on how corporations are maintaining and managing debate on the issues – see Welford (1997a) and Beder (1997).

[23] Appendix 1.1 makes this point; the material later in this chapter extends it. For further development see, for example, Gray (1992), Gray and Morrison (1991, 1992) and the publications from Bebbington and Gray (1995), Bebbington and Thomson (1996), Daly (1980, 1985, 1989), Daly and Cobb (1990), Dauncey (1988), Ekins (1986, 1992a,b), Goldsmith (1988), Goldsmith *et al.* (1972) and Robertson (1978, 1984, 1985, 1990).

Figure 14.4

Ekins/Hueting conception of sustainability

Unsustainability arises from the activities of production and consumption which rise beyond the point where there is no competition for the different functions of the environment – e.g. habitat, food provider, space, etc. Thus unsustainability may be of three types:

- Qualitative: when excessive emissions/wastes lead to excessive concentrations which lead to unsustainable effects.
- Quantitative: when excessive extraction/use leads to excessive depletion which leads to unsustainable effects.
- Spatial: when excessive occupation leads to congestion which leads to unsustainable effects.

Source: Taken from a working paper by Paul Ekins based upon Hueting (1980)

> We challenge the notion that any business can ever be 'environmentally friendly'. This is just not possible. All business involves some environmental damage. The best we can do is clear up our own mess while searching hard for ways to reduce our impact on the environment.
>
> *Source:* Body Shop's *Green Book* (1992)

admirable and difficult progress made by organizations towards the development and integration of environmental management systems (see Chapter 5) *may* be a necessary condition for sustainability *but it is most certainly not a sufficient condition.*[24] Only under the most optimistic of assumptions about technological change and planet carrying capacity and/or the most brutal assumptions about the rights of non-Western peoples and non-human species are we likely to come even close to any sort of sustainable future.

We can illustrate this point by trying to operationalize the concept of sustainability. To do so, we will come back into *relatively* conventional economic and accounting frameworks. Furthermore, as we mentioned earlier in the chapter, we will examine the environmental

---

[24] For illustration see IISD (1992), which represents a brave and thorough examination of the development of environmental management systems and reporting but which purports to be a treatise on sustainability without any examination of why the one should lead to the other. Such lacunae should be highly disturbing if one has any doubts about the optimism of the basic assumption. We would wish to adopt such optimism but see no grounds for doing so. For further illumination see Elkington (1995) and Elkington and Dimmock (1991). For examples of this more 'positive' attitude, see Schmidheiny (1992), Schmidheiny and Zorraquin (1996).

dimension in rather more detail and simply touch upon the social (eco-justice) dimension at the end of the chapter.

14.5 Operationalizing Sustainability

If we are concerned with practicable action as a way forward we must try to find some realistic exposition of sustainability that can be articulated in ways that enable real-world policy to be derived from it. There are a group of environmental economists – including Daly, Pearce and Turner – who have sought to do just this.[25] It is their views of sustainability – or at least *environmental* sustainability – which will be used here to enable us to move forward.[26]

Pearce et al. have produced what is probably the most widely quoted and accepted principle of sustainable development. That is, sustainable development must meet the necessary condition of:

> *constancy of natural capital 'stock'. More strictly, the requirement for non-negative changes in the stock of natural resources such as soil and soil quality, ground surface waters and their quality, land biomass, water biomass, and the waste assimilation capacity of receiving environment.*
>
> (Pearce et al., 1988; quoted in Pearce et al., 1989)

Pearce et al. and then Turner further developed this by employing the concepts of 'capital' and we can relate this to Daly's work using the concept of 'income'.

The 'capital' available to humanity can be thought of as falling into three categories.[27]

(1) *Critical natural capital:* those elements of the biosphere that are essential for life and which, for sustainability, must remain inviolate (examples include the ozone layer, a critical mass of trees, etc.).

---

[25] Examples of their work are included in the bibliography.

[26] We should be honest here and mention that although the work of Daly, Pearce and Turner is excellent and very important in many ways we have some profound hesitations about some of its bases; see, for example, Gray (1992).

[27] Sustainability is a concept rather wider than just the physical environment. It refers to ways of life, societies and communities and the general quality of life of humanity. Included in what follows there should also be, therefore, reference to 'social' capital – qualities of lives, education, culture, built environment, etc. The analysis without these things is difficult enough and we, in following Turner and Daly, have also left them out. Most 'deep greens' see sustainability as embracing these wider social (and it must be said, spiritual) concepts through a realigning of Western values and the pursuit of smaller community levels of activity.

(2) *Other (sustainable, substitutable or renewable) natural capital:* those
    elements of the biosphere which are renewable (e.g. non-extinct
    species, woodlands) or for which reasonable (however defined)
    substitutes can be found (perhaps, for example, energy from
    fossil fuels versus energy from renewable sources, given the right
    capital investment).

(3) *Artificial capital:*[28] those elements created from the biosphere
    which are no longer part of the harmony of the natural ecology,
    which includes such things as machines, buildings, roads, prod-
    ucts, wastes, human know-how and so on.

The general point is that artificial capital (which is largely covered
by priced transactions and thus is dealt with and measured in conventional economics and accounting) is created and expanded at the
expense of the natural capitals. It is artificial capitals that are measured by GNP and by profit and which Western capitalism has been
excessively successful at creating and expanding. But, as artificial
capital expands so it becomes almost inevitable that the natural capital
must decline – unless some way of managing sustainably can be
found. It then follows that for sustainability to be achieved, the critical
capital *must* not be touched and all diminutions in other natural
capital must be replaced, renewed or substituted for.[29] Under current
economics and accounting that cannot happen. Further, Daly's point
(which can be added to this analysis) is the commonly accepted notion
in economics, business and accounting that prudent behaviour suggests we take as income only that which is left over after maintaining
our capital intact – capital maintenance. What we currently measure
as 'income' does *not* leave our *natural* capital intact – it leaves it
depleted. It must follow, therefore, that our measure of income is
wrong and the level of consumption that we have enjoyed has been

---

[28] The more common term is 'man-made' capital. In deference to the gender
implications of this we have used the word 'artificial'. Other terms include 'constructed'
or just 'made' capital.

[29] One point of departure from the economists' approach would be the notion that
one *can* substitute for natural capital. Whilst, for example, the energy use in coal (non-
renewable natural capital) could be substituted by the energy use of solar panels
(artificial capital) there is no way in which the total 'use-value' that future generations
may derive from coal can be known. Until that is known, future generations cannot be
compensated for our use of their coal. Other aspects of natural capital, species for
example, cannot be substituted for. Attempts to put a financial value on all of the
natural capital leads to arguments about how that valuation should be done, whether it
is ethical and whether we really want to be in a position to trade *n* canisters of
underarm deodorant for *m* golden eagles. Finally, there is a critical problem of deciding
what is really critical capital. For the 'deep green' observer, a considerable major
proportion, if not all, of the biosphere is critical capital.

paid for out of capital. Sustainability requires that we maintain our capital and only spend the income that allows us to do so.[30]

The operationalization of a concept as complex as sustainability is bound to oversimplify the concept and, in the process, perhaps lose some of the essential ingredients. As societies show no inclination to revert to a level of peasant existence where sustainability is much easier to achieve, it is necessary to devise some method that can be seen to approximate the concept of sustainability in a practical way within our current institutional and structural arrangements. This is what Pearce, Turner and Daly achieve. The concepts can then be translated to a corporate level. This is where *accounting and reporting for sustainability* can perhaps help and to which the next section of this chapter is directed.

14.6 Accounting for Environmental Sustainability

Ultimately, reporting for (at least *environmental*) sustainability must consist of statements about the extent to which corporations are reducing (or increasing) the options available to future generations. This is a profoundly complex, if not impossible, task. However, there do appear to be three major ways in which any organization could try to approximate this in a fairly practicable and systematic way that would potentially lend itself to reporting. These are the *'inventory approach'* and the *'sustainable cost approach'* – which are both based around the categorization of artificial and natural capital discussed earlier – and the *'resource flow-through/input–output approach'*, which is more general. (In a broad sense, one might bear in mind that the first two are attempts to report *about* sustainability and the last an attempt to move towards reporting *for* sustainability.) These will be briefly examined in turn *but* it must be stressed that each is still highly experimental.[31,32]

---

[30] For more detail see Daly (1980, 1985, 1989), Daly and Cobb (1990), Pearce et al. (1989), Turner (1987, 1988, 1989, 1990), Turner and Pearce (1990). See also Gray (1991, 1992).

[31] See, for example, Rubenstein (1994), the Ontario Hydro experiment (EPA, 1996) and Bebbington and Tan (1996) for insight into both developments in these approaches and alternative approaches to the issues.

[32] It should mentioned here that no reporting can take place until it has a related accounting/information system to back it up and supply the data. Further, it should be recalled that the thinking behind the reporting we have discussed in this book is related to providing information to which society has a right and which will enable society – in the broadest sense – to make judgements about the activities of its organizations. It is, thus, an utterly *democratic* approach which sees accountability in general and sustainability reporting in particular as part of the dialogue between a society and its organizations. (This is discussed in the penultimate section of this chapter.)

The Inventory Approach

The *inventory approach is* concerned with identifying, recording, monitoring and then reporting, probably in non-financial quantities, the different categories of natural capital and their depletion and/or enhancement. The different elements of critical, non-renewable/non-substitutable, non-renewable/substitutable, and renewable natural capital which could be thought of as being under the control of the organization would first be identified by the corporation. These would then be reported with changes therein. In addition, likely impacts of those changes upon the categories of capital, the steps taken to mitigate those effects and/or any action to replace/renew/substitute the elements involved could then also be reported. Figure 14.5 provides a tentative illustration of the way this might look.[33]

The Environmental Sustainable Cost Approach

The second of the approaches to *accounting for (environmental) sustainability* mentioned above is the *sustainable cost approach*. This is easier to explain but proves to be exceptionally difficult in practice.[34] Its attractions, though, are that it can fit within current reporting practice, it *is* a simple concept and the accuracy of the actual sustainable cost is probably not important.

The notion of sustainable cost derives directly from accounting concepts of capital maintenance and the need, within all the definitions of sustainability, to maintain the natural capital for future generations. Translating the most basic concept of sustainability to the level of the organization we could say that *a sustainable organization is one that leaves the biosphere no worse off at the end of the accounting period than it was at the beginning*. It must be the case that the vast majority of, if not all, organizations do not comply with this. The extent of this 'failure' can – potentially – be quantified. That is, it is theoretically possible to calculate the amount of money an organization *would* have to spend at the end of an accounting period to place the biosphere in the position it was in at the start. We are, thus, dealing with a *notional* amount but one that is based on *costs* not *values*. The resultant number could be shown on the income statement as a notional reduction of profit or notional addition to operating expenditure. It is probable that

---

[33] As with some of the environmental reporting approaches discussed in Chapter 12, there may well be a need for some means of providing summaries but with detailed back-up data available to serious enquirers.

[34] One of the authors has worked with a New Zealand organization on the development of this method for some time. Please contact CSEAR for further details.

Figure 14.5

Inventory of X Corporation's environmental sustainability interactions

CRITICAL NATURAL CAPITAL

Ozone depletion: The level of CFC use/emission for 2000 was XXX (1999, YYY). The corporation is committed to total elimination of CFCs by 2002 and HCFCs by 2005.

Tropical hardwood: The corporation has eliminated all use of tropical hardwood in its own processes (1999, YYY used). Supplier audits have established that all hardwood use by suppliers is from sustainably managed sources as accredited by ABC&Co.

Greenhouse gases: . . . (See also Compliance-with-standards report on emissions)

Critical habitats/species: . . . etc.

NON-RENEWABLE/NON-SUBSTITUTABLE NATURAL CAPITAL

Oil and petroleum products:

Product 1 – Use, comparative figures, plans for reduction or substitution, funds or efforts expended to provide substitutes.

Product 2 – ditto, etc.

Other minerals and mineral products:

etc.

NON-RENEWABLE/SUBSTITUTABLE NATURAL CAPITAL

Energy usage: Use details, changes in usage, plans to change, efforts towards renewable sources.

Disposal of wastes: Levels of wastes produced and types, changes and plans.

Efforts towards (a) discovery and access to new sources of resources (typically minerals) and (b) extending longevity of use, repairability and recycling might appear here.

etc.

RENEWABLE NATURAL CAPITAL

Timber products: Use, harvesting, recycling, etc.

Species exploitation: ditto.

Habitat destruction/remediation:

Leisure and visual environment, built environment, water, air, noise, etc.

---

the number would be very large and would wipe out any profit the organization had earned in the (or any previous) year; dividends will have been paid out of 'capital'. But broadly speaking, that is the 'right' answer. It is widely accepted that current organizational activity is *not* sustainable and the calculation of sustainable cost provides some broad 'ball-park' quantification of the degree to which this is the case.

This will not be a simple matter. First, any use of 'critical natural capital' will, by definition, have to be included at infinite cost because it is irreplaceable. Although that might be an uncomfortable conclusion it strikes us as being morally correct (and, perhaps, practically correct in terms of the survival of humanity). Secondly, there may be a very large number of ways of replacing a part of the biosphere; equally there may be no simple way. (What, for example, is the cost of replacing a net-full of cod?) Thirdly, there is no simple agreement on the level at which resources can be sustainably harvested. Fourthly, and perhaps most crucially, the very nature of ecology means that one rapidly finds oneself in an infinite regress. That is, each disturbance to the natural capital must have a potentially infinite number of other ripples in the pond.[35]

These are major practical problems with the sustainable cost approach but progress *is* being made in the application of the idea – even if the answer it produces is not one that businesses, in particular, find attractive.[36]

The Resource Flow/Input–Output Approach

The third and final suggestion for approaching the problem of *reporting for sustainability is* the *resource flow/input–output approach.* This is derived from both a method well established in economics and the *mass balance* approach to environmental reporting which we met in Chapters 9 and 12. It is based upon a systems conception of the organization and attempting to report its resource flows. *It does not directly report sustainability* but provides a transparency to the organization which focuses upon resource use. This is done in a way that will enable participants to assess resource use – and, ultimately, therefore the sustainability of the organization's activities.

What one is seeking here is a catalogue of the resources flowing into an organization, those flowing out of it and the 'losses' or leakages (wastes and emissions, for example) from the process.[37] Such an 'account' would again be quantified – probably in both financial and non-financial numbers (including the profit and other distributions generated). The non-financial numbers would, in many ways, be the most useful, being the most easily accessible and understandable, but the use of financial numbers may help in providing summary data. Figure 14.6 is a tentative outline illustration of how a summary of this might look for a small hotel.[38]

Such a summary would probably need to be backed up by detail that analysed each of the categories and each category would need quantification – in simple numbers, in weights and measures or in

---

[35] This is exactly the same problem as was encountered in life cycle assessment.

[36] For more detail see Bebbington and Gray (1997) and Bebbington and Tan (1996).

[37] As we saw with the mass balance.

[38] The hotel referred to is an actual organization and the example is used because it allowed access and a degree of experimentation with its resources and flows. The same organization is featured in Chapter 5 and provides the illustration of a simple environmental audit.

Figure 14.6

Resource flow statement for XYZ Lodge Ltd (extract)

INPUTS brought f/d	LEAKAGES			OUTPUTS carried f/d
	loss/theft breakages	emissions	wastes	
Building				Building
Fixtures	Deterioration			Fixtures
Furniture				Furniture
Fittings				Fittings
Furnishings	Deterioration			Furnishings
Sheets				Sheets
Crockery	Breakages			Crockery
etc.				etc.
additions to				
non-consumables				
Repairs				
New sheets			packaging	
New crockery			packaging	
etc.				
consumables				
Meat			scraps	
Groceries			packaging	2,700
Canned food			cans	bed-
Canned drink			alu cans	nights
Milk			bottles	
Bottled drink			bottles	
Cleaning materials		sewage	plastics	
Electricity		heat		
Oil		gases, heat		
Gas		gases, heat		
Car miles		gases		
Laundry		water		
etc.				
				Profit/loss
				Taxation paid

As far as possible all inputs, leakages and outputs would be described and/or quantified.

---

financial numbers. Whilst perhaps *the* major problems with this suggestion are that it is cumbersome and would probably be wholly unacceptable to organizations on the grounds of confidentiality, the method could be used for internal reporting and *it could fulfil the requirements of transparency and of allowing society to make choices about resource use* (see below).

The resource flow/input–output approach was independently pursued for a time by Paul Ekins and New Consumer Ltd. Their approach was much more refined and developed than the approach described above. Under the Ekins/New Consumer proposal, the resources used by an organization/product and their flow would be further separated into their source of origin, their function in the organization and their ultimate destination. The idea was to produce product/organization data sheets which could provide references for consumers and others wishing to assess the potential sustainability of an organization or product they intend dealing with. Yet again, the idea was experimental and the data shown in Figure 14.7 was collated from the public domain.[39]

In its concern with transparency, with informing the public and allowing society to decide, the *New Consumer* approach is clearly not a reporting *of* sustainability but a move towards reporting *for* sustainability.

These three broad suggestions represent only some of the ways in which accounting for environmental sustainability might be taken forward. We can expect many more as we are in a period when experimentation and research are critical.[40] Much though it may not please organizations, we must develop means of assessing sustainability that do not trivialize the notion (as is happening in, for example, the recent crop of 'sustainability reports'). The organizations that we must, of necessity, continue to work for, buy from and own are blatantly unsustainable. There is only one conclusion to such practice. The sooner we formally recognize this the sooner we can attempt to do something about it.

14.7 Accounting for Both Social and Environmental Sustainability?

If progress, albeit slow, is being made towards an understanding of what environmental sustainability might mean for organizations – and how we might account for it – this does not, directly, deal with the eco-justice demands of sustainability. As far as we are aware, there has been little systematic (as opposed to piecemeal) examination of what

[39] This figure was taken from a 1990 New Consumer Ltd research proposal. The similarity with the methodology of the eco-labelling studies and the LCA methodology discussed in Chapter 9 is worth noting and, in this regard, the development of the use of the mass balance in, for example, Schaltegger (1996) is highly relevant.

[40] Other methods to approximate sustainability can be considered though. In addition to those already referenced, there are highly novel approaches as outlined in, for example, Jones (1996) and Tomimasu (1996). Another suggestion is that compliance with a public environmental charter such as the CERES Principles (Chapter 4) could be taken as an approximation of sustainable activity. Actions could then be assessed against the charter in terms of whether they brought one closer to or moved one further away from the principles. Estimates of the costs of reaching this approximate sustainability could also be reported. (We acknowledge Paul Ekins's influence here as well.)

Figure 14.7 Example of Ekins/New Consumer sustainability report proposal

Emulsion paint Dulux, ICI		Raw materials/ Extraction	Processing/ Manufacture	Packaging	Use	Disposal
Resources	Renewable	Water Brine Sulphur dioxide Hydrogen sulphate	Chlorine gas Sulphuric acid			
	Non-renewable	Titanium dioxide, (ilmenite, rutile) Oil (Acrylates) Mercury	Oil (Acrylates) Gas Coal (coke)	Metal (tin) Oil (plastic)		Chalk (to neutralize metal salts)
Wastes	Emissions		Acrylic acid Sulphuric acid Chlorine gas Sulphur dioxide			
	Pollution		Acrylic acid Sulphuric acid Chlorine gas Sulphur dioxide			Sulphuric acid Heavy Metal Salts
Impacts	Global services/ Species/ Eco-systems	Mining (open cast & dredge)				Marine life Marshland Landfill sites
	Amenity	Mining (open cast & dredge)		Landfill sites		
Policy	I		Tioxide to spend £220 m over 5–10 yrs on environmental improvements. ICI spends 10% of the capital cost on safety and environmental protection			
	II		ICI's initatives include developing alternatives to CFCs, Aquabase car paint and Biopol, a biodegradable plastic.			

social sustainability would mean for an organization and what any resulting account might look like. What seems increasingly clear, however, is that *social accounting* (Chapter 13) has an important role to play here. Certainly social accounting can contribute to reporting *for* sustainability even if we have, as yet, little idea of what social reporting *about* sustainability might comprise.

It is this sort of thinking which has prompted John Elkington to coin the phrase 'triple bottom line'.[41] He argues that a sustainable organization will perform in three dimensions, economic, social and environmental, and, consequently, must account for all three. Thus, alongside the financial statements we need to see environmental and social accounts. Current thinking suggests that the environmental and social accounts would comprise a mass-balance-based environmental account (see Chapter 12) and a stakeholder-based, compliance and performance social report.[42]

There are, inevitably, dangers with this approach – it doesn't, for example, necessarily question the central tenet of the organization or necessarily demonstrate the unsustainability of financially driven economic activities. However, such reporting *for* sustainability would certainly be a major and productive advance over current practice and is to be applauded for that.

And company reporting, albeit at a rather simple and naive level, is beginning to respond to this change in the agenda. Just as we have seen the rise in environmental reporting followed by rise in social reporting, the turn of the century saw the first attempts to produce 'sustainability reports'.[43] Some of these were simply environmental reports, renamed, with a little social data added – certainly *not* sustainability reports whatever they said on the front cover. Others were relatively serious attempts to begin a process of moving towards sustainability reporting. The key, we believe, to determining whether or not a report is a *real* attempt at a move towards sustainability reporting is the extent to which the reporting organization finds the task daunting to the point of near impossibility.[44] As a small but significant and increasing number of companies are finding, sustainability is simply not a possible option for them and trying to report about their sustainability must, by definition, cast into doubt their economic, social and environmental legitimacy. We should not be surprised if organizations are reluctant to do this.

---

[41] See Elkington (1997).

[42] See Gray, Dey, Owen, Evans and Zadek (1997) for one suggestion of how the social account might be developed.

[43] One of the most celebrated, although still relatively trivial in its data reporting, was that from Interface – the North American carpet company.

[44] See Bebbington and Thomson (1996) for further exploration of this.

14.8 Accountability and Transparency

The essence of environmental and social accountability and transparency is that social and environmental matters are too complex and crucial to be left entirely in the already overburdened hands of corporations. Not only is it unreasonable to ask corporations to take even more decisions that affect our futures but nobody has the information upon which to make such decisions in any unique and 'rational' way. As we have seen, the sustainability or otherwise of an organization cannot be reliably described.

Furthermore, it seems difficult to deny that those who are affected by the environmental actions of business have a right to information about those actions. This essential concept seems appropriate whether one is thinking in terms of democratic rights or concerned to help markets function – after all, neither democracy nor markets can function usefully without information.[45] The idea then is to 'open up' the organizations in order to educate and inform stakeholders and thus enable them, rather than the management of organizations, to express their choices about critical environmental and social issues – to be given information on which to make personal judgements as to the sustainability or otherwise of the organization. In the absence of 'expert opinion'[46] this seems an inevitable and probably critically important road to travel.

The questions of how to fulfil this environmental and social accountability and the sorts of information that would be needed could also be resolved relatively simply – at least in principle. (We have seen examples in this and preceding chapters.) But such matters will not be resolved whilst companies remain reluctant to accept the necessity for legislation requiring such disclosure. Voluntary initiatives have achieved a great deal (as we have seen) but they can only take us so far. At least one reason for this is the problem of 'markets'. Financial markets the world over have demonstrated – in general at least – an awesome indifference to the social and environmental activities of the companies they own. Indifferent, that is, except in so far as the social or environmental activities can be seen to have direct and fairly immediate financial implications.[47] Therefore we find very little financial market pressure (or encouragement) to discharge

[45] For more detail on these ideas see Gray (1989, 1990d, 1991, 1992), Gray, Owen and Adams (1996) and Gray, Owen and Maunders (1987, 1988, 1991).

[46] Or the less defensible concerns about secrecy in defence of the national or corporate interest – survival of our and other species must surely transcend such petty concerns.

[47] For more detail see Gray, Owen and Adams (1996), Gray, Owen and Maunders (1987, 1988, 1991), Mathews (1987), Mintzberg (1983), Owen, Gray and Maunders (1987).

environmental and social accountability. Whilst there is some change here, most obviously in the ethical investment area (see Chapter 10), the increasing recognition that financial markets are crucial to any moves away from unsustainability is not being matched by changes in attitudes or practice.[48]

A faith in voluntary development of the mechanisms for environmental and social accountability is therefore misplaced. It, like all substantial developments in reporting and accountability, will require regulation.[49] Whilst this might be heresy in the present climate, that does not, of itself, make it incorrect. Attachments to voluntary rather than regulatory solutions (at least in the accounting and reporting arena) can be held only if one chooses not to let mere evidence get in the way of a good prejudice.

14.8 Conclusions

The pursuit of sustainability represents an awesome challenge to humanity. Its definition raises enough problems, trying to understand it raises more. It is, however, the central concept by which humans may attempt to provide themselves (and the rest of the planet) with a future. Sadly, however, the term is being treated as a comfortable and easily circumscribed word. We hope that this chapter has shown that this is unlikely to be a defensible posture. We have also emphasized that with the current failures of global agreement on sustainability, more local agreement will be necessary; an essential element of this will be the actions of corporations. One way of operationalizing the concept of sustainability has been outlined – derived from the environmental economics literature. We then used this basis to illustrate four approaches to accounting for the environment. Each of these approaches could be a useful management tool but their real value will lie in their publication. One might have hoped that a small matter like planetary survival might have transcended a concern with publicity effects of a company's information disclosure. Until the West in general, and Western corporations in particular, are able seriously to address sustainability in a climate of accountability and transparency we cannot see how substantive measures to mitigate environmental

---

[48] See Schmidheiny and Zorraquin (1996) for a recognition of the issues – even if their optimism about change has little evidence to support it.

[49] It should be reinforced that whilst a number of companies do, from time to time, respond to desires for new information – be it social, employee or value-added, for example – none of these voluntary efforts is either widespread or of sufficiently long life to become part of reporting orthodoxy without legislation. (See Burchell et al., 1985, for an examination of the value-added story – one of the 'successes' of voluntary reporting.)

crisis can be developed. We deeply envy the optimistic protestations of Western business people and politicians that sustainability will be achieved without it hurting – in the sense of not costing us anything substantial in the short run in economic terms. This case has not been made and until some careful analysis can show that the matters discussed in this chapter are irrelevant, mis-specified, misunderstood or in some other way grossly inappropriate we are forced to continue to assume that such optimism is devastatingly misplaced. The *Titanic* did go down, the *Exxon Valdez* did happen, the ozone is thinning . . . etc., etc. No amount of optimism, no growth in share price, no leaps in profitability can deny – or compensate – for that.

Further Reading

There is now a considerable and increasingly sophisticated literature on the issues involved in and surrounding sustainability. That literature falls, very broadly, into two types: that which sees sustainability as really no more than one more challenge for modern businesses and eminently achievable within current forms of financial capitalism; and that which takes a wider view and sees sustainability as challenging the very core of organizational life and the traditional success indicators of modern business. The WBCSD publications are the champions of the first view.

Daly, H.E. and J.B. Cobb (1990) *For the Common Good* (London: Greenprint)

Elkington, J. (1995) *Who Needs It? Market Implications of Sustainable Lifestyles* (London: SustainAbility)

Elkington, J. (1997) *Cannibals with Forks: The Triple Bottom Line of 21st Century Business* (Oxford: Capstone Publishing)

Jacobs, M. (1991) *The Green Economy: Environment, Sustainable Development and the Politics of the Future* (London: Pluto)

Turner, K. (ed.) (1988) *Sustainable Environmental Management* (London: Belhaven)

Weizsäcker, E. von, A.B. Lovins and L.H. Lovins (1997) *Factor Four: Doubling Wealth, Halving Resource Use* (London: Earthscan)

Welford, R. (ed.) (1997) *Hijacking Environmentalism: Corporate Responses to Sustainable Development* (London: Earthscan)

CHAPTER 15

A CHANGE OF PARADIGM?

15.1 Introduction

'The Earth Summit's real agenda is to bring it home to world leaders and politicians that we have no option but to change our ways.' Only last year [1991] he was heralding the Earth Summit as a 'last chance to save the world'. He is now more realistic. 'There will be failures. I see this just as a step on the way.' Privately, he admits he could make a philosophical case for saying there is no chance on earth of saving the earth; professionally, he cannot.[1]

At the start of this book we identified the initial major environmental problem as being one of belief. Attitude to and debate about the environment hung upon belief about the extent to which the planet was (or was not) in crisis; belief about whose responsibility it might be; belief about whether or not economic and business thought was responsible for causing the crisis; belief about whether or not the Western economic/business model could solve the crisis. But the behaviour by developed world political leaders and major business leaders in the run-up to and during the 1992 United Nations Conference of Environment and Development in Rio de Janiero (UNCED – the 'Earth Summit') suggested conflicting views about such beliefs. That is, the preliminary manoeuvring and eventual lukewarm response by most G7 leaders to the Rio agenda was entirely commensurate with a belief that the planet was in no real crisis – and if it was, it wasn't really G7's responsibility. The behaviour by very many businesses in lobbying to get elements of the Rio agenda diluted (e.g. on global warming) and businesses's success in getting the whole issue of MNE (multinational enterprise) control removed entirely from the agenda suggested a similar belief.[2] Throughout this book we have also seen the really very low level of response to the environmental crisis which has been undertaken by business at large across the world.

Such evidence leads us to conclude that:

(1) business as a whole does not believe in the seriousness of the environmental crisis; and/or

---

[1] Adapted from *Summitry*, in Vidal (1992), which was written incorporating the views of and quoting from Maurice Strong, Organizer of the United Nations Conference on Environment and Development.

[2] See Beder (1997) and Mayhew (1997) for penetrating analyses of this process.

(2) it does not (or cannot) see business as part of the problem; and/or

(3) it is unable to take steps to do anything about it.

We tend to think that the present situation consists of a combination of all three.[3] Whatever, a conclusion such as this has very serious consequences for our environmental future.

15.2 Can Business Really be Part of the Solution?

One of the few positive results of UNCED was the public recognition by Maurice Strong and Stephan Schmidheiny[4] (among others) that the problems facing the planet were critical for human, let alone non-human, existence. When two successful and 'hard-nosed' business people side with the environmentalists, then perhaps the twenty-plus years of pressure from environmentalists are starting to pay off.[5] But such views are not especially widespread and, even when there is apparent agreement on the depth of the crisis, the deeper green environmentalists and the greener business people part company over the identification of causes of, solutions to, and timescales for the crisis[6] (see Figure 15.1).

We have carefully avoided anything that might smack of explicit theory throughout this book. Throughout much of the English-speaking world at least, the business person's contempt for theory is widely applauded as part of a recognition of the pre-eminence of the

---

[3] See, for example, Bebbington and Gray (1995).

[4] Maurice Strong is a self-made businessman of considerable wealth based on energy and mining corporations. He was secretary-general to the 1972 Stockholm UN conference on the human environment as well as organizer of UNCED in Rio de Janiero, 1992. He is a member of the World Economic Forum with Stephan Schmidheiny, who founded the (now World) Business Council for Sustainable Development and is himself a millionaire many times over. These are unlikely – and possibly implausible – champions of the environment and sustainability. (See, for example, John May, *The Independent on Sunday: The Sunday Review*, May 1992, pp. 6–7.) For illustrations of Schmidheiny's thoughts on the issues, see Schmidheiny (1992) and Schmidheiny and Zorraquin (1996).

[5] The positive inference to draw is that when any individual chooses to review such evidence as exists about the state of the planetary environment, they will come to share the views of the deeper green environmentalists. Other inferences are always possible.

[6] Remember that most commentators are speaking from the comfort of the 'developed' world where, apart from occasional minor droughts, algal bloom and the odd health scare, the 'environment' has little, apparent, direct effect on life. In many lesser developed countries the effect of the 'environment' is brutally direct and apparent in that it is quite likely to kill one and/or one's children – and in many parts of the world is doing just that. Our somewhat precious Western concerns might look self-centred and callous in such a context.

Figure 15.1

Some questions over which the deeper green and the greener business person tend to disagree

In essence, this difference of opinion centres upon:

(1)   Are the causes of the problems business- and economic-related?
(2)   If so, to what degree?
(3)   Are the causes of the crisis distinct and separable or systemic?
(4)   If the modern economic system and its baggage are part of the problem, can they also be part of the solution?
(5)   Can the modern economic system be changed?
(6)   Is there any will to try?

---

practical, the pragmatic and the 'realistic'. Of course, no individual is free from theory[7] but as long as that theory stays implicit and unexamined then, for example, unexamined assertions such as that economic growth will lead to sustainability, or that the lesser developed countries must adopt Western standards of achievement, are taken as self-evident truths when, in fact, they are no such thing. They are simply the remaining tatters of a particular brand of economic thinking which is largely unsubstantiated.[8]

This economic thinking might not matter if it had not pervaded business, provided justifications for actions, justified 'business ethics' that would be unacceptable in the individual, and provided the high moral tone that is adopted by governments and business people when talking of 'free markets' and 'level playing fields'.[9] Such economic thinking – and the business which has followed it – has also contributed mightily to the environmental crisis.

But debate upon such issues, upon such 'self-evident truths' as economic growth, would appear to be impossible because, at a minimum, even to discuss such matters requires an acceptance of the *possibility – in principle –* that what is 'good for business' may perhaps not always be necessarily good for all life forms. For much of Western business and politics this is unthinkable, and so their world constructs the business and economics agenda under which we all live. That social construction continues into the environmental agenda.

[7] We might echo John Maynard Keynes's observation that every man who considers himself to be a free-thinker will usually be the slave to some defunct economist. This is exactly the case here.

[8] See, for example, Gray, Owen and Adams (1996).

[9] See, for example, any of the Henderson, Ekins, Daly, Robertson, Schumacher references. See, also, Jackall (1988).

Here the confusion begins. Businesses may be apparently leading the environmental agenda whilst simultaneously seeking profits and growth above all else; corporations may be striking important stands on the sustainability debate while lobbying, for example, British, EU or US governments to avoid any legislation on global warming,[10] to support the motor car, or to tie environmental aid to the south into trade restrictions; or threatening to pull out of a country if an energy tax is introduced.[11] Whilst we can certainly speak positively about how far many organizations have advanced on the environmental agenda, it is difficult really to believe the assurances of 'business' when such duplicity is self-evident and, more importantly, to believe that the environmental agenda is safe in the hands of 'business'.

Of course, it would be foolish to fall into the trap of seeking simple, tidy explanations. 'Business' – despite the propaganda – is not a homogeneous lump; individual organizations are frequently enormous and do not, unsurprisingly, speak with a single voice; and business exists within a system that is explicitly immoral, exploitative and combative and which frequently rewards behaviour wholly unacceptable in the individual (or punishes the absence of such behaviour). So whilst some who work in business and politics may believe that the planet faces a life-threatening crisis, a great many do not. And for those who do hold such beliefs, the cultural and institutional structure within which business operates makes substantial environmental, social and/or ethical initiative very difficult indeed. To expect the business world – as presently constituted – to solve the environmental crisis is naive in the extreme. Substantial, systemic change in the frameworks of business and the intellectual concepts within which business operates is an essential prerequisite for a more environmentally benign economic system. The quotation from Body Shop captures the issue exactly – what it fails to recognize are the implications that arise from the observation.

15.3 Environmental (and Social) Accounting?

What has been said for business applies with at least equal force to accounting and accountants. Whilst it is almost certainly true that business cannot change substantially until accounting does so, it is far

[10] As was clearly the well-documented case with respect to the Kyoto conference on global warming.

[11] Examples of these instances are widely and publicly reported. These contentions are also supported by the way in which business has lobbied for the terms of GATT (General Agreement on Tariffs and Trade – now the World Trade Organization) to override environmental considerations by reference to 'free market' motherhood statements, which are unexamined assertions at best and dishonest at worst.

from clear that accounting can change – or that accountants wish to change. Indeed, evidence and theory are against us.[12] There are a number of strands of theory which suggest that not only can accounting not change in the ways we have suggested as necessary, but that in attempting to address the environmental agenda accounting may do more harm than good.[13] It is impossible not to be sensitive to such points – in an ideal world.

However, we do not live in such a world and, seeing the environmental crisis as requiring action of some sort, cannot see any likely force for benign systemic change in the immediate future. So one works with the tools to hand: business and accounting are those available. If the business and accounting environmental agenda is the only game in town, one can choose to play or not play. We choose to play – in the hope that it may be possible to change that agenda to reflect, more obviously, the real environmental exigencies and develop an accounting that *is* environmentally benign.

As the 1992 EU plan *Towards Sustainability* suggested,[14] for any really significant environmental response from business, it will be necessary to redefine 'accounting concepts, rules, conventions and methodology' in order to permit accounting 'to internalize all external environmental costs'.[15] Radical, and welcome, though such a suggestion might be, genuinely environmentally sensitive business and environmentally sensitive accounting will require far more fundamental changes. The very framework of conventional accounting will have to be rebuilt from scratch. After all, the conventional accounting framework is hardly a roaring success for conventional business transactions and to expect it to incorporate environmental and social considerations sensitively – as a long-term prospect – is unwarrantedly optimistic.

In terms of this book, our view is that we hope to see three phases of development in accounting thought and accounting practice. First, we hope to see some development that clearly falls within conventional accounting – this is essentially the principal message of Chapters 1 to 9. The second develops from the first: that is, the evolutionary process – within which accounting begins to recognize environmental considerations – will produce changes in the accounting itself. There

[12] For illustration see Bebbington et al. (1994) and Gray, Bebbington, Walters and Thomson (1995).

[13] Different strands of work from UK accounting academics Richard Laughlin, Michael Power and Christine Cooper all suggest this – from differing theoretical perspectives and with differing degrees of vitriol. But see also Bebbington (1997), Gray (1992), Lehman (1995, 1999), Owen et al. (1997).

[14] See Bebbington (1993) for a summary.

[15] COM (92) 23, Vol. II, *Towards Sustainability*, from DG XI, reported in *World Accounting Report*, May 1992, p. 1.

were hints of this in Chapters 1 to 9 and it becomes a little more explicit in Chapters 10 to 13. But it should be obvious that conventional accounting cannot really be fully responsive to the change in culture that comes with greater environmental sensitivity, and (the third phase) we introduced a few developmental possibilities in Chapter 14. How will this happen? How might this look? We have no crystal ball. We are simply convinced that change is essential because any system – such as accounting – which reflects an economic theory that is so fundamentally socially and environmentally malign cannot itself lay legitimate claim to being socially and environmentally benign.

15.4 Conclusions

It is clear that the environmental crisis requires something far more profound than a green gloss to existing practices. It is increasingly apparent that what is needed – what is essential – is little short of a complete overhaul of our Western intellectual frameworks and a complete rethink of the institutional and ethical structure of our economic activity. Even if business believed in the necessity for this, there is no way in which business, by itself, could achieve it. It requires change throughout education, the professions, economics, politics, the ethics of modern society, and so on. And we do not come to such radical prescription lightly. This is not some anti-business knee-jerk or the rantings of the disadvantaged but the reluctant conclusion from a great deal of thought, reading, work and observation. Increasing numbers of individuals, from all walks of life, from countries around the world, are coming to the same reluctant conclusion. If fundamentally well-meaning individuals – be they politicians or business people – can operate a system which is intended to produce the greatest good for the greatest number but, instead, produces awesome inequality, profound poverty and destitution, staggering planetary damage, and a dehumanizing effect on people and communities – then we must eventually begin to suspect, however reluctantly, that there is something wrong with that system. Nothing short of basic and fundamental change can offer any hope to these problems.

But, in the meantime, whilst we start to wonder how such fundamental change might be set in motion, we are faced with the here-and-now. There is a need for immediate, practicable solutions to urgent issues. Preferably, such solutions might point towards the possibilities of future change – as opposed to simply a sticking plaster on the wounds of a fatally injured system. That is what this book has tried to be. We have laid out practicable possibilities, experiments and solutions, derived from considerable contact with organizations of all sorts whose help we are delighted to acknowledge. These we have derived in recognition of the immediacy of the problems. But each chapter has been written in the explicit recognition that none of these ideas is a final solution. Each is just a small step towards (hopefully) a more fundamental change.

We can see no alternative. We must develop and introduce such incremental change as we can in order to mitigate the worst excesses of the system and sensitize us all to the issues at stake – this book suggests a large number of possibilities for this. But such incremental change will mean little without fundamental systemic change. Only a complete change of paradigm is likely to allow humanity to become part of the 'environment' rather than its exploiter. Such a paradigm shift might save the human species from extinction – or at least, if we are to become dinosaurs, it would permit us to go extinct causing less widespread human and non-human suffering in the process and let us leave behind us a planet that has not been totally desecrated.

APPENDIX

Selected Contact Addresses

Introduction

The following are just some of the organizations currently active in the environmental field and from whom further information, advice or encouragement can be obtained. In general the organizations have been chosen on the grounds that they constitute useful places to begin in the search for further information and contacts. The names and addresses were correct at the time of writing. They are in alphabetical order. *No endorsement of the quality of the organization or its information or advice is implied by its listing here. Furthermore, no interpretation other than oversight should be made concerning the omission of any relevant and non-aligned body.*

In addition, a number of the newsletters, such as CSEAR's *Social and Environmental Accounting*, provide news items and contact details for various organizations and initiatives.

American Institute of Certified Public Accountants (AICPA), 1211 Avenue of the Americas, New York, NY 10036–8775, USA
www.aicpa.org

Asia-Pacific Centre for Environmental Accountability (APCEA), Victoria University of Technology, Department of Accounting & Finance, F005 Footscray Campus, Box 14428 MCMC, Melbourne, Victoria 8001, Australia
e.mail   garyod@dingo.vut.edu.au
www.efs.mq.edu.au/accg/apcea/index.html

The Association of Chartered Certified Accountants (ACCA), 29 Lincoln's Inn Fields, London WC2A 3EE
e.mail   joanne.hemmings@acca.co.uk
www.acca.co.uk

Australian Society of Certified Public Accountants (ASCPA), CPA House, 170 Queen Street, Melbourne, Victoria 3000, Australia
e.mail   ascpa@natoff.cpaonline.com.au
www.cpaonline.com.au

The British Library, Environmental Information Service, 96 Euston Road, London NW1 2DB
e.mail   eis@bl.uk
www.bl.uk/index.html

Business and The Environment, Cutter Information Corporation, 37 Broadway, Arlington, MA 02174–5552, USA
e.mail   dcrowley@cutter.com
www.cutter.com/envibusi/

Business in the Environment, 137 Shepherdess Walk, London N1 7RQ
e.mail   information@bitc.org.uk
www.bitc.org.uk

Business Information Marketplace, Business Information Review, Headland Press, 1 Henry Smith's Terrace, Headland, Cleveland TS24 OPD, UK

Business Network, 18 Well Walk, Hampstead, London NW3 1LD

Business Strategy in the Environment, John Wiley & Sons, Ltd, Baffins Lane, Chichester, West Sussex, PO19 1UD, UK and ERP Environment, PO Box 75, Shipley, West Yorkshire, BD17 6EZ, UK
 e.mail jpeirce@wiley.co.uk
 www.interscience.wiley.com

Centre for Alternative Technology, Machynlleth, Powys, Wales, SY20 9AZ, UK
 e.mail help@catinfo.demon.ac.uk
 www.cat.org.uk/

Centre for Economic and Environmental Development (CEED), 12 Upper Belgrave Street, London SW1X 8BA
 e.mail info@ukceed.org
 www.ukceed.org/

Center for Human Ecology, PO Box 1972, Edinburgh EH1 1YG, UK
 e.mail che@clan.com
 www.clan.environment/che

Centre for Social and Economic Research on the Global Environment (CSERGE), School of Environmental Sciences, University of East Anglia, Norwich, Norfolk, NR4 7TJ, UK
 e.mail a.howe@uea.ac.uk
 www.uea.ac.uk/env/cserge/

Centre for Social and Environmental Accounting Research (CSEAR), 65–73 Southpark Avenue, Department of Accounting & Finance, University of Glasgow, Glasgow G12 8LE, UK
 e.mail csear@accfin.gla.ac.uk
 www.gla.ac.uk/departments/accounting/csear

Chartered Institute of Canadian Accountants, 277 Wellington Street West, Toronto, Ontario M5V 3H2, Canada
 e.mail customer.service@cica.ca
 www.cica.ca/

Chartered Institute of Management Accountants (CIMA), 63 Portland Place, London W1N 4AB
 e.mail randt@cima.org.uk
 www.cima.org.uk

CMA – The Society of Management Accountants of Canada, PO Box 176, Hamilton, Ontario, Canada
 www.cma-canada.org

Coalition for Environmentally Responsible Economies (CERES), 11 Arlington Street, 6th Floor, Boston, MA 02116–3411, USA
 e.mail muzila@ceres.org
 www.ceres.org

Confederation of British Industry (CBI), Environment, Health & Safety Group, Centre Point, 103 New Oxford Street, London WC1A lDU
 www.cbi.org.uk/

Council on Economic Priorities (CEP), 30 Irving Place, New York, NY 10033, USA
 e.mail info@cepnyc.org
 www.cepnyc.org/

Deloitte Touche Tohmatsu, Stonecutter Court, 1 Stonecutter Street, London EC4A 4TR
 www.dttus.com

Department of the Environment, Transport and the Regions (DETR), Eland House, Bressenden Place, London SW1E 5DU
 www.detr.gov.uk/

Department of Trade and Industry (DTI), The Business and the Environment Unit (BEU), Ashdown House, Victoria Street, London SW1E ORB
www.dti.gov.uk

The Ecologist, Ecosystems Ltd, 1st Floor, Corner House, Station Road, Sturminster Newton, Dorset, UK
e.mail   ecologist@gn.apc.org

Ecology Building Society, 18 Station Road, Keighley, West Yorks, BD20 7EH, UK
Tel: 01535 635933
e.mail   info@ecology.co.uk

The Ecumenical Council for Corporate Responsibility (ECCR), PO Box 4317, Bishop's Stortford CM22 7GZ, UK
e.mail   ECCR@Geo2.poptel.org.uk

Environment Agency, Rio House, Waterside Drive, Aztec West, Almondsbury, Bristol BS32 4UD, UK
e.mail   enquiries@environment-agency.gov.uk
www.environment-agency.gov.uk

Environment Council, 212 High Holborn, London WC1V 7VW
e.mail   info@envcouncil.org.uk
www.greenchannel.com/tec

Environmental Accounting and Auditing Reporter, Monitor Press Ltd, Suffolk House, Church Field Road, Sudbury, Suffolk, CO10 6YA, UK
e.mail   enquiries@monitorpress.co.uk
www.monitorpress.co.ukq

Environmental Data Services (ENDS) Ltd, Unit 24, Finsbury Business Centre, 40 Bowling Green Lane, London EC1R 0NE
e.mail   post@ends.co.uk
www.ends.co.uk/

Environmental Finance, Executive Enterprises Publications Co., Executive Enterprises Building, 22 W. 21st St, New York, NY 10010–6904, USA

Environmental Finance, Fulton Publishing, 22–24 Corsham Street, London, N1 6DR
e.mail   info@environmental-finance.com

Environmental Protection Agency (US), Ariel Rios Building, 1200 Pennsylvania Avenue, N.W., Washington, DC 20460, USA
www.epa.gov/

Ethical Consumer, ECRA Publishing Ltd, Unit 21, 41 Old Birley Street, Manchester, UK
e.mail   ethicon@mcr1.poptel.org.uk
www.ethical consumer.org

Ethical Investment Research & Information Service (EIRIS), 80–84 Bondway, London SW8 1SF
e.mail   ethics@eiris.win-uk.net

Ethical Performance, Dunstans Publishing, PO Box 590, 8 New Street, St Dunstans, Canterbury, Kent, CT2 8GF, UK
e.mail   town@btinternet.com

The European Environment Review, Graham & Trotman Ltd, Sterling House, 66 Wilton Road, London SW1V IDE

Fondazione Eni Enrico Mattei (FEEM), Corso Magenta, 63, 20123 Milano, Italy
e.mail   letter@feem.it
www.feem.it

Forum for the Future, 227a City Road, London EC1V 1JT and 9 Imperial Square, Cheltenham GL50 1QB, UK
Fax: 01242 262757

Friends of the Earth, 26–28 Underwood Street, London NW1 7SQ
e.mail info@foe.co.uk
www.foe.co.uk
Friends of the Earth Scotland, Bonnington Mill, 72 Newhaven Road, Edinburgh
EH6 5QG, UK
e.mail foescotland@gn.apc.org
www.foe-scotland.org.uk/
The Global Reporting Initiative www.globalreporting.org
also accessible through both ACCA and CERES
The Green Alliance, 40 Buckingham Palace Road, London SW1W 0RE
e.mail ga@green-alliance.demon.co.uk
www.green-alliance.demon.co.uk
Green Party, 1A Waterlow Road, London N19 5NJ
e.mail gptyoffice@gn.apc.org.uk
www.gn.apc.org/greenparty
GreenLEAP, Independent Association of Legal Engineering and Accounting Professionals for the Environment, 70 Richmond St East, Suite 400, Toronto, Ontario, M5C 1N8,
Canada
Tel: 416 363 5577; Fax: 416 367 2653
Greenpeace UK, Canonbury Villas, London N1 2PN
e.mail gp-info@uk.greenpeace.org.uk
www.greenpeace.org.uk
Groundwork Foundation, 85–87 Cornwall Street, Birmingham B3 3BY, UK
Tel: 0121 236 8565
Her Majesty's Inspectorate of Pollution, Environment Agency, Rio House, Waterside
Drive, Aztec West, Almondsbury, Bristol BS12 4UD
e.mail enquiries@environment-agency.-gov.uk
www.environment-agency.gov.uk
Institute of Chartered Accountants in Australia, GPO Box 3921, Sydney, NSW 2001,
Australia
Tel: 61 29290 5680; Fax: 61 29299 1689
Institute of Chartered Accountants in England and Wales (ICAEW), PO Box 433,
Chartered Accountants Hall, Moorgate Place, London EC2P 2BJ
www.icaew.co.uk
Institute of Chartered Accountants of Scotland (ICAS), 27 Queen Street, Edinburgh
EH2 1LA, UK
e.mail research@icas.org.uk
www.icas.org.uk
Institute of Environmental Management & Assessment (IEMA), 63 Northumberland
Street, Edinburgh EH3 6JQ, UK
e.mail info@iema.net
www.iema.net
Institute for European Environmental Policy London (IEEP), Dean Bradley House, 52
Horseferry Road, London SW1P 2AG
e.mail central@iceplondon.org.uk
www.greenchannel.com/ieep/ieep.htm
Institute of Social and Ethical Accountability (ISEA), Thrale House, 44–46 Southwark
Street, London SE1 1UN
e.mail Secretariat@AccountAbility.org.uk
www.AccountAbility.org.uk
International Chamber of Commerce (ICC), 14/15 Belgrave Square, London SW1X 8PS
www.iccwbo.org
International Chamber of Commerce (ICC), 9 rue d'Anjou, 75008, Paris, France
www.iccwbo.org

International Environment Reporter, Bureau of National Affairs Inc., 1231 25th St. NW., Washington, DC 20037, USA
Tel: (202) 452 4200
www.bna.com/

International Institute for Environment and Development (IIED), 3 Endsleigh Street, London WC1H 0DD
e.mail   mailbox@iied.org
www.oneworld.org/iied

International Institute for Sustainable Development (IISD), 161 Portage Avenue East, Winnipeg, Manitoba, R3B 0Y4, Canada
e.mail   info@iisd.ca
http://iisd.ca/

Jupiter Environmental Research Unit, Knightsbridge House, 197 Knightsbridge, London SW7 1RB
Tel: 020 7 412 0703; Fax: 020 7 581 3857

KPMG, Management Consultants, 8 Salisbury Square, London EC4Y 8BB
Tel: 020 7 311 1000; Fax: 020 7 311 3311

London Environmental Economics Centre (LEEC), 3 Endsleigh Street, London WC1H 0DD

Management Institute for Environment and Business (MEB), 10G Street NE (Suite 800), Washington, DC 20002, USA
www.wriorg/wri/meb/

The Natural Step, Thornbury House, 18 High Street, Cheltenham, Gloucester GL50 1DZ, UK
www.globalideasbank.org/

New Academy of Business, 17–19 Clare Street, Bristol BS1 1XA, UK
e.mail   info@new-academy.ac.uk
www.new-academy.ac.uk

New Economics Foundation (NEF), Cinnamon House, 6–8 Cole Street, London SE1 4YH
e.mail   info@neweconomics.org
www.neweconomics.org

NPI, 48 Gracechurch Street, London EC3P 3HH
www.npi.co.uk

Pensions & Investment Research Consultants Ltd, Crusader House, 145–157 St John Street, London EC1V 4QJ
e.mail   info@pirc.co.uk
www.pirc.co.uk

PricewaterhouseCoopers, Southwark Towers, 32 London Bridge, London SE1 9SY
www.pwcglobal.com

Shared Interest Society, 25 Collingwood Street, Newcastle upon Tyne NE1 1JE, UK
Tel: 0191 233 9100

Social Investment Forum, 1612 K-Street NW St, 650 Washington, DC 20006, USA
e.mail   info@socialinvest.org
www.socialinvest.org/

Social Investment Forum (UK), Suite 308, 16 Baldwins Gardens, London EC1N 7RJ
e.mail   uksif@gn.apc.org

Socially Responsible Investment Network, *c/o* Pensions Investment Resource Centre, 40 Bowling Green Lane, London EC1R 0NE

Strategic Research Centre for Environmental Accountability (SRCEA), University of Tasmania, GPO Box 252–86, Hobart, TAS, Tasmania 7001, Australia
e.mail   SRCEA@utas.edu.au
www.comlaw.utas.edu.au/srcea/

SustainAbility Ltd, 49–53 Kensington High Street, London W8 5ED
  e.mail info@sustainability.co.uk
  www.sustainability.co.uk
Tomorrow Global Environment Business, Tomorrow Publishing AB, Saltmätargatan 8A,
  SE-113 59 Stockholm, Sweden
  e.mail info@tomorrowpub.se
  www.tomorrow-web.com
Traidcraft, Kingsway, Gateshead, Tyne and Wear, NE11 0NE, UK
  e.mail tcexchange@gn.apc.org
  www.globalnet.co.uk/~traidcraft
United Nations, Conference on Trade and Development (UNCTAD), Palais des
  Nations, 1211 Geneva 10, Switzerland
  Tel: (22) 9071234; Fax: (22) 9070057
United Nations Environment Programme (UNEP), Tour Mirabeau – 39–43, quai André
  Citroën, 75739 Paris Cedex 15, France
  Tel: 33(1) 4437 1450; Fax: 33(1) 4437 1474
US Environmental Protection Agency, Public Affairs Office (A-107), Washington,
  DC 20460, USA
  www.epa.gov
Washington State Department of Ecology, Northwest Regional Office, 3190 160th Ave.
  SE, Bellvue, WA 98008–5452, USA
  www.wa.gov/ecology/
World Business Council for Sustainable Development, 160 route de Florissant,
  CH-1231 Conches-Geneva, Switzerland
  e.mail info@wbcsd.ch
  www.wbcsd.ch
World Resources Institute (WRI), 1709 New York Avenue NW., Washington, DC 20006,
  USA
  www.wri.org/wri
Worldwatch Institute, 1776 Massachusetts Ave. NW, Washington, DC 20036–1904,
  USA
  Tel: (202) 452 1999; Fax: (202) 296 7365
  e.mail worldwatch@worldwatch.org
  www.worldwatch.org
Worldwide Fund for Nature, Panda House, Weyside Park, Godalming, Surrey,
  GU7 1XR, UK
  e.mail wwf-uk@wwf-uk.org
  www.panda.org/
Wuppertal Institut für Klima Umwelt Energie, Döppersberg 19, 42103 Wuppertal,
  Germany
  www.wupperinst.org

BIBLIOGRAPHY

Abdolmohammadi, M., P. Burnarby, L. Greenlay and J. Thibodeau (1997) 'Environmental account-
   ing in the United States: from control and prevention to remediation', *Asia-Pacific Journal of
   Accounting*, 4 (3), December, pp. 199–217
Abt, C.C. and Associates (1972 *et seq.*) *Annual Report and Social Audit*
Accounting Standards Committee (1975) *The Corporate Report* (London: ICAEW)
Ackoff, R.L. (1960) 'Systems, organisations and interdisciplinary research', *General Systems Theory
   Yearbook*, vol. 5, pp. 1–8
Ackoff, R.L. (1972) 'A note on systems science', *Interfaces*, August, pp. 40–41
Adams, C.A., W.Y. Hill and C.B. Roberts (1995) *Environmental, Employee and Ethical Reporting in
   Europe* (London: ACCA)
Adams, C.A., W.-Y. Hill and C.B. Roberts (1998) 'Corporate social reporting practices in West-
   ern Europe: legitimating corporate behaviour?', *British Accounting Review*, 30 (1), pp. 1–21
Adams, R. (1989) *Who Profits?* (Oxford: Lion)
Adams, R. (1990) 'The greening of consumerism', *Accountancy*, June, pp. 80–83
Adams, R., J. Carruthers and C. Fisher (1991) *Shopping for a Better World* (London: Kogan
   Page)
Adams, R., J. Carruthers and S. Hamil (1991) *Changing Corporate Values* (London: Kogan Page)
Adams, R., D. Owen and R. Gray (1997) 'The greening of company accounts', *Certified Accountant*,
   May, pp. 22–26
Advisory Committee on Business and the Environment (1996) *Environmental Reporting and the
   Financial Sector* (London: DoE/DTI)
Ahmad, Y.J., S. El-Serafy and E. Lutz (eds) (1989) *Environmental Accounting for Sustainable Develop-
   ment* (Washington, DC: UNEP/World Bank)
American Accounting Association (1973) 'Report of the committee on environmental effects of
   organizational behaviour', *The Accounting Review*, Supplement to Vol. XLVIII
American Institute of Certified Public Accountants (1977) *The Measurement of Corporate Social
   Performance* (New York: AICPA)
American Institute of Certified Public Accountants (1991) *Audit Risk Alert: General Update on
   Economic, Regulatory and Accounting and Auditing Matters* (New York: AICPA)
Anderson, V. (1991) *Alternative Economic Indicators* (London: Routledge)
Angell, D.J.R., J.D. Comer and M.L.N. Wilkinson (eds) (1990) *Sustaining Earth: Response to the
   Environmental Threats* (London: Macmillan)
Annighöfer, F. (1997) 'Insurers and sustainable development', *Environmental Stategy Europe 1997*
   (London: Campden Publishing), pp. 109–110
Arthur Andersen (1990) *Environmental Liabilities: Is Your Company at Risk?* (Houston: Arthur
   Andersen)
Association of Chartered Certified Accountants and Aspinwall and Co. (1997) *Guide to Environ-
   ment and Energy Reporting and Accounting 1997* (London: ACCA)

Auditing Practices Board (1992) *The Future Development of Auditing: A Paper to Promote Public Debate* (The MacFarlane Report) (London: APB)

Ayres, R.U. (1998) *Turning Point: The End of the Growth Illusion* (London: Earthscan)

Bailey, P.E. (1991) 'Full Cost Accounting for life-cycle costs: a guide for engineers and financial analysis', *Environmental Finance*, Spring, pp. 13–29

Ball, A., D.L. Owen and R.H. Gray (2000) 'External transparency or internal capture? The role of third party statements in adding value to corporate environmental reports', *Business Strategy and the Environment*, 9 (1), Jan/Feb, pp. 1–23

Ball, S. (1991) 'BATNEEC: BAT v. NEEC?', *Integrated Environmental Management*, No. 3, October, pp. 4–6

Ball, S. (1991) 'Implementation of the Environmental Assessment Directive in Britain', *Integrated Environmental Management*, No. 5, August, pp. 9–11

Ball, S. and S. Bell (1991) *Environmental Law* (London: Blackstone Press)

Ball, S. and J. Maltby (1992) 'The accounting implications of new and forthcoming environmental legislation', Paper presented to BAA National Conference, April

Banks, J. (1977) 'Mysteries of a nuclear audit', *Accountancy Age*, 23 September, p. 11

Barbier, E. (1981) 'The concept of sustainable economic development', *Environmental Conservation*, 14 (2), 101–110

Baumhart, R.C. (1961) 'How ethical are businessmen?', *Harvard Business Review*, July/August

Baumol, W.J. (1975) 'Environmental protection at minimum cost: the Pollution Tax', in L.J. Seidler and L.L. Seidler (eds), *Social Accounting: Theory, Issues and Cases* (Los Angeles: Melville)

Baumol, W.J. and W.E. Oates (1979) *Economics, Environmental Policy and the Quality of Life* (New York: Prentice Hall)

Baxter, G. and C. Rarick (1989) 'The manager as Kierkegaard's "Knight of Faith": linking ethical thought and action', *Journal of Business Ethics*, 8 (5), pp. 399–406

Beams, F.A. and P.E. Fertig (1971) 'Pollution control through social cost conversion', *Journal of Accountancy*, November, pp. 37–42

Bebbington, J. (1993) 'The European Community Fifth Action Plan: Towards Sustainability', *Social and Environmental Accounting*, 13 (1), pp. 9–11

Bebbington, J. (1997) 'Engagement, education and sustainability: a review essay on environmental accounting', *Accounting, Auditing and Accountability Journal*, 10 (3), pp. 365–381

Bebbington, K.J. (1999) 'The GRI Sustainability Reporting Conference and Guidelines', *Social and Environmental Accounting*, 19 (2), pp. 8–11

Bebbington, K.J. and R.H. Gray (1990) 'The greening of accountancy: the profession and the environment', *Accountants' Journal (NZ)*, September, pp. 17–20

Bebbington, K.J. and R.H. Gray (1992) 'Where have all the accountants gone?', *Accountancy*, March, pp. 28–29

Bebbington, K.J. and R.H. Gray (1995) 'Incentives and disincentives for the adoption of sustainable development by transnational corporations', *International Accounting and Reporting Issues: 1995 Review* (Geneva: United Nations), pp. 1–39

Bebbington, K.J. and R.H. Gray (1996) 'Sustainable development and accounting: incentives and disincentives for the adoption of sustainability by transnational corporations', in C. Hibbit and H. Blokdijk (eds), *Environmental Accounting and Sustainable Development* (Amsterdam: Limperg Instituut), pp. 107–151

Bebbington, K.J. and R.H. Gray (1997) 'An account of sustainability: failure, success and a reconception', *Interdisciplinary Perspectives on Accounting Conference Proceedings*, Vol 1. (University of Manchester), pp. 1.10.1–1.10.17

Bebbington, K.J. and J. Tan (1996) 'Accounting for sustainability', *Chartered Accountants Journal (NZ)*, July, pp. 75–76

Bebbington, K.J. and J. Tan (1997) 'Accounting for sustainability', *Chartered Accountants Journal (NZ)*, February, pp. 37–40

Bebbington, K.J. and I. Thomson (1996) *Business Conceptions of Sustainability and the Implications for Accountancy* (London: ACCA)

Bebbington, K.J., R.H. Gray, I. Thomson and D. Walters (1994) 'Accountants' attitudes and environmentally sensitive accounting', *Accounting and Business Research*, No. 94, Spring, pp. 51–75

Beder, S. (1997) *Global Spin: The Corporate Assault on Environmentalism* (London: Green Books)

Belkaoui, A. (1984) *Socio-Economic Accounting* (Westport, CT: Quorum Books)

Bell, R. (1992) 'Emissions to explain', *Independent on Sunday*, 16 February, p. 55

Bennett, A. (1988) 'Ethics codes spread despite scepticism', *Wall Street Journal*, 15 July, p. 19

Bennett, M. and P. James (1998a) *Environment under the Spotlight: Current Practice and Future Trends in Environmental-related Performance Measurement for Business* (London: ACCA)

Bennett, M. and P. James (eds) (1998b) *The Green Bottom Line: Environmental Accounting for Management* (Sheffield: Greenleaf)

Benson, G.C.S. (1989) 'Codes of ethics', *Journal of Business Ethics*, 8 (5), May, pp. 305–319

Benston, G.J. (1982a) 'Accounting and corporate accountability', *Accounting, Organizations and Society*, 7 (2), pp. 87–105

Benston, G.J. (1982b) 'An analysis of the role of accounting standards for enhancing corporate governance and social responsibility', *Journal of Accounting and Public Policy*, 1 (1), pp. 5–18

Biffa (1997) *Great Britain plc: The Environmental Balance Sheet* (High Wycombe, Bucks: Biffa Waste Services plc)

Bins-Hoefnagels, I.M.J. and G.C. Molenkamp (1989) *Environmental Auditing* (The Hague: Touche Ross International)

Bins-Hoefnagels, I.M.J., G.C. Molenkamp and K.P.G. Wilschut (1986) 'De milieu-auditor en de accountant' (The environmental auditor and the accountant), *Accountant (Netherlands)*, 92 (10), pp. 446–452

Blumenfeld, K., R. Earle III and J.B. Shopley (1991) 'Identifying strategic environmental opportunities: a life-cycle approach', *Prism*, Third Quarter, pp. 45–58

Bömke, N (1997) 'Banks, the environment and liability', *Environmental Stategy Europe 1997* (London: Campden Publishing), pp. 55–57

Boulding, K.E. (1982) 'The economics of the coming Spaceship Earth', in H. Jarratt (ed.), *Environmental Quality in a Growing Economy* (Baltimore, MD: Johns Hopkins University Press), pp. 3–14

Boulding, K.E. (1982) 'Review of *Ecodevelopment: Economics, Ecology and Development an Alternative to Growth-imperative Models*', *Journal of Economic Literature*, XX (9), pp. 1076–1077

British Standards Institution (1991) *Draft British Standard: Environmental Management Systems (Parts 1–3)* (London: BSI)

British Standards Institution (1994) *British Standard for Environmental Management Systems: BS7750* (London: BSI)

Brophy, M. (1998) 'Environmental policies', in R. Welford (ed.), *Corporate Environmental Management 1: Systems and Strategies* (London: Earthscan), pp. 90–101

Brophy, M. (1998) 'Environmental guidelines and charters', in R.Welford (ed.), *Corporate Environmental Management 1: Systems and Strategies* (London: Earthscan), pp. 102–115

Brown, L.R., C. Flavin and H. French (eds) (1998) *State of the World 1998* (London: Earthscan/Worldwatch Institute)

Brown, L.R., C. Flavin (with others) (1999) *State of the World 1999* (London: Earthscan/Worldwatch Institute)

Bruce, L. (1989) 'How green is your company?', *International Management*, No. 1, pp. 24–29

Bryce, A. (1990) 'Business and law in a cleaner world', *Accountancy*, June, pp. 75–78

Burchell, S., C. Clubb and A. Hopwood (1985) 'Accounting in its social context: towards a history of value added in the United Kingdom', *Accounting, Organizations and Society*, 10 (4), pp. 381–413

Burke, T. and J. Hill (1990) *Ethics, Environment and Company* (London: Institute of Business Ethics)

Burke, T., N. Robins and A. Trisoglio (eds) (1991) *Environment Strategy Europe 1991* (London: Campden)

Burkitt, D. (1990) *The Costs to Industry of Adopting Environmentally Friendly Practices* (London: CIMA)

Burman, V. (1990) 'Budding friends of the earth', *Money Marketing*, 24 May, pp. 9–10

Burritt, R.L. and G. Lehman (1995) 'The Body Shop windfarm: an analysis of accountability and ethics', *British Accounting Review*, 27 (3), pp. 167–186

Business-in-the-Environment (1991a) *Your Business and the Environment: A DIY Review for Companies* (London: BiE/Coopers and Lybrand Deloitte)

Business-in-the-Environment (1991b) *Your Business and the Environment: An Executive Guide* (London: BiE)

Business-in-the-Environment (1992) *A Measure of Commitment: Guidelines for Environmental Performance* (London: BiE/KPMG)

Business-in-the-Environment (1993) *Buying into the Environment: Guidelines for Integrating Environment into Purchasing and Supply* (London: Crown Copyright)

Business-in-the-Environment (1994) *City Analysts and the Environment: A Survey of Environmental Attitudes in the City of London* (London: BiE/Extel)

Business-in-the-Environment/SustainAbility (1993) *The LCA Sourcebook* (London: BiE/SustainAbility/SPOLD)

Cairncross, F. (1991) *Costing the Earth* (London: Business Books/The Economist)

Canadian Institute of Chartered Accountants (1993) *Environmental Costs and Liabilities: Accounting and Financial Reporting Issues* (Toronto: CICA)

Canadian Institute of Chartered Accountants (1994) *The Audit of Financial Statements affected by Environmental Matters* (Toronto: CICA)

Capra, F. and C. Spretnak (1984) *Green Politics: The Global Promise* (London: Hutchinson)

Cardwell, Z. (1991) 'Green Enlightenment', *AA (Accountancy Age)*, January, pp. 30–33

Carson, R. (1962) *Silent Spring* (Boston, MA: Houghton Mifflin)

Cartwright, D. (1990) 'What price ethics?', *Managerial Auditing Journal*, 5 (2), pp. 28–31

CEFIC (1989) *Guidelines for the Communication of Environmental Information to the Public* (Brussels: CEFIC)

CEFIC (1990) *Guidelines on Waste Minimisation* (Paris: CEFIC)

CERES (1995) *Guide to the CERES Principles* (Boston, MA: CERES)

Charlton, C. (1991) 'Lifecycle assessment: making sense of environmental complexities', *CBI Environment Newsletter*, No. 6, pp. 13–14

Chartered Institute of Management Accountants (1982) *The Evaluation of Energy Use: Readings* (London: CIMA)

Chastain, C.E. (1973) 'Environmental accounting: US and UK', *Accountancy*, December, pp. 10–13

Chastain, C.E. (1974) 'Financial accounting for environmental information', *Journal UEC*, 1 January, pp. 46–51

Chechile, A. and S. Carlisle (eds) (1991) *Environmental Decision Making: A Multidisciplinary Perspective* (London: Chapman and Hall)

Choi, J.-S. (1998) 'An evaluation of the voluntary corporate environmental disclosures: Korean evidence', *Social and Environmental Accounting*, 18 (1), April, pp. 2–8

Christophe, B. and K.J. Bebbington (1992) 'The French. Social Balance Sheet: An exploratory note on a possible approach to environmental accounting', *The British Accounting Review*, 24 (2), pp. 149–156

Clayton, A.M.H. and N.J. Radcliffe (1996) *Sustainability: A Systems Approach* (London: Earthscan)

Cmnd 310 (1988) Royal Commission on Environmental Approval *Best Practicable Environment Option* (London: HMSO)

Cmnd 1200 (1990) *This Common Inheritance* (London: HMSO)

Coker, E.W. (1990) 'Adam Smith's concept of the social system', *Journal of Business Ethics*, 9 (2), pp. 139–142

Collison, D.J. (1996) 'The response of statutory financial auditors in the UK to environmental issues: A descriptive and exploratory case study', *British Accounting Review*, 28 (4), pp. 325–349

Collison, D.J. and R.H. Gray (1997) 'Auditors' response to emerging issues: A UK perspective on the statutory auditor and the environment', *International Journal of Auditing*, 1 (2), pp. 135–149

Collison, D.J., R.H. Gray and J. Innes (1996) *The Financial Auditor and the Environment* (London: ICAEW)

Commoner, B. (1971) *The Closing Circle* (New York: Alfred Knopf)

Commoner, B. (1972) 'The social use and misuse of technology', in J. Benthall (ed.), *Ecology: The Shaping Enquiry* (London: Longman), pp. 335–362

Confederation of British Industry (1973) *The Responsibilities of the British Public Company* (London: CBI)

Confederation of British Industry (1986) *Clean Up – It's Good Business* (London: CBI)

Confederation of British Industry (1990) *Narrowing the Gap: Environmental Auditing Guidelines for Business* (London: CBI)

Confederation of British Industry (1991) *Local Authority Air Pollution Control* (London: CBI)

Confederation of British Industry (1992a) *Managing Waste: Guidelines for Business* (London: CBI)

Confederation of British Industry (1992b) *Environment means Business: A CBI Action Plan for the 1990s* (London: CBI)

Confederation of British Industry (1992c) *Corporate Environmental Policy Statements* (London: CBI)

Confederation of British Industry/PA (1990) *Waking Up to a Better Environment* (London: CBI/PA Consulting)

Council for Economic Priorities (1973) *Economic Priorities Report* (New York: CEP)

Counter Information Services (1972 et seq.) *CIS Reports* (London: CIS)

Daly, H.E. (ed.) (1980) *Economy, Ecology, Ethics: Essays Toward a Steady State Economy* (San Francisco: W.H. Freeman)

Daly, H.E. (1985) 'Ultimate confusion: the economics of Julian Simon', *Futures*, 10/85, pp. 446–450

Daly, H.E. (1989) 'Toward a measure of sustainable social Net National Product', in Y.J. Ahmad, S. El-Serafy and E. Lutz (eds), *Environmental Accounting for Sustainable Development* (Washington, DC: UNEP/World Bank), pp. 8–9

Daly, H.E. and J.B. Cobb Jr (1990) *For the Common Good: Redirecting the Economy Towards the Community, the Environment and a Sustainable Future* (London: Greenprint)

Dauncey, G. (1988, 1996) *After the Crash: The Emergence of the Rainbow Economy* (Basingstoke: Greenprint)

Davis, J. (1991) *Greening Business: Managing for Sustainable Development* (Oxford: Basil Blackwell)

Deegan, C. and M. Newson (1997) *Environmental Performance Evaluation and Reporting for Private and Public Organisations* (Sydney: NSW Environmental Protection Agency)

Deegan, C. and M. Rankin (1996) 'Do Australian companies report environmental news objectively? An analysis of environmental disclosures by firms prosecuted successfully by the Environmental Protection Authority', *Accounting, Auditing and Accountability Journal*, 9 (2), pp. 50–67

Deetz, S.A. (1992) *Democracy in an Age of Corporate Colonization* (New York: State University of New York)

Department of the Environment (1989a) *Sustaining Our Common Future* (London: DoE)

Department of the Environment (1989b) *Environment in Trust* (London: DoE)

Department of the Environment (1989c) *Clean Technology* (London: DoE)

Department of the Environment (1989d) *Environmental Assessment: A Guide to Procedures* (London: HMSO)

Department of the Environment (1989e) *Environmental Protection Bill* (London: HMSO)

Department of the Environment (1991a) *The Government's Proposals for the Implementation in UK Law of the EC Directive on Freedom of Access to Information on the Environment. Consultation Paper* (London: DoE)

Department of the Environment (1991b) *Digest of Environmental Protection Statistics 1991* (London: DoE)

Department of the Environment (1991c) *Waste Management. The Duty of Care: A Code of Practice* (London: DoE)

Department of the Environment (1991d) *Giving Guidance to the Green Consumer: Progress on an Eco-labelling Scheme* (London: DoE)

Department of the Environment (1995) *A Waste Strategy for England and Wales* (London: DoE)

Department of Trade and Industry (1989) *Your Business and the Environment* (London: DTI)

Department of Trade and Industry (1990) *Cutting Your Losses: A Business Guide to Waste Minimization* (London: DTI)

Department of Trade and Industry (1991) *The Environment: A Challenge for Business* (London: DTI)

Dewhurst, J. (1989) 'The green resource audit', *The Accountant*, December, pp. 8–9

Dick-Larkham, R. and D. Stonestreet (1977) 'Save it! The accountants' vital role', *Accountants' Weekly*, 15 April, pp. 22–23

Dickson, D. (1974) *Alternative Technology and the Politics of Technical Change* (Glasgow: Fontana)

Dierkes, M. and L.E. Preston (1977) 'Corporate social accounting and reporting for the physical environment: a critical review and implementation proposal', *Accounting, Organizations and Society*, 2 (1), pp. 3–22

Dirks, H.J. (1991) 'Accounting for the costs of environmental clean-up: Where things stand today', *Environmental Finance*, Spring, pp. 89–92

Ditz, D. and J. Ranganathan (1997) *Measuring Up: Toward a Common Framework for Tracking Corporate Environmental Performance* (Washington, DC: World Resources Institute)

Ditz, D., J. Ranganathan and R.D. Banks (1995) *Green Ledgers: Case Studies in Environmental Accounting* (Baltimore, MD: World Resources Institute)

Dobie, C. (1990) 'Green becomes an issue for the fund managers', *The Independent*, 14 May

Dobson, A. (1990) *Green Political Thought* (London: Unwin Hyman)

Donaldson, J. (1988) *Key Issues in Business Ethics* (London: Academic Press)

Douthwaite, R. (1992) *The Growth Illusion* (Devon: Green Books)

DRT International (1991) *Framework for Corporate Reporting on Sustainable Development* (Toronto: DRT/BCSD/IISD)

Duncan, O. and Thomson, I. (1998) 'Waste accounting and cleaner production: a complex evaluation', *APIRA 98 in Osaka: Proceedings Volume II* (Osaka: Osaka City University), pp. 648–656

Dunham, R. (1988) 'Virtue rewarded', *Accountancy*, June, pp. 103–105

Dunham, R. (1990) 'Ethical funds no bar to profit', *Accountancy*, June, p. 111

Earth Works Group (1989) *50 Simple Things You Can Do to Save the Earth* (London: Hodder and Stoughton)

Eden, S. (1996) *Environmental Issues and Business: Implications of a Changing Agenda* (Chichester: John Wiley)

Edgerton, J. (1989) 'Investing: Tanker from hell', *Money*, June, pp. 66–67

EIRIS (1989) *The Financial Performance of Ethical Investments* (London: EIRIS)

Ekins, P. (ed.) (1986) *The Living Economy: A New Economics in the Making* (London: Routledge)

Ekins, P. (1992a) *Wealth beyond Measure: An Atlas of New Economics* (London: Gaia)

Ekins, P. (1992b) *A New World Order: Grassroots Movements for Global Change* (London: Routledge)

Elkington, J. (1978) 'Business through the looking glass', *New Scientist*, 7 September

Elkington, J. (1980) 'The environmental pressure', *Management Today*, January, pp. 62–65

Elkington, J. (1981) 'Converting industry to environmental impact assessment', *Environmental Conservation*, 8 (1), pp. 23–30

Elkington, J. (1982) 'Industrial applications of environmental impact assessment', *Journal of General Management*, 7 (3), pp. 23–33

Elkington, J. (with Tom Burke) (1987) *The Green Capitalists: Industry's Search for Environmental Excellence* (London: Victor Gollancz)

Elkington, J. (1990a) *The Environmental Audit: A Green Filter for Company Policies, Plants, Processes and Products* (London: SustainAbility/World-wide Fund for Nature)

Elkington, J. (1990b) *Community Action: No Thanks, Noah* (London: British Gas)

Elkington, J. (1995) *Who Needs It? Market Implications of Sustainable Lifestyles* (London: SustainAbility)

Elkington, J. (1997) *Cannibals with Forks: The Triple Bottom Line of 21st Century Business* (Oxford: Capstone Publishing)

Elkington, J. and Dimmock, A. (1991) *The Corporate Environmentalists: Selling Sustainable Development: But Can They Deliver?* (London: SustainAbility)

Elkington, J. and J. Hailes (1988) *The Green Consumer Guide: High Street Shopping for a Better Environment* (London: Victor Gollancz)

Elkington, J. and J. Hailes (1989) *The Green Consumer's Supermarket Shopping Guide* (London: Victor Gollancz)

Elkington, J. and J. Hailes (1998) *Manual 2000: Life Choices for the Future You Want* (London: Hodder and Stoughton)

Elkington, J. and V. Jennings (1991) 'The rise of the environmental audit', *Integrated Environmental Management*, No. 1, August, pp. 8–10

Elkington, J., P. Knight and J. Hailes (1991) *The Green Business Guide* (London: Victor Gollancz)

Environmental Protection Agency (1996) *Full Cost Accounting for Decision Making at Ontario Hydro* (Washington, DC: EPA)

Epstein, M.J. (1996) *Measuring Corporate Environmental Performance: Best Practice for Costing and Managing an Effective Environmental Strategy* (Chicago: Irwin)

Ermann, M.D. (1986) 'How managers unintentionally encourage corporate crime', *Business and Society Review*, 59 (Fall), pp. 30–34

Estes, R.W. (1976) *Corporate Social Accounting* (New York: John Wiley)

European Federation of Financial Analysts Societies (with K. Muller, J. deFrutos, K. Schussler and H. Haarbosch) (1994) *Environmental Reporting and Disclosures: The Financial Analyst's View* (Geneva: EFFAS)

Fava, J.A. (1991) 'Product lifecycle assessment: improving environmental quality', *Integrated Environmental Management*, No. 3 (October), pp. 19–21

Fédération des Experts Comptables Européens (1993) *Environmental Accounting and Auditing: Survey of Current Activities and Developments* (Brussels: FEE)

Ferguson, A. (1989) 'Good to be green', *Management Today*, February, pp. 46–52

Field, D., P. Fisher and J. Oldham (1994) *The Environment: An Accountant's Perspective* (Scarborough, Ontario: Carswell)

Flavin, C. and S. Dunn (1998) 'Responding to the threat of climate change', in L.R. Brown et al., *State of the World 1998* (London: Earthscan/Worldwatch Institute)

Foster, A. (1989) 'Decent, clean and true', *Management Today*, April, pp. 56–60

Frankel, M. (1978) *The Social Audit Pollution Handbook* (London: Macmillan)

Frankel, M. (1981) *A Word of Warning* (London: Social Audit)

Frankel, M. (1982) *Chemical Risk* (London: Pluto Press)

Friedman, M. (1962) *Capitalism and Freedom* (Chicago: University of Chicago Press)

Friedman, M. (1970) 'The social responsibility of business is to increase its profits', *The New York Times Magazine*, September 13, pp. 122–126

Friends of the Earth (1989) *The Environmental Charter for Local Government* (London: FoE)

Friends of the Earth (1990) *How Green is Britain?: The Government's Environmental Record* (London: Hutchinson Radius)

Fuller, K. (1991) 'Reviewing UK's Experience in EIA', *Integrated Environmental Management*, No. 1, August, pp. 12–14

Galbraith, J.K. (1973) *Economics and the Public Purpose* (Harmondsworth: Penguin)

Galbraith, J.K. (1991) 'Revolt in our time: the triumph of simplistic ideology', in M. Kaldor (ed.), *Europe from below* (publisher ?)

Gamble, G.O., K. Hsu, C. Jackson and C.D. Tollerson (1996) 'Environmental disclosures in annual reports: an international perspective', *International Journal of Accounting*, 31 (3), pp. 293–331

Gambling, T. (1985) 'The accountants' guide to the galaxy, including the profession at the end of the universe', *Accounting, Organizations and Society*, 10 (4), pp. 415–425

Geddes, M. (1988) *Social Audits and Social Accounting: An Annotated Bibliography and Commentary* (School of Applied Economics and Social Studies, South Bank Polytechnic, London)

Geddes, M. (1992) 'The social audit movement', in D.L. Owen (ed.), *Green Reporting* (London: Chapman and Hall), pp. 215–241

Gelber, M. (1995) 'Eco-balance: an environmental management tool used in Germany', *Social and Environmental Accounting*, 15 (2), pp. 7–9

GEMI (Global Environmental Management Initiative) (1997)

Gilkinson, B. (1992a) 'Economic instruments: positive trend, positive signals', *Accountants Journal (NZ)*, March, pp. 70–71

Gilkinson, B. (1992b) 'What is a green economy?', *Accountants Journal (NZ)*, February, pp. 25–26

Gladwin, T.N., T.-S. Krause and J.J. Kennelly (1995) 'Beyond eco-efficiency: Towards socially sustainable business', *Sustainable Development*, 3, pp. 35–43

Gladwin, T.N., W.E. Newburry and E.D. Reiskin (1997) 'Why is the Northern elite mind biased against community, the environment and a sustainable future?', in M.H. Bazerman, D. Messick, A. Tenbrunsel and K.A. Wade-Benzoni (eds), *Environment, Ethics and Behaviour: The psychology of environmental valuation and degradation* (San Francisco: New Lexington), pp. 234–274

Goldsmith, E. (1988) *The Great U-Turn: De-industrializing Society* (Devon: Green Books)

Goldsmith, E., R. Allen, M. Allaby, J. Davull and S. Lawrence (1972) *Blueprint for Survival* (Harmondsworth: Penguin)

Gonella, C., A. Pilling and S. Zadek (1998) *Making Values Count: Contemporary Experience in Social and Ethical Accounting, Auditing and Reporting* (London: ACCA)

Gorz, A. (1989) *Critique of Economic Reason* (trans. G. Handyside and C. Turner) (London: Verso)

Gray, R.H. (1986) *Accounting for R&D: A Review of Experiences with SSAP13* (London: ICAEW)

Gray, R.H. (1989) 'Accounting and democracy', *Accounting, Auditing and Accountability Journal*, 2 (3), pp. 52–56

Gray, R.H. (1990a) 'The accountant's task as a friend to the Earth', *Accountancy*, June, pp. 65–69

Gray, R.H. (1990b) 'Business ethics and organisational change: building a Trojan horse or rearranging deckchairs on the Titanic?', *Managerial Auditing Journal*, 5 (2), pp. 12–21

Gray, R.H. (1990c) 'Accounting and economics: the psychopathic siblings – A review essay', *British Accounting Review*, 22 (4), pp. 373–388

Gray, R.H. (1990d) *The Greening of Accountancy: The Profession after Pearce* (London: ACCA)

Gray, R.H. (1991) 'Sustainability: Do you REALLY want to know what it means?', *CBI Environment Newsletter*, No. 3 (January), pp. 10–11

Gray, R.H. (1992) 'Accounting and environmentalism: an exploration of the challenge of gently accounting for accountability, transparency and sustainability', *Accounting, Organizations and Society*, 17 (5), pp. 399–426

Gray, R.H. (1996) 'The interesting relationship between accounting research and accounting practice: A personal reply to Professor Whittington', *Journal of Applied Accounting Research*, 3 (1), pp. 5–34

Gray, R.H. and D.J. Collison (1991a) 'Disclosure: the movement towards environmental disclosure', *Environment Strategy Europe 1991* (London: Campden Publishing), pp. 195–198

Gray, R.H. and D.J. Collison (1991b) 'Environmental audit: green gauge or whitewash?', *Managerial Auditing*, 6 (5), pp. 17–25

Gray, R.H. and R.C. Laughlin (1991a) 'The coming of the green and the challenge of environmentalism', *Accounting, Auditing and Accountability Journal*, 4 (3), pp. 5–8

Gray, R.H. and R.C. Laughlin (eds) (1991b) *Green Accounting: A Special Issue of Accounting, Auditing and Accountability* (Bradford: MCB Press)

Gray, R.H. and S. Morrison (1991) 'Accounting for the environment after the Pearce Report', *Radical Quarterly*, No. 19 (Spring), pp. 17–25

Gray, R.H. and S. Morrison (1992) 'The physical environment, accounting and local development', *Local Economy*, pp. 336–350

Gray, R.H. and D.L. Owen (1993) 'The rocky road to reporting', *Certified Accountant*, March, pp. 36–38

Gray, R.H. and I.W. Symon (1992a) 'An environmental audit by any other name . . .', *Integrated Environmental Management*, No. 6, February, pp. 9–11

Gray, R.H. and I.W. Symon (1992b) 'Environmental reporting: BSO/Origin', *Integrated Environmental Management*, No. 7 (March), pp. 8–10

Gray, R.H., K.J. Bebbington, D.J. Collison, R. Kouhy, B. Lyon, C. Reid, A. Russell and L. Stevenson (1998) *The Valuation of Assets and Liabilities: Environmental Law and the Impact of the Environmental Agenda for Business* (Edinburgh: ICAS)

Gray, R.H., K.J. Bebbington and K. McPhail (1994) 'Teaching ethics and the ethics of accounting teaching: educating for immorality and a case for social and environmental accounting education', *Accounting Education*, 3 (1), pp. 51–75

Gray, R.H., K.J. Bebbington, D. Walters and I. Thomson (1995) 'The greening of enterprise: an exploration of the (non) role of environmental accounting and environmental accountants in organisational change', *Critical Perspectives on Accounting*, 6 (3), pp. 211–239

Gray, R.H., C. Dey, D. Owen, R. Evans and S. Zadek (1997) 'Struggling with the praxis of social accounting: stakeholders, accountability, audits and procedures', *Accounting, Auditing and Accountability Journal*, 10 (3), pp. 325–364

Gray, R.H., M. Javad, D.M. Power and C.D. Sinclair (forthcoming) 'Social and environmental disclosure and corporate characteristics: a research note and extension', *Journal of Business Finance and Accounting*, pp. 327–356.

Gray, R.H., R. Kouhy and S. Lavers (1995) 'Corporate social and environmental reporting: a review of the literature and a longitudinal study of UK disclosure', *Accounting, Auditing and Accountability Journal*, 8 (2), pp. 47–77

Gray, R.H., R.C. Laughlin and K.J. Bebbington (1996) *Financial Accounting: Method and Meaning* (London: International Thomson)

Gray, R.H., D.L. Owen and R. Adams (1995) 'Standards, stakeholders and sustainability', *Certified Accountant*, March, pp. 20–224

Gray, R.H., D.L. Owen and C. Adams (1996) *Accounting and Accountability: Changes and Challenges in Corporate Social and Environmental Reporting* (Hemel Hempstead: Prentice Hall)

Gray, R.H., D.L. Owen and K.T. Maunders (1986) 'Corporate social reporting: the way forward?', *Accountancy*, December, pp. 6–8

Gray, R.H., D.L. Owen and K.T. Maunders (1987) *Corporate Social Reporting: Accounting and Accountability* (Hemel Hempstead: Prentice Hall)

Gray, R.H., D.L. Owen and K.T. Maunders (1988) 'Corporate social reporting: emerging trends in accountability and the social contract', *Accounting, Auditing and Accountability Journal*, 1 (1), pp. 6–20

Gray, R.H., D.L. Owen and K.T. Maunders (1991) 'Accountability, corporate social reporting and the external social audits', *Advances in Public Interest Accounting*, 4, pp. 1–21

Gray, Roger (1989) 'Social audit: responding to change?', *Management Accounting*, December, pp. 8–9

Gray, S.J., L.H. Radebaugh and C.B. Roberts (1990) 'International perceptions of cost constraints on voluntary information disclosures: a comparative study of UK and USA multinationals', *Journal of International Business Studies*, Fourth Quarter (Winter), pp. 597–622

Greenpeace (1985) *Whiter Than White?* (London: Greenpeace)

Greer, J. and K.Bruno (1996) *Greenwash: The Reality behind Corporate Environmentalism* (Penang/New York: Third World Network/Apex Press)

Guilding, C. and C. Kirman (1998) 'Environmental accounting in the New Zealand contracting industry', *Accounting Forum*, 10 (1), pp. 27–50

Harker, D., E. Mayo, P. Walker and C. Unsworth (eds) (1997) *Community Works! A guide to community economic action* (London: New Economics Foundation)

Hart, S.L. (1997) 'Beyond greening: stategies for a sustainable world', *Harvard Business Review*, Jan–Feb, pp. 67–76

Harte, G. (1988) 'Ethical investment and corporate reporting', *The Accountants' Magazine*, March, pp. 28–29

Harte, G. and D.L. Owen (1987) 'Fighting de-industrialisation: the role of local government social audits', *Accounting, Organizations and Society*, 12 (2), pp. 123–142

Harte, G. and D.L. Owen (1991) 'Environmental disclosure in the annual reports of British companies: a research note', *Accounting, Auditing and Accountability Journal*, 4 (3), pp. 51–61

Harte, G. and D.L. Owen (1992) 'Current trends in the reporting of green issues in the Annual Reports of UK companies', in D.L. Owen (ed.), *Green Reporting: The Challenge of the Nineties* (London: Chapman and Hall), pp. 166–200

Harte, G., L. Lewis and D.L. Owen (1991) 'Ethical investment and the corporate reporting function', *Critical Perspectives on Accounting*, 2 (3), pp. 227–254

Haughton, G. (1988) 'Impact analysis – the social audit approach', *Project Appraisal*, 3 (1), pp. 21–5

Hawken, P. (1993) *The Ecology of Commerce: A Declaration of Sustainability* (New York: Harper Business)

Hawkshaw, A. (1991) 'Status Quo Vadis', *CA Magazine* (Canada), March, pp. 23–27

Henderson, H. (1978) *Creating Alternative Futures* (New York: Berkley)

Henderson, H. (1981) *The Politics of the Solar Age: Alternatives to Economics* (Doubleday: New York)

Henderson, H. (1991) 'New Markets, New Commons, New Ethics', *Accounting, Auditing and Accountability Journal*, 4 (3), pp. 72–80

Hester, E.J. (1991) 'Environmental issues for insurers and risk managers', *Integrated Environmental Management*, 2 (September), pp. 21–22

Hewgill, J. (1977) 'Can energy become the new currency?', *Accountants' Weekly*, 9 September, p. 13

Hewgill, J. (1979) 'New frontiers: into the unknown', *Accountants' Weekly*, 7 February, p. 11

Hill, J., D. Fedrigo and I. Marshall (1997) *Banking on the Future: A Survey of Implementation of the 'UNEP Statement by Banks on Environment and Sustainable Development'* (London: Green Alliance)

Hindle, P. (1992) '"More from less" in practice', *Moonbeams*, Spring, pp. 14–18

Hines, R.D. (1988) 'Financial accounting: In communicating reality, we construct reality', *Accounting, Organizations and Society*, 13 (3), pp. 251–261

Hines, R.D. (1989) 'The sociopolitical paradigm in financial accounting research', *Accounting, Auditing and Accountability Journal*, 2 (1), pp. 52–76

Hoffman, A.J. (1993) 'The importance of fit between individual values and organisational culture in the greening of industry', *Business Strategy and the Environment*, 2 (4), pp. 10–18

Hoggart, C. (1992) 'Reducing the waste line', *Integrated Environmental Management*, No. 8 (April), pp. 18–19

Holdgate, M. (1990) 'Changes in perception', in D.J.R. Angell, J.D. Comer and M.L.N. Wilkinson (eds), *Sustaining Earth: Response to the Environmental Threats* (London: Macmillan), pp. 79–96

Hopper, T. and A. Powell (1985) 'Making sense of research into the organisational and social aspects of management accounting: A review of its underlying assumptions', *Journal of Management Studies*, 22 (5), September, pp. 429–465

Hopwood, A.G. (1986) 'Economics and the regime of the calculative', in S. Bodington, M. George and J. Michaelson (eds), *Developing the Socially Useful Economy* (London: Macmillan), pp. 69–71

Houldin, M. (1989) 'Can business change to green?', *AA (Accountancy Age)*, November, pp. 34–39

Houldin, M. (1992) 'TQM and environmental management', *Integrated Environmental Management*, No. 9 (May), pp. 5–7

Hueting, R., P. Bosch and B. de Boer (1991) *Methodology for the Calculation of Sustainable National Income* (Voorburg: Netherlands Central Bureau of Statistics)

Huizing, A. and H.C. Dekker (1992) 'Helping to pull our planet out of the red: an environmental report of BSO/Origin', *Accounting Organizations and Society*, 17 (5), pp. 449–458

Humble, J. (1973) *Social Responsibility Audit: A Management Tool for Survival* (London: The Foundation for Business Responsibilities)

Hundred Group of Finance Directors (1992) *Statement of Good Practice: Environmental Reporting in Annual Reports* (London: 100 Group)

Hunt, S.M. (1974) 'Conducting a social inventory', *NAA Management Accounting*, October, pp. 15–16, 26

Hutchinson, C. (1991) *Business and the Environmental Challenge* (Reading: The Conservation Trust)

Innes, J., F. Mitchell, M. Tanaka and T. Yoshikawa (1994) *Contemporary Cost Management* (London: Chapman and Hall)

INSEE (Institut national de la satellites de la statistique et des etudes economiques) (1986) 'Les comptes satellites de l'environnement', *Les collections de l'INSEE*, Serie C, No. 130 (March)

INSEE (1986) 'Les comptes du patrimoine nature!', *Les collections de l'INSEE*, Serie C, No. 137–138 (December)

Institute of Directors (1992) *Members' Opinion Survey: Environment* (London: IOD)

International Auditing Practices Committee (1995) *The Audit Profession and the Environment* (New York: IFAC)

International Chamber of Commerce (1989) *Environmental Auditing* (Paris: ICC)

International Federation of Accountants (1998) *Environmental Management on Organizations: The Role of Management Accounting*, Study No. 6 (March) (New York: IFAC)

International Institute for Sustainable Development (1992) *Business Strategy for Sustainable Development: Leadership and Accountability for the 90s* (Winnipeg: IISD/BCSD/Deloitte Touche)

Irvine, G. (1991) 'Your brother's keeper? Duty of Care under the UK Environmental Protection Act', *Integrated Environmental Management*, No. 2, September, pp. 2–4

Jackall, R. (1988) *Moral Mazes: The World of Corporate Managers* (New York: Oxford University Press)

Jacobs, M. (1991) *The Green Economy: Environment, Sustainable Development and the Politics of the Future* (London: Pluto Press)

Jacobson, R. (1991) 'Economic efficiency and the quality of life', *Journal of Business Ethics*, 101, pp. 201–209

Johnston, R.J. (1996) *Nature, State and Economy: A Political Economy of the Environment* (Chichester: John Wiley)

Kamp-Roelands, N. (1996) *Expert Statements in Environmental Reports* (Brussels: FEE)

Kopitsky, J.J. and E.T. Betzenberger (1997) 'Bankers debate . . . should banks lend to companies with environmental problems?', in P. McDonagh and A. Prothero (eds), *Green Management: A Reader* (London: Dryden), pp. 281–290

Korten, D.C. (1995) *When Corporations Rule the World* (West Hatford/San Francisco: Kumarian/Berrett-Koehler)

KPMG (1996) *UK Environmental Reporting Survey 1996* (London: KPMG)

KPMG (1997) *Environmental Reporting* (Copenhagen: KPMG)

Kretzmann, J.P. and J.L. McKnight (1993) *Building Communities from the Inside Out: A Path Towards Finding and Mobilising a Community's Assets* (Chicago: ACTA Publications)

Krietzman, L. (1988) 'Packaging and design: Air Worthy', *Marketing*, 28 July, p. 49

Krut, R. and H. Gleckman (1998) *ISO14001: A Missed Opportunity for Sustainable Global Industrial Development* (London: Earthscan)

Landbank Consultancy (1992) *The Waste as a Raw Material (WARM) System* (London: Gateway Foodmarkets)

Lander, R. (1989) 'Funds of the Earth', *Management Today*, February, p. 132

Lascelles, D. (1993) *Rating Environmental Risk* (London: Centre for the Study of Financial Innovation)

Laughlin, R. and L.K. Varangu (1991) 'Accounting for waste or garbage accounting: some thoughts from non-accountants', *Accounting, Auditing and Accountability Journal*, 4 (3), pp. 43–50

Laughlin, R.C. (1991) 'Environmental disturbances and organisational transitions and transformations: some alternative models', *Organisation Studies*, 12 (2), pp. 209–232

Lawrence, J. (1991) 'Encouraging cleaner technologies', *Integrated Environmental Management*, No. 4 (November), pp. 15–16

Leggett, J. (ed.) (1996) *Climate Change and the Financial Sector: The Emerging Threat – the Solar Solution* (Munich: Gerling Akademie Verlag)

Lehman, G. (1988) 'Accounting ethics: surviving survival of the fittest', *Advances in Public Interest Accounting*, 2, pp. 71–82

Lehman, G. (1995) 'A legitimate concern for environmental accounting', *Critical Perspectives on Accounting*, 6 (6), pp. 393–412

Lehman, G. (1999) 'Disclosing new worlds: a role for social and environmental accounting and auditing', *Accounting Organizations and Society*, 24 (3), pp. 217–242

Lickiss, M. (1991) 'President's Page: Measuring up to the environmental challenge', *Accountancy*, January, p. 6

Linowes, D. (1972) 'Let's get on with the social audit: a specific proposal', *Business and Society Review*, Winter, pp. 39–42

Litterick, G. (1991) 'Charging for discharging to controlled waters', *Integrated Environmental Management*, No. 5 (December), pp. 2–5

Lovelock, J. (1982) *Gaia: A New look at Life on Earth* (Oxford: Oxford University Press)

Lovelock, J. (1988) *The Ages of Gaia* (Oxford: Oxford University Press)

Lowe, A.E. (1972) 'The finance director's role in the formulation and implementation of strategy', *Journal of Business Finance*, 4 (4), pp. 58–63

Lowe, A.E. and J.M. McInnes (1971) 'Control of socio-economic organisations', *Journal of Management Studies*, 8 (2), pp. 213–227

Luther, R.G. and J. Matatko (1994) 'The performance of ethical unit trusts: choosing an appropriate benchmark', *British Accounting Review*, 26 (1), pp. 77–89

Luther, R.G., J. Matatko and D.C. Corner (1992) 'The investment performance of UK "ethical" unit trusts', *Accounting, Auditing and Accountability Journal*, 5 (4), pp. 57–70

3M/The Environment Council (1991) *A Guide to Policy Making and Implementation* (London: 3M/ Environment Council)

McGoun, E.G. (1997) 'Hyperreal finance', *Critical Perspectives on Accounting*, 8 (1/2), pp. 97–122

McKee, A. (1986) 'The passage from theology to economics', *International Journal of Social Economics*, 13 (3), pp. 5–19

Mackenzie, C. (1997) 'Ethical reasoning in the practice of ethical investment', in G. Moore (ed.), *Business Ethics: Principles and Practice* (Sunderland: Business Education Publishers), pp. 227–240

Macve, R. and A. Carey (eds) (1992) *Business, Accountancy and the Environment: A Policy and Research Agenda* (London: ICAEW)

Magretta, J. (1997) 'Growth through global sustainability: Interview with Robert B. Shapiro', *Harvard Business Review*, Jan–Feb, pp. 81–88

Maltby, J. (1995) 'Not paying for our past: Government, business and the debate on contaminated land in the UK', *Business Strategy and the Environment*, 4 (2), pp. 73–85

Maltby, J. (1997) 'Setting its own standards and meeting those standards: voluntarism *versus* regulation in environmental reporting', *Business Strategy and the Environment*, 6 (2), pp. 83–97

Markandya, A. and D. Pearce (1988) 'Natural environments and the social rate of discount', *Project Appraisal*, 3 (1)

Mathews, M.R. (1987) 'Social responsibility accounting disclosure and information content for shareholders', *British Accounting Review*, 19 (2), pp. 161–168

Maunders, K.T. and R. Burritt (1991) 'Accounting and ecological crisis', *Accounting, Auditing and Accountability Journal*, 4 (3), pp. 9–26

Maunders, K.T., R.H. Gray and D.L. Owen (1991) 'Managerial social accounting in developing countries: towards the operationalisation of social reporting', *Research in Third World Accounting*, 1, pp. 87–101

Mayhew, N. (1997) 'Fading to grey: the use and abuse of corporate executives' "representational power"', in R. Welford (ed.), *Hijacking Environmentalism: Corporate Response to Sustainable Development* (London: Earthscan), pp. 63–95

Mayo, E. (ed.) (1993) *Bank Watch* (London: New Economics Foundation)

Meadows, D.H., D.L. Meadows, J. Randers and W.H. Behrens (1972) *The Limits to Growth* (London: Pan)

Medawar, C. (1976) 'The social audit: a political view', *Accounting, Organizations and Society*, 1 (4), pp. 389–394

Medawar, C. (1978) *The Social Audit Consumer Handbook* (London: Macmillan Press)

Merlin Research Unit (1992) *The Assessment Process for Green Investment* (London: Jupiter Tarbutt Merlin)

Miller, A. (1992) 'Green Investment', in D. Owen (ed.), *Green Reporting: Accountancy and the Challenge of the Nineties* (London: Chapman and Hall), pp. 242–255

Milne, M.J. (1991) 'Accounting, environmental resource values and non-market valuation techniques for environmental resources: a review', *Accounting, Auditing and Accountability Journal*, 4 (3), pp. 81–109

Mintzberg, H. (1983) 'The case for corporate social responsibility', *Journal of Business Strategy*, 4 (2), pp. 3–15

Mishan, E.J. (1969) *The Costs of Economic Growth* (Harmondsworth: Penguin)

Mitchell, F., I. Sams and P. White (1990) 'Ethical investment: current trends and prospects', *The Accountants' Magazine*, January, pp. 12–15

Molinero, L. (ed.) (1991) *Accounting and the Environment: Readings and Discussion* (Washington, DC: Management Institute for Environment and Business)

Moretz, S. (1981) 'Industrial hygiene auditing: Allied Signal takes the "extra step"', *Occupational Hazards*, 5 (May), pp. 73–76

Napier, C. (1992) 'A reticence to lend and invest? A case study of financial institutions and environmental liability – Part two', *Integrated Environmental Management*, No. 9, May, pp. 11–13

Neale, C.W. (1989) 'Post-auditing practices by UK firms: aims, benefits and shortcomings', *British Accounting Review*, 21 (4), pp. 309–328

Netherwood, A. (1996) 'Environmental Management Systems', in R. Welford (ed.), *Corporate Environmental Management: Systems and Strategies* (London: Earthscan), pp. 35–58

Newell, G.E., J.G. Kreuze and S.J. Newell (1990) 'Accounting for hazardous waste: does your firm face potential environmental liabilities?', *Management Accounting (US)*, May, pp. 58–61

Newton, T. and G. Harte (1997) 'Green business: Technist kitsch?', *Journal of Management Studies*, 34 (1), pp. 75–98

Nikolai, L.A., J.D. Bazley and R.L. Brummett (1976) *The Management of Corporate Environmental Activity* (Washington, DC: National Association of Accountants)

Niskala, M. and R. Matasaho (1996) *Environmental Accounting* (Helsinki: WSOY, Ekonomia)

Nixon, B. and A. Lonie (1990) 'Accounting for R&D: the need for change', *Accountancy*, February, pp. 90–91

Nixon, W.A. (1991) 'R&D disclosure: SSAP13 and after', *Accountancy*, February, pp. 72–73

Nixon, W.A. (1996) 'The new technology investment-decision process: some empirical evidence of accounting influence', in R. Mason, L.A. Lefebvre and T.M. Khali (eds), *Management of Technology V: Technology Management in a Changing World* (Oxford: Elsevier), pp. 461–467

O'Connor, J. (1997) 'Is sustainable capitalism possible?', in P. McDonagh and A. Prothero (eds), *Green Management: A Reader* (London: Dryden), pp. 93–111

Odum, H.T. (1996) *Environmental Accounting: Energy and Environmental Decision Making* (New York: John Wiley)

OECD (1989) *Energy technologies for reducing emissions of greenhouse gases* (Paris: OECD)

Opschoor, J.B. and H.B. Vos (1989) *Economic Instruments for Environmental Protection* (Paris: OECD)

Ordre des experts-comptables et des comptables agrées (1980) *'L'evaluation des avantages et couts sociaux la responsabilité socio-economique de l'entreprise'* (Paris: Conseil superieur de l'Ordre des experts-comptables)

O'Riordan, T (ed.) (1997) *Ecotaxation* (London: Earthscan)

O'Riordan, T. and R.K. Turner (1983) *An Annotated Reader in Environmental Planning and Management* (Oxford: Pergamon Press)

Owen, D.L. (1990) 'Towards a theory of social investment: a review essay', *Accounting, Organizations and Society*, 15 (3), pp. 249–266

Owen, D.L. (1992) *Green Reporting: The Challenge of the Nineties* (London: Chapman and Hall)

Owen, D.L. and R.H. Gray (1994) 'Environmental Reporting Awards: profession fails to rise to the challenge', *Certified Accountant*, April, pp. 44–48

Owen, D.L., R.H. Gray and R. Adams (1992) 'A green and fair view', *Certified Accountant*, April, pp. 12–15

Owen, D.L., R.H. Gray and R. Adams (1996) 'Corporate environmental disclosure: slow but steady progress', *Certified Accountant*, March, pp. 18–22

Owen, D., R. Gray and K.J. Bebbington (1997) 'Green accounting: cosmetic irrelevance or radical agenda for change?', *Asia-Pacific Journal of Accounting*, 4 (2), pp. 175–198

Owen, D., R. Gray and K. Maunders (1987) 'Researching the information content of social responsibility disclosure: a comment', *British Accounting Review*, 19 (2), pp. 169–176

Owens, S., V. Anderson and I. Brunskill (1990) *Green Taxes: A Budget Memorandum* (Green Paper No. 2) (London: Institute for Public Policy Research)

Packard, V. (1965) *The Waste Makers* (Harmondsworth: Pelican)

Papworth, J. (1990a) 'White into Green', *AA (Accountancy Age)*, April, pp. 41–42

Papworth, J. (1990b) 'Finding the green balance', *AA (Accountancy Age)*, May, pp. 44 and 47

Pearce, D. (1977) 'Accounting for the future', *Futures*, 9, pp. 365–374 (reprinted in O'Riordan and Turner, 1983)

Pearce, D. (1985) 'Resource scarcity and economic growth in poor developing countries', *Futures*, 10/1985, pp. 440–445

Pearce, D. (ed.) (1991a) *Blueprint 2: Greening the World Economy* (London: Earthscan)

Pearce, D. (1991b) 'Towards a sustainable economy: environment and economics', *The Royal Bank of Scotland Review*, No. 172 (December), pp. 3–15

Pearce, D., A. Markandya and E.B. Barbier (1989) *Blueprint for a Green Economy* (London: Earthscan)

Pearce, J. (1993) *At the Heart of the Community: Community Enterprise in a Changing Society* (London: Caloustie Gulbenkian Foundation)

Pearce, J. (1996) *Measuring Social Wealth: A Study of Social Audit Practice for Community and Cooperative Enterprises* (London: New Economics Foundation)

Perks, R.W., D. Rawlinson and L. Ingram (1992) 'An exploration of ethical investment in the UK', *British Accounting Review*, 24 (1)

Pezzey, J. (1989) *Definitions of Sustainability*, No. 9 (UK CEED)

Pimm, D. (1990) 'Environmental issues for auditors', *Audit Briefing*, 2 (1), pp. 1–3

Plant, C and D.H. Albert (1991) 'Green business in a gray world – can it be done?', in C. Plant and J. Plant (eds), *Green Business: Hope or Hoax?* (Devon: Green Books), pp. 1–8

Plant, C. and J. Plant (1991) *Green Business: Hope or Hoax?* (Devon: Green Books)

Pollock, J. (1992) 'Contaminated land: keep out?', *CA Magazine* (Scotland), February, pp. 22–24

Porritt, J. (1990) *How Green is Britain? The Government's Environmental Record* (London: Hutchinson Radius/Friends of the Earth)

Porritt, J. (ed.) (1991) *Save the Earth* (London: Dorling Kindersley)

Porter, M.E. and C. van der Linde (1995) 'Green and competitive: ending the stalemate', *Harvard Business Review*, September/October, pp. 120–134

Power, M. (1991) 'Auditing and environmental expertise: between protest and professionalisation', *Accounting, Auditing and Accountability*, 4 (3), pp. 30–42

Power, M. (1992) 'After calculation? Reflections on *Critique of Economic Reason* by Andre Gorz', *Accounting, Organizations and Society*, 17 (5), pp. 477–500

Power, M. (1994a) 'Constructing the responsible organisation: accounting and environmental representation', in G. Teubner, L. Farmer and D. Murphy (eds), *Environmental Law and Ecological Responsibility: The Concept and Practice of Ecological Self-organisation* (London: John Wiley), pp. 370–392

Power, M. (1994b) *The Audit Society* (London: Demos)

Power, M. (1997) *The Audit Society: Rituals of Verification* (Oxford: Oxford University Press)

Prakash, P. and A. Rappaport (1977) 'Information inductance and its significance for accounting', *Accounting, Organizations and Society*, 2 (1), pp. 29–38

Price Waterhouse (1991) *Energy: Containing the Costs* (London: Energy Efficiency Office)

Price Waterhouse (1992) *Accounting for Environmental Compliance: Crossroad for GAAP, Engineering and Government* No. 2 (New York: Price Waterhouse)

Price Waterhouse (1994) *Progress on the Environmental Challenge: A Survey of Corporate America's Environmental Accounting and Management* (New York: Price Waterhouse)

Purkiss, A. (1992) 'Gone with the wind', *Accountancy*, January, pp. 70–72

Rabinowitz, D.L. and M. Murphy (1991) 'Environmental disclosure: what the SEC requires', *Environmental Finance*, Spring, pp. 31–43

Raines, J.P. and C.R. Jung (1986) 'Knight on religion and ethics as agents of social change', *American Journal of Economics and Sociology*, 45 (October), pp. 429–439

Ramphal, S.S. (1990) 'Endangered Earth', in D.J.R. Angell, J.D. Comer and M.L.N. Wilkinson (eds) *Sustaining Earth: Response to the Environmental Threats* (Basingstoke: Macmillan), pp. 3–14

Rawls, J. (1972) *A Theory of Justice* (Oxford: Oxford University Press)

Redclift, M. (1992) 'Sustainable development and global environmental change', *Global Environmental Change*, March, pp. 32–42

Redmond, S. (1988) 'Greens roll on after ozone win', *Marketing*, 28 July, p. 15

Reilly, B.J. and M.J. Kyj (1990) 'Economics and ethics', *Journal of Business Ethics*, 9 (9), pp. 691–698

Rich, B. (1994) *Mortgaging the Earth: The World Bank, Environmental Impoverishment and the Crisis of Development* (Boston, MA: Beacon Press)

Ridgers, B. (1979) 'The use of statistics in counter-information', in I.G. Irvine et al. (eds), *Demystifying Social Statistics* (London, Pluto Press)

Roberts, R.Y. (1993) 'Overview of environmental liability disclosure requirements, recent developments and materiality', presented to the American Bar Association 1993 Annual Meeting, New York

Robertson, J. (1978) *The Sane Alternative* (London: James Robertson)

Robertson, J. (1984) 'Introduction to the British Edition', in F. Capra and C. Spretnak, *Green Politics: the global promise* (London: Hutchinson), pp. xxiii–xxx

Robertson, J. (1985) *Future Work: Jobs, Self Employment and Leisure after the Industrial Age* (London: Gower/Temple Smith)

Robertson, J. (1990) *Future Wealth: A New Economics for the 21st Century* (London: Cassell)

Rockness, J. and P.F. Williams (1988) 'A descriptive study of social responsibility mutual funds', *Accounting, Organizations and Society*, 13 (4), pp. 397–411

Rowley, D.A. and Witmer T.L. (1988/9) 'Assessing environmental risks before booking a loan', *Commercial Lending Review*, 4 (1), pp. 53–64

Rubenstein, D.B. (1994) *Environmental Accounting for the Sustainable Corporation: Strategies and Techniques* (Westport, CT: Quorum Books)

Ryding, Sven-Olof (1991) 'Environmental priority strategies in product design (EPS)', *Integrated Environmental Management*, No. 4 (November), pp. 18–19

Sadgrove, K. (1995) *The Green Guide to Profitable Management* (Aldershot: Gower)

Salamitou, J. (1991) 'The environmental index: an environmental management tool for Rhône Poulenc', *Integrated Environmental Management*, No. 4 (November), pp. 7–9

Sarokin, D. and J. Schulkin (1991) 'Environmental concerns and the business of banking', *Journal of Commercial Bank Lending*, February, pp. 6–19

Sattar, D. (with A. Gozzi and C. Church) (1997) *Green and Ethical Pensions: A Report for Local Authorities* (London: UNED-UK)

de Savornin Lohman, A.F. (1991) 'Financial incentives: an idea whose time has come?', *Integrated Environmental Management*, No. 4 (November), pp. 4–5

Scapens, R.W. and J.T. Sale (1981) 'Performance measurement and formal capital expenditure controls in divisionalised companies', *Journal of Business Finance and Accounting*, Autumn, pp. 389–419

Schaltegger, S. (with K. Mueller and H. Hindrichsen) (1996) *Corporate Environmental Accounting* (New York: John Wiley)

Schanzenbächer, B. (1997) 'UNEP signs up the insurance industry', *Environmental Strategy Europe 1997* (London: Campden Publishing), pp. 61–63

Schmidheiny, S. (1992) *Changing Course* (New York: MIT Press)

Schmidheiny, S. and F.J. Zorraquin (1996) *Financing Change: the financial community, eco-efficiency and sustainable development* (Cambridge, MA: MIT Press)

Schumacher, E.F. (1968) 'Buddhist economics', *Resurgence*, 1 (11), reprinted in H.E. Daly (ed.) (1980) *Economy, Ecology, Ethics: Essays Toward a Steady State Economy* (San Francisco: W.H. Freeman), pp. 138–145

Schumacher, E.F. (1973) *Small is Beautiful* (London: Abacus)

Schumacher, E.F. (1974) *The Age of Plenty: A Christian View* (Edinburgh: St Andrews Press), reprinted in H.E. Daly (ed.) (1980) *Economy, Ecology, Ethics: Essays Toward a Steady State Economy* (San Francisco: W.H. Freeman), pp. 126–137

Sellen, J.W. (1980) 'Positive savings from energy plans', *Accountant's Weekly*, 18 January, pp. 22–23

Shane, P. and B. Spicer (1983) 'Market response to environmental information produced outside the firm', *The Accounting Review*, July, pp. 521–538

Sheldon, C. (1997) *ISO 14000 and Beyond* (Sheffield: Greenleaf Publishing)

Sikka, P., H.C. Willmott and E.A. Lowe (1989) 'Guardians of knowledge and the public interest: evidence and issues of accountability in the UK Accountancy Profession', *Accounting, Auditing and Accountability Journal*, 2 (2), pp. 47–71

Sikka, P., H.C. Willmott and E.A. Lowe (1991) '"Guardians of knowledge and the public interest": a reply to our critics', *Accounting, Auditing and Accountability Journal*, 4 (4), pp. 14–22

Simpson, S. (1990) *The Times Guide to the Environment* (London: Times Books)

Singh, J. (1989) 'Pollution risks may hamper acquisitions', *National Underwriter*, 93 (15), 10 April, pp. 31, 33

Smith, D. (1991) 'The Kraken wakes: the political dynamics of the hazardous waste issue', *Industrial Crisis Quarterly*, 5 (3), pp. 189–207

Social Audit Ltd (1973–1976) *Social Audit Quarterly* (London: Social Audit Ltd)

Society of Environmental Toxicology and Chemistry (SETAC) (1991) *A Technical Framework for Life-Cycle Assessments* (Washington, DC: SETAC)

Society of Management Accountants of Canada (CMA) (1992) *Accounting for the Environment* (Hamilton: CMA)

Sparkes, R. (1995) *Ethical Investor* (London: Harper Collins)

Spreckley, F. (1997) 'Has social audit a role in community enterprise and cooperative organisations?', *Social and Environmental Accounting*, 17 (2), pp. 16–18

Stead, W.E. and J.G. Stead (1992) *Management for a Small Planet* (Newbury Park, CA: Sage)

Stephenson, L. (1973) 'Prying open corporations: tighter than clams', *Business and Society Review*, Winter, pp. 66–73

Stevenson, M.A. and T.M. Dowell (1990) 'Energy for sustainable development', *Journal of Business Ethics*, 9 (10), pp. 829–836

Stone, C.D. (1975) *Where the Law Ends* (New York: Harper and Row)

Stone, C.D. (1987) *Earth and Other Ethics: The Case for Moral Pluralism* (New York: Harper and Row)

Surma, J.P. and A.A. Vondra (1992) 'Accounting for environmental costs: a hazardous subject', *Journal of Accountancy*, March, pp. 51–55

SustainAbility/UNEP (1997) *Engaging Stakeholders: The 1997 Benchmark Survey* (London: Sustain-Ability)

SustainAbility/UNEP (1998) *Engaging Stakeholders: The Non-Reporting Report* (London: Sustain-Ability)

Tennant, T., T. Belsom and C. Thomas (1997) *Creating a Standard for a Corporate Global Warming Indicator* (London: NPI Global Care Investments)

Thompson, H.J. (1992) 'The need for a secured lender exemption', *Integrated Environmental Management*, 7 (March), p. 20

Tinker, A.M. (ed.) (1984) *Social Accounting for Corporations* (Manchester: Manchester University Press)

Tinker, A.M. (1985) *Paper Prophets: A Social Critique of Accounting* (Eastbourne: Holt Saunders)

Tinker, A.M., C. Lehman and M. Neimark (1991) 'Corporate social reporting: falling down the hole in the middle of the road', *Accounting, Auditing and Accountability Journal*, 4 (1), pp. 28–54

Tomimasu, K. (1996) 'Sustainability and accounting: Toward deep green financial statements', in C. Hibbitt and H. Blokdijk (eds), *Proceedings of the Environmental Management and Accounting Conference: Volume IV – Sustainability* (Amsterdam: Limberg Instituut)

Trades Union Congress (1991) *Greening the Workplace* (London: TUC)

Turner, R.K. (1987) 'Sustainable global futures: common interest, interdependence, complexity and global possibilities', *Futures*, 10, pp. 574–82

Turner, R.K. (ed.) (1988) *Sustainable Environmental Management: Principles and Practice* (London: Belhaven Press)

Turner, R.K. (1989) 'Interdisciplinarity and holism in the environmental training of economists and planners', Symposium on education for economists and planners, International Environment Institute, University of Malta, December 1989

Turner, R.K. (1990) *Towards an Integrated Waste Management Strategy* (London: Business Gas)

Turner, R.K. and D.W. Pearce (1990) 'Ethical foundations of sustainable economic development', International Institute for Environment and Development/ London Environmental Economics Centre Paper 90–01, March

Ullmann, A.E. (1976) 'The corporate environmental accounting system: a management tool for fighting environmental degradation', *Accounting, Organizations and Society*, 1 (1), pp. 71–79

United Nations Centre for Transnational Corporations (1992) *International Accounting and Reporting* (New York: UNCTC)

United Nations Conference on Trade and Development (UNCTAD) (1996) 'Sustainable development and accounting: Incentives and disincentives for the adoption of sustainability by transnational corporations', *International Accounting and Reporting Issues: 1995 Review* (Geneva: United Nations), pp. 1–39

United Nations Environment Programme (1995) *Environmental Policies and Practices of the Financial Sector* (Geneva: United Nations)

United Nations World Commission on Environment and Development (1987) *Our Common Future* (The Brundtland Report) (Oxford: Oxford University Press)

Vidal, J. (ed.) (1992) *Earth* (London: The Guardian/Oxfam)

Wackernagel, M. and R. Rees (1996) *Our Ecological Footprint: Reducing Human Impact on the Earth* (Gabriola Island, BC: New Society Publishers)

Walley, N. and B. Whitehead (1994) 'It's not easy being green', *Harvard Business Review*, May/June, pp. 46–52

Walton, C.W. (1983) 'Corporate social responsibility: the debate revisited', *Journal of Economics and Business*, 3 (4), pp. 173–187

Ward, B. (1966) *Spaceship Earth* (Harmondsworth: Penguin)

Ward, B. (1979) *Progress for a Small Planet* (Harmondsworth: Penguin)

Ward, B. and R. Dubos (1972) *Only One Earth: The Care and Maintenance of a Small Planet* (Harmondsworth: Penguin)

Ward, S. (1991) *Socially Responsible Investment*, 2nd edn (London: Directory for Social Change)

Weizsäcker, E. von (1994) *Earth Politics* (London: Zed Books)

Weizsäcker, E. von, A.B. Lovins and L.H. Lovins (1997) *Factor Four: Doubling Wealth, Halving Resource Use* (London: Earthscan)

Welford, R. (1994) *Cases in Environmental Management and Business Strategy* (London: Pitman)

Welford, R. (1996) *Corporate Environment Management: Systems and Strategies* (London: Earthscan)

Welford, R. (ed.) (1997a) *Hijacking Environmentalism: Corporate Response to sustainable development* (London: Earthscan)

Welford, R. (ed.) (1997b) *Corporate Environmental Management 2: Culture and Organisations* (London: Earthscan)

Welford, R. (ed.) (1998) *Corporate Environmental Management 1: Systems and Strategies* (London: Earthscan)

Welford, R. and A. Gouldson (1993) *Environmental Management and Business Strategy* (London: Pitman)

Welford, R. and R. Starkey (eds) (1996) *The Earthscan Reader in Business and the Environment* (London: Earthscan)

Weston, D. (1991) 'The rules of lucre', *Geographical Magazine*, April, pp. 38–40

Wheatley, D. (1991) 'Greener than green?', *New Law Journal*, 15 February, pp. 208–209

Wheeler, D. and M. Silanpaa (1997) *The Stakeholder Corporation: A Blueprint for Maximising Shareholder Value* (London: Pitman)

White, M.A. and B. Wagner (1996) 'Lessons from Germany: the "eco-balance" as a tool for pollution prevention', *Social and Environmental Accounting*, 16 (1), April, pp. 3–6

Whittington, G. (1995) *Is Accounting Becoming too Interesting?* Sir Julian Hodge Lecture, University of Aberystwyth

Winter, G. (1988) *Business and the Environment* (Hamburg: McGraw-Hill)

WM Research (1996) *Is There a Cost to Ethical Investing?* (Edinburgh: WM Company)

Wright, C. and E. Kaposi (1992) 'Reports: could do better', *AA (Accountancy Age)*, March, pp. 35–36

Yankelovich, D. (1972) *Corporate Priorities: A Continuing Study of the New Demands on Business* (Stamford, CT: Daniel Yankelovich)

Zadek, S., P. Pruzan and R. Evans (1997) *Building Corporate Accountability: Emerging Trends in Social and Ethical Accounting, Auditing and Reporting* (London: Earthscan)

Zaikov, G. (1986) 'Political and economic problems of accounting for ecological factors in social production', *Problems of Economics*, 28 (9)

Zyber, G.R. and C.G. Berry (1992) 'Assessing environmental risk', *Journal of Accountancy*, March, pp. 43–48

INDEX